THE KOVELS'
COMPLETE BOTTLE
PRICE LIST

12/80

Ray
This book will
show you how your investment
in Beam bottles is doing.
Merry Christmas.
Lee & Mary Ann

BOOKS BY RALPH AND TERRY KOVEL

Dictionary of Marks—Pottery and Porcelain

A Directory of American Silver, Pewter and Silver Plate

American Country Furniture, 1780–1875

Know Your Antiques,® Revised

The Kovels' Complete Antiques Price List

The Kovels' Complete Bottle Price List

The Kovels' Collector's Guide to American Art Pottery

Kovels' Organizer for Collectors

The Kovels' Price Guide for Collector Plates, Figurines, Paperweights, and Other Limited Editions

THE KOVELS' COMPLETE BOTTLE PRICE LIST

Fifth Edition

By Ralph M. and Terry H. Kovel

Illustrated

Crown Publishers, Inc., New York

Library of Congress Catalog Card Number: 75-12542

ISBN: 0-517-535599

AN IMPORTANT ANNOUNCEMENT TO COLLECTORS AND DEALERS

Every second year *The Kovels' Complete Bottle Price List* is completely rewritten. Every entry and every picture is new because of the rapidly changing antiques market. The only way so complete a revision can be accomplished is by using a computer, making it possible to publish the book two months after the last price is received.

Yet many price changes occur between editions of *The Kovels' Complete Bottle Price List*. Important sales produce new record prices each day. Inflation, the changing price of silver and gold, and the international demand for some types of antiques influence sales in the United States.

The serious collector will want to keep up with developments from month to month rather than from year to year. Therefore, we call your attention to a new service to provide price information almost instantaneously: "Kovels On Antiques and Collectables," a nationally distributed illustrated newsletter, published monthly.

This monthly newsletter reports the best places and ways to buy or sell, the current prices, collecting trends, landmark auction results, and tax, estate, security, and other pertinent news for collectors.

Additional information about the newsletter is available from the authors at P.O. Box 22200, Beachwood, Ohio 44122.   v

HOW TO USE THIS BOOK

Bottle clubs and bottle shows have set the rules for this edition of *The Kovels' Complete Bottle Price List*. We have taken the terms from those in common usage and tried to organize the thousands of listings in easy-to-use form. Many abbreviations have been included that are part of the bottle collector's language. The Tibbits' abbreviations appear throughout the book.

ABM means automatic bottle machine.

BIMAL means blown in mold, applied lip, open pontil.

FB means free-blown.

SC means sun-colored.

SCA means sun-colored amethyst.

OP means open pontil.

IP means iron pontil.

To make the descriptions of the bottles as complete as possible, in some categories an identification number has been added to the description. The serious collector knows the important books about a specialty and these books have numbered lists of styles of bottles. Included in this book are identification numbers for milk glass from Belknap, flasks from Van Rensselaer and McKearin, bitters from Watson, and ink bottles from Covill. The full titles of the books used are included in the bibliography and listed in the introductory paragraph for each category.

Medicine bottles include all medicine or drugstore bottles, except those under the more specific headings of bitters or sarsaparilla. Modern liquor bottles are listed under the brand name if more than five of the bottles are in the collectible series. If you are not a regular at bottle shows, it may take a few tries to become accustomed to the method of listing. If you cannot find a bottle, try several related headings. For instance, hair dye is found under "household" bottles; many named bottles are found under "medicine," "food," "fruit jar," etc. If your fruit jar has several names, such as "Ball, Mason," look under "fruit jar, Ball," or "fruit jar, Mason." If no color is listed the bottle is clear.

The prices shown for old bottles are the actual prices asked for bottles during the past year. A few bottles have been included to complete a listing of new bottles. When this has been done, the prices are estimates based on known prices of the past two years. The estimated prices appear only for modern bottles in a series. Pre–World War I bottles are all listed at actual sale prices.

Prices may vary in different parts of the country, so a range is given. Because of the idiosyncrasies of the computer, it was impossible to place a range of prices on bottles that are illustrated. The price listed is an average.

Spelling is meant to help the collector. If the original bottle spelled "catsup" as "ketchup," that is the spelling that appears. If the period was omitted from "Dr" or the apostrophe from "Jones' sarsaparilla," that is the way it appears. A few bottles are included that had errors in the original spelling; these are listed under "error." "Whiskey" is used even if the bottle held Scotch or Canadian and should be spelled "whisky." Whiskey includes Kummel, Bourbon, Scotch, and liqueurs.

Every bottle illustrated in black and white is indicated by the word "illus" in the text. Every bottle pictured in color is indicated by the word "color" in the listing.

There are a number of the color illustrated bottles shown without prices. These bottles have a price listing of XXXX.XX. They are so rare that obtaining current market prices is not practical.

We welcome any information about clubs, prices, or content for future books, but cannot give appraisals by mail. We have tried to be accurate, but we cannot be responsible for any errors in pricing.

Ralph M. Kovel, Senior Member, American Society of Appraisers.
Terry H. Kovel, Senior Member, American Society of Appraisers.

PICTURE ACKNOWLEDGMENTS

To the following companies and collectors, our thanks for their help in obtaining pictures: Dick Abbott; Avon; Ballantine; Paul and Mary Ballantine; Norman Barnett; John Bartley; Joe Blum; Donald Burkett; Bruce Burwell; Doug Butler; Tom and Deena Caniff; Phyllis Christ; Jim Coffman; Jess Cook; Cyrus Noble; Jim Duquid; Roger Durflinger; Don and Barb Dzuro; Ezra Brooks Distilling Co; Famous Firsts (Richard Magnus); Ray Farrell; Fleischmann Distilling Co. (Joseph Tremont); Doc Ford; Bob and Sue Gilbert; Grenadier Spirits Co.; Hass Brothers (Summer Burrows); Joyce Hawkins; Hoffman Originals (William Ukrainetz); John Horn; Calvin Howard; J. W. Dant; Jack Daniel Distillery; James Beam Distilling Co. (Nancy Walters); Jim Kamerer; Bill Knepp; Mike Kolb; Kontinental Spirits Kompanie; Lionstone Distillers, Ltd.; Luxardo; Sonny Mallory; Paul Mansour; James Maxwell; McCormick (Richard Cray); Michter's (Mr. Romito); Millville Art (Ed and Inge Johnson); Bill Morris; Old Fitzgerald; Raintree; Frank Recards; Kenneth Redmond; Ken Roat; Joe Sabo; Dennis Scott; Ski Country; Hoosier J. Smith; Paul Snyder; Roy Thacker; Charley Thompson; Edith Underwood; Norm Velie; Al Vianon; Mary Villmagna; Steve Vittitoe; Kirby Ward; Donald Wallingford; Wheaton Commemoratives; Wild Turkey (Carol Bauman).

Special thanks to Maxie Harper, Jack Lyons, and the Chillicothe and Central Ohio Bottle Clubs for permitting photographs to be taken at the 1979 Antique Bottle Show and Sale, Columbus, Ohio.

BOTTLE CLUBS

There are hundreds of bottle clubs that welcome new members. This list is arranged by state and city so you can find the club nearest your home. If no club is listed nearby we suggest you contact the national organizations (see below). New clubs are formed each month. Members of the Federation of Historical Bottle Clubs are interested in old bottles. Modern bottles such as Avon, Ezra Brooks, and Beam have their own clubs in many areas.

For more information on local Avon club meetings see *Western World Avon Quarterly* or *World Wide Avon News.*

For last-minute information on bottle club meetings see *Old Bottle Magazine,* Box 243, Bend, Oregon 97701, the publisher of which assisted with this listing.

Any active bottle club that is not listed and wishes to be included in future editions of *The Kovels' Complete Bottle Price List* should send the necessary information to the authors, c/o Crown Publishers, One Park Avenue, New York, New York 10016.

NATIONAL CLUBS

BUD HASTIN'S NATIONAL
AVON CLUB
P.O. Box 9686
Kansas City, Missouri 64134

FEDERATION OF HISTORICAL
BOTTLE CLUBS
MEMBER-AT-LARGE
APPLICATION
10118 Schuessler
St. Louis, Missouri 63128

INTERNATIONAL
ASSOCIATION OF JIM BEAM
BOTTLE AND SPECIALTIES
CLUB
1650 South Amphlett Boulevard,
No. 121
San Mateo, California 94402

LIONSTONE BOTTLE
COLLECTORS OF AMERICA
P.O. Box 75924
Los Angeles, California 90075

MILKBOTTLES ONLY
ORGANIZATION (MOO)
P.O. Box 5456
Newport News, Virginia 23605

NATIONAL ASSOCIATION OF
MINIATURE ENTHUSIASTS
(N.A.M.E.)
1309 West Valencia, Suite H
Fullerton, California 92633

NATIONAL EZRA BROOKS
BOTTLE & SPECIALTIES CLUB
420 W. 1st Street
Kewanee, Illinois 61443

NATIONAL GRENADIER
BOTTLE CLUB
3108A W. Meineche Avenue
Milwaukee, Wisconsin 53210

WESTERN WORLD AVON
CLUB
P.O. Box 27587
San Francisco, California 94127

STATE CLUBS

Alabama
ALABAMA BOTTLE
COLLECTORS' SOCIETY
2768 Hanover Circle
Birmingham, Alabama 35205

ROCKET CITY, 1776 CLUB,
AVON
7115 Crine Drive
Huntsville, Alabama 35802

MONTGOMERY BOTTLE &
INSULATOR CLUB
2021 Merrily Drive
Montgomery, Alabama 36111

MOBILE BOTTLE
COLLECTORS CLUB
6927 Historic Mobile Parkway
Theodore, Alabama 36582

Alaska
ALASKA BOTTLE CLUB
(formerly the Anchorage Beam
Club)
8510 E. 10th Street
Anchorage, Alaska 99504

Arizona
KACHINA EZRA BROOKS
BOTTLE CLUB
3818 W. Cactus Wren Drive
Phoenix, Arizona 85021

PICK & SHOVEL ANTIQUE
BOTTLE CLUB OF ARIZONA
P.O. Box 7476
Phoenix, Arizona 85011

ARIZONA TERRITORY
ANTIQUE BOTTLE &
COLLECTIBLES CLUB, INC.
P.O. Box 26312
Tucson, Arizona 85726

SOUTHERN ARIZONA
HISTORICAL COLLECTORS'
ASSOCIATION, LTD.
6211 Piedra Sega
Tucson, Arizona 85718

Arkansas
FORT SMITH AREA BOTTLE
COLLECTORS ASSOCIATION
5809 Apache Trail
Fort Smith, Arkansas 72904

NORTHEAST ARKANSAS
ANTIQUE BOTTLE CLUB
529 N. Church
Jonesboro, Arkansas 72401

LITTLE ROCK ANTIQUE
BOTTLE CLUB
610 N. Polk
Little Rock, Arkansas 72205

California
GOLDEN GATE HISTORICAL
BOTTLE SOCIETY
P.O. Box 2129
Alameda, California 94501

SUPERIOR CALIFORNIA
BOTTLE CLUB
P.O. Box 555
Anderson, California 96007

KERN COUNTY ANTIQUE
BOTTLE CLUB
P.O. Box 6724
Bakersfield, California 93306

PENINSULA BOTTLE CLUB
P.O. Box 886
Belmont, California 94402

SAN BERNARDINO
HISTORICAL BOTTLE &
COLLECTIBLE CLUB
P.O. Box 127
Bloomington, California 92316

MONTEREY BAY BEAM
BOTTLE & SPECIALTIES CLUB
P.O. Box 11
Carmel, California 93921

BIDWELL BOTTLE CLUB
c/o Don Harned
Box 546
Chico, California 95927

ORIGINAL SIPPIN' COUSINS
BROOKS SPECIALTIES CLUB
5823 Bartmus Street
City of Commerce, California
90040

AVON SPECIALTIES
COLLECTORS CLUB
Box 23
Claremont, California 91711

NATIONAL JIM BEAM BOTTLE
& SPECIALTY CLUB
4298 Callan Blvd.
Daly City, California 94015

MT. BOTTLE CLUB
422 Orpheus
Encinitas, California 92024

SAN JOAQUIN VALLEY
JIM BEAM BOTTLE &
SPECIALTIES CLUB
P.O. Box 11624
Fresno, California 93774

ORANGE COUNTY AVON
CLUB
P.O. Box 505
Garden Grove, California 92642

SOUTHERN CALIFORNIA
AVON COLLECTORS
1350 S. Bender
Glendora, California 91740

SAN FRANCISCO BAY AREA
MINIATURE BOTTLE CLUB
160 Lower Via Casitas #8
Kentfield, California 94904

SEQUOIA ANTIQUE BOTTLE
SOCIETY
1900 Fourth Avenue
Kingsburg, California 93631

LILLIPUTIAN BOTTLE CLUB
5626 Corning Avenue
Los Angeles, California 90056

LOS ANGELES HISTORICAL
BOTTLE CLUB
P.O. Box 60762 Terminal Annex
Los Angeles, California 90060

MADERA AVON COLLECTORS
CLUB
P.O. Box 705
Madera, California 93637

MODESTO AVON
COLLECTORS CLUB
Box 6392
Modesto, California 95355

AVON COLLECTORS OF SAN
DIEGO
202 Avenue Marguarita
Oceanside, California 92054

49ER HISTORICAL BOTTLE
ASSOCIATION
Box 91, Station A
Old Town Auburn, California
95603

QUEEN MARY BEAM &
SPECIALTIES CLUB
1307 Jamestown Way
Orange, California 92669

SAN LUIS OBISPO BOTTLE
SOCIETY (SLOBS)
124 21st Street
Paso Robles, California 93446

TEHAMA COUNTRY ANTIQUE
BOTTLE CLUB
Route 1, Box 775
Red Bluff, California 96080

WEST VALLEY AVON
COLLECTORS
19331 Lorne
Reseda, California 91335

LIVERMORE AVON CLUB
6385 Clarment Avenue
Richmond, California 94805

MORNING AVON CLUB
Box 8323
Riverside, California 92505

RIVERSIDE AVON BOTTLE
CLUB
Box 8445
Riverside, California 92515

LIONSTONE COLLECTABLE
BOTTLE CLUB
3148 N. Walnut Grove
Rosemead, California 91770

MISSION BELLS JIM BEAM
BOTTLE CLUB, INC.
3221 N. Jackson
Rosemead, California 91770

SKI COUNTRY BOTTLE CLUB
OF SOUTHERN CALIFORNIA
3148 N. Walnut Grove
Rosemead, California 91770

YOUNG COLLECTORS OF
AMERICA, AVON
5350 70th Street
Sacramento, California 95820

GOLDEN BEAR EZRA BROOKS
CLUB
8808 Capricorn Way
San Diego, California 92126

SAN DIEGO ANTIQUE BOTTLE
CLUB
P.O. Box 5137
San Diego, California 92105

SAN DIEGO BEAM CLUB
c/o Jack B. Mills
3253 Ogalala Avenue
San Diego, California 92117

GOLDEN GATE EZRA BROOKS
CLUB
1337 Natoma Street
San Francisco, California 94103

SAN JOSE ANTIQUE BOTTLE
COLLECTORS ASSOCIATION
P.O. Box 18548
Saratoga, California 95070

SIERRA GOLD SKI COUNTRY
BOTTLE CLUB
5081 Rio Vista Avenue
San Jose, California 95129

ANTIQUE BOTTLE
COLLECTORS OF ORANGE
COUNTY
223 E. Ponona
Santa Ana, California 92707

AVON TREASURES
UNLIMITED
Box 6412
Santa Ana, California 92706

CALIFORNIA PERFUME
COMPANY CLUB
3130 South Rita Way
Santa Ana, California 92704

MISSION TRAILS CLUB, INC.
1254 Crowley Avenue
Santa Clara, California 95051

SANTA MARIA VALLEY AVON
CLUB
815 N. Palisades Drive
Santa Maria, California 93454

NORTHWESTERN BOTTLE
COLLECTORS ASSOCIATION
P.O. Box 1121
Santa Rosa, California 95402

MISSION TRAIL HISTORICAL
BOTTLE CLUB
P.O. Box 721
Seaside, California 93955

STOCKTON HISTORICAL
BOTTLE & COLLECTIBLE
SOCIETY
P.O. Box 8584
Stockton, California 95208

CHIEF SOLANO BOTTLE CLUB
4-D Boynton Avenue
Suisun, California 94585

Canal Zone
CANAL ZONE BOTTLE
COLLECTORS ASSOCIATION
Box 2232
Balboa, Canal Zone

Colorado

AVON CLUB OF COLORADO
SPRINGS, COLORADO
707 N. Farragut
Colorado Springs, Colorado
80909

FOUR CORNERS BOTTLE &
GLASS CLUB
Box 45
Cortez, Colorado 81321

ANTIQUE BOTTLE CLUB OF
COLORADO
Box 63
Denver, Colorado 80201

WESTERN SLOPE BOTTLE
CLUB
2533 Droad
Grand Junction, Colorado 81501

ROCKY MOUNTAIN AVON
CLUB
8612 W. Warren Lane
Lakewood, Colorado 80227

COLORADO MILE-HIGH EZRA
BROOKS BOTTLE CLUB
7401 Decatur Street
Westminster, Colorado 80030

Connecticut
GREENWICH ANTIQUE
BOTTLE COLLECTORS CLUB
18 Pond Place
Cos Cob, Connecticut 06807

EAST COAST MINI BOTTLE
CLUB
156 Hillfield Road
Hamden, Connecticut 06514

NUTMEG STATE EZRA
BROOKS BOTTLE CLUB
191 W. Main Street
Meriden, Connecticut 06450

ANTIQUE BOTTLE CLUB OF
MIDDLETOWN
15 Elam Street, Apt. #10
New Britain, Connecticut 06053

SOMERS ANTIQUE BOTTLE
CLUB, INC.
Box 373
Somers, Connecticut 06071

CENTRAL CONNECTICUT
ANTIQUE BOTTLE
COLLECTORS
38 Village Road
Southington, Connecticut 06489

SOUTHERN CONNECTICUT
ANTIQUE BOTTLE
COLLECTORS ASSOCIATION
29 Ida Lane
West Haven, Connecticut 06516

NUTMEG STATE EZRA
BROOKS CLUB
279 Andrews Road
Wolcott, Connecticut 06716

Delaware
TRI-STATE BOTTLE
COLLECTORS & DIGGERS
CLUB, INC.
730 Papermill Road
Newark, Delaware 19711

Florida
M-T BOTTLE COLLECTORS
ASSOCIATION
P.O. Box 1581
Deland, Florida 32720

HARBOR CITY
1232 Causeway
Eau, Florida 32935

ANTIQUE BOTTLE
COLLECTORS OF FLORIDA,
INC.
2512 Davie Boulevard
Ft. Lauderdale, Florida 3312

EVERGLADES ANTIQUE
BOTTLE & COLLECTORS CLUB
400 S. 57 Terrace
Hollywood, Florida 33023

ANTIQUE BOTTLE CLUB OF
NORTH FLORIDA
Box 14796
Jacksonville, Florida 32210

CROSS ARMS COLLECTORS
CLUB
1756 N. W. 58th Avenue
Lauderhill, Florida 33313

MID-STATE ANTIQUE BOTTLE
COLLECTORS, INC.
88 Sweetbriar Branch
Longwood, Florida 32750

ANTIQUE BOTTLE
COLLECTORS OF FLORIDA
5901 S. W. 16th Street
Miami, Florida 33144

SOUTH FLORIDA JIM BEAM
BOTTLE & SPECIALTIES CLUB
P.O. Box 011764
Miami, Florida 33101

PENSACOLA BOTTLE & RELIC
COLLECTORS ASSOCIATION
1004 Fremont Avenue
Pensacola, Florida 32505

SANFORD ANTIQUE BOTTLE
COLLECTORS CLUB
2656 Grandview Avenue South
Sanford, Florida 32771

ANTIQUE BOTTLE
COLLECTORS ASSOCIATION
Route 1, Box 74-136
Sarasota, Florida 33583

WEST COAST FLORIDA EZRA
BROOKS CLUB
6583 Bluewater Avenue
Sarasota, Florida 33581

WEST COAST FLORIDA EZRA
BROOKS BOTTLE CLUB
1360 Harbor Drive
Sarasota, Florida 33579

SUNCOAST ANTIQUE BOTTLE
COLLECTORS ASSOCIATION
P.O. Box 12712
St. Petersburg, Florida 33733

TAMPA ANTIQUE BOTTLE
COLLECTORS
P.O. Box 4232
Tampa, Florida 33607

Georgia
SOUTHEASTERN ANTIQUE
BOTTLE CLUB
Box 441
Fairborn, Georgia 30213

MACON ANTIQUE BOTTLE
CLUB
P.O. Box 5395
Macon, Georgia 31208

ROME ANTIQUE BOTTLE CLUB
527 Broad Street
Rome, Georgia 30161

COASTAL EMPIRE BOTTLE
CLUB
P.O. Box 3714 Station B
Savannah, Georgia 31402

Hawaii
HAWAII BOTTLE COLLECTORS
CLUB
6770 Hawaii Kai Drive, Apt. 708
Hawaii Kai, Hawaii 96825

Idaho
GEM ANTIQUE BOTTLE CLUB,
INC.
1630 Londoner Avenue
Boise, Idaho 83706

ROCK & BOTTLE CLUB
Route 1
Fruitland, Idaho 83619

EM TEE BOTTLE CLUB
Box 62
Jerome, Idaho 83338

POCATELLO ANTIQUE
BOTTLE COLLECTORS
ASSOCIATION
4530 S. 5th Street
Pocatello, Idaho 83201

Illinois
ALTON AREA BOTTLE CLUB
2448 Alby Street
Alton, Illinois 62035

FLIGHT TO BEAUTY AVON
CLUB
RR #1
Beason, Illinois 62512

METRO-EAST BOTTLE & JAR
ASSOCIATION
309 Bellevue Park Drive
Belleville, Illinois 62223

CHICAGO EZRA BROOKS
BOTTLE & SPECIALTY CLUB
3635 W. 82nd Street
Chicago, Illinois 60652

FIRST CHICAGO BOTTLE
CLUB
P.O. Box A3382
Chicago, Illinois 60690

ANTIQUE BOTTLE CLUB OF
NORTH ILLINOIS
P.O. Box 23
Ingleside, Illinois 60041

AVON CALLING COLLECTORS
CLUB
P.O. Box 182
Joliet, Illinois 60431

NATIONAL EZRA BROOKS
BOTTLE & SPECIALTIES CLUB
420 N. First Street
Kewanee, Illinois 61443

PEKIN BOTTLE COLLECTORS
ASSOCIATION
P.O. Box 372
Pekin, Illinois 61554

ILLINOIS AVON COLLECTORS
CLUB
Box 188
Peoria, Illinois 61650

LINCOLN LAND AVON CLUB
1137 W. Elliott
Springfield, Illinois 62702

Indiana
INDIANA EZRA BROOKS
BOTTLE CLUB
72 N. 14th Street
Beech Grove, Indiana 46107

KENTUCKIAN ANTIQUE
BOTTLE & OUTHOUSE
SOCIETY
554 Andalusia Avenue
Clarksville, Indiana 47130

THE MIDWEST ANTIQUE
FRUIT JAR & BOTTLE CLUB
P.O. Box 38
Flat Rock, Indiana 47234

FORT WAYNE HISTORICAL
BOTTLE CLUB
5124 Roberta Drive
Fort Wayne, Indiana 46806

LAFAYETTE ANTIQUE BOTTLE
CLUB
3664 Redondo Drive
Lafayette, Indiana 47905

STEEL CITY JIM BEAM
BOTTLE & SPECIALTY CLUB
74 S. Smoke Road
Valparaiso, Indiana 46383

Iowa
CEDAR VALLEY AVON
COLLECTORS
1551 C Avenue, NE
Cedar Rapids, Iowa 52402

IOWA ANTIQUE BOTTLEERS
2865 Second Avenue
Marion, Iowa 52302

Kansas
WALNUT VALLEY EZRA
BROOKS CLUB
P.O. Box 631
Arkansas City, Kansas 62005

SOUTHEAST KANSAS BOTTLE
& RELIC CLUB
P.O. Box 835
Chanute, Kansas 66720

KANSAS CITY ANTIQUE
BOTTLE CLUB ASSOCIATION
5528 Aberdeen
Shawnee Mission, Kansas 66205

Kentucky
KENTUCKY WISE CHOICE
CLUB, AVON
1028 Franelm Road
Louisville, Kentucky 40214

Louisiana
CELNA BOTTLE CLUB
Route 1, Box 463
Dry Prong, Louisiana 71423

NORTHEAST LOUISIANA
BOTTLE & INSULATOR CLUB
P.O. Box 4192
Monroe, Louisiana 71201

BAYOU EZRA BROOKS
BOTTLE CLUB
733 Wright Avenue
Gretna, Louisiana 70053

NEW ORLEANS ANTIQUE
BOTTLE CLUB
4336 Palmyra
New Orleans, Louisiana 70119

SHREVEPORT ANTIQUE
BOTTLE CLUB
1157 Arncliffe Drive
Shreveport, Louisiana 71107

Maine

NEW ENGLAND ANTIQUE
BOTTLE CLUB
Box 118
Alfred, Maine 04002

DIRIGO BOTTLE
COLLECTORS' CLUB
24 Maple Street
Dexter, Maine 04930

WALDO COUNTY
BOTTLENECKS CLUB
Head-of-the-Tide
Belfast, Maine 04915

Maryland
BLUE & GRAY EZRA BROOKS
BOTTLE CLUB
2106 Sunnybrook Drive
Frederick, Maryland 21201

BALTIMORE ANTIQUE BOTTLE
HOUNDS
421 Sixth Avenue N.E.
Glen Burnie, Maryland 21061

BALTIMORE ANTIQUE BOTTLE
HOUNDS
1528 York Road
Lutherville, Maryland 21093

Massachusetts
MERRIMACK VALLEY BOTTLE
CLUB
16 Algonquin Avenue
Andover, Massachusetts 01810

BERKSHIRE ANTIQUE BOTTLE
ASSOCIATION
P.O. Box 753
Lenox, Massachusetts 01240

NEW ENGLAND BOTTLE
COLLECTORS ASSOCIATION
7a Broad Street
Lynn, Massachusetts 01902

SATUIT BOTTLE CLUB
54 Cedarwood Road
Scituate, Massachusetts 02066

CAPE COD ANTIQUE BOTTLE
CLUB
262 Setuket Road
Yarmouth, Massachusetts 02675

Michigan
HURON VALLEY BOTTLE &
INSULATOR CLUB
7582 DiBrova Drive
Brighton, Michigan 48116

AVON BOTTLE OF MT. CLEMO
15521 N. Park
East Detroit, Michigan 48021

GREAT LAKES MINIATURE
BOTTLE CLUB
P.O. Box 245
Fairhaven, Michigan 48023

METRO EAST BOTTLE & JAR
ASSOCIATION
309 Bellevue Park Drive
Fairview Heights, Michigan

METRO DETROIT ANTIQUE
BOTTLE CLUB
28860 Balmoral Way
Farmington Hills, Michigan
48018

ROYAL ORB AVON CLUB
9490 Bennett Lake Road
Fenton, Michigan 48430

FLINT ANTIQUE BOTTLE CLUB
450 Leta Avenue
Flint, Michigan 48507

YE OLD CORKERS
P.O. Box 7
Gaastra, Michigan 49927

CENTRAL MICHIGAN KRAZY
KORKERS BOTTLE CLUB
Mid-Michigan Community
College
Clare Avenue
Harrison, Michigan 48625

CHIEF PONTIAC ANTIQUE
BOTTLE CLUB
755 Scottwood
Pontiac, Michigan 48058

INTERNATIONAL AVON CLUB
22708 Wick Road
Taylor, Michigan 48180

Minnesota
NORTH STAR AVON
COLLECTORS CLUB
273 Yosemite Circle
Golden Valley, Minnesota 55427

VIKING AVON CLUB
4017 Highway 194
Hermantown (Duluth), Minnesota
55811

MINNESOTA'S FIRST ANTIQUE
BOTTLE CLUB
5001 Queen Avenue N
Minneapolis, Minnesota 55430

NORTH STAR HISTORICAL
BOTTLE ASSOCIATION
P.O. Box 30343
St. Paul, Minnesota 55175

MINNESOTA 1ST AVON CLUB
524 Central Avenue
White Bear Lake, Minnesota
55110

Mississippi

SOUTH MISSISSIPPI
HISTORICAL BOTTLE CLUB
165 Belvedere Drive
Biloxi, Mississippi 39530

MISS AVON BOTTLE CLUB
101 Sproles Street
Clinton, Mississippi 39056

THE MAGNOLIA STATE
BOTTLE & SPECIALTIES CLUB
2918 Larchmont
Jackson, Mississippi 39209

MIDDLE MISSISSIPPI ANTIQUE
BOTTLE CLUB
5528 Crepe Myrtle Drive
Jackson, Mississippi 39206

Missouri
ST. LOUIS ANTIQUE BOTTLE
COLLECTOR ASSOCIATION
306 N. Woodlawn Avenue
Kirkwood, Missouri 63122

ANTIQUE BOTTLE & RELIC
CLUB OF CENTRAL MISSOURI
726 W. Monroe
Mexico, Missouri 65265

PACK RATS UNITED
Route 6
Wardsville, Missouri 65101

Montana
HELLGATE ANTIQUE BOTTLE
CLUB
P.O. Box 7411
Missoula, Montana 59807

Nebraska
NEBRASKA ANTIQUE BOTTLE
& COLLECTORS CLUB
P.O. Box 37021
Omaha, Nebraska 68137

Nevada
LINCOLN COUNTY ANTIQUE
BOTTLE CLUB
P.O. Box 191
Caliente, Nevada 89008

LAS VEGAS BOTTLE CLUB
3115 Las Vegas Boulevard N.
North Las Vegas, Nevada 89030

RENO-SPARKS ANTIQUE
BOTTLE COLLECTORS
ASSOCIATION
P.O. Box 1061
Verdi, Nevada 89439

New Hampshire
YANKEE BOTTLE CLUB
P.O. Box 702
Keene, New Hampshire 03431

New Jersey
BURLINGTON ANTIQUE
BOTTLE CLUB
38 Yorktown Road
Bordentown, New Jersey 08505

NEW JERSEY EZRA BROOKS
BOTTLE CLUB
Sayers Neck Road
Cedarville, New Jersey 08311

AVON BOTTLE CLUB OF
CLIFTON
100 Harding Avenue
Clifton, New Jersey 07011

SOUTH JERSEY'S HERITAGE
BOTTLE & GLASS CLUB
P.O. Box 122
Glassboro, New Jersey 08028

JERSEY DEVIL BOTTLE CLUB
14 Church Street
Mt. Holly, New Jersey 08042

LAKELAND ANTIQUE BOTTLE
CLUB
18 Alan Lane, Mine Hill
Dover, New Jersey 07801

THE JERSEY SHORE BOTTLE
CLUB
P.O. Box 995
Toms River, New Jersey 08753

NORTH NEW JERSEY
ANTIQUE BOTTLE
COLLECTORS ASSOCIATION
P.O. Box 617
Westwood, New Jersey 07675

New York
AUBURN BOTTLE CLUB
297 South Street Road
Auburn, New York 13021

NORTH COUNTY BOTTLE
COLLECTORS ASSOCIATION
Road 1
Canton, New York 13617

TWIN COUNTIES OLD BOTTLE
CLUB
R.D. #2 Box 270E
Catskill, New York 12414

THE MUSCOOT BOTTLE &
INSULATOR COLLECTORS
CLUB
Box 427
Golden Bridge, New York 10526

FINGER LAKES BOTTLE CLUB
ASSOCIATION
Box 815
Ithaca, New York 14850

WESTERN NEW YORK
BOTTLE COLLECTORS
62 Adams Street
Jamestown, New York 14701

WEST VALLEY BOTTLETIQUE
COLLECTORS ASSOCIATION
P.O. Box 204
Killbuck, New York 14748

STEEL CITY AVON CLUB
52 E. Milnor
Lackawanna, New York 14218

THE GREATER CATSKILL
ANTIQUE BOTTLE CLUB
Loch Sheldrake, New York
12759

EMPIRE STATE BEAM BOTTLE
& SPECIALTIES CLUB
P.O. Box 484
Lynbrook, New York 11563

HUDSON VALLEY BOTTLE
CLUB
Mt. Zion Road
Marlboro, New York 12542

SUFFOLK COUNTY ANTIQUE
BOTTLE ASSOCIATION OF
LONG ISLAND
Box 943
Melville, New York 11746

EMPIRE STATE BOTTLE
COLLECTORS ASSOCIATION
102 Clarton Street
North Syracuse, New York
13212

THE GENESEE VALLEY
BOTTLE COLLECTORS
ASSOCIATION
P.O. Box 7528
West Ridge Station
Rochester, New York 14610

NIAGARA AREA AVON CLUB
5231 Townline Road
Sanborn, New York 14132

RENSSELAER COUNTY
ANTIQUE BOTTLE CLUB, INC.
Box 792
Troy, New York 12181

WARWICK VALLEY BOTTLE
CLUB
Box 393
Warwick, New York 10990

North Carolina
GOLDSBORO BOTTLE &
COLLECTORS CLUB
2406 E. Ash Street
American Savings & Loan
Goldsboro, North Carolina 27530

BOTTLE COLLECTORS CLUB
OF NORTH CAROLINA
4201 Live Oak
Raleigh, North Carolina 27604

WILSON BOTTLE &
ARTIFACTS CLUB
Route 1, Box 59
Wilson, North Carolina 27893

Ohio
OHIO BOTTLE CLUB, INC.
P.O. Box 585
Barberton, Ohio 44203

CENTRAL OHIO BOTTLE CLUB
931 Minerva Avenue
Columbus, Ohio 43229

GOLDEN SLIPPER AVON CLUB
159 E. Apple Street
Dayton, Ohio 45409

SOUTHWESTERN OHIO
ANTIQUE BOTTLE & JAR CLUB
5888 Executive Boulevard
Dayton, Ohio 45424

TRI-STATE HISTORICAL
BOTTLE CLUB
P.O. Box 609
East Liverpool, Ohio 43920

FINDLAY ANTIQUE BOTTLE
CLUB
P.O. Box 1329
Findlay, Ohio 45840

FIRST CAPITAL BOTTLE CLUB
Route 1, Box 94
Laurelville, Ohio 43135

HEART OF OHIO BOTTLE
CLUB
P.O. Box 353
New Washington, Ohio 44854

SOUTHWESTERN OHIO
ANTIQUE BOTTLE & JAR CLUB
P.O. Box 53
North Hampton, Ohio 45349

JEFFERSON COUNTY
ANTIQUE BOTTLE CLUB
1223 Oak Grove Avenue
Steubenville, Ohio 43952

BUCKEYE BOTTLE DIGGERS
CLUB
Route 2, Box 77
Thornville, Ohio 43076

GLASS CITY AVON CLUB
609 Prouty Avenue
Toledo, Ohio 43609

Oklahoma
T-TOWN BOTTLE & RELIC
NEWS
8921 S. 200th East Avenue
Broken Arrow, Oklahoma 74012

BIG RED AVON CLUB
822 Wylie Road
Norman, Oklahoma 73069

SOONER AVON COLLECTORS
CLUB
6706 E. 9th Street, Box 15435
Tulsa, Oklahoma 74112

TULSA ANTIQUE BOTTLE &
RELIC CLUB
P.O. Box 4278
Tulsa, Oklahoma 74104

CENTRAL PAYNE AVON CLUB
Rt. 2, Box 49
Yale, Oklahoma 74085

Oregon
CENTRAL OREGON BOTTLE &
RELIC CLUB
671 N.E. Seward
Bend, Oregon 97701

OREGON BOTTLE
COLLECTORS ASSOCIATION
3661 S.E. Nehalem Street
Portland, Oregon 97202

Pennsylvania
BEDFORD COUNTY ANTIQUE
BOTTLE CLUB
107 Seifert Street
Bedford, Pennsylvania, 15522

WASHINGTON COUNTY
BOTTLE & INSULATOR CLUB
Route 1, Box 118
Cannonsburg, Pennsylvania
15317

CLASSIC GLASS BOTTLE
COLLECTORS
R.D. #2
Cogan Station, Pennsylvania
17728

FORKS OF THE DELAWARE
BOTTLE CLUB
P.O. Box 693
Easton, Pennsylvania 18042

DELAWARE VALLEY BOTTLE
CLUB
12 Belmar Road
Hatboro, Pennsylvania 19040

DEL VAL BOTTLE CLUB
Route 152 at Hilltown Park
Hilltown, Pennsylvania 18927

INDIANA BOTTLE CLUB
R.D. #5 Box 138
Indiana, Pennsylvania 15701

CAMOSET BOTTLE CLUB
Box 252
Johnstown, Pennsylvania 15907

LAUREL VALLEY BOTTLE
CLUB
618 Monastery Drive
Latrobe, Pennsylvania 15650

MIDDLETOWN AREA BOTTLE
COLLECTORS ASSOCIATION
P.O. Box 1
Middletown, Pennsylvania 17057

PITTSBURGH ANTIQUE
BOTTLE CLUB
209 Palomina Drive
Oakdale, Pennsylvania 15071

PHILADELPHIA BOTTLE CLUB
8445 Walker Street
Philadelphia, Pennsylvania
19136

PHILADA COLLECTORS' CLUB
P.O. Box 8302
Philadelphia, Pennsylvania
19111

VIEW OF NOSTALGIA AVON
CLUB
2 E. Fifth Street
Pottstown, Pennsylvania 19464

KISKI MINI BOTTLE CLUB
Box 3, Freedom Road
Rochester, Pennsylvania 15074

CLASSIC GLASS BOTTLE
CLUB
1720 Memorial Avenue
Williamsport, Pennsylvania
17701

DEL-VAL MINIATURE BOTTLE
CLUB
Cedarbrook Hill Apts. B-PH-12
Wyncote, Pennsylvania 19095

PENNSYLVANIA BOTTLE
COLLECTORS ASSOCIATION
P.O. Box 156
York, Pennsylvania 17362

Rhode Island
LITTLE RHODY BOTTLE CLUB
3161 W. Shore Road
Warwick, Rhode Island 02886

South Carolina
SOUTH CAROLINA BOTTLE
CLUB
Route 1, Box 66
Irmo, South Carolina 29063

Tennessee
GOODLETTSVILLE ANTIQUE
BOTTLE CLUB
128 E. Lawn Drive
Goodlettsville, Tennessee 37072

COTTON CARNIVAL BEAM
CLUB
P.O. Box 17951
Memphis, Tennessee 38117

MEMPHIS BOTTLE
COLLECTORS CLUB
232 Tilton
Memphis, Tennessee 38111

MIDDLE TENNESSEE BOTTLE
COLLECTORS CLUB
P.O. Box 120083
Nashville, Tennessee 37205

Texas
THE AUSTIN BOTTLE &
INSULATOR COLLECTORS
1614 Ashberry Drive
Austin, Texas 78723

EXPLORATION SOCIETY
603 9th Street
Corpus Christi, Texas 78419

AVON SUN CITY CLUB
5715 Waycross
El Paso, Texas 79924

AVON COLLECTORS OF
TEXAS
P.O. Box 53356
Houston, Texas 77052

AVON LONE STAR
COLLECTORS CLUB
4418 Woodvalley
Houston, Texas 77096

EXCALIBUR AVON
COLLECTORS CLUB
2332 Triway
Houston, Texas 77043

TEXAS LONGHORN BOTTLE
CLUB
P.O. Box 5346
Irving, Texas 75062

GULF COAST BOTTLE & JAR
CLUB
P.O. Box 1754
Pasadena, Texas 77501

VICTORIAN AVON
COLLECTORS CLUB
1809 Melrose, #C
Victoria, Texas 77901

Utah
UTAH ANTIQUE BOTTLE &
RELIC CLUB
1594 West 500 North
Salt Lake City, Utah 84116

Virginia
METRO-WASHINGTON
BOTTLE COLLECTORS
4305 Guinea Road
Annandale, Virginia 22003

POTOMAC BOTTLE
COLLECTORS CLUB
5100 N. 25th Place
Arlington, Virginia 22207

YE OLD BOTTLE CLUB
P.O. Box 688
Clarksville, Virginia 23987

METROPOLITAN ANTIQUE
BOTTLE CLUB
109 Howard Street
Dumfries, Virginia 22026

POTOMAC BOTTLE
COLLECTORS
6602 Orland Street
Falls Church, Virginia 22043

HISTORICAL BOTTLE
DIGGERS OF VIRGINIA
2043 E. Court
Harrisonburg, Virginia 22801

DIXIE BEAM BOTTLE CLUB
P.O. Box 267
Leesburg, Virginia 22075

RICHMOND AREA BOTTLE
COLLECTORS ASSOCIATION
614 Park Drive
Mechanicsville, Virginia 23111

HAMPTON ROADS AREA
BOTTLE COLLECTORS
ASSOCIATION
4012 Winchester Drive
Portsmouth, Virginia 23707

HAMPTON ROADS AVON
CLUB
2837 N. Nansemond Drive
Suffolk, Virginia 23435

APPLE VALLEY BOTTLE
COLLECTORS CLUB, INC.
P.O. Box 2201
Winchester, Virginia 22601

Washington
CAPITOL BOTTLE
COLLECTORS & BOTTLE CLUB
P.O. Box 202
Olympia, Washington 98507

PACIFIC NW AVON
COLLECTORS CLUB
12540 Phinny Avenue N.
Seattle, Washington 98133

WASHINGTON BOTTLE
COLLECTORS ASSOCIATION
P.O. Box 80045
Seattle, Washington 98108

WASHINGTON APPLE
BLOSSOM CLUB, AVON
Rt 2. Box 2226
Selah, Washington 98942

YOUR AVON KLUB OF
SPOKANE
P.O. Box 2551
Spokane, Washington 99220

West Virginia
WILD & WONDERFUL WEST
VIRGINIA EZRA BROOKS
BOTTLE & SPECIALTY CLUB
1929 Pennsylvania Avenue
Weirton, West Virginia 26062

Wisconsin
AVON CLUB OF CUDAHY
P.O. Box 384
Cudahy, Wisconsin 53110

BUCKEN BEAMERS BOTTLE
CLUB
North 95 West 16548 Richmond
Drive
Menomonee Falls, Wisconsin
53051

NATIONAL GRENADIER
BOTTLE CLUB OF AMERICA
3108A W. Meinecke Avenue
Milwaukee, Wisconsin 53210

MILWAUKEE ANTIQUE
BOTTLE CLUB, INC
2343 Met-To-Wee Lane
Wauwatosa, Wisconsin 53226

Wyoming
CHEYENNE ANTIQUE BOTTLE
CLUB
4417 E. 8th Street
Cheyenne, Wyoming 82001

CANADIAN CLUBS

Alberta
WILD ROSE ANTIQUE BOTTLE
COLLECTORS
P.O. Box 1471, Main Post Office
Edmonton, Alberta, Canada

RANGELAND COLLECTORS
CLUB
P.O. Box 724
Lethbridge, Alberta
T1J 3Z6 Canada

British Columbia
PRINCE RUPERT OLDE TYME
BOTTLE & COLLECTABLES
CLUB
P.O. Box 622
Prince Rupert, British Columbia,
Canada

THE OLD TIME BOTTLE CLUB
OF BRITISH COLUMBIA
P.O. Box 77154, Postal Station 5
Vancouver/6, British Columbia,
Canada

Manitoba
MANITOBA AVON BOTTLE
COLLECTORS
#1113 Winnipeg General P.O.
Winnipeg, Manitoba
R3C 2X4 Canada

New Brunswick
THE SAINT JOHN ANTIQUE
BOTTLE CLUB
25 Orange Street
Saint John, New Brunswick
E2L 1L9, Canada

Nova Scotia
LAND OF EVANGELINE
ANTIQUE BOTTLE CLUB
Cambridge Station
Kings County, Nova Scotia,
Canada

Ontario
QUINTE BOTTLE
COLLECTORS
637 Bridge Street
East Belleville, Ontario, Canada

TORONTO AVON
COLLECTORS CLUB
20 Castlebury Crescent
Willowdale, Toronto, Ontario
M2H 1W6, Canada

ESSEX COUNTY ANTIQUE
BOTTLE & INSULATOR CLUB
9767 Ridge Road
Windsor, Ontario
N8R 1G5, Canada

Saskatchewan
BRIDGE CITY COLLECTORS'
CLUB
111–115th Street East
Saskatoon, Saskatchewan
57N 2E1, Canada

INTERNATIONAL CLUBS

England
OLD BOTTLE CLUB OF GREAT
BRITAIN
14 Derwent Crescent
Whitehill, Kidsgrove, England

PUBLICATIONS OF INTEREST TO BOTTLE COLLECTORS

Many of the publications listed are regional in content. We suggest you see a copy before you subscribe. Some of these publications will send a sample copy on request.

NEWSPAPERS

Antique Trader Weekly
P.O. Box 1050
Dubuque, Iowa 52001

Collector's News
P.O. Box 156
Grundy Center, Iowa 50638

The Collector
Drawer C
Kermit, Texas 79745

Maine Antique Digest
RFD 3, Box 76
Waldoboro, Maine 04572

Ohio Antique Review
72 E. North Street
Worthington, Ohio 43085

Southeast Trader
P.O. Box 1068
W. Columbia, S. Carolina 29169

NEWSLETTERS

Kovels on Antiques and Collectables
P.O. Box 22200
Beachwood, Ohio 44122

The Milking Parlor (MOO)
P.O. Box 5456
Newport News, Virginia 23605

Miniature Bottle Mart
24 Gertrude Lane
West Haven, Connecticut 06516

Western World Avon Quarterly
511 Harrison Street
San Francisco, California 94105

World Wide Avon News
P.O. Box 27587
San Francisco, California 94127

MAGAZINES

Antique Bottle Collector
Chapel House Farm, Newport Road
Albrighton, N. Wolverhampton
Staffs, England

Antique Bottle World
5003 W. Berwyn
Chicago, Illinois 60630

Antiques Journal
P.O. Box 1046
Dubuque, Iowa 52001

Bottle News
P.O. Box 1000
Kermit, Texas 79745

Federation of Historical Bottle Clubs
10118 Schuessler
St. Louis, Missouri 63128

The Miniature Bottle Collector
P.O. Box 2161
Palos Verdes Peninsula
California 90274

Old Bottle Magazine
525 E. Revere
Bend, Oregon 97701

Pictorial Bottle Review
Brisco Publications
P.O. Box 2161
Palos Verdes Peninsula
California 90274

BIBLIOGRAPHY

This list includes most of the books about bottles available in bookstores or through the mail. Out-of-print books or price books published before 1976 are not included unless of importance as research tools.

GENERAL
Belknap, E. M. *Milk Glass*. New York: Crown Publishers, Inc., 1959.

Freeman, Dr. Larry. *Grand Old American Bottles*. Watkins Glen, New York: Century House, 1964.

Ketchum, William C., Jr. *A Treasury of American Bottles*. Indianapolis: The Bobbs-Merrill Company, 1975.

Klamkin, Marian. *The Collector's Book of Bottles*. New York: Dodd, Mead & Company, 1971.

Kovel, Ralph and Terry. *Know Your Antiques*. New York: Crown Publishers, Inc., 1973.

————.*The Kovels' Complete Antiques Price List*. New York: Crown Publishers, Inc., 1979.

McKearin, George L. and Helen. *Two Hundred Years of American Blown Glass*. New York: Crown Publishers, Inc., 1950.

Munsey, Cecil. *The Illustrated Guide to Collecting Bottles*. New York: Hawthorn Books, Inc., 1970.

Neal, Nelson and Marna. *Common Bottles for the Average Collector*. Wolfe City, Texas: The University Press, 1975.

Ohio Bottle Club, The. *Ohio Bottles, Bicentennial Edition*. (Order from The Ohio Bottle Club, P.O. Box 585, Barberton, Ohio 44203.)

Ohio Bottle Club, The. *10th Anniversary Edition Ohio Bottles*. Barberton, Ohio: Ohio Bottle Club, 1978.

Potomac Bottle Collectors. *Washington D.C. Bottles*. 1976. (Order from Tom & Kaye Johnson, 7722 Woodstock Street, Manassas, Virginia 22110.)

Toulouse, Julian Harrison. *Bottle Makers and Their Marks*. Camden, New Jersey: Thomas Nelson, Inc., 1971.

Unitt, Doris and Peter. *Bottles in Canada*. Petersborough, Ontario, Canada: Clock House Publications, 1972.

GENERAL ENGLISH
Davis, Derek C. *English Bottles & Decanters 1650–1900*. New York: The World Publishing Company, 1972.

Fletcher, Edward. *Bottle Collecting: Finding, Collecting and Displaying Antique Bottles*. London, England: Blandford Press Ltd., 1972.

BITTERS
Watson, Richard. *Bitter Bottles*. Fort Davis, Texas: Thomas Nelson & Sons, 1965.

————. *Supplement to Bitters Bottles*. Camden, New Jersey: Thomas Nelson & Sons, 1968.

CANDY CONTAINERS
Eikelberner, George, and Agadjanian, Serge. *American Glass Containers.* Privately printed, 1967. (Order from Serge Agadjanian, River Road, Belle Mead, New Jersey 08502.)
———. *More American Glass Candy Containers.* Privately printed, 1970.

FIGURAL
Revi, Albert Christian. *American Pressed Glass and Figure Bottles.* New York: Thomas Nelson & Sons, 1964.
Umberger, Jewel and Arthur L. *Collectible Character Bottles.* Privately printed, 1969. (Order from Corker Book Company, 819 W. Wilson, Tyler, Texas 75701.)
Wearin, Otha D. *Statues That Pour: The Story of Character Bottles.* Denver, Colorado: Sage Books (2679 South York Street), 1965.

FLASKS
McKearin, Helen, and Wilson, Kenneth M. *American Bottles & Flasks and Their Ancestry.* New York: Crown Publishers, Inc., 1978.
McKearin, George L. and Helen. *American Glass.* New York: Crown Publishers, Inc., 1959.
Thomas, John L. *Picnics, Coffins, Shoo-Flies.* Privately printed, 1974. (Order from author, P.O. Box 446, Weaverville, California 96093.)
Van Rensselaer, Stephen. *Early American Bottles & Flasks*—Revised. Privately printed, 1969. (Order from J. Edmund Edwards, 61 Winton Place, Stratford, Connecticut 06497.)

FRUIT JARS
Brantley, William F. *A Collector's Guide to Ball Jars.* 1975. (Order from Ball Corporation, Consumer Publications, Muncie, Indiana 47302.)
Creswick, Alice. *The Red Book of Fruit Jars No. 3.* Michigan: ABC Printing, Inc., 1977.
Milligan, Harry J. *Canning Jars of Canada. A "Colcasea's" Record Book and Price Guide.* Privately printed, 1975. (Order from author, 121 Admiral Avenue, Sarnia, Ontario N7T 5L6, Canada.)
Peters, Frank. *Fruit Jar Manual and Price Guide.* Bend, Oregon: Old Bottle Magazine, 1973.
Toulouse, Julian Harrison. *Fruit Jars: A Collector's Manual.* Jointly published by Camden, New Jersey: Thomas Nelson & Sons, and Hanover, Pennsylvania: Everybody's Press, 1969.

INKWELLS
Covill, William E., Jr. *Ink Bottles and Inkwells.* Taunton, Massachusetts: William S. Sullwold, Publishing, 1971.

MEDICINE
Baldwin, Joseph K. *A Collector's Guide to Patent and Proprietary Medicine Bottles of the Nineteenth Century.* New York: Thomas Nelson, Inc., 1973.
Blasi, Betty. *A Bit About Balsams. A Chapter in the History of Nineteenth Century Medicine.* Privately printed, 1974. (Order from author, 5801 River Knolls Drive, Louisville, Kentucky 40222.)

MILK

Rawlinson, Fred. *Make Mine Milk.* Privately printed, 1970. (Order from FAR Publications, Box 5456, Newport News, Virginia 23605.)

MINIATURES

Cembura, Al, and Avery, Constance. *A Guide to Miniature Bottles.* Vol. 1, sections 1–3. Privately printed, 1972 and 1973. (Order from authors, 139 Arlington Avenue, Berkeley, California 94708.)

MODERN

Montague, H. F. *Montague's Modern Bottle Identification and Price Guide.* 1st edition. Overland Park, Kansas: H. F. Montague Enterprises, Inc., 1978.

Avon

Hastin, Bud. *Bud Hastin's Avon Bottle Encyclopedia.* 1976–77 ed. Privately printed, 1976. (Order from author, Box 9868, Kansas City, Missouri 64134.)

Schneider, Dee. *Avon's Bottles: By Any Other Name.* Glendale, California: Avon Research, 1974.

Triangle Books. *Avon's Glass Figural Bottles.* 1975. (Order from Triangle Books, P.O. Box 1406, Mesa, Arizona 85201.)

Underwood, Beatrice and Judith Ann. *Pacific Coast Avon Museum Catalogue.* 1974 edition. (Order from Pacific Coast Avon Museum, 137 Park Way South, Santa Cruz, California 95060.)

Western World. *Avon: Western World Handbook & Price Guide to Avon Bottles.* 1978. (Order from Western World Publishers, 511 Harrison Street, San Francisco, California 94105.)

Beam

Cembura, Al, and Avery, Constance. *Jim Beam Bottles, Identification and Price Guide.* 1978 (9th) edition. Privately printed, 1978. (Order from authors, 139 Arlington Avenue, Berkeley, California 94707).

POISON BOTTLES

Durflinger, Roger L. *Poison Bottles Collectors Guide.* Vol. 1. Privately printed, 1972. (Order from author, 132 W. Oak Street, Washington C.H., Ohio 43160.)

SARSAPARILLA

Shimko, Phyllis. *Sarsaparilla Bottle Encyclopedia.* Privately printed, 1969. (Order from author, Box 117, Aurora, Oregon 97002.)

SEAL

Morgan, Roy. *Sealed Bottles: Their History and Evolution (1630–1930).* Burton upon Trent, England: Midlands Antique Bottle Publishing, 1976.

SODA AND MINERAL WATER

Herr, J. A. *Breweries & Soda Works of St. Thomas, Ont., 1833–1933: An Illustrated History for Bottle Collectors.* Vol. 1. Ontario Series. Privately printed, 1974. (Order from Canada West Publishing Company, 175 Alma Street, St. Thomas, Ontario N5P 3B5, Canada.)

————. *The Ontario Soda Water Bottle Collector's Index and Price Guide.* Vol. 2. Ontario Series. Privately printed, 1975. (Order from Canada West Publishing Company.)

————. *The Ontario Stone Ginger Beer Collector's Index and Price Guide.* Vol. 3. Ontario Series. Privately printed, 1975. (Order from Canada West Publishing Company.)

Markota, Peck and Audia. *Western Blob Top Soda and Mineral Water Bottles,* Revised Edition. Privately printed, 1972. (Order from authors, 8512 Pershing Avenue, Fair Oaks, California 95628.)

SOFT DRINKS

Coca-Cola Company, The. *The Coca-Cola Company . . . An Illustrated Profile.* Atlanta, Georgia: The Coca-Cola Company, 1974. (Order from The Coca-Cola Company, P.O. Drawer 1734, Atlanta, Georgia 30301.)

Goldstein, Shelly and Helen. *Coca-Cola Collectibles with Current Prices and Photographs in Full Color.* Vols. 1–4. Privately printed, 1971–75. (Order from author, P.O. Box 301, Woodland Hills, California 91364.)

Munsey, Cecil. *The Illustrated Guide to the Collectibles of Coca-Cola.* New York: Hawthorn Books, Inc. 1972.

————, and Petretti, Allan. *Official Coca-Cola Collectibles Price Guide.* Hackensack, New Jersey: The Nostalgia Publishing Company, 1978.

Paul, John R., and Parmalee, Paul W. *Soft Drink Bottling: A History with Special Reference to Illinois.* Springfield, Illinois: Illinois State Museum Society, 1973.

Pitcock, Florene. *Soft Drink Bottle Guide.* Privately printed, 1975. (Order from author, 30 N. Powell Avenue, Columbus, Ohio 43204.)

Rawlingson, Fred. *Brad's Drink: A Primer for Pepsi-Cola Collectors.* Privately printed, 1976. (Order from FAR Publications, Box 5456, Newport News, Virginia 23605.)

Sidlow, Peter J. *The Real Thing Price Guide,* 3rd edition. Privately printed, 1975. (Order from The Real Thing, 11702 Ventura Blvd., Studio City, California 91604.)

WHISKEY AND BEER

Anderson, Sonja and Will. *Andersons' Turn-of-the-Century Brewery Dictionary.* Privately printed, 1968. (Order from author, 1 Lindy Street, Carmel, New York 10512.)

Anderson, Will. *The Beer Book: An Illustrated Guide to American Breweriana.* Princeton, New Jersey: The Pyne Press, 1973.

Martin, Byron and Vicky. *Here's to Beers, Blob Top Beer Bottles 1880–1910.* Privately printed, 1973. (Order from Achin' Back Saloon, 8400 Darby Avenue, Northbridge, California 91324.)

Thomas, John. *Whiskey Bottles of the Old West.* Bend, Oregon: Maverick Publications, 1977.

Most of the books not published privately and listed in the bibliography can be obtained at local bookstores. Specialized shops that carry many books not normally stocked are:

Antique Publications
Emmitsburg, Maryland 21727

Hotchkiss House
18 Hearthstone
Pittsford, New York 14534

Collector Books
P.O. Box 3009
Paducah, Kentucky 42001

Old Bottle Magazine
Box 243
Bend, Oregon 97701

Alpa, Speedy Gonzales, 1977 .... 22.00
Alpa, Sylvester, 1977 .... 22.00
Alpa, Tweety Bird, 1978 .... 22.00
Alpha, see Lewis & Clark
Apothecary, Ammonia Carbon, Gold Leaf Label, 9 In. 10.50
Apothecary, Cylinder, Free-Blown, Open Pontil, Amethyst, 10 1/2 In. 200.00
Apothecary, Free-Blown, Leans 20 Degrees, Amethyst Tint, 2 Gallon 24.50
Apothecary, Glass Stopper, Bubbles, Cobalt Blue 15.00
Apothecary, Lin., Tereb., Acet., Stopper & Label, Ribbed, Cobalt, 8 In. 27.50
Apothecary, Millville, Mushroom Stopper, Honey Amber, 6 3/4 In. 8.50
Apothecary, P.Sennae, Gold Leaf Label, 9 In. 10.50
Auchinloch, Jug 7.00
Austin Nichols, see Wild Turkey
Avon started in 1886 as the California Perfume Company. It was not
until 1929 that the name Avon was used. In 1939 it became Avon
Products, Inc. Each year Avon sells many figural bottles filled with
cosmetic products. Ceramic, plastic, and glass bottles are made in limited
editions.
Avon, Abraham Lincoln, 1971, Full & Boxed 3.00
Avon, After Shave Caddy, 1968 .... 20.00
Avon, After Shave Lotion, 1958, 1/2 Oz. 5.00
Avon, After Shave On Tap, 1974, Amber 1.00
Avon, After Shave Soother, 1968, Full & Boxed 2.00
Avon, Airplane, see Avon, Spirit of St. Louis
Avon, Aladdin's Lamp, 1971-72, Gold Cap, 7 1/2 In. 8.00
Avon, Alaskan Moose, 1974 .... 7.00
Avon, Alpine Flask, Full & Boxed 45.00
Avon, American Beauty Fragrance, Jar, 1934 .... 3.50
Avon, American Belle, 1976 .... 5.00
Avon, American Eagle, 1971-75, Gold Plastic Head, Black, 6 In. 2.50
Avon, American Schooner, 1972-73, Blue Plastic Cap, 7 1/2 In. 4.00
Avon, Angel, see Avon, Golden Angel, Avon, Heavenly Angel
Avon, Angler, Fishing Reel, 1970, Silver Plastic Cap, Blue 5.00
Avon, Antiseptic, 7 Oz., 1956 .... 8.00
Avon, Anvil, 1972 .... 4.00
Avon, Ariane, 1977, First Edition On Bottle, Full & Boxed 4.50
Avon, At Point 4.00
Avon, Atlantic 4-4-2, 1973-75, Train, Silver Plastic Parts, Silvered, 8 In. 6.50
Avon, Auto Horn, see Avon, It's A Blast
Avon, Auto Lantern, 1973-74, Gold Cap, Amber Windows, 6 In. .... 10.00 To 13.00
Avon, Avon Calling For Men, 1969 .... 10.00
Avon, Avon Calling, Phone, 1973 .... 8.50
Avon, Avon Lady 1896, 1976 .... 35.00
Avon, Avon Lady 1906, 1977 .... 30.00
Avon, Avon Lady, 1916 .... 16.00
Avon, Avon Open, 1972-75 .... 6.00
Avon, Baby Grand Piano, 1971 .... 15.00
Avon, Baby Shoe, 1973 .... 5.00
Avon, Barber Bottle, see Avon, Close Harmony
Avon, Barometer, see Avon, Weather-Or-Not
Avon, Barrel, see Avon, After Shave On Tap
Avon, Baseball Mitt, see Avon, Fielder's Choice
Avon, Bath Oil For Men, 1968, Full & Boxed 2.00
Avon, Bath Urn, 1963, Opal Glass 12.00
Avon, Bathcare Sets, Bath Bouquet, 1965, Full & Boxed 25.00
Avon, Bay Rum Jug, 1962, White Enamel, Light Green Neck .... 6.00 To 15.00
Avon, Beautiful Awakening, Clock 5.00
Avon, Beauty Course Records, 1971 .... 10.00
Avon, Ben Franklin, 1974, Full & Boxed 6.00
Avon, Betsy Ross, 1976 .... 8.00
Avon, Big Game Rhino, 1972-73, Green Plastic Head, Green, 6 In. 6.00
Avon, Big Whistle, 1972-73, Silver Plastic Cap, Blue, 5 1/2 In. 3.00
Avon, Bird Feeding, 1967, Full & Boxed 7.00
Avon, Bird Of Paradise Bath Oil Emollient, 6 Oz., 1969, Full & Boxed 4.00
Avon, Bird Of Paradise Cologne, Clear Glass, 4 Oz., 1969, Full & Boxed 4.00
Avon, Bird Of Paradise Mist, 3 Oz., 1970 .... 2.00

Avon, Bird Of Paradise Skin Freshener, 1970 .... 1.00
Avon, Blue Eyes, Cat 4.00
Avon, Blue Lotus Bath Freshener, 1967, Full & Boxed 3.00
Avon, Bon Bon Cologne, 1973 .... 2.00
Avon, Book, First Edition, 1967 .... 6.00
Avon, Book, First Edition, 1967-68 .... 3.00
    Avon, Boot, see also Avon, Miss Lollypop Cologne Boot, Avon,
    High Button Shoe, Avon, Western Boot
Avon, Boot, Gold Top, 1966 .... 3.00
Avon, Boot, Silver Top, 1965 .... 7.00
    Avon, Bowling Pin, see Avon, King Pin
Avon, Breath Fresh, 1968 .... 1.00
Avon, Bright Night Cologne ,1954, Full & Boxed 10.00
Avon, Bright Night Cologne Mist, 3 Oz., 1958 .... 12.00
Avon, Bright Night Powder Sachet, 1954 .... 6.00
Avon, Brilliantine Bottle, 1936-54 .... 22.00
Avon, Bristol Blue, Full & Boxed 25.00
Avon, Bud Vase Cologne, 1968 .... 2.50
Avon, Buffalo Nickel, 1971-72, Silver Cap, Silvered, 5 In. 4.00
Avon, Bulldog, Pipe, Black Stem, Beige Milk Glass, 1972-73 .... 4.00 To 7.00
Avon, Bullet Perfume Oil, 1965 .... 10.00
Avon, Butter Dish, 1973, Full & Boxed 8.00
Avon, Butterfly, 1972, Full & Boxed 3.00
Avon, Cable Car, 1974, Full & Boxed 6.00
Avon, Caddy, 1968 .... 15.00
Avon, California Perfume Company, Baby Toilet Water, Dabber .... 25.00 To 80.00
Avon, California Perfume Company, Factory Club 40.00
Avon, California Perfume Company, Fruit Flavors, Iridescent 80.00
Avon, California Perfume Company, Vernafleur Adherent Face Powder, 1925 .... 40.00
Avon, California Perfume Company, 1908, Original Label 150.00
Avon, California Perfume Company, 1925 .... 95.00
Avon, Camper, 1972-74, Truck, Beige Plastic Top, Green, 7 1/2 In. 5.00
Avon, Canadian Goose, 1973-74, Black Plastic Head, Amber, 6 1/2 In. 7.00
    Avon, Cannon, see also Avon, Defender Cannon, Avon, Revolutionary
    Cannon
Avon, Cannon, 1966, Full & Boxed 8.00
Avon, Cannonball Express, 1976 .... 5.00
Avon, Capital, 1970, Full & Boxed 5.00
Avon, Captain's Choice, 1964 .... 10.00 To 12.00
Avon, Captain's Pride, 1970 .... 6.00
Avon, Car, Cable, 1974 .... 5.00
Avon, Car, Cadillac, Gold Plastic Cap, Gold Gilded, Full & Boxed, 1969-73 .... 20.00
Avon, Car, Cadillac, Solid Gold, Full, Box, 1969 .... 6.00
Avon, Car, Duesenberg, Silver, Full, Box, 1970 .... 5.00
Avon, Car, Electric Charger, Black Enameled, 6 In., 1971-72 .... 5.00
Avon, Car, Electric Charger, Full, Box 4.00
Avon, Car, Electric Charger, 1970 .... 3.00
Avon, Car, Packard Roadster, Amber, 6 1/2 In., 1970-72 .... 5.00
Avon, Car, Red Depot Wagon, Black Plastic Top, Amber, 5 In., 1972-73 .... 5.00
Avon, Car, Rolls Royce, Brown Plastic Hood, Beige Enameled, 8 In., 1972-75 .... 6.00
Avon, Car, Sterling Six, Black Plastic Tire Cap, Amber Shades, 1968-73 .... 10.00
Avon, Car, Stock Car Racer, Red & Blue Plastic Trim, 6 1/2 In., 1974-76 .... 4.00
Avon, Car, Straight Eight, Full, Box, 1969 .... 4.00
Avon, Car, Touring T, Black Plastic Top, Black Enameled, 7 In., 1969-73 .... 8.00
Avon, Car, Volkswagon, Blue, 1970-72 .... 4.00
Avon, Car, Volkswagon, Blue, 1973-74 .... 4.00
Avon, Car, Volkswagon, Red, 1972 .... 7.00
Avon, Car, 1936 M.G., White Plastic Top, Red Enameled, 7 In., 1974-75 .... 3.00
Avon, Casey's Lantern, 1966-67, Gold Caps & Enameling, Amber 40.00
Avon, Casey's Lantern, 1966-67, Gold Caps & Enameling, Green 50.00
Avon, Casey's Lantern, 1966-67, Gold Caps & Enameling, Red 35.00
    Avon, Cat, see Avon, Blue Eyes, Avon, Tabatha, Avon, Kitten
    Little, Avon, Kitten Petite, Avon, Ming Cat
Avon, Charisma Cologne Mist, 3 Oz., 1968 .... 2.00
Avon, Charisma Perfume Rollette, 1968 .... 1.00
Avon, Charisma Skin Softener, 1968 .... 1.00

Avon, **Charmlight Lamp,** Full & Boxed	7.00
Avon, **Chess Piece,** Original Set	4.00
Avon, **Chimney Lamp,** 1973-74, White Frosted Shade, Pressed Glass, 5 In.	5.00
Avon, **Christmas Cologne,** 1969-73, Faceted, Silver With Green	7.00
Avon, **Christmas On The Farm,** 1974, Full & Boxed	22.50
Avon, **Christmas Ornament,** Bubble Bath, Red, 1970	1.00
Avon, **Christmas Ornament,** Bubble Bath, 1967, Silver, Red, Round	3.00
Avon, **Christmas Sparkler,** Green, 1968-69	7.00
Avon, **Christmas Sparkler,** Purple, 1968	21.00
Avon, **Christmas Tree,** Bubble Bath, 1968, Red, Green, Silver	4.00
Avon, **Classic Lion,** 1973-75, Green Plastic Head, Green, 4 1/2 In.	6.00
Avon, **Clock,** see Avon, Beautiful Awakening, Avon, Daylight Shaving Time, Avon, Enchanted Hours, Avon, Fragrance Hours	
Avon, **Close Harmony After Shave Barber Bottle,** 1963	15.00
Avon, **Close Harmony,** 1963	10.00
Avon, **Coffee Mill,** see Avon, Country Store Coffee Mill	
Avon, **Cologne & Perfume Sets,** Bath Classic Cologne Only, 1962	5.00
Avon, **Cologne & Perfume Sets,** Fragrance Gold Trio, Set, 1964	18.00
Avon, **Cologne Classic,** 1967, Full & Boxed	5.00
Avon, **Cologne Gem,** 1967	2.00
Avon, **Cologne Mist,** Here's My Heart, 1958	5.00
Avon, **Cologne Mist,** 1963, Full & Boxed	5.00
Avon, **Cologne Mist,** 1966	5.00
Avon, **Cologne Mist,** 1968	2.00
Avon, **Cologne Mist,** 1969	2.00
Avon, **Cologne Riviera,** 1968, Full & Boxed	6.00
Avon, **Cologne Silk,** 1966	2.00
Avon, **Cologne Spray,** Wild Country, 1970, Full, Box	6.00
Avon, **Cologne Trilogy,** 1966, Full & Boxed	15.00
Avon, **Cologne,** Bravo, 1969, Full, Box	3.00
Avon, **Compact Set,** High Fashion, 1 Dram Perfume, Compact, Rouge, 1951	10.00
Avon, **Compote,** Gold Cap, Milk Glass, 5 1/2 In., 1972-75	5.00
Avon, **Corncob Pipe,** 1974	3.00
Avon, **Cotillion Bath Oil Bottle,** 1954	9.00
Avon, **Cotillion Body Powder,** 1957	10.00
Avon, **Cotillion Cologne Mist,** White Bottom, 1961	2.00
Avon, **Cotillion Cologne,** Gray Top, 1961	2.00
Avon, **Cotillion Cologne,** White Top, 1961	1.00
Avon, **Cotillion Cologne,** 1/2 Oz., 1970	1.50
Avon, **Cotillion Cologne,** 1953, Full & Boxed	20.00
Avon, **Cotillion Cologne,** 1956, Full & Boxed	18.00
Avon, **Cotillion Cream Sachet,** Pink Top & Bottom, 1954	7.00
Avon, **Cotillion Powder Sachet,** 1937, Full & Boxed	11.75
Avon, **Cotillion Powder Sachet,** 1961	5.00 To 6.00
Avon, **Cotillion Spray Perfume,** 1960	7.00
Avon, **Cotillion Talc Bottle,** 1956	8.00
Avon, **Cotillion Talc,** Painted Label, 1954	10.00
Avon, **Cotillion Toilet Water,** Pink Label, 1954	10.00
Avon, **Country Kitchen,** 1973-75	6.00
Avon, **Country Pump,** 1975	4.00
Avon, **Country Store Coffee Mill,** 1972-75, Milk Glass, 6 In.	5.00
Avon, **Courting Lamp,** 1970-71, Milk Glass Shade, Blue	8.00
Avon, **Courting Lamp,** 1970-71, Milk Glass Shade, Green	25.00
Avon, **Courting Rose,** 1974, Gold Cap & Stem, Red	8.00
Avon, **Cream Hair Lotion,** 1949	4.00
Avon, **Cruet,** Decanter, 1970	12.00
Avon, **Crystal Cologne,** 1966, 4 Oz., Full, Box	4.00
Avon, **Cupid's Bow,** 1955, Full & Boxed	45.00
Avon, **Dachshund,** 1973-74	3.00
Avon, **Daisy Pin Glace,** 1969	8.00
Avon, **Daphne Talcum,** 1936, 2.75 Oz.	12.00
Avon, **Daylight Shaving Time,** 1968, Full, Box	6.00
Avon, **Daylight Shaving Time,** 1970	3.00
Avon, **Dazzling Perfume,** 1969	1.00
Avon, **Decanter,** Greek Woman	10.00
Avon, **Decisions,** 1965	25.00

Avon, Decoy Duck, Silver Head .... *Illus*   7.50
Avon, Defender Cannon, 1966, Plastic Stand, Amber, 9 1/2 In. .... 12.00 To 15.00
Avon, Deodorant For Men, 1958 .... 5.00
Avon, Dew Kiss, 1960 .... 2.00
Avon, Dew Kiss, 1966 .... 1.00
     Avon, Dog, see Avon, At Point, Avon, Bon Bon, Avon,
     Dachshund, Avon, Lady Spaniel, Avon, Noble Prince, Avon, Old
     Faithful, Avon, Queen of Scots, Avon, Snoopy Surprise, Avon,
     Suzette
Avon, Dollars & Scents, 1966-67, Green Dollar, Silver Cap .... 10.00 To 25.00
Avon, Dolphin, 1967, Full & Boxed 3.00
Avon, Dolphin, 1968, Gold Plastic Tail Cap, Frosted, 9 In. .... 2.50 To 8.00

Avon, Decoy Duck, Silver Head

Avon, Dr.Hoot, 1975 .... 6.00
Avon, Dream Garden Perfume, Full & Boxed 10.00
Avon, Dream Garden, 1972-73, Watering Can, Gold Cap, Pink Frosted, 2 In. 5.00
     Avon, Dueling Pistols, see Avon, Twenty Paces
     Avon, Duesenberg, see Avon, Car, Duesenberg
Avon, Dutch Girl, 1973-74, Light Blue Top, Dark Blue Skirt, 7 In. 8.00
Avon, Dutch Pipe, 1973-74, Meerschaum, Blue Delft Scene, Milk Glass, 6 In. 5.00
Avon, Eiffel Tower, 1970, Pressed Glass, Gold Cap, 9 In. 4.00
     Avon, Electric Charger, see Avon, Car, Electric Charger
Avon, Electric Preshave Lotion, Spicy, 1962, Full, Box 7.00
Avon, Electric Preshave, 1967, Full, Box 3.00
Avon, Elegante Cologne, 1957, 4 Oz. 15.00
Avon, Elegante Cream Sachet, 1957 .... 6.00
Avon, Elegante Sachet, 1957 .... 8.00
Avon, Elizabethan, 1972, Fashion Figure, Pink Skirt, 10 In. .... 5.00 To 12.00
Avon, Elusive Cologne, 1/2 Oz., 1969 .... 1.50
Avon, Elusive Cream Sachet, 1969 .... 1.00
Avon, Enchanted Hours, 1973-74, Swiss Cuckoo Clock, Gold Top, 5 In. 3.00
Avon, Even Tone, 1961 .... 1.00
Avon, Evening Glow Lamp, Full & Boxed 7.00
Avon, Excalibur, Cologne, 1969, Full, Box 4.00
Avon, Eye & Throat Oil, 1964 .... 1.00
Avon, Factory, 1974 .... 50.00
Avon, Fan Rocker, 1962 .... 4.00
Avon, Fielder's Choice, 1971-72 .... 2.50
Avon, Fire Fighter, 1975, Red Enameled, 7 1/2 In. 5.00
Avon, First Class Male, 1970-71, Red Plastic Top, Blue, 4 1/2 In. 7.00
Avon, First Down, 1970 .... 4.00
     Avon, First Edition, see Avon, Book, First Edition
     Avon, Fish, see Avon, Dolphin, Avon, Sea Spirit
Avon, Flaming Tulip, 1973, Full & Boxed 9.00
Avon, Flamingo Brocade, 1971 .... 4.00
Avon, Flat Top Rocker, 1959 .... 4.00
Avon, Flight To Beauty, 1974, Full & Boxed 5.00
Avon, Flower Maiden, 1973-75, Yellow Skirt, 5 1/2 In. .... 2.50 To 8.00
Avon, Flowertime Perfume, 1949, 1 Dram 8.00
Avon, Flowertime Powder Sachet, 1951 .... 4.00

Avon, Fly-A-Balloon Boy, 1975, Holding Red Balloon, 8 1/2 In.	10.00
Avon, Football, see Avon, First Down	
Avon, Football Helmet, see Avon, Opening Play	
Avon, Forever Spring Cologne, 1950	15.00
Avon, Fragrance Bell, 1965, Full & Boxed	7.00 To 15.00
Avon, Fragrance Bell, 1968, Full & Boxed	7.00
Avon, Fragrance Chest, For Men, Full & Boxed	25.00
Avon, Fragrance Fling, 1968, Full & Boxed	2.00
Avon, Fragrance Hours, Clock, Grandfather, 1971-73	5.00
Avon, Fragrance Ornament, 1965, Full & Boxed	45.00
Avon, Fragrance Splendor, 1971, Full & Boxed	5.00
Avon, Fragrance Touch, Hand Holding Bottle, 1969-70, White Stopper	5.00
Avon, French Frosting, 1957	7.00
Avon, French Telephone, see Avon, Telephone, French	
Avon, Frosted Warrior, 1968, Full, Box	5.00
Avon, Futura Excaliber, 1969	10.00
Avon, Futura, 1969, Full & Boxed	18.00 To 20.00
Avon, Garden Girl, 1975, Plastic Top, Yellow Skirt, 6 1/2 In.	7.00
Avon, Garnet, Bud Vase, 1973-74, Diamond Quilted, Garnet Red, 6 1/2 In.	5.00
Avon, Gavel, 1967	20.00
Avon, Gavel, 1967-68, Brown Plastic Handle, Dark Amber, 8 In.	15.00
Avon, Gay 90s Figurine, see Avon, Victorian Lady	
Avon, Gaylord Gator, 1967	6.00
Avon, General 4-4-0	5.00
Avon, Gentleman's Choice, Black Cap, Tribute, 1969, Full, Box	7.00
Avon, Gentleman's Choice, Red Labels, 1969, 5 Different, Full, Box	3.00
Avon, Gentleman's Selection, 1970, Full, Box	2.00
Avon, Gift Cologne, 1969, Full & Boxed	4.00
Avon, Gold Cap Rocker, 1967	3.00
Avon, Gold Coast, 1974	27.50
Avon, Golden Angel, 1968-69	4.00
Avon, Golden Cadillac, Label	5.50
Avon, Golden Charmer, 1968, Full & Boxed	12.00
Avon, Golden Promise Cologne, 1947, Full & Boxed	15.00
Avon, Golden Rocket, 0-2-2, 1971-75, Train, Gilded, 5 1/2 In.	8.00
Avon, Golden Vanity, 1966	15.00
Avon, Golf, see Avon, Avon Open, Avon, Long Drive, Avon,	
Perfect Drive, Avon, Swinger, Avon, Tee Off	
Avon, Good Luck Elephant	3.00
Avon, Grape, 1973, Bud Vase, Purple Grapes, 8 In.	6.00
Avon, Grecian, 1972-76, Pitcher, Milk Glass, 6 1/2 In.	4.00
Avon, Hana Gasa Cologne, 1/2 Oz., 1970	1.50
Avon, Handy Frog, 1975, Red Top Hat, White, 5 1/2 In.	5.00
Avon, Hawaiian Ginger Bath Freshener, 1965, Full & Boxed	6.00
Avon, Hawaiian Ginger Bath Freshener, 1968, Full & Boxed	2.00
Avon, Head, see Avon, Warrior Head	
Avon, Hearth Lamp, 1973, Full & Boxed	5.00
Avon, Heavenly Angel, 1974-75	3.00
Avon, Helmet, see Avon, Opening Play	
Avon, Her Prettiness Talc, 1970	1.50
Avon, Here's My Heart Cologne Mist, 3 Oz., 1959	2.00
Avon, Here's My Heart Cologne, 2 Oz., 1958	2.00
Avon, Here's My Heart Cream Sachet, Full & Boxed	1.50
Avon, Here's My Heart Perfume Spray, 1958	7.00
Avon, Here's My Heart Skin Softener, 1964	1.00
Avon, Here's My Heart Soap, 1959, Full & Boxed	12.50
Avon, High Button Shoe, 1975-76, Gold Plastic Cap, 5 In.	2.00
Avon, High Top Button Shoe, 1975, Full & Boxed	3.00
Avon, Hobnail Bud Vase	4.00
Avon, Hobnail Decanter, 1972-74, Milk Glass, 5 1/2 In.	3.50 To 8.00
Avon, Honeysuckle Bath Freshener, 1967	1.50
Avon, Honeysusckle Talc, 1967	1.50
Avon, Hunter's Stein, 1972	15.00
Avon, Hurricane Lamp, 1973-74	10.00
Avon, Icicle, 1967	6.00
Avon, Independence Hall, 1973, Full & Boxed	25.00

Avon, Indian Chieftan, 1972-75, Gold Plastic Cap, Amber, 3 1/2 In. 3.00
Avon, Indian Head Penny, 1970-72, Bronze Plastic Cap, Bronzed, 4 In. 4.00
Avon, Indian Head Penny, 1970, Full & Boxed 5.00
Avon, Indian Head Penny, 1973, Full & Boxed 4.00
Avon, Ink Bottle ....*Color* 4.00
Avon, Island Line Cologne, 1969, Full, Box 4.00
Avon, It's A Blast, 1970-71, Black Rubber Bulb, Gold Gilded, 8 1/2 In. 5.00
Avon, Jar, Frosted, Rose Fragrance 40.00
Avon, Jasmine Bath Freshener, 1967 .... 2.00
Avon, Jewel Collection, 1964, Full & Boxed 35.00
Avon, Key Note, 1967, Key, Gold Plastic Cap, Full & Boxed 20.00
Avon, King Pin, 1969 .... 2.00
Avon, King Pin, 1969, Full, Box 4.00
Avon, Kitten Little, 1975-76, Black Plastic Head, 3 1/2 In. .... 3.00 To 6.00
Avon, Kitten Petite, 1973-74 .... 3.00
Avon, Kitten's Hideaway, 1974-76, White Plastic Cap, Dark Amber, 3 1/2 In. 3.00
Avon, Kodiak, 1977 .... 5.00
Avon, Koffee Klatch, 1971 .... 5.00
Avon, La Belle Telephone, 1974-76, Gold Plastic Top & Receiver, 5 In. 6.50
Avon, Lady Slipper Soap, 1965, Full & Boxed 12.00
Avon, Lady Spaniel, 1974-76 .... 3.00
Avon, Ladybug, 1975-76, Gold Plastic Head, 2 In. 5.00
    Avon, Lamp, see Avon, Courting Lamp, Avon, Hurricane Lamp,
    Avon, Ming Blue Lamp, Avon, Parlor Lamp, Avon, Tiffany
    Lamp
    Avon, Lantern, see Avon, Casey's Lantern
Avon, Lavender Cologne, 1970 .... 3.00
Avon, Lavender Powder, Sachet, 1961, Full & Boxed .... 4.00 To 8.00

Avon, Lavender Sachet, 4 In.

Avon, Lavender Sachet, 4 In. ....*Illus* 6.00
Avon, Leather Aerosol Deodorant, 1966, Full & Boxed 3.00
Avon, Leisure Hours Bath Oil Decanter, 1970 .... 2.00
Avon, Liberty Bell, 1973, Full & Boxed 35.00
Avon, Liberty Bell, 1976, Full & Boxed 6.00
Avon, Liberty Dollar, 1970, Full & Boxed 4.50
Avon, Lights And Shadows, 1969, Full & Boxed 5.00
Avon, Lilac, Sachet, 1967 .... .50
Avon, Lilac, Talc, 1963 .... 1.50
Avon, Liquid Hair Lotion, 1966, Full & Boxed 1.50
Avon, Little Kate, 1973-74, Girl With Muff, Apricot Enameled, 5 1/2 In. 10.00
Avon, Long Drive, 1973-75 .... 6.00
Avon, Longhorn Steer, 1975, Brown Plastic Head, White Horns, Amber, 7 In. 8.00
Avon, Lotion Lovely, 1964 .... 7.00
Avon, Lovebird, 1969-70, Frosted, Silver Cap, Full & Boxed, 2 1/2 In. 10.00

Avon, Magic Mushroom, 1969	50.00
Avon, Mallard, 1967-68, Silver Plastic Head, 6 1/2 In.	8.00
Avon, Mallard, 1974-75, In Flight, Green Plastic Head, 6 1/2 In.	4.50 To 8.00
Avon, Man's World, 1969-70, World Globe, Brown Plastic Stand, Gold Gilded	5.00
Avon, Marblesque Cologne Mist, 1974, Urn, Green, Marbleized, 5 1/2 In.	5.00
Avon, Marine Binoculars, 1973-74, Black Enameled Glass Gold Cap, 6 In.	9.00
Avon, Memory Book Glace, 1971	7.00
Avon, Men's Fragrance, Spicy, 1965, 1/2 Full	4.00
Avon, Milk Glass, Nesting Dove, 1970	6.00
Avon, Ming Blue Lamp, 1974-76, White Fluted Shade, Cobalt, 7 In.	7.00
Avon, Ming Cat, 1971	4.50 To 7.00
Avon, Mini-Cologne, 1969, Full & Boxed	1.50
Avon, Mini-Snowman Petite Perfume, 1973, Full & Boxed	6.00
Avon, Minuette Cologne, 1969	1.50
Avon, Miss Lollypop Cologne Boot, 1967-69	2.00
Avon, Modern Avon Lady, 1975	25.00
Avon, Nearness, Body Powder, 1954	8.00
Avon, Nearness, Cream Sachet, 1954	7.00
Avon, Nearness, Dusting Powder, 1959	8.00
Avon, Nearness, Powder Sachet, 1954	6.00
Avon, Nesting Dove, see Avon, Milk Glass	
Avon, Noble Prince, 1975-76, German Shepard, Amber, 6 1/2 In.	5.00
Avon, Occur, Cologne Mist	2.00
Avon, Occur, Cream Lotion, 1963	4.00
Avon, Occur, Cream Sachet, 1963	.50
Avon, Occur, Perfume Oil, 1/2 Oz., 1964	3.00
Avon, Oland Cologne, 1970, Full, Box	3.00
Avon, Old Faithful, 1972-73, St.Bernard, Gold Keg, Amber, 4 1/2 In.	7.00
Avon, Opening Play, Gold, 1968	15.00
Avon, Opening Play, 1968-67, Gold, Blue Glass, No Stripes	15.00
Avon, Original, 1965	10.00
Avon, Ornament, see Avon, Christmas Ornament, Avon, Christmas Sparkler	
Avon, Owl, see Avon, Dr. Hoot, Avon, Precious Owl, Avon, Wise Choice	
Avon, Parlor Lamp, 1971-72	8.00
Avon, Partridge, 1973-75, Milk Glass, 4 In.	7.00
Avon, Patterns, Cream Sachet, 1969	1.00
Avon, Perfect Drive, Golfer, 1975	5.00
Avon, Perfection Cake Chest, 1938	15.00 To 30.00
Avon, Perfume Flagon, 1966	7.00
Avon, Perfume Oil, 1969, Full & Boxed	3.00
Avon, Persian Wood, Cologne Mist, 1959	2.00
Avon, Persian Wood, Cologne, 2 Oz., 1959	6.00
Avon, Persian Wood, Lotion Sachet, 1957	5.00
Avon, Pert Penguin, 1975-76, Gold Plastic Head, 4 n.	2.00
Avon, Petite Mouse, 1970, Full & Boxed	10.00 To 15.00
Avon, Petti Fleur, 1969-73, Gold Leaf Cap, Full & Boxed	2.00
Avon, Piano, 1972, White Plastic Top, Amber, 4 In.	2.00
Avon, Picture Frame, 1970-71, Gold Plastic Frame & Cap, Gold Gilded, 4 In.	5.00
Avon, Piglet, 1972	5.00
Avon, Pin Bottle, see Avon, King Pin	
Avon, Pinecone, 1970, Full & Boxed	6.00
Avon, Pipe, see also Avon, Pony Express Rider Pipe, Avon, Uncle Sam Pipe	
Avon, Pipe Dream, 1966, Full & Boxed	18.00
Avon, Pipe Full, Amber, Full & Boxed	4.00
Avon, Pistols, see Avon, Twenty Paces	
Avon, Plus My Pet, Full & Boxed	30.00
Avon, Pony Express Rider, Pipe, 1971, Full & Boxed	4.00
Avon, Pony Post, Amber, Canadian	3.00
Avon, Pony Post, Green, Brass Ring, 10 In.	10.00
Avon, Pot Belly Stove, Full & Boxed	6.00
Avon, Precious Owl, 1972-74	3.00
Avon, Precious Swan, 1974-76, Gold Plastic Head, 2 In.	5.00
Avon, Precious Turtle, 1975-76	3.00

Avon, Pretty Girl Pink, 1975, Flower Girl, Pink Plastic Top, 6 In. 7.00
Avon, Pretty Peach, Cologne, 1964, Full & Boxed 18.00
Avon, Pretty Peach, Cream Sachet, 1964 .... 4.00
   Avon, Pump, see Avon, Country Pump, Avon, Town Pump
Avon, Pyramid Of Fragrance, 1969, Full & Boxed 15.00
Avon, Quail, 1973-75, Amber, Gold Plastic Head, 6 In. .... 4.00 To 5.00
Avon, Quaintance Cologne, 1948 .... 22.00
Avon, Quaintance Cream Lotion, 1949 .... 11.00
Avon, Quaintance Perfume, 1948 .... 22.00
Avon, Queen Of Scots, 1973, Full & Boxed 3.00
Avon, Rainbow Trout, 1973-74, Green Plastic Head, Green, 7 1/2 In. 6.00
Avon, Ram's Head, 1975-76, Black Plastic Base, Milk Glass, 4 In. 3.00
Avon, Rapture, Cologne, 1/2 Oz., 1970 .... 1.50
Avon, Rapture, Cologne, 2 Oz., 1964 .... 2.00
Avon, Rapture, Cream Sachet, 1964 .... .50
Avon, Rapture, Dark Blue Glass, 1966 .... 6.00
Avon, Rapture, Powder Sachet, 1964 .... 7.00
Avon, Regal Peacock, 1973 .... 6.00
Avon, Regence, Cologne Mist, 1966 .... 2.00
Avon, Regence, Cologne Silk, 1968 .... 2.00
Avon, Regence, Cologne, 2 Oz., 1966 .... 1.00
Avon, Regence, Skin Softener, 1966 .... 1.00
Avon, Remember When, School Desk, 1972-74, Red Apple Cap, Black, 3 1/2 In. 5.00
Avon, Revolutionary Cannon, 1975-76 .... 4.00
Avon, Roaring Twenties Girl, 1972 .... 8.00
Avon, Roll-A-Fluff, 1967 .... 17.00
   Avon, Rooster, see Avon, Country Kitchen
Avon, Rose Cold Cream, Jar, 1936 .... 4.00
Avon, Rose Fragrance, 1946 .... 60.00
Avon, Rose Fragrance, 1947 .... 35.00
Avon, Royal Apple, 1972-73, Red Frosted, Gold Leaf Cap, 3 1/2 In. 4.00
Avon, Royal Ark, 1965 .... 10.00
Avon, Royal Coach, 1973-74, Gold Cap, Full & Boxed, 3 In. 5.00
Avon, Scimitar, 1968-69, Gold Cap, Red Jewel Windows, Full, Boxed .... 10.00 To 22.00
Avon, Scottish Lass, 1975-76, Blue Plastic Top, Plaid Skirt, 6 In. 8.00
Avon, Sea Garden, Emollient Bath Oil, 1970 .... 1.00
Avon, Sea Garden, Spray Oil, 1970 .... 1.00
Avon, Sea Horse, 1970-72, Gold Head Cap, 9 In. .... 2.50 To 6.00
Avon, Sea Maiden, 1971-72, Mermaid, Gold Cap, 7 In. 6.50
Avon, Sea Spirit, 1973-75, Carp, Green Milk Glass, 7 1/2 In. 5.00
Avon, Sea Treasure, 1971-72, Seashell, Gold Cap, 7 In. 5.00
   Avon, Seashell, see Avon, Sea Treasure
Avon, Senorita, 1971 .... 5.00
Avon, Sewing Notions, 1975, Spool Of Thread, Thimble Top, Pink, 3 In. 3.50
Avon, Short Pony Head, 1968, Full, Box 4.00
Avon, Side Wheeler Steamboat, 1971-72, Amber, Gold Plastic Cap, 6 In. 5.00
Avon, Silk & Honey, 1969 .... 1.00 To 4.00
Avon, Skin Conditioner For Men, 1966 .... 3.00
Avon, Skin Conditioner For Men, 1969 .... 1.00
Avon, Skin Freshener, Blue, 1967 .... 1.00
Avon, Skin Freshener, 1956 .... 2.00
Avon, Skin So Soft, Bath Urn, 1963, Full 9.00
Avon, Skin So Soft, Blue Demi-Cup Bath Oil, Gold Top, 1968, Full & Boxed 8.00
Avon, Skin So Soft, Blue Demi-Cup Bath Oil, White Top, 1968, Full & Boxed 4.00
Avon, Skin So Soft, Golden Angel, 1968 .... 4.00
Avon, Skin So Soft, Leisure Hours, 1970, Full & Boxed 5.00
Avon, Skin So Soft, Painted Leaf, 1 Oz., 1966 .... 2.00
Avon, Skin So Soft, Scented Bath Oil, 1969, Full & Boxed 3.00
Avon, Skin So Soft, Skin So Soft, 1962, Full & Boxed 12.00
Avon, Skin So Soft, Skin So Soft, 1964, Full & Boxed 12.00
Avon, Skin So Soft, Skin So Soft, 1965, Full 8.00
Avon, Skin So Soft, Skin So Soft, 1966, Full & Boxed 10.00
Avon, Skin So Soft, Skin So Soft, 1967 .... 7.00
Avon, Skin So Soft, Strawberries & Cream, Orange, 1970, Full & Boxed 4.00
Avon, Skin So Soft, Strawberries & Cream, Red, 1970, Full & Boxed 8.00
Avon, Skin So Soft, Strawberries & Cream, 1969, Full & Boxed 8.00

Avon, Skin So Soft, Three Embossed S's, 4 Oz., 1966	1.00
Avon, Skin So Soft, Three Embossed S's, 8 Oz., 1966	1.50
Avon, Skin So Soft, 1972, Delft Blue, Full & Boxed	18.00
Avon, Small Wonder, 1972, Full	7.00
Avon, Smart Move, see Avon, Chess Piece	
Avon, Snail, 1968	5.00
Avon, Snail, 1969, Gold Head, Full & Boxed, 6 In.	8.00
Avon, Snail, 1973-75, Gold Head, Full & Boxed, 6 In.	6.00
Avon, Snoopy Surprise, 1969-71, Blue Plastic Hat, Milk Glass, 5 1/2 In.	6.00
Avon, Snow Bunny, 1975-76, Rabbit, Gold Plastic Head, 4 In.	3.00
Avon, Snowman Petite, 1973	7.00
Avon, Snowmobile, 1974-75, Black & Yellow Plastic Parts, Blue, 8 In.	5.00
Avon, Solid Gold Cadillac, see Avon, Car	
Avon, Somewhere, Cologne, Jeweled Lid, 1961	5.00
Avon, Somewhere, Cologne, 2 Oz., 1966	1.00
Avon, Somewhere, Cream Lotion, 4 Oz., 1961	4.00
Avon, Somewhere, Cream Sachet, 1961	3.00
Avon, Somewhere, Dream Castle, 1964, Full & Boxed	15.00
Avon, Somewhere, Powder Sachet, 1961	7.00
Avon, Somewhere, Skin Softener, 1966	1.00
Avon, Song Of Love, 1974, Full & Boxed	3.00
Avon, Spanish Senorita, 1975, Different Skirt Patterns, 6 In.	8.00
Avon, Spicy, Black Top, 1967, Full, Box	3.00
Avon, Spicy, Orange Top, 4 Oz., Full	8.00
Avon, Spirit Of St.Louis, 1970-72, Plane, Silver Glass, 7 1/2 In.	5.50 To 9.00
Avon, Sport Of Kings, 1975-76, Thoroughbred Horse, Amber, 6 In.	4.00
Avon, Spray Deodorant, White Plastic, 1962	2.00
Avon, Spray Essence, 1959	6.00
Avon, Spray Essence, 1966	6.00
Avon, Spray Essence, 1967	2.00
Avon, Spray Essence, 1969	2.00
Avon, Stagecoach, 1960, Gold Cap, Dark Amber, 4 1/2 In.	6.00
Avon, Stagecoach, 1961, Gold Cap, Dark Amber, 6 In.	18.00
Avon, Stagecoach, 1970, Full, Box	4.00
Avon, Stanley Steamer, 1972	3.00
Avon, Stein, 1965, Silvered Glass Holding Plastic Bottle, 8 Oz., Full	9.00
Avon, Stein, 1966, Silvered Glass Holding Plastic Bottle, 6 Oz.	12.00
Avon, Stein, 1968, Silvered Glass Holding Plastic Bottle, 6 Oz., Full, Box	6.00
Avon, Stein, 1976, Full & Boxed	30.00
Avon, Straight Eight, Car, see Avon, Car	
Avon, Sunshine Rose, 1973, Full & Boxed	9.00
Avon, Super Cycle, 1971-72, Motorcycle, Silver Handlebars, Gray, 7 In.	5.00
Avon, Super Rich Cream, 1936, Full & Boxed	5.00
Avon, Suzette, 1973-76	5.00
Avon, Swan Lake Cologne, 1972-76, Milk Glass, 8 In.	5.00
Avon, Swinger Golf Bag, 1969, Full, Box	5.00
Avon, Swinger, 1969-71	5.00
Avon, Sword, see Avon, Scimitar	
Avon, Tabatha, Cat, 1975-76	6.00
Avon, Tale For Men, 1939	8.00
Avon, Tee Off, 1973-75	4.00
Avon, Telephone, see Avon, Avon Calling, Avon, La Belle	
Telephone, Avon, Telephone, French	
Avon, Telephone, French, 1971, Full & Boxed	15.00 To 25.00
Avon, Ten-Point Buck, 1973-74, Deer, Gold Antlers, Red Amber, 4 1/2 In.	7.00
Avon, Theodore Roosevelt, 1975, Full & Boxed	6.00
Avon, Tiffany Lamp, Full & Boxed	9.00
Avon, Tiffany Lamp, 1972-74, Pink Leaded Shade, Amber, 8 1/2 In.	5.00
Avon, To A Wild Rose, see Avon, Wild Rose	
Avon, Tooth Powder, 1943-46, Paper Box	25.00
Avon, Topaze, Cologne, 2 Oz., 1960	1.50
Avon, Topaze, Powder Sachet, 1959	7.00
Avon, Topaze, Talc, 1960	5.00
Avon, Touring T Car, see Avon, Car	
Avon, Town Pump, 1968, Full, Box	3.00 To 5.00
Avon, Trailing Arbutus, Gold Cap, Label, 1930s	25.00

Avon, Train, see Avon, General 4-4-0

Avon, Treasure Chest, 1973	40.00
Avon, Treasure Turtle, 1971-73, Gold Head, Amber, Full & Boxed, 3 1/2 In.	3.00
Avon, Treasure Turtle, 1971, Full & Boxed	3.00
Avon, Tribute After Shave, 1968, Full & Boxed	2.50
Avon, Tribute Talc, 1963, Full & Boxed	5.00
Avon, Trilogy, 1969, Full & Boxed	18.00
Avon, Trout, 1973	5.00
Avon, Turtle, see Avon, Precious Turtle, Avon, Treasure Turtle	
Avon, Twenty Paces, 1967-69, Red Box, Full & Boxed	20.00 To 40.00
Avon, Ultra Sheer, 1967	1.00
Avon, Uncle Sam Pipe, Black Stem, Milk Glass, 6 In., 1975	5.00

Ballantine, Duck, Mallard, 1969

Avon, Unforgettable, Cologne Mist, 1965	2.00
Avon, Unforgettable, Skin Softener, 1965	1.00
Avon, Unicorn, 1974-75, Gold Plastic Cap, 5 1/2 In.	3.00
Avon, Venetian Pitcher, 1973-75, Silver, 3 Handled Top, Black Plastic Coated	5.00
Avon, Victorian Girl, 1971, White	10.00
Avon, Victorian Lady, 1972	7.00
Avon, Victorian Manor, 1972-73, Pink Roof, White Enameled, 4 1/2 In.	5.00
Avon, Viking Horn, 1966-67, Gold Plastic Cap, Dark Amber	20.00
Avon, Warrior, see also Avon, Tribute	
Avon, Warrior, Head, Silver Cap, Blue, Full & Boxed, 1967	15.00
Avon, Weather Vane, 1969, Full, Box	5.00
Avon, Weather-Or-Not, 1969-71, Dark Amber, Gold Eagle Cap	5.00
Avon, Western Boot, 1973-75	4.00
Avon, Western Choice, 1967, Steer Horns, Plastic Base, Red Center	10.00 To 12.00
Avon, Whale Oil Lantern, 1971	3.00
Avon, Whale Oil Lantern, 1975, Silver Base & Handle, Green, 7 In.	6.00
Avon, Wild Country Cologne, 1967	1.00
Avon, Wild Country Spray Cologne, 1968, Full & Boxed	2.00
Avon, Wild Rose, Body Powder, 1954	3.00 To 7.00
Avon, Wild Rose, Cologne, 2 Oz., 1961	3.00
Avon, Wild Rose, Cream Lotion, 4 Oz., 1954	8.00
Avon, Wild Rose, Skin Softener, 1964	1.00
Avon, Wild Rose, Toilet Water, 1950, Full & Boxed	15.00 To 25.00
Avon, Wild Turkey, 1974-75, Silver Head, Light Amber, 8 In.	5.00 To 7.00
Avon, Windjammer Cologne, Paper Label, 1969, Full & Boxed	4.00
Avon, Windjammer, 1972	5.00
Avon, Wings Of Beauty, 1975, Full & Boxed	3.50
Avon, Wise Choice, 1969-70, Silver Plastic Head, Amber, Full & Boxed	4.00
Avon, Wishing, Cream Sachet, 1963	1.00
Avon, Wishing, Powder Sachet, 1963	8.00
Avon, Women's Soap, Dolphin, 1970	7.00
Avon, Women's Soap, Lady Slipper, 1970	4.00
Avon, Women's Soap, Partridge & Pear, 1968, Full & Boxed	3.00
Avon, Women's Soap, Soap Jar, 1965	10.00 To 15.00
Avon, World's Greatest Dad, 1971, Full & Boxed	2.00
Ballantine, Charioteer, 1969	4.00
Ballantine, Discus Thrower, 1969	4.00
Ballantine, Duck, Mallard, 1969 .... Illus	15.00

Ballantine, Fisherman, 1969 .... *Illus* 19.00
Ballantine, Gladiator, 1969 .... 4.00
Ballantine, Golf Bag .... *Illus* 15.00
Ballantine, Knight, Gold, 1969 .... 17.00
Ballantine, Knight, Silver, 1969 .... 15.00
    Ballantine, Mallard, see Ballantine, Duck
Ballantine, Mercury, 1969 .... 4.00
Ballantine, Zebra, 1970 .... 8.00 To 14.00
Bank, Atlas, Strong Shoulder, Mason 11.00
Bank, Bear, Original Slotted Cap, 8 1/2 In. 6.00
Bank, Clown, Grapette, Slotted Cap, 7 1/2 In. .... 5.00 To 10.00
Bank, Iron, Man On Motorcycle With Sidecar, Cop 30.00
Bank, Lincoln .... 7.00 To 15.00
Bank, Lucky Joe 6.00
Bank, New York World's Fair, Watch Your Savings Grow, Globe, 1939, Slot 15.00
Bank, Radio Bank, 4 In. .... *Illus* 30.00
Bar, Cavalier Rye, Enamel, Fifth 12.00
Bar, Gensing Gin, Embossed, Gold Leaf Lettering 50.00
Bar, Hayner Whiskey 18.00
Bar, Hayner, Combination Lock Stopper 25.00
Bar, Kentucky Oaks, White Enamel Lettering, Quart 40.00
Bar, Malmo, Enamel Lettering, Quart 60.00
Bar, Pure Kentucky Brook, J.W.Flood & Co., White Enameling, Clear 37.00

*Barber bottles were used either at the barbershop or in the home. They
held hair tonic. These special, fancy bottles were popular in the last half
of the 19th century.*

Barber, Bay Rum, Cobalt, 12 In. 25.00
Barber, Cologne, Painted Decoration, Milk Glass, 10 1/2 In. .... *Illus* 85.00
Barber, Hand-Painted Daisies, Bell Shaped, OP, Black Amethyst 75.00

Ballantine, Fisherman, 1969

Ballantine, Golf Bag

Barber, Cologne, Painted
Decoration, Milk Glass,
10 1/2 In.

Bank, Radio Bank, 4 In.

Barber, Hobnail, Polished Pontil, Vaseline 45.00
Barber, Lyon's Kathairon For The Hair, N.Y., Aqua, Open Pontil 13.50
Barber, Milk Glass, Sandwich Glass Co., 9 1/2 In. .... *Illus* 125.00
Barber, Opaque Blue, Open Pontil, 10 1/2 In. 65.00
Barber, Spanish Lace .... *Illus* 27.50

Barber, Spanish Lace

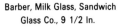

Barber, Milk Glass, Sandwich
Glass Co., 9 1/2 In.

Barney O'Killarney, Knuckles Muldoon 18.00
Barrel, Chapin & Gore, Amber 42.00
Barrel, Kelly's, Medium Amber 525.00
Barrel, Lancaster Glass Works, Puce 100.00
Barrel, Mist Of The Morning, Yellow Amber 150.00
Barsottini, Fruit Basket 15.00
Barsottini, Monk 10.00
Barsottini, Pheasant Rooster 15.00
Barsottini, Roman Warrior 12.00
Barton, Canadian Mounted Police 10.00

*Beam bottles are made as containers for the Kentucky Straight Bourbon
made by the James Beam Distilling Company. The Beam ceramics were
first made in 1953. Executive series bottles started in 1955. Regal china
specialties were started in 1955 and political figures in 1956. Customer
specialties were first made in 1956, trophy series in 1957, state series in
1958.*

Beam, ABC, Florida, 1973 .... 12.00 To 15.00
Beam, Ahepa, 1972, Club Series 6.00
Beam, Alaska Purchase, Centennial, 1966 .... 8.00 To 11.00
Beam, Alaska, State, 1958 .... 65.00 To 71.00
Beam, Alaska, State, 1959, Reissue 50.00
Beam, Alaska, State, 1964, Reissue .... 50.00 To 79.00
Beam, Alaska, State, 1965, Reissue 50.00
Beam, Amaretto, Glass Specialty, 1975, 11 1/4 In. 4.00
Beam, American Gothic, 1968, Collectors Edition Vol.III 4.00
Beam, Amvets, 1970 .... 6.00
Beam, Antioch, Centennial, 1967 .... 6.00
Beam, Appaloosa, 1974, Trophy 9.00
Beam, Aristide Bruant, 1966, Collectors Edition Vol.I 5.00
Beam, Arizona, State, 1968 .... 5.00
Beam, Armanetti Award Winner, 1969 .... 6.00
Beam, Armanetti Vase, 1968 .... 6.00
Beam, Artist Before Easel, 1966, Collectors Edition Vol.I 5.00
Beam, Ashtray, Ivory, 1955 .... 22.00
Beam, Au Cafe, 1970, Collectors Edition Vol.V 3.00
Beam, Australia, Kangaroo, 1977, Foreign Countries Series 22.00

Beam, Australia, Koala Bear, 1973, Foreign Countries Series .... 9.00 To 12.00
Beam, Australia, Magpie, 1977, Foreign Countries Series 22.00
Beam, Australia, Opera House, 1977, Foreign Countries Series 31.00
Beam, Australia, Tiger, 1977 .... 20.00
Beam, B.P.O.Does, Club 7.00
Beam, B.P.O.Does, 1971 .... 6.00
Beam, Bag Piper, 1972, Collectors Edition Vol.VII 4.00
Beam, Balcony, 1969, Collectors Edition Vol.IV 3.00
Beam, Bartenders Guild, 1973 .... 5.00 To 7.00
Beam, Baseball, Centennial, 1969 .... 5.00 To 7.00
Beam, Bass, Largemouth, 1973 .... *Illus* 9.00
Beam, Bass, Smallmouth, Trophy, 1973 .... 8.00
Beam, Beatty Burro, 1970, Glass Specialty 14.00
Beam, Beaver Valley Club, 1977 .... 16.95 To 27.00
Beam, Bell Ringer No.1, Tartan, 1970 .... 10.00
Beam, Bell, Zimmerman, Cobalt, 1976 .... 12.00
Beam, Bell, Zimmerman, Light Blue, 1976 .... 12.00
Beam, Ben Franklin, Rockwell, 1975, Glass Specialty 4.00
Beam, Bicentennial, 1975, Norman Rockwell .... *Illus* 4.00
Beam, Bighorn Sheep, 1976, Collectors Edition Vol.XI 4.00
Beam, Bing Crosby, 29th Pro-Am, 1970, Golf Series .... 5.00 To 8.00
Beam, Bing Crosby, 30th Pro-Am, 1971, Golf Series .... 7.00 To 8.00
Beam, Bing Crosby, 31st Pro-Am, 1972, Golf Series .... 22.00 To 35.00
Beam, Bing Crosby, 32nd Pro-Am, 1973, Golf Series .... 25.00 To 35.00

Beam, Bass, Largemouth, 1973

Beam, Bicentennial, 1975,
Norman Rockwell

Beam, Bing Crosby, 33rd Pro-Am, 1974, Golf Series 35.00
Beam, Bing Crosby, 34th Pro-Am, 1975, Golf Series .... 80.00 To 85.00
Beam, Bing Crosby, 35th Pro-Am, 1975, Golf Series 25.00
Beam, Bing Crosby, 36th Pro-Am, 1976, Golf Series .... 25.00 To 30.00
Beam, Bing Crosby, 37th Pro-Am, 1977, Golf Series .... 35.00 To 40.00
Beam, Binion's Horseshoe, 1970 .... 8.00 To 13.00
Beam, Black Crystal, Glass Specialty, 1974 .... 4.00
Beam, Black Katz, 1967, Customer Specialty 11.00
Beam, Black Katz, 1968 .... 12.00
Beam, Blue Beauty, Zimmerman, 1969 .... 12.00 To 14.00
Beam, Blue Boy, 1966, Collectors Edition Vol.I 5.00
Beam, Blue Crystal, 1971, Glass Specialty 5.00
Beam, Blue Fox, 1967 .... 110.00 To 130.00
Beam, Blue Gill, 1974, Trophy .... *Illus* 9.00
Beam, Blue Goose, 1979 .... 20.00
Beam, Blue Jay, 1969, Trophy * 7.00 To 10.00
Beam, Blue Slot Machine, Harolds Club, 1967 .... 13.00
Beam, Boating Party, 1970, Collectors Edition Vol.V 3.00

Beam, Bob Hope, 14th Desert Classic, 1973, Golf Series 12.00
Beam, Bob Hope, 15th Desert Classic, 1974, Golf Series 15.00
Beam, Bobby Unser Olsonite Eagle, 1975, Automotive Series .... 29.95 To 36.00
Beam, Bohemian Cafe Girl 15.00
Beam, Bohemian Girl, 1974 .... 16.00 To 18.00
Beam, Bonded Gold, 1975 .... 5.00
Beam, Bonded Silver, 1975 .... 5.00
Beam, Bowling Pin, 1952 .... 6.86
Beam, Bowling Proprietors, 1974, Club Series 6.00
Beam, Boy Holding Flute, 1971, Collectors Edition Vol.VI 4.00
Beam, Boy With Cherries, 1969, Collectors Edition Vol.IV 3.00
Beam, Boys Town Of Italy, 1973, Regal China .... 4.00 To 7.00
Beam, Broadmoor Hotel, Regal China, 1968 .... 5.00
Beam, Broadmoor Hotel, 1968, Regal China 6.00
Beam, Buffalo Bill, 1974 .... 4.00 To 6.00
Beam, Buffalo Hunt, 1968, Collectors Edition Vol.III 3.00
Beam, C.P.O., Mess, 1974 .... 10.00 To 18.00
Beam, C.R.L.D.A., 1973 .... 7.95
Beam, Cable Car, 1968 .... 5.00
Beam, Cal-Neva, 1969 .... 6.00
Beam, California Derby, Glass Specialty, 1971 .... 10.00

Beam, Blue Gill, 1974, Trophy
(See Page 13)

Beam, Centennial, 1976,
Martha Washington Bicentennial

Beam, California Mission, 1970 .... 18.00 To 24.00
Beam, Cameo Blue, Glass Specialty, 1965 .... 5.00
Beam, Cannon 3.00
Beam, Cannon, Glass Specialty, 1970 .... 4.00
Beam, Cardinal, 1968, Trophy .... 48.00 To 50.00
Beam, Cardinal, 1973, Female, Trophy .... 18.00 To 22.00
Beam, Cardinal, 1974, Collectors Edition Vol.IX 4.00
Beam, Carmen, 1978 .... 200.00 To 400.00
Beam, Cat, 1967, Burmese, Trophy .... 6.00 To 11.00
Beam, Cat, 1967, Siamese, Trophy .... 6.00 To 11.00
Beam, Cat, 1967, Tabby, Trophy 11.00
Beam, Cedars Of Lebanon, 1971 .... 5.00
Beam, Centennial, 1960, Santa Fe 220.00
Beam, Centennial, 1961, Civil War, North .... 30.00 To 42.00
Beam, Centennial, 1961, Civil War, South 65.00
Beam, Centennial, 1964, St.Louis Arch .... 12.00 To 42.00
Beam, Centennial, 1966, Alaska Purchase .... 8.00 To 11.00
Beam, Centennial, 1967, Antioch 6.00
Beam, Centennial, 1967, Cheyenne 6.00
Beam, Centennial, 1967, St.Louis Arch, Reissue .... 15.00 To 22.00

Beam, Centennial, 1968, Laramie 5.00
Beam, Centennial, 1968, Reno 5.00
Beam, Centennial, 1968, San Diego 5.00
Beam, Centennial, 1969, Baseball 6.00
Beam, Centennial, 1969, Lombard Lilac Festival 5.00
Beam, Centennial, 1970, Preakness Pimlico .... 5.00 To 7.00
Beam, Centennial, 1971, Chicago Fire .... 14.00 To 17.00
Beam, Centennial, 1971, Indianapolis 5.00
Beam, Centennial, 1972, Colorado Springs 6.00
Beam, Centennial, 1972, Dodge City, Boot Hill 5.00
Beam, Centennial, 1972, Key West 7.00
Beam, Centennial, 1972, Yellowstone 5.00
Beam, Centennial, 1973, Ohio State Fair .... 7.00 To 12.00
Beam, Centennial, 1973, Phi Sigma Kappa 7.00
Beam, Centennial, 1973, Reidsville .... 6.00 To 9.00
Beam, Centennial, 1974, Kentucky Derby, 100th 8.00
Beam, Centennial, 1975, Red Mile 9.00
Beam, Centennial, 1976, Colorado Centennial 12.00
Beam, Centennial, 1976, George Washington, Bicentennial ....*Illus* 12.00
Beam, Centennial, 1976, Martha Washington, Bicentennial ....*Illus* 12.00
Beam, Centennial, 1976, New Mexico, Bicentennial .... 6.95 To 10.00

Beam, Charlie McCarthy,
1976, Fantasy Series

Beam, Centennial, 1976, Statue Of Liberty, Bicentennial 7.00
Beam, Centennial, 1976, Washington State, Bicentennial .... 12.00 To 14.00
Beam, Charles I, 1971, Collectors Edition Vol.VI 4.00
Beam, Charlie McCarthy, 1976, Fantasy Series ....*Illus* 25.00
Beam, Cherry Hills Country Club, 1973 .... 7.00
Beam, Cherub, Lavender, Zimmerman, 1968 .... 8.00
Beam, Cherub, Salmon, Zimmerman, 1969 .... 8.00
Beam, Cheyenne, 1967, Centennial 6.00
Beam, Chicago Bottle Show, 1977 .... 35.00 To 50.00
Beam, Chicago Fire, 1971, Centennial .... 14.00 To 17.00
Beam, Chicago, Art Museum, 1972 .... 12.00 To 40.00
Beam, Chipmunk, 1976, Collectors Edition Vol.XI 4.00
Beam, Churchill Downs, 100th, 1974 .... 10.00
Beam, Churchill Downs, 95th, Pink Roses, 1969 .... 5.00
Beam, Churchill Downs, 95th, Red Roses, 1969 .... 10.00
Beam, Churchill Downs, 96th, 1970 .... 10.00 To 20.00
Beam, Churchill Downs, 97th, 1971 .... 5.00
Beam, Churchill Downs, 98th, 1972 .... 6.00 To 8.00
Beam, Civil War, North, Centennial, 1961 .... 33.00 To 42.00
Beam, Civil War, South, Centennial, 1961 .... 65.00

Beam, **Clear Crystal Bourbon,** Glass Specialty, 1967 .... 6.00
Beam, **Clear Crystal Scotch,** Glass Specialty, 1966 .... 10.00
Beam, **Clear Crystal Vodka,** Glass Specialty, 1967 .... 6.00
Beam, **Cleopatra,** Rust, Glass Specialty, 1962 .... 4.00
Beam, **Cleopatra,** Yellow, Glass Specialty, 1962 .... 13.00 To 15.00
Beam, **Clint Eastwood,** 1973 .... 5.00 To 10.00
Beam, **Cocktail Shaker,** Glass Specialty, 1953 .... 5.00 To 6.00
Beam, **Coffee Warmer,** 1954 .... 4.00 To 10.00
Beam, **Coho Salmon,** 1976, Trophy ....*Color* 7.00
Beam, **Collector's Edition,** Largemouth Bass, Vol.X, 1975 ....*Illus* 5.00

Beam, Collector's Edition,
Largemouth Bass, Vol.X, 1975

Beam, Executive, 1976,
Floro De Oro, Case

Beam, **Colorado Springs,** Centennial, 1972 .... 6.00
Beam, **Colorado,** State, 1959 .... 38.00 To 45.00
Beam, **Convention,** 1st Denver, 1971 .... 12.00 To 16.00
Beam, **Convention,** 2nd Anaheim, 1972 .... 45.00
Beam, **Convention,** 3rd Detroit, 1973 .... 20.00 To 25.00
Beam, **Convention,** 4th Lancaster, 1974 .... 40.00
Beam, **Convention,** 5th Sacramento, 1975 .... 16.00 To 19.00
Beam, **Convention,** 6th Hartford, 1976 .... 15.00 To 18.00
Beam, **Convention,** 7th Louisville, 1977 .... 16.00 To 20.00
Beam, **Covered Wagon,** Harolds Club, 1968 .... 6.00
Beam, **Crispus Attucks,** Glass Specialty, 1976 .... 5.00
Beam, **CRLDA,** 1973 .... 6.00
Beam, **Dancing Scot Couple,** 1964, Glass Specialty 200.00
Beam, **Dancing Scot,** Short, 1963, Glass Specialty 35.00
Beam, **Dancing Scot,** Tall, 1964, Glass Specialty 9.00
Beam, **Decanter,** Gold Bonded, 1975, Regal China 4.00
Beam, **Decanter,** Silver Bonded, 1975, Regal China 4.00
Beam, **Decanter,** Teal Blue, 1973, Glass Specialty 5.00
Beam, **Delaware,** State, 1972 .... 5.00 To 9.00
Beam, **Delft Blue,** 1963, Glass Specialty 4.00
Beam, **Delft Rose,** 1963, Glass Specialty .... 4.00 To 6.00
Beam, **Denver-Rush To The Rockies,** 1970 .... 8.00 To 17.00
Beam, **Dodge City,** Boot Hill, Centennial, 1972 .... 5.00
Beam, **Doe,** 1963, Trophy .... 30.00 To 33.00
Beam, **Doe,** 1967, Trophy, Reissue 30.00
Beam, **Dog,** 1959, Trophy, Setter .... 47.00 To 65.00
Beam, **Donkey,** Boxer, Political, 1964 .... 15.00
Beam, **Donkey,** Campaigner, Political, 1960 .... 14.00
Beam, **Donkey,** Clown, Political, 1968 .... 6.00
Beam, **Donkey,** Drum, Political, 1976 .... 10.00
Beam, **Donkey,** Football, Political, 1972 .... 6.00
Beam, **Donkey,** New York, Political, 1976 .... 6.00
Beam, **Duck,** 1957, Trophy 32.00
Beam, **Ducks & Geese,** 1955, Glass Specialty 7.00

Beam, **Ducks Unlimited,** No.1, Mallard, 1974	14.00
Beam, **Ducks Unlimited,** No.2, Wood Duck, 1975	14.00
Beam, **Ducks Unlimited,** No.3, 40th, 1977	13.00
Beam, **Ducks Unlimited,** No.4, 1978	16.00
Beam, **Eagle,** 1966, Trophy	12.00
Beam, **Eldorado,** Zimmerman, 1978	19.95
Beam, **Elect Casey,** Rockwell, 1975, Glass Specialty	4.00
Beam, **Elephant,** Agnew, Political, 1970	2000.00
Beam, **Elephant,** Boxer, Political, 1964	15.00
Beam, **Elephant,** Campaigner, Political, 1960	15.00
Beam, **Elephant,** Clown, Political, 1968	6.00
Beam, **Elephant,** Drum, Political, 1976	10.00
Beam, **Elephant,** Football, Miami Beach, Political, 1972	750.00
Beam, **Elephant,** Football, San Diego, Political, 1972	6.00 To 18.00
Beam, **Elephant,** Football, Washington, D.C., Political, 1972	700.00 To 850.00
Beam, **Elephant,** Kansas City, Political, 1976	6.00 To 12.00
Beam, **Elks Club,** 1968	5.00
Beam, **Emerald Crystal,** 1968, Glass Specialty	5.00
Beam. **Emile Zola,** 1969, Collectors Edition, Vol.IV	3.00
Beam, **Emmett Kelly,** 1973, Regal China	15.00 To 16.00
Beam, **Ernie's Flower Cart,** 1976, Regal China	13.96 To 19.00
Beam, **Evergreen,** 1974, Club Series	12.00 To 20.00
Beam, **Executive,** 1956, Royal Gold Round	125.00 To 135.00
Beam, **Executive,** 1957, Royal De Monte	60.00 To 75.00
Beam, **Executive,** 1958, Grey Cherub	400.00 To 425.00
Beam, **Executive,** 1960, Blue Cherub	115.00 To 145.00
Beam, **Executive,** 1963, Royal Rose	45.00 To 48.00
Beam, **Executive,** 1965, Marbled Fantasy	60.00 To 71.00
Beam, **Executive,** 1966, Majestic	34.00 To 40.00
Beam, **Executive,** 1973, Phoenician	10.00 To 11.00
Beam, **Executive,** 1975, Reflections In Gold	10.00 To 21.00
Beam, **Executive,** 1976, Floro De Oro, Case *Illus*	20.00

Beam, Executive, 1978,
Yellow Rose

Beam, Fire Engine, 1978, Regal China

Beam, **Executive,** 1977, Golden Jubilee	12.00 To 24.00
Beam, **Executive,** 1978, Yellow Rose *Illus*	24.00
Beam, **Expo 74,** Regal China	5.00 To 9.00
Beam, **Fiesta Bowl,** 1971, Glass Specialty	12.00 To 14.00
Beam, **Figaro,** 1977, Opera Series	395.00 To 584.00
Beam, **Fiji Islands,** 1971, Foreign Countries Series	5.00
Beam, **Fire Engine,** 1978, Regal China *Illus*	50.00
Beam, **First National Bank,** 1964	130.00 To 320.00
Beam, **Fleet Reserve Association,** 1974	5.00 To 10.00
Beam, **Florida,** Bronze Shell, State, 1968	5.00
Beam, **Florida,** White Shell, State, 1968	5.00

Beam, Football Hall Of Fame, 1972, Regal China .... 6.00 To 8.00
Beam, Foremost, Black And Gold, 1956 .... 180.00
Beam, Foremost, Grey & Gold, 1956 .... 208.00
Beam, Foremost, Pink Speckled Beauty, 1956 .... 650.00
Beam, Fox, Blue, 1967 .... 100.00 To 130.00
Beam, Fox, Distillery, Red Coat, 1973 .... 2500.00
Beam, Fox, Gold Coat .... 65.00 To 90.00
Beam, Fox, Renee, 1974 .... 11.00
Beam, Fox, Rennie The Runner, 1974 .... 11.00
Beam, Fox, Rennie The Surfer, 1975 .... 20.00 To 22.00
Beam, Fox, Uncle Sam, 1971 .... 8.00 To 12.00
Beam, Fox, White Coat, 1969 .... 40.00 To 45.00
Beam, Fox, 1965, Green, Trophy .... 30.00 To 40.00
Beam, Fox, 1967, Trophy, Green, Reissue .... 35.00 To 40.00
Beam, Franklin Mint, 1970, Regal China .... 6.00 To 9.00
Beam, Frederick Francois Chopin, 1973, Collectors Edition, Vol.VIII 4.00
Beam, Fruit Basket, 1969, Collectors Edition, Vol.IV 3.00
Beam, Game Called, Rockwell, 1975, Glass Specialty 4.00
Beam, Gare Saint Lazare, 1970, Collectors Edition, Vol.V 3.00
Beam, General Stark, 1972, Regal China .... 12.00 To 14.00
Beam, George Gisze, 1967, Collectors Edition, Vol.II 4.00
Beam, George Washington, 1976, Bicentennial .... *Illus* 12.00
Beam, German Short-Haired Pointer, 1977, Collectors Edition, Vol.XII 3.00
Beam, Germany, Wiesbaden, 1973, Foreign Countries Series 7.00
Beam, Germany, 1970, Foreign Countries Series 4.00

Beam, Glen Campbell, Los Angeles Open,　　　　Beam, Great Dane, 1976, Trophy
51st Pro-Am, 1976

Beam, Glen Campbell, Los Angeles Open, 51st Pro-Am, 1976 .... *Illus* 12.00
Beam, Golden Amber, Crystal, Glass Specialty, 1973 .... 5.00
Beam, Golden Amber, 1973, Glass Specialty 4.00
Beam, Golden Gate Las Vegas, 1969 .... 12.00 To 50.00
Beam, Golden Gate Las Vegas, 1970 .... 16.00
Beam, Grand Canyon, 1969, Regal China .... 9.00 To 13.00
Beam, Great Dane, 1976, Trophy .... *Illus* 13.00
Beam, Green China Jug, 1965, Regal China 5.00
Beam, Grey Slot Machine, Harolds Club, 1968, Regal China 5.00
Beam, Hannah Dustin, 1973, Regal China .... 20.00 To 24.00
Beam, Hansel And Gretel, 1971, Fantasy Series 4.00
Beam, Harolds Club, Blue Slot Machine, 1967 .... 13.00
Beam, Harolds Club, Covered Wagon, 1968 .... 6.00
Beam, Harolds Club, Nevada Grey, 1963, Customer Specialty .... 145.00 To 160.00
Beam, Harolds Club, Nevada Silver, 1964, Customer Specialty .... 145.00 To 165.00
Beam, Harolds Club, Reno Or Bust, 1974 .... 15.00
Beam, Harolds Club, V.I.P., 1969, Customer Specialty 182.00
Beam, Harolds Club, V.I.P., 1975, Customer Specialty .... 12.95 To 27.00
Beam, Harolds Club, V.I.P., 1977, Customer Specialty .... 30.00 To 50.00

Beam, Harrah's Club, Nevada Grey, 1963, Customer Specialty 758.00
Beam, Harrah's Club, Nevada Silver, 1963 .... 11.96
Beam, Harvey's Glass, 1969, Glass Specialty 6.00
Beam, Hauling In The Gill Net, 1968, Collectors Edition, Vol.III 3.00
Beam, Hawaii, State, 1959 .... 50.00 To 55.00
Beam, Hawaii, State, 1967, Reissue .... 30.00 To 44.00
Beam, Hawaiian Open, 1972, 7th, Pineapple, Golf Series 8.00
Beam, Hawaiian Open, 1973, 8th, Golf Ball, Golf Series 8.00
Beam, Hawaiian Open, 1974, 9th, Tiki God, Golf Series 8.00
Beam, Hawaiian Open, 1975, 10th, Menehone, Golf Series 8.00
Beam, Hawaiian Open, 1975, 11th, Outrigger, Golf Series ....*Illus*   15.00

Beam, International
Chili Society, 1976

Beam, Hawaiian Open, 1975,
11th, Outrigger, Golf Series

Beam, King Kong, 1976
(See Page 20)

Beam, Hawaiian Open, 1975, 11th, UA & Emblem, Golf Series 28.00
Beam, Hawaiian Open, 1976, 12th, Disk, Golf Series 14.00
Beam, Hemisfair, 1968, Regal China .... 7.00 To 9.00
Beam, Herre Bros., 1972, Glass Specialty 25.00
Beam, Hoffman, Regal China, 1969 .... 6.00 To 12.00
Beam, Homecoming, Rockwell, 1975, Glass Specialty 4.00
Beam, Horse, 1962, Black, Trophy 24.00
Beam, Horse, 1962, Brown, Trophy 24.00
Beam, Horse, 1962, White, Trophy .... 20.00 To 24.00
Beam, Horse, 1967, Black, Trophy, Reissue .... 20.00 To 22.00
Beam, Horse, 1967, Brown, Trophy, Reissue .... 20.00 To 22.00
Beam, Horse, 1967, White, Trophy, Reissue .... 20.00 To 22.00
Beam, Horseshoe Club, Reno, 1969 .... 6.00 To 8.00
Beam, Hula Bowl, 1975, Golf Series 13.00
Beam, Humboldt County Fair, 1970, Glass Specialty 10.00
Beam, Hyatt House, Chicago, 1971, Customers Specialty 17.00
Beam, Hyatt Regency, New Orleans, 1976 .... 30.00
Beam, Idaho, State, 1963 .... 60.00 To 65.00
Beam, Illinois, State, Embossed Stopper, 1968 .... 8.00
Beam, Illinois, State, 1968 .... 5.00 To 7.00
Beam, Indian Maiden, 1968, Collectors Edition, Vol.III 4.00
Beam, Indianapolis 500, 1970, 54th Anniversary, Regal China 4.00
Beam, Indianapolis, Sesquicentennial, 1971 .... 5.00
Beam, International Chili Society, 1976 ....*Illus*   12.00
Beam, International Petroleum, 1971, Regal China 5.00
Beam, Irish Setter, 1977, Collectors Edition, Vol.XII 3.00
Beam, Jackelope, 1971, Fantasy Series .... 6.00 To 35.00
Beam, Jester, 1967, Collectors Edition, Vol.II 4.00
Beam, Jewel Tea Wagon, 1974 .... 27.00 To 36.00
Beam, Jewish Bride, 1970, Collectors Edition, Vol.V 3.00
Beam, John Henry, 1972, Fantasy Series .... 68.00 To 75.00
Beam, Judge, 1969, Collectors Edition, Vol.IV 3.00

Beam, Jug, Two Handled, Zimmerman, Green, 1965 .... 115.00
Beam, Kaiser International, 1971, Golf Series 5.00
Beam, Kansas, State, 1960 .... 57.00 To 66.00
Beam, Kentuckian, 1968, Collectors Edition, Vol.III 4.00
Beam, Kentucky Colonel, 1970 .... 5.00
Beam, Kentucky Derby, Centennial, 1974 .... 8.00
Beam, Kentucky, Black Head, State, 1967 .... 14.00
Beam, Kentucky, Brown Head, State, 1967 .... 22.00
Beam, Kentucky, White Head, State, 1967 .... 20.00 To 65.00
Beam, Key West, Centennial, 1972 .... 5.00 To 7.00
Beam, King Kamehameha, 1972, Regal China .... 17.00 To 21.00
Beam, King Kong, 1976 .... Illus 15.00
Beam, Labrador Retreiver, 1977, Collectors Edition, Vol.XII 3.00
Beam, Laramie, Centennial, 1968 .... 5.00
Beam, Largemouth Bass, 1975, Collectors Edition, Vol.X .... 5.00 To 8.00
Beam, Las Vegas, 1969, Regal China 5.00
Beam, Laughing Cavalier, 1966, Collectors Edition, Vol.I 5.00
Beam, Lombard Lilac Festival, Centennial, 1969 .... 5.00
Beam, London Bridge, Medallion, 1971 .... 50.00
Beam, London Bridge, 1971, Regal China 5.00
Beam, Louisiana Superdome, 1975, Regal China 8.00
Beam, Louisville Downs, Pro-Am, 1977 .... Illus 13.00
Beam, Ludwig Van Beethoven, 1973, Collectors Edition, Vol.VIII 4.00
Beam, Madama Butterfly, Gold Base, 1977, Opera Series 50.00
Beam, Madama Butterfly, Paperweight & Base, 1977, Opera Series .... 800.00 To 1000.00
Beam, Madama Butterfly, 1977, Opera Series .... Color 550.00
Beam, Maidservant Pouring Milk, 1972, Collectors Edition, Vol.VII 4.00
Beam, Maine, State, 1970 .... 5.00
Beam, Man On Horse, 1967, Collectors Edition, Vol.II 4.00
Beam, Marbleized, Crystal, Glass Specialty, 1972 .... 4.00
Beam, Mardi Gras, 1966, Collectors Edition, Vol.I 5.00
Beam, Marina City, 1962 .... 32.00 To 37.00
Beam, Marine Corps, 1975 .... 45.00 To 60.00
Beam, Mark Anthony, 1962, Glass Specialty 16.00
Beam, Martha Washington, Centennial, 1976 .... Illus 12.00
Beam, McCoy, 1973, Regal China 25.00
Beam, Merry Lute Player, 1971, Collectors Edition, Vol.VI 4.00
Beam, Metallic Gold, 1976, Glass Specialty 4.00
Beam, Metallic Silver, 1976, Glass Specialty 4.00
Beam, Michigan, State, 1972 .... 5.00 To 8.00
Beam, Milwaukee Club Stein, 1972 .... 30.00 To 50.00
Beam, Mint 400, 3rd, 1970, Ceramic Stopper 12.00
Beam, Mint 400, 3rd, 1970, Metal Stopper 12.00
Beam, Mint 400, 4th, 1971, Motorcycle Stopper 7.00
Beam, Mint 400, 5th, 1972, Helmet Stopper, Regal China 7.00
Beam, Mint 400, 6th, 1973 .... 10.00
Beam, Mint 400, 7th, 1975 .... 5.00
Beam, Mint 400, 8th, 1976 .... 6.00
Beam, Model A Ford, Black, 1978 .... 44.95
Beam, Model A Ford, Red, 1978 .... Color 44.95
Beam, Model T Ford, Black, 1974, Automotive Series .... 24.00 To 32.00
Beam, Model T Ford, Green, 1974, Automotive Series .... 24.00 To 32.00
Beam, Momence Gladiolas Festival, 1974, Regal China 6.00
Beam, Montana, State, 1963 .... 73.00 To 81.00
Beam, Monterey Bay Club, 1977 .... 22.00
Beam, Mortimer Snerd, 1976, Fantasy Series .... 14.00 To 15.95
Beam, Musicians On Wine Cask, 1964, Regal China 6.00
Beam, National Licensed Beverage Assoc., 1975 .... 7.00 To 8.00
Beam, Navy, C.P.O., 1974 .... 6.00 To 12.00
Beam, Nebraska No.1, Coach Devanay, 1972 .... 8.00
Beam, Nebraska, State, 1967 .... 6.00 To 8.00
Beam, Nevada Grey, Harolds Club, 1963 .... 157.00 To 160.00
Beam, Nevada Silver, Harolds Club, 1964 .... 160.00 To 165.00
Beam, Nevada, State, 1963 .... 40.00 To 51.00
Beam, New Hampshire, Gold Eagle, 1971, Regal China .... 35.00 To 41.00
Beam, New Hampshire, State, 1967 .... 5.00 To 8.00

Beam, New Jersey, Grey, State, 1963 .... 65.00 To 77.00
Beam, New Jersey, Yellow, State, 1963 .... 55.00 To 60.00
Beam, New Mexico, Bicentennial, 1976 .... 6.95 To 10.00
Beam, New Mexico, State, 1972 .... 12.00 To 17.00
Beam, New York World's Fair, 1964, Regal China .... 18.00 To 24.00
Beam, New Zealand, Kiwi, 1974, Backwards, Foreign Countries Series 17.00
Beam, New Zealand, Kiwi, 1974, Foreign Countries Series .... 6.00 To 8.00
Beam, Night Watch, 1967, Collectors Edition, Vol.II 4.00
Beam, North Dakota, State, 1964 .... 80.00 To 105.00
Beam, Northern Pike, 1978.Trophy 8.00
Beam, Nurse And Child, 1967, Collectors Edition, Vol.II 4.00
Beam, Oatmeal China Jug, 1966, Regal China 63.00
Beam, Ohio State Fair, Centennial, 1973 .... 7.00 To 12.00
Beam, Ohio, State, 1966 .... 8.00 To 12.00
Beam, Old Peasant, 1970, Collectors Edition, Vol.V 3.00
Beam, Oldsmobile, 1972, Automotive Series .... 60.00 To 80.00
Beam, Olympian, 1960, Glass Specialty 4.00
Beam, On The Terrace, 1966, Collectors Edition, Vol.I 6.50
Beam, On The Trail, 1968, Collectors Edition, Vol.III 3.00
Beam, Opaline, Crystal, Glass Specialty, 1969 .... 4.00
Beam, Oregon, State, 1959 .... 36.00 To 45.00
Beam, Oriental Jade, Glass Specialty, 1972 .... 5.00
Beam, P.G.A., Club, 1971 .... 5.00
Beam, Paul Bunyan, 1970, Fantasy Series .... 6.00 To 8.00
Beam, Pearl Harbor Survivors, No.1, 1972 .... 18.00 To 25.00
Beam, Pearl Harbor Survivors, No.2, 1976 .... 6.00 To 12.00
Beam, Peddler, Zimmerman, 1971 .... 12.00 To 15.00
Beam, Pennsylvania Dutch Club, 1974 .... 18.00 To 20.00
Beam, Pennsylvania, State, 1967 .... 6.00 To 9.00
Beam, Pheasant, 1960, Trophy .... 18.00 To 26.00
Beam, Pheasant, 1961, Trophy, Reissue 18.00
Beam, Pheasant, 1963, Trophy, Reissue .... 16.00 To 22.00
Beam, Pheasant, 1966, Trophy, Reissue 18.00
Beam, Pheasant, 1967, Reissue, Trophy 18.00

Beam, Louisville Downs, Pro-Am, 1977

Beam, Political, Donkey, 1976, Drum

Beam, Political, Elephant, 1976, Drum
(See Page 22)

Beam, Pheasant, 1968, Trophy, Reissue 18.00
Beam, Phi Sigma Kappa, Centennial, 1973 .... 6.00
Beam, Pied Piper, 1974, Fantasy Series 5.00
Beam, Pinwheel, Harolds Club, 1965 .... 65.00 To 68.00
Beam, Pioneers, Rockwell, 1975, Glass Specialty 6.00
Beam, Political, Donkey, 1956, Ashtray 14.00
Beam, Political, Donkey, 1960, Campaigner 14.00
Beam, Political, Donkey, 1964, Boxer 15.00
Beam, Political, Donkey, 1968, Clown 6.00
Beam, Political, Donkey, 1972, Football 6.00
Beam, Political, Donkey, 1976, Drum .... Illus 10.00

Beam, Political, Donkey, 1976, New York 6.00
Beam, Political, Elephant, 1956, Ashtray 14.00
Beam, Political, Elephant, 1960, Campaigner 15.00
Beam, Political, Elephant, 1964, Boxer 15.00
Beam, Political, Elephant, 1968, Clown 6.00
Beam, Political, Elephant, 1970, Agnew 2000.00
Beam, Political, Elephant, 1972, Football, Miami Beach, Prestige Award 750.00
Beam, Political, Elephant, 1972, Football, San Diego .... 6.00 To 18.00
Beam, Political, Elephant, 1976, Drum ....*Illus* 10.00
Beam, Political, Elephant, 1976, Kansas City .... 6.00 To 12.00
Beam, Ponderosa Ranch, 1969, Regal China .... 5.00 To 16.00
Beam, Pony Express, 1968, Regal China 5.00
Beam, Poodle, 1970, Grey, Trophy 7.00
Beam, Poodle, 1970, White, Trophy 7.00
Beam, Portland Rose Festival, 1972, Regal China .... 5.00 To 9.00
Beam, Portola Trek, 1969, Glass Specialty 5.00
Beam, Powell Expedition, 1969, Glass Specialty .... 6.00 To 8.00
Beam, Preakness, Centennial, 1975, Reissue .... 5.66 To 7.00
Beam, Preakness, 100th Anniversary, Centennial, 1970 .... 7.00
Beam, Prima Donna, 1969 .... 6.00
Beam, Prince Baltasor Carlos, 1972, Collectors Edition, Vol.VII 4.00

Beam, Short Timer,
1975, Regal China

Beam, Spenger's
Fish Grotto, 1977

Beam, Pronghorn Antelope, 1976, Collectors Edition, Vol.VII 4.00
Beam, Rainbow Trout, 1975, Collectors Edition, Vol.X .... 5.00 To 10.00
Beam, Ralph's Market, Centennial, 1973 .... 12.00 To 16.00
Beam, Ram, 1958, Trophy .... 144.00 To 155.00
Beam, Ramada Inn, 1976, Regal China .... 6.00 To 8.00
Beam, Red Mile, Centennial, 1976 .... 9.00
Beam, Redwood, 1967, Regal China .... 4.00 To 6.00
Beam, Reidsville, Centennial, 1973 .... 6.00 To 9.00
Beam, Reno Or Bust, Harolds Club, 1974 .... 15.00
Beam, Reno, Centennial, 1968 .... 5.00
Beam, Richard's New Mexico, 1967 .... 5.00
Beam, Ring-Neck Pheasant, 1974, Collectors Edition, Vol.IX 4.00
Beam, Riverside Centennial, 1970, Glass Specialty 10.00
Beam, Robin, 1969, Trophy .... 7.00 To 11.00
Beam, Rocky Marciano, 1973, Regal China .... 5.00 To 11.00
Beam, Royal Crystal, Glass Specialty, 1957 .... 4.00
Beam, Royal Emperor, 1958, Glass Specialty 6.00
Beam, Royal Opal, 1957, Glass Specialty 8.00
Beam, Royal Reserve, 1953, Glass Specialty 4.00
Beam, Rubber Capital, Akron, 1973, Club Series .... 22.00 To 28.00
Beam, Ruby, Crystal, Glass Specialty, 1967 .... 10.00
Beam, Ruidoso Downs, Pointed Ears, 1968, Regal China 22.00
Beam, Ruidoso Downs, 1968, Regal China 5.00
Beam, Sahara Invitational, 1971, Golf Series 5.00
Beam, Sailfish, 1957, Trophy 34.00
Beam, Sailfish, 1974, Collectors Edition, Vol.X 5.00

Beam, Samoa, 1973, Foreign Countries Series 7.00
Beam, San Diego, Centennial, 1968 .... 5.00
Beam, Santa Fe, 1960, Centennial 220.00
Beam, Scout, 1968, Collectors Edition, Vol.III 4.00
Beam, Seafair, 1972, Regal China .... 7.00 To 10.00
Beam, Seattle World's Fair, 1962, Regal China .... 15.00 To 18.00
Beam, Sheraton Hotel, 1975, Regal China .... 10.00 To 12.95
Beam, Short Timer, 1975, Regal China ....Illus   11.00
Beam, Shriners, El Kahir, 1975 .... 10.00 To 18.00
Beam, Shriners, Indiana, 1970 .... 5.00
Beam, Shriners, Moila No.1, 1972 .... 24.00
Beam, Shriners, Moila No.2, 1975 .... 20.00
Beam, Shriners, Ra Juh, 1977 .... 20.00
Beam, Sigma Nu, Kentucky, 1977 .... 13.00
Beam, Sigma Nu, Michigan, 1977 .... 5.66
Beam, Smith's North Shore Club, 1972 .... 12.00
Beam, Smoked Crystal, Geni, 1964, Glass Specialty 10.00
Beam, Smoked Crystal, 1964, Glass Specialty 5.00
Beam, Snow Goose, 1979 .... 20.00
Beam, Soldier And Girl, 1967, Collectors Edition, Vol.II 4.00
Beam, South Carolina, State, 1970 .... 5.00
Beam, South Dakota, Mt.Rushmore, State, 1969 .... 6.00
Beam, Spenger's Fish Grotto, 1977 ....Illus   18.00
Beam, Sports Car Club Of America, 1976 .... 7.56 To 12.00
Beam, Springer Spaniel, 1977, Collectors Edition, Vol.XII 3.00
Beam, St.Louis Arch, 1964, Centennial .... 12.00 To 42.00
Beam, St.Louis Arch, 1967, Centennial, Reissue .... 15.00 To 17.00
Beam, St.Louis, Club, 1972 .... 20.00
Beam, State, Alaska, 1958 .... 65.00 To 71.00
Beam, State, Alaska, 1959, Reissue 50.00
Beam, State, Alaska, 1964, Reissue .... 50.00 To 69.00
Beam, State, Alaska, 1965, Reissue 50.00
Beam, State, Arizona, 1968 .... 5.00
Beam, State, Colorado, 1959 .... 38.00 To 45.00
Beam, State, Delaware, 1972 * 5.00 To 8.00
Beam, State, Florida, Bronze Shell, 1968 .... 5.00
Beam, State, Florida, White Shell, 1968 .... 5.00
Beam, State, Hawaii, 1959 .... 50.00 To 55.00
Beam, State, Hawaii, 1967, Reissue .... 30.00 To 44.00
Beam, State, Idaho, 1963 .... 60.00 To 66.00
Beam, State, Illinois, 1968 .... 5.00 To 7.00
Beam, State, Illinois, 1968, Embossed Stopper 8.00
Beam, State, Kansas, 1960 .... 57.00 To 66.00
Beam, State, Kentucky, Black Head, 1967 .... 13.00
Beam, State, Kentucky, Brown Head, 1967 .... 22.00
Beam, State, Kentucky, White Head, 1967 .... 20.00 To 65.00
Beam, State, Maine, 1970 .... 5.00
Beam, State, Michigan, 1972 .... 5.00 To 8.00
Beam, State, Montana, 1963 .... 73.00 To 81.00
Beam, State, Nebraska, 1967 .... 6.00 To 8.00
Beam, State, Nevada, 1963 .... 40.00 To 51.00
Beam, State, New Hampshire, 1967 .... 5.00 To 8.00
Beam, State, New Jersey, Grey, 1963 .... 65.00 To 77.00
Beam, State, New Jersey, Yellow, 1963 .... 55.00 To 60.00
Beam, State, New Mexico, 1972 .... 12.00 To 17.00
Beam, State, North Dakota, 1964 .... 80.00 To 105.00
Beam, State, Ohio, 1966 .... 8.00 To 12.00
Beam, State, Oregon, 1959 .... 36.00 To 45.00
Beam, State, Pennsylvania, 1967 .... 6.00 To 9.00
Beam, State, South Carolina, 1970 .... 5.00
Beam, State, South Dakota, Mt.Rushmore, 1969 .... 6.00
Beam, State, Washington, 1975 .... 9.00 To 16.00
Beam, State, West Virginia, 1963 .... 222.00 To 232.00
Beam, State, Wyoming, 1965 .... 57.00 To 67.00
Beam, Statue Of Liberty, Bicentennial, 1976 .... 7.00 To 9.00
Beam, Stone Mountain, 1974, Regal China .... 6.00 To 10.00

Beam, Stutz Bearcat, Grey And Black, 1977, Automotive Series 29.95
Beam, Stutz Bearcat, Yellow And Black, 1977, Automotive Series 37.00
Beam, Submarine Redfin, 1970, Regal China 5.00
Beam, Sunburst Amaretto, 1975, Glass Specialty 4.00
Beam, Sunburst Amaretto, 1976, Glass Specialty 4.00
Beam, Sunburst Azur-Glo, 1975, Glass Specialty 4.00
Beam, Sunburst Chocolomi, 1976, Glass Specialty 4.00
Beam, Sunburst Expresso, 1976, Glass Specialty 4.00
Beam, Sunburst Jubilee, 1976, Glass Specialty 4.00
Beam, Sunburst Multi-Glo, 1975, Glass Specialty 4.00
Beam, Sunburst Onyx, 1976, Glass Specialty 4.00
Beam, Sunburst Smoke-Glo, 1975, Glass Specialty 4.00
Beam, Sunburst, Blue, Glass Specialty, 1974 .... 4.00
Beam, Sunburst, Green, Glass Specialty, 1974 .... 4.00
Beam, Sunburst, Red, Glass Specialty, 1974 .... 4.00
Beam, Sunflowers, 1969, Collectors Edition, Vol.IV 3.00
Beam, Teal Blue Crystal, 1973, Glass Specialty 6.00
Beam, Telephone, Pioneers, 1977 .... 14.00 To 21.95
Beam, Texas Rabbit, 1971, Trophy 11.00
Beam, Thailand, 1969, Foreign Countries Series 5.00
Beam, Thomas Flyer, Blue, 1976, Automotive Series 37.00
Beam, Thomas Flyer, White, 1976, Automotive Series .... 30.00 To 37.00
Beam, Titus At Writing Desk, 1970, Collectors Edition, Vol.V 3.00
Beam, Tobacco Festival, 1973, Regal China 9.00
Beam, Tombstone, 1970, Regal China .... 5.00 To 8.00
Beam, Travel Lodge, 1972, Regal China .... 5.00 To 8.00
Beam, Trophy, 1957, Duck .... 32.00 To 35.00
Beam, Trophy, 1957, Sailfish .... 30.00 To 35.00
Beam, Trophy, 1958, Ram .... 135.00 To 155.00
Beam, Trophy, 1959, Dog, Setter 55.00
Beam, Trophy, 1960, Pheasant 18.00
Beam, Trophy, 1961, Pheasant, Reissue .... 18.00 To 22.00
Beam, Trophy, 1962, Horse, Black 24.00
Beam, Trophy, 1962, Horse, Brown .... 22.00 To 24.00
Beam, Trophy, 1962, Horse, White 20.00
Beam, Trophy, 1963, Doe .... 28.00 To 33.00
Beam, Trophy, 1963, Pheasant, Reissue 22.00
Beam, Trophy, 1965, Fox, Green .... 38.00 To 40.00
Beam, Trophy, 1966, Eagle .... 10.00 To 15.00
Beam, Trophy, 1966, Pheasant, Reissue 18.00
Beam, Trophy, 1967, Cat, Burmese 10.00
Beam, Trophy, 1967, Cat, Siamese 10.00
Beam, Trophy, 1967, Cat, Tabby 10.00
Beam, Trophy, 1967, Doe, Reissue .... 32.00 To 33.00
Beam, Trophy, 1967, Fox, Green, Reissue .... 35.00 To 40.00
Beam, Trophy, 1967, Horse, Black, Reissue 22.00
Beam, Trophy, 1967, Horse, Brown, Reissue 21.00
Beam, Trophy, 1967, Horse, White, Reissue 22.00
Beam, Trophy, 1967, Pheasant, Reissue 18.00
Beam, Trophy, 1968, Cardinal 50.00
Beam, Trophy, 1968, Pheasant, Reissue 18.00
Beam, Trophy, 1969, Blue Jay .... 7.00 To 10.00
Beam, Trophy, 1969, Robin .... 7.00 To 10.00
Beam, Trophy, 1969, Woodpecker .... 7.00 To 15.00
Beam, Trophy, 1970, Poodle, Grey 7.00
Beam, Trophy, 1970, Poodle, White .... 7.00 To 8.00
Beam, Trophy, 1971, Texas Rabbit .... 9.00 To 11.00
Beam, Trophy, 1971, Wisconsin Muskie 22.00
Beam, Trophy, 1973, Cardinal, Female .... 18.00 To 22.00
Beam, Trophy, 1974, Appaloosa 9.00
Beam, Trophy, 1974, Blue Gill 9.00
Beam, Trophy, 1976, Coho Salmon 7.00
Beam, Trophy, 1976, Great Dane .... 6.00 To 13.00
Beam, Trophy, 1977, Walleye Pike 10.00
Beam, Trophy, 1978, Northern Pike 8.00
Beam, Trout Unlimited, 1977, Club Series .... 14.00 To 17.00

Beam, **Truth Or Consequences**, 1974, Regal China .... 5.00 To 7.00
Beam, **Turquoise China Jug**, Regal China, 1966 .... 5.00
Beam, **Turtle**, 1975, Club Series .... 9.00 To 12.00
Beam, **Twin Bridges**, 1971, Club Series .... 50.00 To 62.00
Beam, **U.S.Open**, 1972, Golf Series .... 12.00 To 14.00
Beam, **V.F.W.**, 1971, Club Series .... 8.00 To 16.00
Beam, **V.I.P.**, 1967, Harolds Club, Customer Specialty .... 49.00 To 55.00
Beam, **V.I.P.**, 1968, Harolds Club, Customer Specialty .... 50.00 To 55.00
Beam, **V.I.P.**, 1969, Harolds Club, Customer Specialty 182.00
Beam, **V.I.P.**, 1970, Harolds Club, Customer Specialty .... 57.00 To 60.00
Beam, **V.I.P.**, 1971, Harolds Club, Customer Specialty .... 70.00 To 75.00
Beam, **V.I.P.**, 1972, Harolds Club, Customer Specialty .... 37.00 To 40.00
Beam, **V.I.P.**, 1973, Harolds Club, Customer Specialty .... 15.00 To 35.00
Beam, **V.I.P.**, 1974, Harolds Club, Customer Specialty .... 20.00 To 32.00
Beam, **V.I.P.**, 1975, Harolds Club, Customer Specialty .... 12.95 To 27.00
Beam, **V.I.P.**, 1976, Harolds Club, Customer Specialty .... 25.00 To 35.00
Beam, **V.I.P.**, 1977, Harolds Club, Customer Specialty .... 30.00 To 50.00
Beam, **V.I.P.**, 1978, Harolds Club, Customer Specialty 35.00
Beam, **Vase**, Brown, Zimmerman, 1972 .... 22.00
Beam, **Vase**, Green, Zimmerman, 1972 .... 15.00
Beam, **Vendome Drummer's Wagon**, 1975, Automotive Series .... *Illus* 39.00

Beam, Vendome Drummer's Wagon,
1975, Automotive Series

Beam, **Volkswagon**, Blue, 1973, Automotive Series .... 17.95 To 25.00
Beam, **Volkswagon**, Red, 1973, Automotive Series .... 15.00 To 22.00
Beam, **W.G.A.**, 1971, Golf Series 5.00
Beam, **Walleye Pike**, 1977, Trophy 11.00
Beam, **Washington**, Bicentennial, 1976 .... 12.00 To 14.00
Beam, **Washington**, State, 1975 .... 9.00 To 16.00
Beam, **West Virginia**, State, 1963 .... 232.00
Beam, **Whistler's Mother**, 1968, Collectors Edition, Vol.III 3.00
Beam, **Wisconsin Muskie**, 1971, Trophy .... 13.00 To 22.00
Beam, **Wolfgang Mozart**, 1973, Collectors Edition, Vol.VIII 4.00
Beam, **Wolverine**, 1975, Club Series .... 18.00 To 20.00
Beam, **Woodcock**, 1974, Collectors Edition, Vol.IX 4.00
Beam, **Woodpecker**, 1969, Trophy .... 7.00 To 15.00
Beam, **Wyoming**, State, 965 .... 57.00 To 67.00
Beam, **Ye Pipe & Bowl**, Rockwell, 1975, Glass Specialty 4.00
Beam, **Yellow Katz**, 1967, Customer Specialty 25.00
Beam, **Yellowstone**, Centennial, 1972 .... 6.00
Beam, **Yosemite**, 1967, Regal China .... 4.00 To 6.00
Beam, **Yuma Rifle**, Club Series .... 20.00 To 32.00
Beam, **Z**, Zimmerman, 1970 .... 9.00
Beam, **Zimmerman Bell**, Cobalt, 1976 .... 12.00
Beam, **Zimmerman Bell**, Light Blue, 1976 .... 12.00
Beam, **Zimmerman Blue Beauty**, 1969 .... 12.00 To 14.00
Beam, **Zimmerman Cherub**, Lavender, 1968 .... 8.00
Beam, **Zimmerman Cherub**, Salmon, 1969 .... 8.00
Beam, **Zimmerman Eldorado**, 1978 .... *Illus* 15.95
Beam, **Zimmerman Jug**, Two-Handled, 1965 .... 115.00
Beam, **Zimmerman Peddler**, 1971 .... 12.00 To 15.00

Beam, Zimmerman Vase, Green, 1972 .... 15.00
Beam, Zimmerman Z, 1970 .... 9.00
Beam, Zimmerman, 1969, Glass Specialty 7.00
Beam, Zouave, 1969, Collectors Edition, Vol.IV 3.00
Beam, 101st Airborne Div., Screaming Eagles, 1977, Club Series .... 10.00 To 14.00

> Beer was bottled in all parts of the United States by the time of the
> Civil War. Stoneware and the standard beer bottle shape of the 1870s
> are included in this category.

Beer, A.Haas Brewing Co., Amber, Quart 5.00
Beer, Anheuser-Busch Brewing Assn., Washington, D.C., BIMAL, Amber, 9 In. 7.00
Beer, Anheuser-Busch, A & Eagle, Richmond, Va., Squat Blob, Amber 49.50
Beer, Anheuser-Busch, Amber ....Color xxxx.xx
Beer, Anheuser-Busch, Quart ....Color xxxx.xx
Beer, Anheuser-Busch, St.Louis ....Color xxxx.xx
Beer, Barbarossa, Aqua, 9 1/2 In. ....Illus 8.50
Beer, Bayview Brewing Co., Seattle, Wash., Green, Quart 75.00
Beer, Ben Franklin Brewing Co., Columbus, Amber, 10 In. ....Illus 30.00

Beam, Zimmerman Eldorado, 1978
(See Page 25)

Beer, Barbarossa, Aqua,
9 1/2 In.

Beer, Ben Franklin Brewing Co.,
Columbus, Amber, 10 In.

Beer, Boba 45.00
Beer, Budweiser, Amber ....Color xxxx.xx
Beer, Budweiser, Ruby Red, Quart, 9 1/2 In. 8.00
Beer, Buffalo Beer Brewing Co., Amber, 1/2 Pint 10.00
Beer, Buffalo Beer Brewing Co., Clear, Pint 35.00
Beer, Buffalo Beer Brewing Co., Green, Quart 100.00
Beer, Buffalo Beer Brewing Co., Red, Quart 50.00
Beer, Buffalo Brewing Co., San Francisco Agency, Amber, Pint 12.00
Beer, Butch Porter, Stretched Neck, H In Pontil, 12 In. 70.00
Beer, C.Conrad & Co., Original Budweiser Patent No.6376, Aqua, 11 1/2 In. 18.00
Beer, C.Maurer, Amber, Quart 35.00
Beer, Charles Hoblemans, Green, Iron Pontil ....Color xxxx.xx
Beer, Clarke & White, N.Y., Olive 20.00
Beer, Claus Wreden Brewing Co., San Francisco 10.00
Beer, Coburn & Lang & Co., XX Boston, Mushroom Top, C.1864, Cobalt 200.00
Beer, Consumer's Brewing, Erie, Pa., Amber 5.00
Beer, Cooperstown, N.Y., Blob Top 3.50
Beer, D.Carnegie & Co., Contents Wired In Cork, Labeled, Amber 8.50
Beer, Davenport, Iowa, Blob Top, Wired-Down Stopper 10.00
Beer, Dr.Bell's Peptonized Port, School Bell Shape 425.00
Beer, Dr.Earl's Premium Beer, Stoneware, 9 1/2 In. 28.50
Beer, Duffy's Malt, Amber, Sample 6.00
Beer, Duffy's Malt, Rectangular, Amber 3.00
Beer, Dukehart & Co., Maryland Brewery & Co., 8 In. ....Illus 41.50

Beer, Dutch Porter, C.1700, Open Pontil, Laid On Ring Lip	47.00
Beer, Dutch Porter, C.1740, Olive Green, Open Pontil	45.00
Beer, Eagle Brewing	65.00
Beer, Eigenbrot Brewery, The, Baltimore, Md.	7.50
Beer, Enterprise Brewing Co., San Francisco, Quart	4.50
Beer, Florida Brewing Co., Tampa, Fla., Aqua, 6 1/2 In.	10.00
Beer, Foss, Schneder, Cincinnatti, Crown Top, Lime Green	20.00
Beer, Frank's Bros., San Francisco, Amber, Quart	12.00 To 14.00
Beer, Franklin Brewing Co., Columbus, O., Bust Of Franklin, Amber, Pint	25.00
Beer, Fredericksburg Bottling Co., Blob Top, Porcelain Stopper, Amber, Pint	14.00
Beer, Fredericksburg Bottling Co., Green, Quart	15.00
Beer, Fredericksburg Bottling Co., Lager, Blob Top, Clear	9.50
Beer, Fredericksburg Bottling Co., San Francisco, Green, Pint	20.00
Beer, Fredericksburg Bottling Co., San Francisco, Green, Quart	15.00
Beer, Fredericksburg Lager, Blumke & Reich, Lightning Stopper, Amber, Quart	22.00
Beer, G.E.Flanagan, Roanoke, Va., Aqua Blue, 9 1/4 In.	15.00
Beer, Glass, Stemmed, Anthony & Kuhn XXX Brewing Co., St.Louis, Clear	18.50

Beer, Dukehart & Co.,
Maryland Brewery & Co., 8 In.

Beer, Hoster, Columbus,
Amber, 10 1/2 In.

Beer, J.C.Buffum & Co's,
Pittsburg, Brown, 10 In.

Beer, Jas.Powers,
Pittsburg, 11 In.

Beer, Globe Brewery, Baltimore, Md., Honey Amber	12.50
Beer, Golden Gate	65.00
Beer, Grace Bros., Brewing Co., Santa Rosa, Cal., 4-Piece Mold, Amber, 7 Oz.	7.00
Beer, Guinness Extra Stout, Label, 3-Piece Mold, Italian Green	6.00
Beer, Hanson Kaher, Oakland, Quart	7.00
Beer, Henry Becker, Terre Haute, Ind., Green Aqua, Quart	6.00
Beer, Hoag & Alexander, Kinderhook, N.Y., Squat, Bail, Aqua	35.00
Beer, Hochgreve Brewing Co., Green Bay, Wisc., Stopper, Dark Amber, Quart	35.00
Beer, Home Brewing, Richmond, Va., Aqua Blob, Amber	24.50
Beer, Honolulu Brewing Co., Honolulu, Aqua, Quart	25.00
Beer, Honolulu Brewing Co., Honolulu, Blob Top	15.00
Beer, Hoster, Columbus, Amber, 10 1/2 In. .... Illus	6.00
Beer, Hoster, Columbus, O., Flying H, Crown Top, Amber, Pint	15.00
Beer, Hoster, Columbus, Ohio, H With Eagle Wings, Amber, Pint	10.00
Beer, I.Beck Hutch, Braddock, Pa., Ground Glass Stopper, Clear, 8 1/2 In.	12.00
Beer, Indianapolis Brewing Co., Embossed Winged Woman, Crown Top, Pint	7.00
Beer, J.C.Buffum & Co's, Pittsburg, Brown, 10 In. .... Illus	3.00
Beer, J.F.Deininger, Vallejo, Gold Edge Bottling Works, Aqua, 1/2 Pint	12.00
Beer, J.G.B.Siegert & Sons, BIM, Medium Green, 5 In.	4.00
Beer, Jacob Wirth & Co., Rhode Island, Aqua, 9 1/4 In.	15.00
Beer, Japan Brewing Co., San Francisco, Aqua, Quart	15.00
Beer, Jas.Powers, Pittsburg, 11 In. .... Illus	5.50
Beer, Jno.Wyeth & Bros., Philadelphia, Liquid Extract Malt	5.00

Beer, John Eichler Brewing, N.Y., Aqua 5.00
Beer, John Kuhlman Brewing Co., Ellenville, N.Y., Pale Green 6.00
Beer, John Lucas In., Rock Springs, Wyo., Wire Closure, Amber, 1/2 Gallon 12.00
Beer, John Rapp & Son, San Francisco, Amber, Quart 10.00
Beer, John Wieland's, Red Amber, Split 25.00
Beer, Kirchner & Manter, Oakland, Quart 8.00
Beer, Lager, Cherubs, Jug, Pottery, Cincinnati, Ohio 39.50
Beer, Miller Brewing Co., Milwaukee, Aqua 5.00
Beer, Miller, Fred, Amber, C.1900 ....*Illus* 18.00
Beer, Miller, Porcelain Stopper, C.1910 ....*Illus* 15.00
Beer, Milwaukee Lager, 8 Sided, Base Picture Of Beer Mug, Amber 6.00
 Beer, Miniature, see Miniature, Beer
Beer, Mirrasoul Bros., Amber, 1/2 Pint 5.00
Beer, Moerlein's Old Jug Lager, Cincinnati, Stoneware, Cherubs, 10 1/4 In. 18.50
Beer, Moerlein's Old Jug Lager, Pottery, 9 In. ....*Illus* 12.00
Beer, National Bottling Works, Fulton St., Embossed Eagle, Quart 27.00
Beer, National Bottling, 525 Grove St. 90.00
Beer, Northern Brewing Co., Superior, Wis., Paper Label 3.00
Beer, Oakland Bottling Co., Blob Top, Pint 7.00
Beer, Old Dutch, Paper Label, 9 In. ....*Color* 4.00
Beer, Pabst B., Milwaukee, Amber, 9 1/4 In. 18.00
Beer, Pabst B., Milwaukee, E.O.Jones Co., Youngstown, Ohio, Amber, 9 1/2 In. 15.00
Beer, Pabst Extract, The Best Tonic, Amber 15.00

Beer, Miller,
Porcelain Stopper, C.1910

Beer, Miller, Fred,
Amber, C.1900

Beer, Moerlein's
Old Jug-Lager,
Pottery, 9 In.

Beer, Pabst Milwaukee, Blob Top, Green 3.50
Beer, Pabst, BIM, Aqua 4.00
Beer, People's Brewing Co., Terre Haute, Ind., Embossed Eagle, Crown Top, Qt. 7.00
Beer, People's Brewing Co., Terre Haute, Ind., Embossed Eagle, Pint 6.00
Beer, Peter Mugler Brewer, Sisson, Cal., 1/2 Pint 14.00
Beer, Philadelphia Porter & Ale, Honesdale Glassworks, Pa., IP, Green 65.00
Beer, Philadelphia XXX Porter & Ale, Iron Pontil, Green 40.00
Beer, Phoenix Bird, Embossed, Olive, BIMAL 2.00
Beer, Pilsen Extract, Sun-Colored Amethyst, 6 In.Square 10.00
Beer, Pittsburg Brewing Co., Pittsburg, Pa. 10.00
Beer, Property Of Rochester Brewing Co., Embossed, Slanting Letters 5.00
Beer, Quandt Brewing Co., Embossed Indian, Troy, N.Y., Green, 9 1/4 In. 10.00
Beer, Red Enterprize, 1/2 Pint 40.00
Beer, Reinhardt Salvador Lager, Toronto, Aqua 25.00
Beer, Reno, Nev., Brewing Co., Blob Top, Amber 10.00
Beer, Republic Pale, Republic Brewing Co., Washington, Crown Top, Aqua, Pint 10.00
Beer, Robert Portner, Blob Top, Vaseline Green 49.50
Beer, Rochester Brewing Co., N.Y., Amber 10.00
Beer, Rock Island Brewing, Ill., Blob Top, Wired Down Stopper 10.00

Beer, Rock Island Brewing, Ill., 1/2 Gallon	15.00
Beer, Royal Bury, Anchor Glass, Quart	8.00
Beer, Rudolph Scherf, San Jose, Quart	6.00
Beer, S.L., Monogram In Oval Slug Plate, Glop Top, Aqua, Quart	15.00
Beer, Scarboro & Whitby, Inside Threads, Amber	3.00
Beer, Schlitz, Ruby Red	10.00
Beer, Schultz, Walker, N.Y., Amber	15.00
Beer, Seattle Brewing & Malting, Seattle, Wash., Olive Green, Pint	70.00
Beer, Sonoma Brewing Co.	10.00
Beer, Squat Onion, Open Pontil, Quart	90.00
Beer, St.Louis Bottling Co., McC. & B., Vallejo, Cal., Amber, Quart	5.00
Beer, St.Louis Bottling Co., Vallejo, Cal., Amber, Pint	6.00
Beer, Standard Bottling, Pawtucket, Rhode Island, Embossed Flag, Clear	15.00
Beer, Taylor Bate Lager, St.Catherines, Amber	50.00
Beer, Terre Haute Brewing Co., Crown Top, Green Aqua, Pint	5.00
Beer, Texas Splits, Galveston Brewing Co.	7.00
Beer, The Gerke Brewing Co., Cincinnati, O., U.S.A., Aqua	3.50
Beer, The Germania Brewing Co., Charleston, S.C.	5.00
Beer, The Jung Brewing Co., Cincinnati	4.50
Beer, Trommer Extract Of Malt Co., Fremont, Ohio, Amber, 7 3/4 In.	10.00
Beer, W.Eagle, Canal St., N.Y., Philadelphia Porter, Green	50.00
Beer, Warner's Log Cabin, Hops & Buch Remedy, Amber	170.00
Beer, Weiss, St.Louis Brewery, 1870, Amber, Quart	150.00
Beer, William Schellhas Brewing Co., Picnic Blob, Amber	21.00
Beer, Wonder Bottling Co., San Francisco, Monogram, Light Amber, Quart	5.00
Bell's, Scotch, 1969	8.00
Bennington, Coachman, Yellow, Brown Glaze	298.00
Bennington, Departed Spirits, Rocking Ham Glaze, 5 1/2 In.	130.00
Bininger & Co., Whiskey, Barrel, Amber, 3/4 Quart	70.00
Bininger, Barrel, Amber, Open Pontil, Pint	155.00
Bininger, Barrel, Kentucky Bourbon, Open Pontil, Amber	110.00
Bininger, Barrel, Old Kentucky Bourbon, Amber	155.00
Bininger, Barrel, Old Kentucky Bourbon, 1849 Reserve, Amber, 8 In.	150.00
Bininger, Cannon, Light Honey Amber	325.00
Bininger, Cannon, Medium Amber	385.00
Bininger, Cannon, Spangler Display, Amber	75.00
Bininger, Clock, Golden Amber, Pint	250.00
Bininger, Clock, Open Pontil, Yellow Amber	325.00
Bininger, Clock, Regulator, Light Amber	310.00
Bininger, Jug, Handled, Amber	120.00
Bininger, Jug, Handled, Reddish Amber	195.00
Bininger, Knickerbocker, Whiskey Jug, Bulbous Handles, Amber, Pint	550.00
Bininger, London Dock Gin, Amber	45.00
Bininger, London Dock Gin, Green, Quart	45.00
Bininger, London Dock Gin, Olive Green	55.00
Bininger, Night Cap, Open Pontil, Amber	250.00
Bininger, Old Dominion Wheat Tonic, Olive Green	70.00
Bininger, Old Dominion Wheat Tonic, Surface Scratches	32.00
Bininger, Old Dominion Wheat, Green	95.00
Bininger, Old Kentucky Bourbon, Barrel, Amber, OP	165.00 To 175.00
Bininger, Old Kentucky Bourbon, Barrel, Honey Amber, Open Pontil	150.00
Bininger, Old Kentucky Bourbon, Distilled In 1848, Olive Green	85.00
Bininger, Old Kentucky Bourbon, Golden Amber	55.00
Bininger, Old Kentucky Bourbon, 1849	40.00 To 49.50
Bininger, Old Kentucky Bourbon, 1849, Deep Golden Amber, Quart	65.00
Bininger, Old London Dock Gin, Amber, Pint	45.00 To 50.00
Bininger, Old London Dock Gin, Amber, Quart	50.00
Bininger, Old London Dock Gin, Dark Amber	37.00
Bininger, Old London Dock Gin, Light Amber	34.00
Bininger, Old London Dock Gin, N.Y., Orange Amber, Quart	32.00
Bininger, Old London Dock Gin, Olive Green	55.00 To 85.00
Bininger, Old London Dock Gin, Olive Yellow, Quart	45.00
Bininger, Old London Dock Gin, Quart, Honey Amber	54.50
Bininger, Old London Dock Gin, Yellow Olive	36.00
Bininger, Regulator Clock, Amber	385.00
Bininger, Regulator, Deep Amber	350.00

Bininger, Regulator, Light Amber, Open Pontil	385.00
Bininger, Regulator, Open Pontil, Amber	325.00
Bininger, Regulator, Open Pontil, Aqua	825.00
Bininger, Regulator, Whiskey, Deep Amber	295.00
Bininger, Regulator, Whiskey, Embossed, Amber, Pint	120.00
Bininger, Regulator, 19 Broad St., Yellow Amber, Open Pontil	325.00
Bininger, Traveler's Guide, Amber	185.00
Bininger, Traveler's Guide, Flask, Honey Amber	165.00
Bininger, Urn, Light Honey Amber	735.00

Bischoff Company has made fancy decanters since it was founded in 1777 in Trieste, Italy. The modern collectible Bischoff bottles have been imported to the United States since about 1950. Glass, porcelain, and stoneware decanters and figurals are made.

Bischoff, African Head, 1962	13.00
Bischoff, Alabaster Dob, 1969	20.00
Bischoff, Amber Flower, 1952	33.00
Bischoff, Amber Leaf, 1952	33.00
Bischoff, Bell House, 1960	37.00
Bischoff, Bell Tower, 1959	20.00
Bischoff, Black Cat, 1969	13.00
Bischoff, Blue Gold, 1956	48.00
Bischoff, Chinese Boy, 1962	36.00
Bischoff, Chinese Girl, 1962	37.00
Bischoff, Christmas Tree, 1957	48.00
Bischoff, Clown, Handstand	8.00
Bischoff, Clown, Low, 1963	36.00
Bischoff, Clown, Tall, 1963	36.00
Bischoff, Columbian Mask, 1963	18.00
Bischoff, Dachshund, 1966	38.00
Bischoff, Deer, 1969	10.00
Bischoff, Duck, 1964	47.00
Bischoff, Emerald Rose, 1952	48.00
Bischoff, Festival, 1957	48.00
Bischoff, Fruit Bowl, 1966	27.00
Bischoff, Gold Dust, 1958	37.00
Bischoff, Gold Flower, 1956	48.00
Bischoff, Gold Rose, 1952	28.00
Bischoff, Gold Topaz, 1955	24.00
Bischoff, Gold Violet, 1954	23.00
Bischoff, Golden Fish, 1964	46.00
Bischoff, Green Rose, 1954	33.00
Bischoff, Green Striped, 1958	33.00
Bischoff, Jungle Scene, Ruby, 1952	25.00
Bischoff, Jungle Scene, Topaz, 1952	28.00
Bischoff, Opaline, 1957	48.00
Bischoff, Pink Rose, 1953	33.00
Bischoff, Pirate	20.00
Bischoff, Porcelain Cameo, 1953	15.00
Bischoff, Red Bell, 1957	43.00
Bischoff, Red Rose, 1957	48.00
Bischoff, Red Striped, 1958	33.00
Bischoff, Roman Urn	12.00
Bischoff, Ruby Fish, 1969	16.00
Bischoff, Spanish Boy, 1961	26.00
Bischoff, Spanish Girl, 1961	27.00
Bischoff, Topaz Basket, 1958	33.00
Bischoff, Tower Of Fruit	18.00
Bischoff, Venetian Blue, 1953	28.00
Bischoff, Venetian Green, 1953	28.00
Bischoff, Venetian Violet, 1953	28.00
Bischoff, Watchtower, 1960	9.00

Bitters bottles held the famous 19th-century medicine called bitters. It was often of such a high alcohol content that the user felt healthier with each sip. The word bitters must be embossed on the glass or a paper label must

be affixed for the collector to call the bottle a bitters bottle. Most
date from 1840 to 1900. The numbers used in the entries in the form
W-0 or W-L-0 refer to the books "Bitters Bottles" and "Supplement
to Bitters Bottles" by Richard Watson.

Bitters, A.Watson's, Coca One Side, Best Tonic Other, BIMAL, Amber	350.00
Bitters, Abbott's Aromatic, Full Labels, Sample Size	20.00
Bitters, Amazon, Peter McQuade, New York, Amber, W-7	75.00
Bitters, Andrew Lee Compound Cathartic, Manchester, Mass., Aqua	48.00
Bitters, Angostura Bark, Eagle, Globular, Amber, W-11	58.00 To 118.00
Bitters, Angostura, Embossed, Amber, Sample Size	8.00
Bitters, Angostura, Sample Size	15.00
Bitters, Appetine, Geo.Benz, Amethyst, W-383	600.00
Bitters, Appetine, Geo.Benz, Medium Amber, W-383	300.00
Bitters, Arberle Westheimer, Wines & Liquors, St.Paul, Embossed Horseshoe	30.00
Bitters, Ash, Partial Label, Honey Amber	40.00
Bitters, Atwood's Genuine, Round, Aqua, W-15	20.00
Bitters, Atwood's Jaundice, Double Band Collar, ABM	1.75
Bitters, Atwood's Jaundice, 12 Sided, Aqua	3.00 To 10.00
Bitters, Atwood's Quinine Tonic, Aqua, W-18	38.00
Bitters, Atwood's Wild Cherry, Label, N.Wood, Portland, Me., Aqua	25.00
Bitters, Augauer's, ABM, Kelly Green, W-21	50.00
Bitters, B. & L., Cincinnati, Label	12.00
Bitters, Baker's Orange Grove, Golden Amber, 3/4 Quart, W-23	90.00
Bitters, Baker's Orange Grove, Light Yellow Amber, 3/4 Quart, W-23	130.00
Bitters, Baker's Orange Grove, Medium Amber, W-23	180.00
Bitters, Baker's Orange Grove, Roped Corners, Label, Amber, W-23	135.00 To 150.00
Bitters, Barrel, Burnt Umber	600.00
Bitters, Barrel, Deep Sapphire Blue, 3/4 Quart ....*Illus*	975.00
Bitters, Barrel, 20 Rings, Sapphire Blue, Mouth Chips, 3/4 Quart ....*Illus*	625.00
Bitters, Beef, Wine & Iron, Light Green	5.00
Bitters, Beggs Dandelion, Amber, W-30	30.00
Bitters, Beggs Dandelion, Flat Sides, Amber, W-390	30.00
Bitters, Bell's Cocktail, Lady's Leg, Amber, W-72	250.00
Bitters, Ben-Hur Celebrated Stomach, New Orleans	70.00
Bitters, Bennet's Celebrated Stomach, San Francisco, Green Amber	200.00
Bitters, Bennet's Celebrated, San Francisco, Yellow Amber	190.00
Bitters, Bennett & Carroll, Barrel, Amber	325.00
Bitters, Bennett & Carroll, Pittsburgh, Barrel	150.00
Bitters, Berliner Magen, Amber, W-39	32.50
Bitters, Big Bill's Best, Amber, W-41	95.00
Bitters, Big Bill's Best, Medium Amber, W-41	100.00
Bitters, Bissell's Tonic Bitters, O.P.Bissell Reverse, Square, Amber	150.00
Bitters, Bitters, Angostura, Green, 4 1/4 In.	20.00
Bitters, Blue Mountain, Waynesboro, Pa.	54.00
Bitters, Boerhave's Holland, Rectangular, Clear, W-48	30.00
Bitters, Boff's Herb, Light Aqua	10.00
Bitters, Botanic, Herzberg Bros., N.Y., Embossed Sphinx	205.00
Bitters, Bourbon Whiskey Bitters, Barrel, Light Puce, W-52	400.00
Bitters, Bourbon Whiskey, Apricot Puce, 3/4 Quart, W-52	185.00
Bitters, Bourbon Whiskey, Barrel, Burgundy, 3/4 Quart, W-52	140.00
Bitters, Bourbon Whiskey, Barrel, Burnt Orange, W-52	180.00
Bitters, Bourbon Whiskey, Barrel, Medium Claret, W-52	180.00
Bitters, Bourbon Whiskey, Barrel, Puce, W-52	180.00 To 225.00
Bitters, Bourbon, Whiskey, Barrel, Smoky Olive, W-52	350.00
Bitters, Bourbon Whiskey, Barrel, Smoky Puce, 3/4 Quart, W-145	175.00
Bitters, Bourbon Whiskey, Barrel, Smoky Yellow Olive, 3/4 Quart, W-52	175.00
Bitters, Bower, Olney, Gravitating Stopper	18.00
Bitters, Boyer's Stomach, Cincinnati	25.00
Bitters, Brown Sarsaparilla & Tomato, Aqua, Pontil, W-58	85.00
Bitters, Brown's Celebrated Indian Herb, Amber, W-57	240.00 To 345.00
Bitters, Brown's Celebrated Indian Herb, Amber, 3/4 Quart, W-57 ....*Illus*	170.00
Bitters, Brown's Celebrated Indian Herb, Bird's Wing In Base, Amber	350.00
Bitters, Brown's Celebrated Indian Herb, Deep Golden Amber, 3/4 Quart, W-57	245.00
Bitters, Brown's Celebrated Indian Herb, Honey Amber	290.00 To 350.00
Bitters, Brown's Celebrated Indian Herb, Light Amber, W-57B	335.00
Bitters, Brown's Celebrated Indian Herb, Patent 1868, Amber, W-57B	2000.00

Bitters, Brown's Celebrated Indian Herb, Rolled Lip, Amber Green 1000.00
Bitters, Brown's Iron, Burlington, Vt., Indented Panels 35.00
Bitters, Brown's Iron, Deep Amber, W-399 .... 24.00
Bitters, Brown's Iron, Honey Amber, W-399 .... 35.00
Bitters, Brown's Iron, W-399 .... 20.00 To 24.00
Bitters, Buhrer's Gentian, Light Amber, W-402 .... 59.00
Bitters, Burdock Blood, Aqua .... 7.50 To 15.00
Bitters, Burdock Blood, Side, T.Milburn & Co., Toronto, Deep Aqua 15.00
    Bitters, Byrne, see Bitters, Professor Geo. J. Byrne
Bitters, Byrne's, Great Universal Compound, 3/4 Quart, W-63 .... *Illus* 1000.00
Bitters, C.Gates & Co., Life Of Man, Original Label 50.00
Bitters, C.Heimsteet & Co., Troy, N.H., Open Pontil, 8 Sided, Cobalt Blue 115.00
Bitters, C.K.Wilson's Wa-Hoo, Rectangular, Label, W-L147 .... 15.00
Bitters, C.W.Abbott, Amber 4.00
    Bitters, C.W.Roback's, see also Bitters, Dr.C.W.Roback's
Bitters, C.W.Roback's Stomach, Barrel, Amber, W-280 .... 150.00
    Bitters, Cabin, see Bitters, Drake's Plantation, Bitters, Golden,
    Bitters, Kelly's Old Cabin, Bitters, Old Homestead Wild
    Cherry

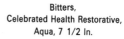

Bitters,
Celebrated Health Restorative,
Aqua, 7 1/2 In.

Bitters, Barrel, 20 Rings,
Sapphire Blue, Mouth Chips,
3/4 Quart
(See Page 31)

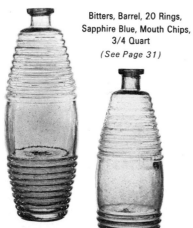

Bitters, Barrel,
Deep Sapphire Blue,
3/4 Quart
(See Page 31)

Bitters, Byrne's,
Great Universal Compound,
3/4 Quart, W-63

Bitters, Caldwell's Herb, Light Amber, W-65 .... 175.00
Bitters, Caldwell's Herb, Yellow Amber, Iron Pontil, W-65 .... 250.00
Bitters, California Fig & Herb, Amber, 10 In., W-67 .... 45.00
Bitters, California Fig & Herb, Light Amber, Quart, W-67 .... 35.00 To 60.00
Bitters, Canton, Star, Lady's Leg, Amber, W-69 .... 245.00
Bitters, Capitol, Label 35.00
Bitters, Caracas, Olive Green, W-406 .... 18.00 To 20.00
Bitters, Carmeliter For All Kidney & Liver Complaints, N.Y., Amber, W-71 .... 85.00
Bitters, Caroni, BIMAL, Sample, Emerald Green 20.00
Bitters, Caroni, Olive Amber, 5 1/4 In., W-72 .... 40.00
Bitters, Caroni, Olive Green, Sample Size 25.00
Bitters, Caroni, Olive Green, Sample Size, W-72 .... 18.00
Bitters, Carpathian Herb, Braddock, Pa., Amber, W-73 .... 26.00
Bitters, Carter's Spanish Mixture, Pontil, Olive Green 115.00
Bitters, Celebrated Health Restorative, Aqua, 7 1/2 In. .... *Illus* 50.00
Bitters, Celectrated Crown, F.Chevalier & Co., Sole Agents, W-80 .... 125.00
Bitters, Clark's California Sherry Cordial, Rectangular, Amber 45.00
Bitters, Clark's Giant, Philadelphia, Prickly Ash 33.00
Bitters, Clark's Syrup, Green 120.00

Bitters, Clarke's Compound Mandrake, Oval, Aqua, W-85 .... 35.00 To 55.00
Bitters, Clarke's Sherry Wine, Gallon, W-88 .... 135.00
Bitters, Clarke's Sherry Wine, Open Pontil, Quart, W-87 .... 50.00
Bitters, Clarke's Sherry Wine, Open Pontil, 1/2 Gallon, W-87 .... 95.00
Bitters, Clarke's Sherry Wine, 25 Cents, Sharon, Mass., W-88D 90.00
Bitters, Clarke's Sherry Wine, 8 1/2 In., W-88A 30.00
Bitters, Clarke's Vegetable Sherry Wine, Aqua, Gallon, W-88C 90.00
Bitters, Clarke's Vegetable Sherry Wine, 1/2 Gallon, W-88C 180.00
Bitters, Cole Bros., Vegetable, Aqua, W-413 .... 35.00
Bitters, Columbo Peptic, L.E.Jung Cordial, New Orleans, Amber, W-93 .... 15.00
Bitters, Columbo Peptic, Square, Amber, W-13 .... 20.00 To 38.00
Bitters, Columbo Peptic, Stain & Bruise On Base, W-93 .... 16.00
Bitters, Constitution, Seward & Bentley, Honey Amber, W-95 .... 525.00
Bitters, Constitution, Seward & Bentley, Medium Amber, W-95 .... 340.00
Bitters, Constitution, Seward & Bentley, Olive Amber, W-95 .... 375.00
Bitters, Corwitz Stomach, Square, Aqua 20.00
Bitters, Cundurango, Old Amber 75.00
Bitters, Curtis & Perkins Wild Cherry, Open Pontil, Aqua, W-102 .... 60.00 To 110.00
Bitters, Damiana, Baja, California, Aqua, W-103 .... 45.00
Bitters, Damiana, Lewis Hess, Baja, California, Dark Aqua, W-103 .... 23.00
Bitters, Dandelion, XXX, W-105 .... 49.00
Bitters, David Andrews Vegetable Jaundice, OP, Aqua, W-10 .... 375.00 To 450.00
Bitters, DeWitt's Stomach Bitters, Chicago, Amber, Original Label, W-426 .... 35.00
Bitters, DeWitt's, Ghost Letters, Rectangular, W-107 .... 23.00
Bitters, Doctor Fisch's, Amber, 3/4 Quart, W-124 .... 140.00
Bitters, Doctor Fisch's, Golden Amber, 3/4 Quart, W-124 .... 110.00 To 140.00
Bitters, Doctor Fisch's, Golden Yellow, W-124 .... 300.00
Bitters, Doctor Fisch's, Medium Amber, W-124 .... 137.00
Bitters, Doyle's Hop Bitters, Amber, W-110 .... 18.50 To 20.00
Bitters, Doyle's Hop Bitters, 1872, Square, Golden Amber 30.00
Bitters, Doyle's Hop, Dark Amber, W-110 .... 25.00
Bitters, Doyle's Hop, Light Amber, W-110 .... 20.00
Bitters, Doyle's Hop, Light Reddish Amber, W-110 .... 23.00
Bitters, Doyle's Hop, Medium Gold Amber, W-110 .... 48.00
Bitters, Doyle's Hop, Yellow Amber, W-110 .... 35.00
Bitters, Dr.A.H.Smith's, W-309 .... 50.00
Bitters, Dr.A.S.Hopkins Union Stomach, Honey Amber, Open Pontil, W-177 .... 35.00
Bitters, Dr.Ball's Vegetable Stomachic, Aqua, OP, W-25 .... 125.00 To 135.00
Bitters, Dr.Baxter's Mandrake, Clear, W-29 .... 6.00 To 9.25
Bitters, Dr.Baxter's, Aqua, W-29 .... 4.00
Bitters, Dr.Bell's, Blood Purifier, Amber, W-31 .... 85.00 To 250.00
Bitters, Dr.Bernard's Dandelion Yellow Docks, Aqua 18.00
Bitters, Dr.Bishops Wahoo, Medium Golden Amber, 6 Star, W-43 .... 275.00 To 285.00
Bitters, Dr.Blake's Aromatic, Open Pontil, Aqua, W-45 .... 80.00 To 90.00
Bitters, Dr.C.D.Warner's German Hop, Michigan, Honey Amber, W-355 .... 35.00
Bitters, Dr.C.W.Roback's Stomach, Barrel, Honey Amber, W-280 .... 135.00
Bitters, Dr.C.W.Roback's Stomach, Barrel, Light Amber, W-280 .... 110.00
Bitters, Dr.C.W.Roback's Stomach, Barrel, Light Golden Amber, Small Size 285.00
Bitters, Dr.C.W.Roback's Stomach, Golden Amber, Quart 140.00
Bitters, Dr.C.W.Roback's Stomach, Yellow Amber, 3/4 Quart, W-280 .... 80.00
Bitters, Dr.Carey's Mandrake, Elmira, N.Y., 12 Sided, Aqua, W-407 .... 30.00
Bitters, Dr.Carson's Stomach, Aqua, W-74 .... 45.00
Bitters, Dr.Chandler's Ginger Root, Barrel, Amber, W-82 .... 1950.00
Bitters, Dr.Fenner's Capitol, Aqua, W-122 .... 25.00
Bitters, Dr.Fiske Alternative 9.00
Bitters, Dr.Flint's Quaker, Providence, R.I., Bubbles, 9 1/2 In., W-126 .... 30.00
Bitters, Dr.George Pierce's Indian Restorative, Lowell, Mass., W-258 .... 35.00
Bitters, Dr.Gillmore's, Laxative, Kidney & Liver, Amber, W-436 .... 95.00
Bitters, Dr.Harter's Wild Cherry, Amber, 4 1/2 In., W-158 .... 20.00 To 25.00
Bitters, Dr.Harter's Wild Cherry, Ohio, Amber, 4 1/2 In., W-158d .... 16.00 To 25.00
Bitters, Dr.Harter's Wild Cherry, Ohio, Label & Contents, Large, W-158d 50.00
Bitters, Dr.Harter's Wild Cherry, St.Louis, Dark Amber, Large Size 200.00
Bitters, Dr.Harter's Wild Cherry, St.Louis, Honey Amber, 7 1/2 In. 25.00
Bitters, Dr.Harter's Wild Cherry, St.Louis, 4 1/2 In. 16.00
Bitters, Dr.Harter's, St.Louis, Small, W-158c 18.00
Bitters, Dr.Henley's California, IXL, Rectangle, Aqua, 10 In., W-163 .... 30.00

Bitters, Dr.Henley's IXL Wild Grape Root, Medium Green, W-164 .... 300.00
Bitters, Dr.Henley's Wild Grape Root, Lime Green, W-164 .... 100.00
Bitters, Dr.Henley's, California, Rectangle, Aqua, 10 In., W-163 .... 30.00
Bitters, Dr.Hoofland's German, Liver Complaint, Philadelphia, Aqua, 7 In. 38.00
Bitters, Dr.Hoofland's German, Open Pontil, Aqua .... 45.00 To 50.00
Bitters, Dr.Hoofland's German, Rectangular, Aqua, W-174 .... 10.00 To 23.00
Bitters, Dr.Hopkin's Union Stomach, Hartford, Conn., Amber 39.00
Bitters, Dr.Hopkin's Union Stomach, Yellow Olive, Quart, W-177 .... 35.00 To 60.00
    Bitters, Dr. Hostetter, see Bitters, Dr. J. Hostetter
Bitters, Dr.J.G.B.Seigert & Hijos, Olive 5.00
Bitters, Dr.J.G.B.Siegert's & Sons, Angostura, Label, Green, BIMAL 5.00
Bitters, Dr.J.Hostetter's Stomach, Black Amber, W-179 .... 95.00
Bitters, Dr.J.Hostetter's Stomach, C.1860s, Black Glass, Green, W-179 .... 65.00
Bitters, Dr.J.Hostetter's Stomach, Chocolate Brown, W-179 .... 45.00
Bitters, Dr.J.Hostetter's Stomach, Embossed W.M.C. & Co.6, Yellow, W-179 .... 50.00
Bitters, Dr.J.Hostetter's Stomach, L. & W.On Bottom, Yellow Green, W-179 .... 30.00
Bitters, Dr.J.Hostetter's Stomach, Lancaster Mark, Olive Green, W-179 .... 100.00
Bitters, Dr.J.Hostetter's Stomach, Red Amber, W-179 .... 9.00
Bitters, Dr.J.Hostetter's, ABM, W-179 .... 5.00
Bitters, Dr.J.Hostetter's, Amber, BIMAL, W-179 .... 2.00
Bitters, Dr.J.Hostetter's, Black Glass, W-179 .... 65.00
Bitters, Dr.J.Hostetter's, Citron, W-179 .... 55.00
Bitters, Dr.J.Hostetter's, 13 On Back & Base, W-179 .... 8.00
Bitters, Dr.Kaufman's Sulpher, The Greatest Discovery Of The Ages, Label 15.00
Bitters, Dr.Langley's Root & Herb, Amber, Large, W-206 .... 58.00
Bitters, Dr.Langley's Root & Herb, Aqua, W-206 .... 20.00 To 25.00
Bitters, Dr.Langley's Root & Herb, 76 Union St., Boston, Aqua, 6 3/4 In. 25.00
Bitters, Dr.Langley's Root & Herb, 99 Union St., Boston, Aqua, W-206B 40.00
Bitters, Dr.Loew's Celebrated Stomach, Emerald Green, 3 7/8 In., W-217 .... 100.00
Bitters, Dr.Loew's, Cleveland, Label, 4 In., W-217 .... 84.00
Bitters, Dr.Lyford's, C.P.Herrick, Tilton, N.H., Aqua, 8 1/4 In., W-222 .... 50.00
Bitters, Dr.Lyon's, Amber, Paper Label, 11 1/2 In. ....Color xxxx.xx
Bitters, Dr.M.C.Ayer Restorative, Aqua, Rectangular, W-386 .... 18.00
Bitters, Dr.Manly Hardy's Genuine Jaundice, Bangor, Me., W-155 .... 100.00 To 135.00
Bitters, Dr.Petzolds Genuine German, Amber, Large, W-256 .... 95.00
Bitters, Dr.Petzolds Genuine German, Inopt.1862, Light Honey Amber, W-256 .... 140.00
Bitters, Dr.Petzolds Genuine German, Yellow, W-256 .... 150.00
Bitters, Dr.Petzolds Genuine German, 6 1/2 In., W-256 .... 65.00
Bitters, Dr.Petzolds, Amber, 6 3/4 X 2 1/2 X 1 1/2 In. 130.00
Bitters, Dr.Renz's Herb, Barrel, Light Amber, W-273 .... 190.00
Bitters, Dr.Renz's Herb, Chocolate Amber, W-273 .... 140.00
Bitters, Dr.Renz's Herb, Yellow Green Amber, W-273 .... 135.00
Bitters, Dr.Ryder's Clover, Syracuse, Label, Amber, W-291 .... 70.00
Bitters, Dr.Sims' Anti-Constipation, Amber, 6 In., W-305 .... 47.00 To 50.00
Bitters, Dr.Skinner's Celebrated, 25 Cent, W-306 .... 125.00
Bitters, Dr.Skinner's Sherry Wine, S.Reading, Mass., Open Pontil, W-307 .... 135.00
Bitters, Dr.Stanley's South American Indian, W-314 .... 74.00
Bitters, Dr.Stephen Jewett's Celebrated Health Restoring, OP, Aqua, W-193 .... 70.00
Bitters, Dr.Stephen Jewett's, Ice Blue, Pint, W-193 .... 145.00
Bitters, Dr.Stewart's Tonic, Rectangular, Amber, W-500 .... 20.00
Bitters, Dr.Thomas Hall's California Pepsin Wine, Medium Amber, W-153 .... 185.00
Bitters, Dr.Van Hopf's Curaco, Amber, W-343 .... 30.00 To 50.00
Bitters, Dr.Walker's, California Vinegar, W-L-140 .... 6.00
Bitters, Dr.Wheeler's Sherry Tonic, Clear, W-518 .... 100.00
Bitters, Dr.Wilson's Herbine, The Brayley Drug Co., Original Label, W-368 .... 50.00
Bitters, Drake's Plantation, Green, 10 In. ....Color xxxx.xx
Bitters, Drake's Plantation, 4 Log, Amber, W-1116 .... 45.00 To 70.00
Bitters, Drake's Plantation, 4 Log, Dark Amber, W-1116 .... 60.00
Bitters, Drake's Plantation, 4 Log, Front & Back Label, Honey Amber, W-1116 .... 125.00
Bitters, Drake's Plantation, 4 Log, Gold Amber, W-1116 .... 74.50
Bitters, Drake's Plantation, 4 Log, Honey Amber, W-1116 .... 55.00 To 70.00
Bitters, Drake's Plantation, 4 Log, Honey To Reddish, W-1116 .... 74.50
Bitters, Drake's Plantation, 4 Log, Light Yellow, W-1116 .... 150.00
Bitters, Drake's Plantation, 4 Log, Reddish Amber, W-1116 .... 69.50 To 79.50
Bitters, Drake's Plantation, 4 Log, Yellow Amber, W-1116 .... 125.00
Bitters, Drake's Plantation, 4 Log, Yellow, W-1116 .... 165.00

Bitters, Drake's Plantation, 5 Log, Light Golden Yellow, W-1118 .... 525.00
Bitters, Drake's Plantation, 5 Log, Medium Amber, W-1118 .... 150.00 To 250.00
Bitters, Drake's Plantation, 6 Log, Amber, W-111 .... 50.00 To 85.00
Bitters, Drake's Plantation, 6 Log, Chocolate, W-111 .... 80.00
Bitters, Drake's Plantation, 6 Log, Copper Puce, W-111 .... 100.00 To 125.00
Bitters, Drake's Plantation, 6 Log, Dark Chocolate Amber, W-111 .... 95.00
Bitters, Drake's Plantation, 6 Log, Deep Amber, W-111 .... 65.00
Bitters, Drake's Plantation, 6 Log, Deep Apricot, W-111 .... 75.00
Bitters, Drake's Plantation, 6 Log, Deep Puce, W-111 .... 105.00 To 150.00
Bitters, Drake's Plantation, 6 Log, Deep Red, W-111 .... 150.00
Bitters, Drake's Plantation, 6 Log, Honey Amber, W-111 .... 55.00 To 75.00
Bitters, Drake's Plantation, 6 Log, Light Amber, W-111 .... 60.00 To 450.00
Bitters, Drake's Plantation, 6 Log, Light Olive Green, W-111 .... 700.00
Bitters, Drake's Plantation, 6 Log, Medium Apricot, W-111 .... 185.00
Bitters, Drake's Plantation, 6 Log, Medium Green, W-111 .... 725.00
Bitters, Drake's Plantation, 6 Log, Olive Green, W-111 .... 500.00
Bitters, Drake's Plantation, 6 Log, Orangish Puce, W-111 .... 175.00
Bitters, Drake's Plantation, 6 Log, Puce, W-111 .... 112.00 To 165.00
Bitters, Drake's Plantation, 6 Log, Strawberry & Amber, W-111 .... 150.00
Bitters, Drake's Plantation, 6 Log, Yellow Green Amber, W-111 .... 475.00
Bitters, E.Baker's Premium, Richmond, Va., Aqua, W-24 .... 24.50
Bitters, E.E.Hall's, Barrel, Amber, W-151 .... 65.00 To 90.00
Bitters, E.E.Hall's, Barrel, Medium Amber, W-151 .... 130.00
Bitters, E.E.Hall's, Barrel, Medium Orange Amber, W-151 .... 80.00
Bitters, E.J.Rose's Magador, Stomach, Kidney & Liver, Square 25.00
Bitters, Ear of Corn, see Bitters, National Ear of Corn
Bitters, Edw.Wilder's Stomach, Cabin, Clear, W-366 .... 150.00
Bitters, Electric Brand, Amber, BIMAL, W-115 .... 15.00
Bitters, Electric Brand, Amber, W-114 .... 16.00
Bitters, Electric Brand, Embossed & Labeled, W-114 .... 20.00
Bitters, Electric Brand, H.E.Bucklen & Co., ABM, Olive Green, W-115 .... 7.00
Bitters, Electric Brand, H.E.Bucklen & Co., Label, Amber, W-115 .... 29.00
Bitters, Electric Brand, H.E.Bucklen & Co., Square, Amber, BIMAL, W-115 .... 12.00
Bitters, Fero-China Bisieri, Green, BIMAL 3.00
Bitters, Ferro Quina Stomach, Blood Maker, Lady Leg Neck, Amber, W-123 .... 55.00
Bitters, Ferro Quina, Open Pontil, San Francisco, Cal., W-123a 50.00
Bitters, Fish, W.H.Ware, Dark Amber, 3/4 Quart, W-125 .... 130.00 To 150.00
Bitters, Fish, W.H.Ware, Dark Olive Amber, W-125 .... 225.00
Bitters, Fish, W.H.Ware, Deep Golden Amber, W-125 .... 170.00
Bitters, Fish, W.H.Ware, Patent 1866, Amber, W-125 .... 116.00 To 130.00
Bitters, Genuine Bull Wild Cherry, Cloudy, W-59 .... 75.00
Bitters, German Hop, Reading, Mich., Amber, W-130 .... 55.00 To 65.00
Bitters, Globe Tonic, Dark Amber, W-134 .... 45.00
Bitters, Goff's Herb, Aqua, Rectangular, W-139 .... 4.00
Bitters, Goff's, Labels & Contents, Boxed, Trial Size, W-136 .... 10.00
Bitters, Golden, Geo.C.Hubbell Co., Cabin, Aqua, W-138 .... 180.00
Bitters, Granger's, Baltimore, Amber .... 45.00 To 55.00
Bitters, Greeley's Bourbon Whiskey, Aqua, 3/4 Quart, W-145 .... Illus 950.00
Bitters, Greeley's Bourbon Whiskey, Barrel, Dark Puce, W-145 .... 350.00 To 500.00
Bitters, Greeley's Bourbon Whiskey, Copper Amber, W-145 .... 225.00
Bitters, Greeley's Bourbon, Barrel, Amber Puce, W-144 .... 185.00
Bitters, Greeley's Bourbon, Barrel, Copper Puce, W-144 .... 160.00 To 200.00
Bitters, Greeley's Bourbon, Barrel, Dark Red Amber, W-144 .... 60.00
Bitters, Greeley's Bourbon, Barrel, Deep Apricot, W-144 .... 285.00
Bitters, Greeley's Bourbon, Barrel, Green, W-144 .... 325.00
Bitters, Greeley's Bourbon, Barrel, Light Olive, W-144 .... 225.00
Bitters, Greeley's Bourbon, Barrel, Light Puce, W-144 .... 200.00
Bitters, Greeley's Bourbon, Barrel, Puce, W-144 .... 210.00 To 225.00
Bitters, Greeley's Bourbon, Barrel, Smoky Puce, W-144 .... 180.00 To 225.00
Bitters, Greeley's Bourbon, Dark Copper, W-144 .... 200.00
Bitters, Greeley's Bourbon, Green, W-144 .... 350.00
Bitters, Greeley's Bourbon, Olive Green, W-144 .... 275.00
Bitters, Greeley's Bourbon, Smoky Puce, 3/4 Quart, W-144 .... 110.00 To 150.00
Bitters, Greeley's Bourbon, Whiskey, Deep Red, Barrel, W-145 .... 350.00
Bitters, Greeley's Bourbon, Whiskey, Light Puce, W-145 .... 180.00
Bitters, Gregory's Scotch, Label, Amber 22.00

Bitters, Griffith & Hyatt, Handled, Open Pontil, Olive Green 395.00
Bitters, H.P.Herb Wild Cherry, Amber, 3/4 Quart, W-148 .... 140.00
Bitters, H.P.Herb Wild Cherry, Cabin, Green, Scratches, 3/4 Qt. ....*Illus* 750.00
Bitters, H.P.Herb Wild Cherry, Cabin, Light Amber, W-148 .... 180.00
Bitters, H.P.Herb Wild Cherry, Dark Amber, W-148 .... 170.00
Bitters, H.P.Herb Wild Cherry, Honey Amber, W-148 .... 250.00
Bitters, H.P.Herb Wild Cherry, Medium Amber, W-148 .... 165.00
Bitters, Hall's Bitter, Barrel, Light Amber, W-152 .... 350.00
Bitters, Hall's, E.E.Hall, Barrel, Yellow Amber, W-151 .... 70.00 To 110.00
Bitters, Hall's, E.E.Hall, New Haven, Barrel, Amber, W-158 .... 70.00 To 110.00
Bitters, Hall's, E.E.Hall, New Haven, Medium Amber, W-151 .... 100.00
Bitters, Hansard's Genuine Hop, 2 Tone Stencil, Pottery 45.00
Bitters, Hartwig Kantorowicz Posen, Germany, Milk Glass, Label, W-L-84 .... 80.00
Bitters, Hartwig Kantorowicz Posen, Hamburg, Paris, 9 1/2 X 2 1/2 In. 40.00
Bitters, Hartwig Kantorowicz Posen, Old Rye Whiskey Label, W-L-84 .... 55.00
Bitters, Hartwig Kantorowicz, Fish Inside Star, Amber 80.00
Bitters, Hartwig Kantorowicz, Strawberry Puce 87.00
Bitters, Henke's Schnapps Aromatico, Dark Green, Quart 30.00
Bitters, Hentz's Curative, Philadelphia, Square Indented Panels, Aqua, W-165 .... 35.00
Bitters, Hesperdina Bagley, Amber, Quart, Barrel 350.00
Bitters, Hi Hi, Amber, W-167 .... 60.00 To 62.50
Bitters, Hi Hi, Good For What Ails You, 4 Color, Label Under Glass, W-167 .... 450.00
Bitters, Highland Tonic, Medium Amber, W-170 .... 525.00
Bitters, Holtzermann's Patent Stomach, Cabin, Amber, 3/4 Quart ....*Illus* 450.00
Bitters, Holtzermann's Patent Stomach, Dark Amber, W-172A 145.00
Bitters, Holtzermann's Patent Stomach, Golden Amber, 3/4 Quart, W-172 .... 450.00
Bitters, Holtzermann's Patent Stomach, Light Amber, W-172 .... 95.00
Bitters, Holtzermann's Patent Stomach, Medium Amber, W-172 .... 125.00 To 165.00
Bitters, Holtzermann's Patent Stomach, 2-Sided Roof, Dark Amber, W-172A 550.00
Bitters, Holtzermann's Patent Stomach, 2-Sided Roof, Golden Amber, W-172A 525.00

Bitters, H.P.Herb Wild Cherry,
Cabin, Green, Scratches, 3/4 Qt.

Bitters, Greeley's Bourbon Whiskey,
Aqua, 3/4 Quart, W-145

(See Page 35)

Bitters, Holtzermann's Patent Stomach,
Cabin, Amber, 3/4 Quart

Bitters, Home, St.Louis, Amber, W-173 .... 65.00
Bitters, Hop & Iron, Utica, N.Y., Natural Bubbleburst, Amber, W-175 .... 35.00
Bitters, Hops & Malt, Sample, Amber, 4 In., W-176 ....*Color* 145.00
    Bitters, Hostetter's, see Bitters, Dr. J. Hostetter
    Bitters, Hubbell Co., see Bitters, Golden
Bitters, Hutching's Dyspepsia, Iron Pontil, 8 1/2 In. 200.00
    Bitters, Indian Restorative, see Bitters, Dr.George Pierce's
Bitters, Iron Bitters, Brown Chemical Co., Square, Amber, W-186 .... 15.00
Bitters, Iron Tonic, Label 18.00

Bitters, **J.A.Gilka,** Berlin, 8 Sided, Rectangular, Amber 10.00
Bitters, **J.H.Henke's Cinebra Aromatica Azulejo,** Green, Square, Pint 30.00
Bitters, **J.T.Higby Tonic,** Golden Amber, W-331 .... 30.00
Bitters, **Jackson's Aromatic Life,** Olive Green, W-188 .... 450.00
Bitters, **Jacob Pinkerton,** Wahos & Calisaya, Syracuse, N.Y., Amber, W-347 .... 150.00
Bitters, **Jacob's Cholera & Dysentery Cordial,** OP, Embossed, Aqua 80.00
Bitters, **Jenny Lind,** Shuffsy, Barrel, Deep Aqua, Pontil 135.00
Bitters, **Jente's,** Ribon & Munoz, Hueva, York, Iron Pontil 50.00
Bitters, **John Graf,** Milwaukee, Wis., Bottle Not To Be Sold, 8 Sided, Amber 22.00
Bitters, **Johnson's Calisaya,** Burlington, Vt., Olive Amber, 10 In. .... 55.00 To 65.00
Bitters, **Jos.Triner,** Chicago, Amber, 10 1/2 In. 4.00
Bitters, **Kaiser Wilhelm,** Light Scarlet, W-197 .... 75.00
Bitters, **Kaiser Wilhelm,** Sandusky, Label, Clear, W-197 .... 39.00

Bitters, Lutz's German Stomach,
Amber, 3/4 Quart, W-L-86
(See Page 38)

Bitters, Original Pocahontas,
Aqua, Mouth Roughness,
3/4 Quart
(See Page 39)

Bitters, Old Sachem & Wigwam Tonic,
Barrel, 20 Rings, 3/4 Quart
(See Page 39)

Bitters, **Kaufmann's Sulfur,** Label, Aqua 16.00
Bitters, **Kelly's Old Cabin,** Dark Green, W-199 .... 1800.00
Bitters, **Kelly's Old Cabin,** Patent 1870, Dark Amber 800.00
Bitters, **Kelly's Old Cabin,** 1863, Honey Amber, W-199 .... 275.00
Bitters, **Kennedy's East India,** Iller & Co., Omaha, Neb., W-200 .... 20.00
Bitters, **Keystone,** Barrel, Amber, W-201 .... 250.00
Bitters, **Keystone,** Barrel, Light Amber, W-201 .... 325.00
Bitters, **Keystone,** Barrel, Medium Amber, W-201 .... 275.00
Bitters, **Keystone,** Barrel, Medium To Dark Amber, W-201 .... 305.00
Bitters, **Keystone,** Barrel, Yellow Amber, W-201 .... 265.00
Bitters, **Kimball's Jaundice,** Iron Pontil, Olive Amber, W-202 .... 210.00 To 260.00
Bitters, **Kimball's Jaundice,** Tray, N.H., Nail Heads, Olive Amber, IP, W-202 .... 265.00
Bitters, **King Solomon's, Seattle,** Wash., Amber, Quart, W-457 .... 45.00
Bitters, **Knickerbocker,** Seal, Amber, W-515 .... 220.00
Bitters, **Koehler & Hindrichs,** Stomach, Amber, Quart 170.00
Bitters, **Lady's Leg,** Amber, Pint 10.00
Bitters, **Lady's Leg,** Amber, Quart 8.00
Bitters, **Lady's Leg,** Amber, 4 In. 20.00
Bitters, **Lady's Leg,** Amber, 12 1/2 In. 45.00
Bitters, **Lady's Leg,** Honey Amber, 12 In. 24.00

Bitters, Lady's Leg, M On Base, Red	40.00
Bitters, Lady's Leg, Olive Green, 12 In., Quart	55.00
Bitters, Lady's Leg, Olive Green, 14 In.	15.00
Bitters, Landley's, Push-Up Base, Pale Green, 6 1/2 In.	15.00
Bitters, Landsberg's Century, Chicago, Amber, W-205	450.00
Bitters, Lash's Kidney & Liver, Amber, 4 1/2 In., W-208	37.00
Bitters, Lash's Kidney & Liver, Best Cathartic, Amber, 9 1/8 In., W-208	12.50
Bitters, Lash's Kidney & Liver, Light Amber, W-208	8.00
Bitters, Lash's Kidney & Liver, Red Amber, W-208	45.00
Bitters, Lash's L.B.Co., Oval	5.00
Bitters, Lash's Liver, Amber, W-209	12.50
Bitters, Lash's, Natural Tonic Laxative, Honey Amber, W-207B	12.50
Bitters, Lash's, Tonic, Label, W-207	5.00
Bitters, Lediard's Celebrated Stomach, Emerald Green, Iron Pontil	650.00
Bitters, Lewis Red Jacket, New Haven, Conn., Amber, W-213	50.00
Bitters, Lilly Iron, ABM	4.00
Bitters, Lippman's Great German, N.Y. & Savannah, Amber, W-215	10.00
Bitters, Litthauer Stomach, see also Bitters, Hartwig Kantorowicz Posen	
Bitters, Litthauer Stomach, Milk Glass, W-216	88.00
Bitters, Lohengrin, Milk Glass, Case, W-218	150.00
Bitters, Loveridge's Wahoo, Dark Amber	125.00
Bitters, Loveridge's Wahoo, Violet	175.00
Bitters, Lutz's German Stomach, Amber, 3/4 Quart, W-L-86 .....Illus	250.00
Bitters, MacKenzie's Wild Cherry, Chicago, W-463	60.00
Bitters, Magador	40.00
Bitters, Mandrake, see Bitters, Dr. Baxter's	
Bitters, Marshall's Best Laxative & Blood Purifier, Amber, 8 3/4 In., W-227	28.00
Bitters, McKeever's Army, W-228	1800.00
Bitters, McLean's Strengthening Cordial & Blood Purifier, 10 In.	8.00
Bitters, Medicine, R.Wistar Balsam Of Wild Cherry, Open Pontil, Aqua	25.00
Bitters, Mishler's Herb, Dr.S.B.Hartman & Co., Amber, Label, W-229	35.00
Bitters, Mishler's Herb, Dr.S.B.Hartman & Co., Citron, W-229	45.00
Bitters, Mishler's Herb, Dr.S.B.Hartman & Co., Honey Color, W-229	50.00
Bitters, Mishler's Herb, Dr.S.B.Hartman & Co., Yellow Amber, W-229	30.00
Bitters, Mist Of The Morning, Amber, Barrel	210.00
Bitters, Morning Star, Amber, W-272	175.00 To 250.00
Bitters, Morning Star, Burst Bubble, Iron Pontil, Amber, W-232	145.00
Bitters, Morning Star, Dark Amber, W-232	195.00
Bitters, Morning Star, Light Gold, W-272	325.00
Bitters, Moultons Oloroso, Deep Aqua, W-233	250.00 To 275.00
Bitters, Mrs.Kidder's Dysentery Cordial, Round, Aqua, 8 In.	42.50
Bitters, National, Ear Of Corn, Amber, W-236	180.00 To 215.00
Bitters, National, Ear Of Corn, Applied Top, Dark Amber, W-236	205.00
Bitters, National, Ear Of Corn, Aquamarine, W-236	1500.00
Bitters, National, Ear Of Corn, Golden Amber, W-236	180.00 To 200.00
Bitters, National, Ear Of Corn, Label, Light Amber, W-236	235.00
Bitters, National, Ear Of Corn, Medium Golden Amber, W-236	195.00 To 200.00
Bitters, National, Ear Of Corn, Puce, W-236	365.00
Bitters, National, Ear Of Corn, W-236	350.00
Bitters, National, Ear Of Corn, Yellow, Amber, W-236	200.00 To 245.00
Bitters, New York Hop Bitters Co., Embossed Flag, Square, Aqua, W-472	190.00
Bitters, New York Hop, Indented Sides, Aqua	300.00
Bitters, O'leary's 20th Century, Amber, W-245	45.00
Bitters, Old Continental, Cabin, Light Amber, W-240	200.00 To 260.00
Bitters, Old Continental, Golden Amber, W-240	225.00 To 275.00
Bitters, Old Hickory Celebrated Stomach, J.Grossman, N.O., Amber, W-476	75.00
Bitters, Old Homestead Wild Cherry, Amber, W-242	150.00 To 175.00
Bitters, Old Homestead Wild Cherry, Cabin, Medium Amber, W-242	180.00 To 200.00
Bitters, Old Homestead Wild Cherry, Dark Amber, W-242	210.00
Bitters, Old Homestead Wild Cherry, Gold Amber, 3/4 Qt., W-242	170.00 To 190.00
Bitters, Old Homestead Wild Cherry, Light Puce, W-242	400.00
Bitters, Old Sachem & Wigwam Tonic, Barrel, Amber, W-244	150.00 To 190.00
Bitters, Old Sachem & Wigwam Tonic, Barrel, Amethyst, W-244	425.00
Bitters, Old Sachem & Wigwam Tonic, Barrel, Citron, 3/4 Quart, W-244	310.00
Bitters, Old Sachem & Wigwam Tonic, Barrel, Golden Amber, W-244	165.00

Bitters, Old Sachem & Wigwam Tonic, Barrel, Golden Amber, 3/4 Quart, W-244 .... 120.00
Bitters, Old Sachem & Wigwam Tonic, Barrel, Light Amber .... 130.00 To 195.00
Bitters, Old Sachem & Wigwam Tonic, Barrel, Medium Amber 180.00
Bitters, Old Sachem & Wigwam Tonic, Barrel, Medium Amber, W-244 .... 145.00
Bitters, Old Sachem & Wigwam Tonic, Barrel, Puce, W-244 .... 190.00
Bitters, Old Sachem & Wigwam Tonic, Barrel, Strawberry Amber, W-244 .... 140.00
Bitters, Old Sachem & Wigwam Tonic, Barrel, Strawberry, W-244 .... 225.00
Bitters, Old Sachem & Wigwam Tonic, Barrel, 20 Rings, 3/4 Quart ....*Illus* 310.00
Bitters, Old Sachem Wigwam Tonic, Barrel, Apricot, W-244 .... 390.00
Bitters, Orange, Aqua, Label, Fifth 15.00
Bitters, Oregon Grape Root, Small Checks, W-246 .... 130.00
Bitters, Original Pocahontas, Aqua, Mouth Roughness, 3/4 Quart ....*Illus* 1225.00
Bitters, Orruro, Round, Green, W-248 .... 18.00
Bitters, Osgood's India Cholagogue, Swirl Etched, Open Pontil, Aqua 12.00
Bitters, Oswego Bitters, 25 Cents, Amber, W-477 .... 32.00 To 40.00
Bitters, Oxygenated, For Dyspepsia, Asthma & General Debility, 6 In.W-249 .... 45.00
Bitters, Parker's Celebrated Stomach, W-480 .... 75.00
Bitters, Pepsin Calisaya, Dr.Russell Med., Co., Emerald Green, W-253 .... 25.00
Bitters, Pepsin Calisaya, Dr.Russell Med.Co., Green, 4 1/8 In., W-253 .... 60.00
Bitters, Peptinized Wine & Iron, M.F.G.Chemist, Pittsburgh, 9 1/2 In. 75.00
Bitters, Perrin's Apple Ginger 80.00
Bitters, Peruvian, Amber, W-254 .... 50.00
Bitters, Peruvian, Light Amber, W-254 .... 35.00
Bitters, Phoenix, Aqua, Open Pontil.W-257 .... 65.00
Bitters, Phoenix, Jno Moffat, Open Pontil, W-257A .... 200.00 To 275.00
Bitters, Phoenix, New York, Price I Dollar, Olive Green, W-257 .... 275.00
Bitters, Phoenix, Olive Amber, W-257 .... 240.00
Bitters, Phoenix, Olive Amber, 1/2 Pint, W-257 .... 200.00
Bitters, Pineapple Bitters, Barrel, Amber 175.00
Bitters, Pineapple Bitters, W. & Co., N.Y., Barrel, Light Amber, Pontil 375.00

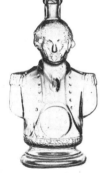

Bitters, Suffolk, Pig, Golden Amber, 3/4 Quart, W-322
(See Page 40)

Bitters, Simon's Centennial,
Washington, Aqua,
3/4 Qt., W-304

(See Page 40)

Bitters, Royal Italian,
Amethyst, 3/4 Quart, W-286

(See Page 40)

Bitters, Pineapple Shape, Amber .... 125.00 To 135.00
Bitters, Pineapple, Green, 9 In. ....*Color* xxxx.xx
Bitters, Pineapple, J.C.& Co., Pontil, Amber 600.00
Bitters, Pond's Kidney & Liver, Square, Amber, BIMAL, W-487 .... 8.00
Bitters, Poor Man's Family, Contents, Label, Circular, W-262 .... 25.00
Bitters, Prickley Ash, ABM 15.00
Bitters, Prickley Ash, Label, Box, Contents, W-263 .... 50.00
Bitters, Professor B.E.Mann's Oriental Stomach, Medium Amber, W-226 .... 1000.00

Bitters, Professor Geo.J.Byrne Stomach, Pat.1870, Barrel, Amber, W-63 .... 725.00
Bitters, Professor Geo.J.Byrne Stomach, Yellow, 3/4 Quart, W-63 .... 2000.00
Bitters, Professor Geo.J.Byrne, Clear, W-63 .... 395.00
Bitters, Prune Stomach & Liver, Cathartic & Blood Purifier, Amber, W-264 .... 35.00
Bitters, Prune Stomach & Liver, Square, Amber, 9 In., W-264 .... 35.00
   Bitters, Quaker, see Bitters, Dr. Flint's
Bitters, Quinine, Dark Aqua 50.00
Bitters, Ramsey's Trinidad, Olive, W-268 .... 15.00 To 20.00
Bitters, Red Cross Laxative, Label & Contents, Square, Amber, Quart 30.00
Bitters, Red Jacket, Monheimer & Co., Amber .... 20.00 To 50.00
Bitters, Reed's Gilt Edge, 1878 .... 28.00
Bitters, Reed's, Lady's Leg, Amber, W-272 .... 140.00 To 175.00
Bitters, Reed's, Lady's Leg, W-272 .... 150.00
Bitters, Remko Tonic, Clear 50.00
Bitters, Rex Kidney & Liver, Square, Amber, W-274 .... 16.00
Bitters, Roback's Stomach, Cincinnati, O., IP, Golden Amber, Large, W-280 .... 200.00
Bitters, Roback's Stomach, Forest Green, Quart 950.00
Bitters, Roback's Stomach, Light Amber, Large, W-280 .... 190.00 To 225.00
Bitters, Roback's Stomach, Light Amber, W-280a 110.00
Bitters, Rocky Mountain Tonic, Amber, W-281 .... 70.00
Bitters, Romaine's Crimean, Amber, W-282 .... 145.00 To 165.00
Bitters, Royal Italian, Amethyst, 3/4 Quart, W-286 .... Illus 325.00
Bitters, Royal Italian, Dark Amethyst, W-286 .... 495.00
Bitters, Royal Italian, Light Plum, Open Pontil, W-286 .... 500.00
Bitters, Royal Pepsin Stomach, Amber, W-287 .... 59.00
Bitters, Royal Pepsin Stomach, Dark Red Amber, Pint, W-287A 65.00
Bitters, Royal Pepsin Stomach, Full Label, Glass Stopper, Amber, W-287 .... 70.00
Bitters, Royal Pepsin Stomach, Stopper, Sample, W-287A 75.00
Bitters, Royce's Sherry Wine, 5 Star, Aqua, W-288 .... 60.00
Bitters, Rush's, A.H.Flanders, M.C., N.Y., OP, Amber, W-289 .... 25.00 To 49.00
Bitters, S. & S., Clear, Quart 35.00
Bitters, S.O.Richardson's, Aqua, Open Pontil, W-275 .... 25.00 To 41.00
   Bitters, S.T. Drake's, see Bitters, Drake's
Bitters, Saint Jacob's, Amber, Square, 8 5/8 In., W-453 .... 40.00
Bitters, Sanborn Kidney & Liver Vegetable Laxative, Amber, W-293 .... 30.00
Bitters, Sarasina Stomach, W-294 .... 35.00
Bitters, Sazerac Aromatic, Lady's Leg, Light Amber, W-296 .... 365.00
Bitters, Sazerac, Block Top, Lady's Leg, Milk Glass, W-296 .... 275.00
Bitters, Schnapp's Aromatic, Green, 1/2 Pint 15.00
Bitters, Schroeder's, Louisville, Ky., Lady's Leg, Amber, W297 .... 99.00 To 265.00
Bitters, Simon's Centennial, Aqua, W-304 .... 525.00 To 950.00
Bitters, Simon's Centennial, Washington, Aqua, 3/4 Qt., W-304 .... Illus 500.00
Bitters, Smith-Druid, Light Apricot Amber, W-308 .... 700.00
Bitters, Solomon's Strengthening, Cobalt, W-313 .... 250.00
Bitters, Somer's Liver & Kidney, Amber 60.00
Bitters, Steele's Niagara Star, Eagle With 13 Stars, Amber, W-316 .... 175.00
Bitters, Steele's Niagara Star, Eagle With 13 Stars, Golden Amber, W-316 .... 180.00
Bitters, Stockton's Port Wine, W-319 .... 75.00
Bitters, Stonsdorfer, Label, Fifth 25.00
Bitters, Suffolk, Pig, Golden Amber, 3/4 Quart, W-322 .... Illus 375.00
Bitters, Suffolk, Pig, Golden Olive Amber, W-322 .... 35.00
Bitters, Suffolk, Pig, Honey Amber, W-322 .... 550.00
Bitters, Suffolk, Pig, Light Orange Amber, W-322 .... 490.00
Bitters, Sunny Castle Stomach, Amber, Square, 8 7/8 In., W-325 .... 55.00
Bitters, Swain's Bourbon, Amber, W-326 .... 65.00 To 90.00
Bitters, Tippecanoe, Chapin & Cone Sour Mash, H.H.Warner, 1867 .... Color xxxx.xx
Bitters, Tippecanoe, H.H.Warner & Co., Amber .... 70.00 To 75.00
Bitters, Tippecanoe, H.H.Warner & Co., Golden Amber, 3/4 Quart .... 65.00 To 75.00
Bitters, Tippecanoe, H.H.Warner & Co., Tree Bark, Amber .... 40.00 To 65.00
Bitters, Tippecanoe, H.H.Warner & Co., Tree Bark, Honey Amber 75.00
Bitters, Tippecanoe, H.H.Warner & Co., Tree Bark, Olive Amber, 3/4 Quart 145.00
Bitters, Toneco Stomach, Amethyst, Stain, W-330 .... 15.00
Bitters, Turner Brothers, Barrel, Burnt Amber 160.00
Bitters, Turner Brothers, N.Y., Barrel, Citron 230.00
Bitters, Tyler's Standard American, Amber, 3/4 Quart, W-337 .... 60.00
Bitters, Udolpho Wolfe's Aromatic Schnapps, Deep Brilliant Green, Pint 35.00

Fire Grenade, California Fire Extinguisher, Amber

Ink, Stoddard, Open Pontil, 12 Sided

Fruit Jar, Mason's Patent Nov. 30, 1858, Amethyst, ½ Gallon

Fruit Jar, J.P. Smith & Co., Philadelphia, Green, ½ Gallon

Zanesville, C. 1815, L. To R.: 10-Diamond
Chestnut Flask, 24-Swirled Rib Globular
Bottle, Chestnut Flask, 24-Rib Flask In
Tight Swirl

Fruit Jar, Ravenna Glass
Works, Airtight, C. 1857

Flask, Ravenna Glass Co. & Traveler's
Companion

Medicine, Wm. Radam's
Fungus Destroyer, ½ Gallon

Figural, Dog, Sterling Silver Head, 8 In.

Figural, Chicken, 3-Mold, Painted, 9½ In.

Flasks, Calabash, Jenny Lind, Ravenna, Ohio

Bitters, Drake's Plantation, Green, 10 In.

Candy Container, Tot Telephone, 2½ In.

Coca-Cola, Seltzer, Winona,
Minnesota

Milk, Painted, 7½ In.

Wine, Face Under Glass, 14 In.

Medicine, Shaker Extract Of Roots, Clear, 5½ In.

Bitters, Tippecanoe, Chapin & Cone Sour Mash, H. H. Warner, 1867

Codd, Milton Aerated Waterworks, Queens, N.S., Aqua, 8½ In.

Wild Turkey, No. 8

Fruit Jar, Petal, Tin Top, Blue

Figural, Moses, 7½ In.

Ink, Signet, Cobalt, 9 In.

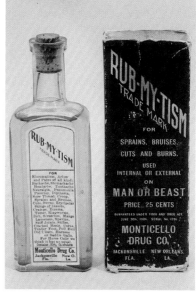

Medicine, Rub-My-Tism, Box, 5½ In.

Medicine, Dr. Pyle's Azoturia, Box, 8½ In.

Household, Stove Polish, Black Silk, 5½ In.

Food, Hellman, Crock, 8 In.

Food, Butler's Ketchup, 8 In.; Food, My Own Catsup, 7 In.

Miniature, Wee Scotch, 5 In.; Miniature,
The Nineteenth Hole, 4 In.

Food, R. T. French,
Mustard, Atlantic, 5 In.

Medicine, Tonic, Vimalt,
Amber, Paper Label, 9 In.

Household, Wavenlock For
Hair, Glass Label, 8½ In.

Bitters, W. & Co., N.Y.,
Pineapple Shape, Yellow Olive, 3/4 Qt.
(See Page 42)

Blown, Midwestern, Globular,
Swirled To Right, Citron, 8 3/4 In.
(See Page 42)

Blown, Midwestern, 16 Ribs Swirled
To Left, Yellow, 9 1/8 In.
(See Page 42)

Candy Container,
Felix The Cat, 5 In.
(See Page 43)

Candy Container, Radio, Chip, 4 1/2 In.
(See Page 43)

Candy Container, Jumbo, 3 3/4 In.
(See Page 43)

Candy Container, Santa
Descending Chimney, 5 In.
(See Page 43)

Candy Container, World's Fair, 6 In.
(See Page 44)

Candy Container.
Telephone, 5 In.
(See Page 43)

Bitters, Udolpho Wolfe's Aromatic Schnapps, IP, Olive Green 45.00
Bitters, Udolpho Wolfe's Aromatic Schnapps, Olive Gree, Pontil, 8 In. 29.50
Bitters, Udolpho Wolfe's Aromatic Schnapps, Oliver Amber, 3/4 Quart 30.00
Bitters, Udolpho Wolfe's Aromatic Schnapps, Yellow, 8 1/2 In. 10.00
Bitters, Udolpho Wolfe's Aromatic Shcnapps, Amber, Quart 20.00
Bitters, Vermo Stomach, ABM, W-342 .... 5.00
Bitters, Voldner's Aromatic Schnapps, Applied Lip 50.00
Bitters, Voldner's Aromatic Schnapps, Olive Green 25.00
Bitters, Von Dunk's Geneva Trade Mark, Barrel, Amber 150.00
Bitters, W. & Co., N.Y., Pineapple Shape, Yellow Olive, 3/4 Qt. ....*Illus* 600.00
Bitters, W. & Co., Pineapple, Deep Golden Amber, 3/4 Quart 140.00
Bitters, W.C.Bitters, Brobst & Rentschler, Reading, Pa., Barrel, Amber, W-347 .... 390.00
Bitters, W.F.Severa Stomach, Amber, W-321 .... 30.00 To 45.00
Bitters, Wahoo & Calisaya, Pinkerton, Semi-Cabin, Light Amber, W-349 .... 110.00
Bitters, Wahoo & Calisaya, W-349 .... 35.00 To 190.00
Bitters, Wait's Kidney & Liver, W-350 .... 25.00
Bitters, Wakefield's Strengthening, Aqua, W-510 .... 30.00
Bitters, Wallace's Tonic, W-353 .... 49.00
Bitters, Warner's Safe Tonic, Amber, W-5 2 .... 400.00
Bitters, Warner's Safe Tonic, Dark Amber, 1/2 Pint, W-512 .... 500.00
Bitters, Warner's Safe, Light Amber, 1/2 Pint, W-356 .... 500.00
Bitters, Webb's Improved, W-358 .... 42.50
Bitters, West India, Stomach, Amber, W-359 .... 45.00
Bitters, West India, Stomach, Light Amber, W-359 .... 45.00
Bitters, Wheat, Beveled Base Corners, Light Amber, 9 3/4 In., W-360 .... 135.00
Bitters, White's Stomach, Square, Amber, Quart, W-363 .... 75.00
Bitters, White's Stomach, Stars Embossed On Indented Panels, Amber 35.00
Bitters, Whitwell's Temperance, Boston, Open Pontil, W-364 .... 135.00
Bitters, Willer, Schenectady, N.Y., Gravitating Stopper 10.00
Bitters, William Allen's Congress, Aqua, W-4 .... 90.00
Bitters, William Allen's Congress, Emerald Green, 3/4 Quart, W-4 .... 250.00
Bitters, William Allen's Congress, Lockport Green 350.00
Bitters, Wishart's Pine Tree Tar Cordial, Green 80.00
Bitters, Wishart's Pine Tree Tar Cordial, 1859, Blue Green, Pint 55.00
Bitters, Wm.H.Daley, Bell, N.Y., Barrel, Green 695.00
Bitters, Wolfe's Schnapps, Label Dated 1852, Amber 15.00
Bitters, Woodbury's, W-373 .... 23.00
Bitters, Wormser Bros., S.R., Barrel, Light Amber 575.00
Bitters, Yamara Cordial, Embossed Globe & Hop Leaves 50.00
Bitters, Yerba Buena, Amber, Pint, W-375 .... 60.00
Bitters, Yerba Buena, Olive Green, 8 1/2 In., W-375 .... 35.00
Bitters, Yerba Buena, San Francisco, Cal., Amber, W-375A 125.00
Bitters, Yochim Bros., W-376 .... 55.00
Bitters, Zadoc Porter Stomach, Aqua 16.00
Bitters, Zingari, W-377 .... 195.00
Black Glass, Ale, Cooper, Portobello, 3 Mold, Squat 5.00
Black Glass, Ale, Crude 1.50
Black Glass, Ale, Woolfale, Quart 6.00
Black Glass, Captain's, C.1700s, Free-Blown Pontil 65.00
Black Glass, Rum, Free-Blown, Pontil, Squat 20.00
Black Glass, Rum, Free-Blown, Quart 14.00
Blacking, see Shoe Polish
Blown, Midwestern, Globular, Swirled To Right, Citron, 8 3/4 In. ....*Illus* 350.00
Blown, Midwestern, 16 Ribs Swirled To Left, Yellow, 9 1/8 In. ....*Illus* 850.00
Bralatta, Column 18.00
Brandy, Landsberg's Pure Blackberry, A.Heller & Bros., N.Y., Aqua 475.00
Brooks, see Ezra Brooks
C.P.C., California Perfume Company, see Avon
Cabin Still, see Old Fitzgerald
Calabash, see Flask
Canadian Mist, Royal Canadian Mounted Policeman, Porcelain, 12 In. 10.00

Candy containers of glass were very popular after World War I. Small glass figural bottles held dime-store candy. Today many of the same shapes hold modern candy in plastic bottles.

Candy Container, Airplane, U.S.P-51 .... 12.00

Candy Container, Army Bomber	7.50
Candy Container, Automobile, Vallerystahl	32.00
Candy Container, Boat, Model Cruiser	4.00
Candy Container, Boot, Santa's	4.00
Candy Container, Bunte, Chicago, Cylinder, 20 Panels, 8 1/2 In.	10.00
Candy Container, Cap, Military	10.00
Candy Container, Chick, Standing	52.00
Candy Container, Chicken On The Nest	7.50 To 11.00
Candy Container, Felix The Cat, 5 In.	Illus 37.00
Candy Container, Fire Engine, With Candy	5.00
Candy Container, Girl With Muff	10.00
Candy Container, Gun, Screw Opening	55.00
Candy Container, Horse With Two Wheeled Cart	3.50
Candy Container, Horseless Carriage, Clear	40.00
Candy Container, Iron	4.00
Candy Container, Jeep	6.00
Candy Container, Jumbo, 3 3/4 In.	Illus 55.00
Candy Container, Liberty Bell, Bottom Closure, Green	25.00
Candy Container, Locomotive 1028	8.50
Candy Container, Owl, 4 X 1 In.	3.00

Coca-Cola, November 16, 1915
(See Page 46)

Coca-Cola, Bottling Co., Birmingham
(See Page 45)

Coca-Cola, Bottling Co., Cleveland, Ohio, Amber
(See Page 45)

Candy Container, Peter Rabbit	8.50
Candy Container, Pistol, Ground Top, Pewter Cap, Clear	12.00
Candy Container, Radio, Chip, 4 1/2 In.	Illus 25.00
Candy Container, Revolver, Round Butt, Closure & Contents, Clear, 8 In.	20.00
Candy Container, Santa Descending Chimney, 5 In.	Illus 42.50
Candy Container, Sign, Don't Park Here	30.00
Candy Container, Sitting Dog	9.00
Candy Container, Spirit Of Goodwill	45.00
Candy Container, Suitcase, Metal Lower Side & Handle	25.00 To 30.00
Candy Container, Telephone, 5 In.	Illus 8.00
Candy Container, Three Swimming Ducks	45.00
Candy Container, Tot Telephone, 2 1/2 In.	Color 22.50
Candy Container, Uncle Sam Hat	15.00

Candy Container, World, Embossed, Round, Clear 20.00
Candy Container, World's Fair, 6 In. .... *Illus* 35.00
    Canning Jar, see Fruit Jar
Chemical, Bobbitt Co., Baltimore, BIMAL, Amber, 7 In. 5.00
Chemical, Borbeck Radium Jar, Federal Radium Lab., St.Louis, Mo. 100.00
Chemical, Dead Stuck For Bugs, Clear 7.00
Chemical, Diamond-Quilted, Dri Gas Fire Extinguisher, Chattanooga, Tenn. 25.00
Chemical, Dr.Blocksom's Chemical Warehouse, Zanesville, 12 Sided, OP 80.00
Chemical, Eastman Kodak Co., Rochester, N.Y., Beaker, Graduated, 4 1/8 In. 10.00
Chemical, Eastman Kodak, Amber 15.00
Chemical, Esco Distinctive Embalming Fluid, BIMAL, 8 In. 4.00
Chemical, Figaro Chemical Co., Dallas, Tex., Aqua, 2 1/2 Pint 18.00
Chemical, Marble's Nitro Solvent, Clear 3.00
Chemical, Munyon's Germicide Solution, Green 7.00
Chemical, Photo, Round, Amber, 1/10 Liter 10.00
Chemical, Reese Chemical Co., For External Use Only, Use 4 Times Daily 5.00
Chemical, Rumford Chemical Works 3.00
Chemical, Rumford Chemical Works, Label 17.00
Chestnut, Blown, Aqua, 10 1/8 In. 35.00
Chestnut, Open Pontil, Green, 7 In. 65.00
Clevenger, Apollo 9 .... 14.00
Clevenger, Bismarck, North Dakota 6.00
Clevenger, Bunker Hill 7.00
Clevenger, C & O Canal 9.00
Clevenger, Charles Gardner 9.00
Clevenger, Charles S.Price 10.00
Clevenger, Chevy Roadster 10.00
Clevenger, Christmas, 1973 .... 8.00
Clevenger, Citizen Ship 10.00
Clevenger, Corvette, 25th Anniversary 10.00
Clevenger, Cowpens 7.00

Cologne, Tappan's Dime, Paper Label, 3 1/2 In.
(See Page 46)

Cologne, Bunker Hill Monument, Figural, 7 In.
(See Page 46)

Clevenger, Delaware 8.00
Clevenger, East Clay Grange 9.00
Clevenger, Eastland Ship 10.00
Clevenger, First Washington Monument 9.00
Clevenger, Freedom Train 19.00
Clevenger, H.H.Humphrey 10.00
Clevenger, Hawaii Bicentennial 10.00
Clevenger, Independence Hall 10.00

Clevenger, Israel, 25th Anniversary	8.00
Clevenger, Jersey Devil	8.00
Clevenger, Kennedy	12.00
Clevenger, Kennedy Memorial	8.00
Clevenger, King Mountain	7.00
Clevenger, Lexington	7.00
Clevenger, New Castle Ferry	8.00
Clevenger, New Jersey	8.00
Clevenger, Paul Revere Ride	8.00
Clevenger, Pennsylvania	8.00
Clevenger, Pomona Hall	8.00
Clevenger, POW	10.00
Clevenger, Silver Dollar	10.00
Clevenger, Space Shuttle	10.00
Clevenger, Spirit Of '76	10.00
Clevenger, SS Columbus	10.00
Clevenger, St.Barnabas Church	10.00
Clevenger, Stewart Cort Ship	10.00
Clevenger, Walt Whitman	8.00
Clevenger, Washington City	9.00
Clevenger, Watergate, Amethyst	25.00
Clevenger, Watergate, Blue	10.00
Clevenger, Watergate, Topaz	8.00
Clevenger, West Maryland RR	9.00
Clevenger, Wright Brothers First Flight	10.00

Coca-Cola was first made in 1886. Since that time the drink has been sold in all parts of the world in a variety of bottles. The "waisted" bottle was first used in 1916.

Coca-Cola, AAR Convention, Red & White	40.00
Coca-Cola, Amelia Earhart	15.00
Coca-Cola, Aqua, Paper Label, 7 In. ....*Color*	xxxx.xx
Coca-Cola, Arizona	19.00
Coca-Cola, Bottling Co., Birmingham ....*Illus*	40.00
Coca-Cola, Bottling Co., Cleveland, Ohio, Amber ....*Illus*	12.00
Coca-Cola, Buffalo, N.Y., Straight Sided, Aqua	10.00
Coca-Cola, Buffalo, N.Y., 1908, Clear	8.00
Coca-Cola, C.E.W.Wright, Greenwood, Miss., Script, Amber	24.00
Coca-Cola, Charlotte, N.C., BIM, Aqua	12.00
Coca-Cola, Clifton Forge, Ice & Bottling Works, Va, Script, Pale Green	10.00
Coca-Cola, Columbus, Ohio, Amber	25.00
Coca-Cola, Columbus, Script, Clear	5.00
Coca-Cola, Cuero Centennial & Turkey Trot, 1872-1972, Green	6.00
Coca-Cola, Diamond Each Side, First No Return, Embossed	4.00
Coca-Cola, Embossed, D-Pat., D105529	3.00
Coca-Cola, Embossed, December 25, 1923	6.00
Coca-Cola, Embossed, November 16, 1915	5.00
Coca-Cola, Embossed, 1955, 12 Ounce	3.00
Coca-Cola, Florida, Straight Sided	7.00
Coca-Cola, Forrest City, Ark., Gold-Plated Silk Screen, 1925, 6 1/2 Oz.	20.00
Coca-Cola, Fort Worth, Tex., Script	8.00
Coca-Cola, Gold, 6 1/2 Oz.	25.00
Coca-Cola, Grostean & Holdawcy, Sacto, Cal., Aqua	15.00
Coca-Cola, Hobble Skirt, Pat., 1923, Providence, R.I.	10.00
Coca-Cola, Huntsville, Alabama, Amber	20.00
Coca-Cola, Hutchinson, Biedenharn Candy Co., 1894, Repro, Handmade	30.00
Coca-Cola, Hygeia Bottling Works, Pensacola, Fla., Straight	8.00 To 15.00
Coca-Cola, Jacksonville, Fla., Straight Sided, Aqua	7.00
Coca-Cola, Japan	6.00
Coca-Cola, Las Vegas, Nevada, Clear	40.00
Coca-Cola, Little Rock, Ark., 1915	5.00
Coca-Cola, Louisville, Ky., Amber	25.00
Coca-Cola, Miniature, 2 1/2 In. ....*Color*	xxxx.xx
Coca-Cola, Nashville, Tenn., Amber	8.00 To 14.00
Coca-Cola, New Mexico	19.00
Coca-Cola, New York, N.Y., Script, BIMAL, Amber	7.00 To 15.00

Coca-Cola, Norfolk, Va., BIMAL, Script, Amber	18.00
Coca-Cola, Norfolk, Va., 1906, Amber, 7 Oz.	15.00
Coca-Cola, November 16, 1915 ....*Illus*	3.00
Coca-Cola, Phoenix, Ariz.	19.00
Coca-Cola, Rome, Ga., Straight Side, Clear	6.00
Coca-Cola, Root Reproduction, 1965, 7 In. ....*Color*	xxxx.xx
Coca-Cola, Seattle, BIMAL Crown	10.00
Coca-Cola, Seltzer, Winona, Minnesota ....*Color*	35.00
Coca-Cola, Springfield, Ill., Amber, 6 1/2 Oz.	10.00
Coca-Cola, Staunton, Va., BIM, Amber	12.00
Coca-Cola, Tampa, Fla., Straight Sided, Aqua	7.50
Coca-Cola, Tennessee Bottling Works, Wytheville, Va., Honey Amber	8.00
Coca-Cola, Toledo, Ohio, Amber	7.00
Coca-Cola, Turkey Trot	6.00
Coca-Cola, Verner Springs, S.C., Straight Sided, 9 In.	30.00
Coca-Cola, Water, Ship On Back, Green	75.00
Coca-Cola, Wilmington, N.C., Stain, Amber	20.00
Coca-Cola, 50th Anniversary, Western	50.00
Coca-Cola, 75th Anniversary, 1974, Printed, 7 In. ....*Color*	4.00
Codd, Milton Aerated Waterworks, Queens, N.S., Aqua, 8 1/2 In. ....*Color*	xxxx.xx
Collectors Art, Brahma Bull	40.00 To 44.95
Collectors Art, Charolais Bull, 1974	31.00
Collectors Art, Corvette Stingray, Blue, Goodyear Tires	25.00
Collectors Art, Corvette Stingray, Red	16.00 To 25.00
Collectors Art, Doberman Pinscher, Black	13.00
Collectors Art, Doberman Pinscher, Red	17.00
Collectors Art, Hereford Bull	12.95 To 42.00
Collectors Art, Longhorn Bull	34.00
Collectors Art, Mexican Fighting Bull	32.00 To 47.95
Collectors Art, Shepherd, Black	20.00
Collectors Art, Shepherd, Brown	14.00
Collectors Art, Shepherd, White	20.00
Collectors Art, Texas Longhorn	35.00
Collectors Bourbon, Cuckoo Clock, 1971	25.00
Collectors Bourbon, Flower Child, 1968	5.00
Collectors Bourbon, Hippie, 1968	5.00
Collectors Bourbon, Queen Anne Clock, 1970	24.00
Collectors Bourbon, Villain, 1969	6.00 To 8.00
Collectors Weekly, Chicago Fire	8.00
Collectors Weekly, Stanley & Livingston	7.00
Cologne, see also Perfume, Scent	
Cologne, Barrel, Clear	20.00
Cologne, Basket Weave Handles, Bulbous Neck	65.00
Cologne, Basket Weave, Open Pontil, Aquamarine, Small	18.00
Cologne, Bellows, Free Blown, Clear, 6 1/2 In.	95.00
Cologne, Bunker Hill Monument, Figural, 7 In. ....*Illus*	22.00
Cologne, Cathedral, Open Pontil, 5 3/4 In. ....*Color*	100.00
Cologne, Dancing Indian, Aqua	45.00
Cologne, Domed Inset Panels, Milk Glass, 3 In.	35.00
Cologne, Eau De Cologne, Label, Clear, 4 1/2 In.	5.00
Cologne, Embossed Eagle With Scroll In Beak, N.Prentiss, N.Y., OP, Clear	90.00
Cologne, Embossed Floral Design, Corrugated Edges, OP, Aqua, 4 In.	25.00
Cologne, Embossed Man, Gothic Pillars & Arches, 4 In.	15.00
Cologne, Fancy Designs, Aqua, 4 In., Pair	60.00
Cologne, Flattened Barrel, Flanged Lip, Pontil, Clear	12.00
Cologne, Floral Design, Cathedral Shape	55.00
Cologne, Floral Design, Side Ribbing	65.00
Cologne, Gothic Column, Open Pontil, Clear, 9 1/4 In.	30.00
Cologne, Indian, Aqua, 4 3/4 X 3 X 2 In.	40.00
Cologne, Larson, Diamond Patter, Amethyst, Pint	120.00
Cologne, Monument, Brickwork, 12 In.Square	35.00
Cologne, Monument, Opalescent, 9 In.	80.00
Cologne, Sandwich Type, Blue, 7 1/2 In.	100.00
Cologne, Tappan's Dime, Paper Label, 3 1/2 In. ....*Illus*	28.00
Cologne, Teardrop, Ground Stopper, Cut Design, Laid Gold Leaf, Clear, 7 In.	35.00
Cologne, Teardrop, Ground Stopper, Cut Design, Laid In Gold Leaf, Blue, 7 In.	35.00

Cologne, Two Dancing Indians, Triangle 90.00
Cologne, Van Ren, Large Pontil, Flint, Clear 49.00
Cordial, Allash Kummel, Gilka Shape, Green 18.00
Cordial, B.Fosgate's Anodyne, Open Pontil, Aqua .... 15.00 To 20.00
Cordial, Charles London Cordial Gin, Seeds, Olive Green, 8 In. 32.00
Cordial, Charles London, Open Pontil, Green 55.00
Cordial, Chas., Backman, Holland, Genever, Square, Squat, Olive Green 55.00
Cordial, Chastenet Freres' Creme De Menthe, Sealed, Nudes, 5 1/2 In. 16.00
Cordial, Cloud's, Tapered, Honey Amber, Quart .... 35.00 To 65.00
Cordial, Dr.G.N.Lambert's Aphrodisiac, Pontil, Green 40.00
Cordial, Hagee's, Label, ABM, Clear 6.00
Cordial, Jacob's Cholera & Dysentery, Open Pontil, Contents, Aqua 80.00
Cordial, McLean's Strengthening, 9 In. 12.50
Cosmetic, Ayer's Hair Vigor, Stopper, Peacock Blue .... 15.00 To 35.00
Cosmetic, Barrow Evan's Hair Restorer, Cornflower Blue 18.00
Cosmetic, Barry's Tricopherous For The Skin & Hair .... 11.50 To 13.00
Cosmetic, Batchelor's Liquid Hair Dye, Aqua .... 1.50 To 8.00
Cosmetic, Batchelor's Liquid Hair Dye, Nos. 1 & 2, Open Pontil, Aqua, Pair 42.00
Cosmetic, Bogle's Hyperion Fluid For The Hair, Aqua, 7 In. 27.00
Cosmetic, Bush's Argentine Hair Dye, Aqua 2.00
Cosmetic, C.Damschinsky Liquid Hair Dye, N.Y., Aqua, 3 1/2 In. 3.00
Cosmetic, C.F.Haskell, Coloris Capilli Restitutor, New Mexico, Iron Pontil 85.00
Cosmetic, Capilania, Hair Restorative, Pontil, Aqua, 6 In. 24.00
Cosmetic, Cherry Tooth Paste, Pot Lid 12.00
Cosmetic, Creme De Damelia For The Complexion, Dark Cobalt, 5 In. 7.00
Cosmetic, Cuticura System, Aqua 1.00
Cosmetic, Cuticura Treatment For Affections Of The Skin, Clear, 7 1/4 In. 10.00
Cosmetic, Dodge Brothers Melanine Hair Tonic, Strawberry Puce 250.00
Cosmetic, Dr.Campbell's Hair Invigorator, Aurora, N.Y., 4 Sided, Embossed 35.00
Cosmetic, Dr.D.Jayne's Hair Tonic, Philada., Open Pontil, Aqua 15.00
Cosmetic, Dr.D.Jayne's Hair Tonic, Philada., Open Pontil, Oval, 4 1/2 In. 19.00
Cosmetic, Dr.Gorham's Gray Hair Restorer, Boston, Mass., Amber, 5 1/2 In. 10.00
Cosmetic, Dr.J.Parker Pray, America's First Manicure, Square, Clear, 4 In. 8.00
Cosmetic, Dr.Tebbett's Physiological Hair Regenerator, Amethyst 100.00
Cosmetic, Dr.Tebbett's Physiological Hair Regenerator, Rose Amethyst 165.00
Cosmetic, Dr.Tebbett's Physiological Hair Restorer, Light Puce 115.00
Cosmetic, Dr.Wilson Hair Restorer, Burnt Orange 15.00
Cosmetic, Famo Retards Greyness, Label 8.00
Cosmetic, Floraplexion 12.00
Cosmetic, Gold Dandruff 9.00
Cosmetic, Great American Hair Discovery, Geo.E.Ormes & Co., Aqua, 6 5/8 In. 32.00
Cosmetic, Hair Oil, Pontil, Label, Embossed, Aqua 20.00
Cosmetic, Hall's Hair Renewer, Glass Stopper, Peacock Green 35.00
Cosmetic, Henry Tetlow Complexion Cream, Phila., Milk Glass 11.00
Cosmetic, Hinds' Honey & Almond Cream, 5 1/2 In. ....*Color* 2.50
Cosmetic, Hover's Hair Dye, Phila., 6 Sided 35.00
Cosmetic, J.Cristadoro's Hair Preservative & Beautifier, Aqua, 5 In. 15.00
Cosmetic, John Hart & Co., Heart-Shaped, Light Amber 250.00
Cosmetic, Lillie Cream, Picture Of Lillie Langtry, London, England 200.00
Cosmetic, Lockeyer's Sulphur Hair Restorer, Oval, Italian Blue, 7 1/8 In. 6.50
Cosmetic, Lyon's Kathairon For The Hair, N.Y., Pontil, 6 1/4 In .... 12.00 To 18.00
Cosmetic, Lyon's Kathairon For The Hair, Open Pontil, Aqua 24.00
Cosmetic, Lyon's Powder, New York, Round, Puce 75.00
Cosmetic, Macassar Oil For The Hair, London, Embossed, Corked, Clear 15.00
Cosmetic, Mahan's Hair Restorer, A.J.Mahan, Prop., Vt., Milk Glass, White 45.00
Cosmetic, Mexican Hair Renewer, Flask Shape, Cobalt 18.00
Cosmetic, Mrs.S.A.Allen's Hair Balsam, Broome St., Embossed 30.00
Cosmetic, Mrs.S.A.Allen's Hair Balsam, New York, Open Pontil, Aqua 25.00
Cosmetic, Mrs.S.A.Allen's Hair Restorer, Black Amethyst 90.00
Cosmetic, Mrs.S.A.Allen's Hair Restorer, Broome St., Light Grape 150.00
Cosmetic, Mrs.S.A.Allen's Hair Restorer, Burgundy 125.00
Cosmetic, Mrs.S.A.Allen's Hair Restorer, Deep Amber 20.00
Cosmetic, Mrs.S.A.Allen's Hair Restorer, Deep Puce 73.00
Cosmetic, Mrs.S.A.Allen's Hair Restorer, Honey Amber 10.00
Cosmetic, Mrs.S.A.Allen's Hair Restorer, Label & Contents, Amber 9.00
Cosmetic, Mrs.S.A.Allen's Hair Restorer, New York, Honey Amber 10.00

Cosmetic, Mrs.S.A.Allen's Hair Restorer, New York, Puce 80.00
Cosmetic, Mrs.S.A.Allen's Hair Restorer, Yellow 6.00
Cosmetic, Nature's Hair Restorative, Lip Nick, Aqua 6.00
Cosmetic, Newbros Herpicide For The Scalp 12.50
Cosmetic, Newbros Herpicide Hair Saver & Dandruff Eradicator, Lady's Leg 18.00
Cosmetic, Newbros Herpicide, The Dandruff Cure, Clear 7.00
Cosmetic, Oldridge's Balsam Of Columbia For Restoring Hair, 1826, Amber 60.00
Cosmetic, Parker's Hair Balsam, Aqua 3.00
Cosmetic, Parker's Hair Balsam, New York, Amber, 6 3/4 In. 1.75
Cosmetic, Perry's Hungarian Balm For The Hair, Open Pontil, Aqua 50.00
Cosmetic, Pinal Genuine Tonic, Promotes Hair Health, Label, 7 In. 50.00
Cosmetic, Pond's Extract, Beveled Corners, Pontil, Aqua, 4 1/4 X 2 1/8 In. 25.00
Cosmetic, Professor Wood's Hair Restorative, St.Louis & N.Y., Open Pontil 20.00
Cosmetic, Ricksecker's Skin Soap, Heals Cures, Oval, Clear, 2 1/2 In. 10.00
Cosmetic, Rosewood Dandruff 7.00
Cosmetic, Royal Hair Restorer, Cobalt 45.00
Cosmetic, Seven Sister's Hair Grower, Aqua 5.00
Cosmetic, Simmon's & Hammond's Imperial Cream 2.00
Cosmetic, Skookum Root Hair Grower, Cobalt 30.00
Cosmetic, St.Clair's Hair Lotion, Cobalt Blue 20.00
Cosmetic, Sterling's Ambrosia For The Hair, Aqua 6.00
Cosmetic, Swanson's Antiseptic Dandruff Cure, Clear 30.00
Cosmetic, Velvetina Skin Beautifier, Goodrich Drug, Milk Glass, 5 1/4 In. 15.00
Cosmetic, Walnut Leaf Hair Restorer, Amber 20.00
Cosmetic, White Clover Cream, 5 In. ....Color xxxx.xx
Cosmetic, Whittall Tatum Talc, Open Pontil, Amethyst, 8 In. 50.00
Cosmetic, Wm.D.Crumbie's Tricopherous Or Hair Restorative, Aqua, 7 In. 55.00
Cosmetic, 7 Sutherland Sisters' Hair Grower, Amethyst 8.00
Cranberry Glass, Bottle, Perfume, Gold Decoration, 4 X 2 In. 100.00
Creative World, Angelica Globe, 1971 .... 24.00
Creative World, Fisherman, 1970 .... 23.00
Creative World, Queen Anne Clock, 1970 .... 24.00
Creative World, Shakespeare Folio, 1970 .... 22.00
    Cure, see Medicine
Cut Glass, Decanter, Captain's, Hobstars, Cane, Fans, Notched Prisms, 9 In. 695.00
Cyrus Noble, Aesop's Fable, Musical 27.00
Cyrus Noble, Animal Series, First Edition, 6 Piece 675.00
Cyrus Noble, Assayer, 1972 .... 135.00 To 225.00
Cyrus Noble, Assayer, 4 Piece Set 1050.00
Cyrus Noble, Bank Exchange Exterior, 1976 .... 16.00
Cyrus Noble, Bank Exchange, Interior, 1976 .... 16.00
Cyrus Noble, Bartender, 1971 .... 140.00 To 162.00
Cyrus Noble, Bartender, 5 Piece Set 0500.00
Cyrus Noble, Bear & Cubs, 1978 .... 70.00 To 83.50
Cyrus Noble, Beaver & Kit, 1978 .... 49.95 To 63.00
Cyrus Noble, Big Horn Sheep Family .... 49.95 To 55.00
Cyrus Noble, Big Red Machine, Baseball Glove With Ball Stopper 22.50
Cyrus Noble, Blacksmith, 1974 ....Color 41.00
Cyrus Noble, Buffalo Cow .... 121.00 To 125.00
Cyrus Noble, Buffalo, Reissue 60.00
Cyrus Noble, Burro, 1973 .... 60.00 To 105.00
Cyrus Noble, Carousel, Black Flyer Horse 52.99
Cyrus Noble, Carousel, Lion 52.95
Cyrus Noble, Carousel, White Charger Horse 53.00
Cyrus Noble, Cat & Barrel Tavern 22.00
Cyrus Noble, Cow With Calf, 1977 .... 91.50
Cyrus Noble, Delta Saloon, Set Of 4 .... 285.00
Cyrus Noble, Desert Sheep Farm 50.00
Cyrus Noble, Doe & Fawn, Musical 55.00
Cyrus Noble, Dog & Shadow, Musical 27.00
Cyrus Noble, Dolphin .... 50.00 To 52.99
Cyrus Noble, Drummer .... 35.00 To 48.00
Cyrus Noble, Eagle, Musical 55.00
Cyrus Noble, Fiddler 39.95
Cyrus Noble, Fighting Rams, Set Of 4 .... 150.00
Cyrus Noble, Gambler, 1974 ....Color 40.00

Cyrus Noble, Gambler's Lady, 1976 .... 34.00 To 40.00
Cyrus Noble, Gold Miner 536.00
Cyrus Noble, Hare & Tortoise, Musical 27.00
Cyrus Noble, Harold's Club, 1970 .... 20.00
Cyrus Noble, Landlady, 1977 .... 38.00 To 50.00
Cyrus Noble, Lion 53.00
Cyrus Noble, Lion & Sheep, Set Of 3 .... 150.00
Cyrus Noble, Middle Of The Piano .... 49.95 To 51.00
Cyrus Noble, Mine, 4/5 .... 49.95 To 52.99
Cyrus Noble, Miner, 1970 .... Color 750.00
Cyrus Noble, Miner's Daughter, 1975 .... Color 46.00
Cyrus Noble, Moose, Reissue 49.00
Cyrus Noble, Mountain Lion, Reissue .... 39.95 To 60.00
Cyrus Noble, Mountain Lion, 1st Issue 128.00

Dant, Alamo, 1969
(See Page 50)

Dant, Boston Tea Party,
Eagle Right, 1968
(See Page 50)

Dant, Fort Sill, Centennial, 1969
(See Page 50)

Dant, Mt.Rushmore, 1969
(See Page 50)

Cyrus Noble, Mr.Lucky, Musical 27.00
Cyrus Noble, Music Man, 1977 .... 35.00 To 41.95
Cyrus Noble, Oklahoma Dancers, 1978 .... 49.95 To 52.99
Cyrus Noble, Penguin Family, 1978 .... 49.95 To 53.00
Cyrus Noble, Prospector 24.00
Cyrus Noble, Rabbit 32.00
Cyrus Noble, Raccoon .... 29.95 To 32.00
Cyrus Noble, Rodeo Clown 38.00
Cyrus Noble, Sea Turtle .... 49.95 To 52.99
Cyrus Noble, Snowshoe Thompson, 1972 .... 175.00 To 350.00
Cyrus Noble, South Of The Border Dancers, 1978 .... 49.95 To 54.00
Cyrus Noble, Tennis Player, Pair, 1976 .... 32.00

Cyrus Noble, Tonopah Saloon, Hexagon, White, 1972 .... 342.00 To 350.00
Cyrus Noble, Trumpet Player, 4/5 .... 49.95 To 52.99
Cyrus Noble, Violinist, 1976 .... 35.95 To 50.00
Cyrus Noble, Walrus Family, 1978 .... 49.95 To 53.00
Cyrus Noble, Whiskey Drummer, 1975 .... 40.00 To 49.95
Cyrus Noble, White Charger .... 49.95 To 52.99
Cyrus Noble, Willits, Frontier Days, 1976 .... 116.00

Dant figural bottles first were released in 1968 to hold J.W.Dant
alcoholic products. The company has made the Americana series, field
birds, special bottlings, and ceramic bottles.
Dant, Alamo, 1969 .... *Illus*   6.00
Dant, American Legion, 1969 ....   6.00
Dant, Atlantic City, 1969 ....   5.00
Dant, Boeing 747 ....   10.00
Dant, Boston Tea Party, Eagle Left, 1968 ....   4.00
Dant, Boston Tea Party, Eagle Right, 1968 .... *Illus*   10.00
Dant, Burr & Hamilton Duel 8.00
Dant, Clear Tip Pinch, 1953 .... 4.00 To 9.00
Dant, Field Bird, Bob White, 1969 ....   9.00
Dant, Field Bird, California Quail, 1969 ....   9.00
Dant, Field Bird, Chucker Partridge, 1969 ....   9.00
Dant, Field Bird, Mountain Quail, 1969 ....   9.00
Dant, Field Bird, Pheasant, 1969 ....   9.00
Dant, Field Bird, Prairie Chicken, 1969 ....   9.00
Dant, Field Bird, Ruffed Grouse, 1969 ....   9.00
Dant, Field Bird, Woodcock, 1969 ....   9.00
Dant, Fort Sill, Centennial, 1969 .... *Illus*   10.00
Dant, Indy 500, 1969 .... 5.00 To 8.00
Dant, Mt.Rushmore, 1969 .... *Illus*   10.50
Dant, Patrick Henry, 1969 ....   6.00
Dant, Paul Bunyan 7.00
Dant, Pot Belly Stove, 1966 ....   7.00
Dant, San Diego Harbor, 1969 ....   4.00
Dant, Washington At Delaware 6.00

Decanters were first used to hold the alcoholic beverages that had been
stored in kegs. At first a necessity, the decanter later was merely an
attractive serving vessel.
Decanter, see also Beam, Bischoff, Kord, etc.
Decanter, Back Bar, Captain's, Old Dorsey Straight Whiskey, Fluted Neck 35.00
Decanter, Back Bar, Massachusetts Pattern 30.00
Decanter, Back Bar, Ruby Flashed Push Up, Flute Neck, Clear 35.00
Decanter, Blown, Cobalt Blue, 8 1/8 In. 80.00
Decanter, Bobby Lee, Pontil, Stopper 50.00
Decanter, Cut & Cased, White & Clear, 6 1/2 In. .... *Illus*   33.00
Decanter, Cut Glass, Captain's, Hobstars, Cane, Fans, Notched Prisms, 9 In. 695.00
Decanter, Decorated Glass, Green & Gold, 13 In. .... *Illus*   35.00
Decanter, Dog, Blown, Green, 9 In. 75.00
Decanter, I.W.Harper, Pinch, Southern Gentleman, Riverboat, Pint 45.00
Decanter, McK G II-006, Blown, 3 Mold, Deep Aqua, Pint .... *Illus* 650.00
Decanter, McK G II-030, Blown, 3 Mold, Yellow Green, Pint 80.00
Decanter, McK G III-002, Blown, 3 Mold, Olive Amber, Pint .... *Illus* 180.00
Decanter, McK G III-009, Blown, 3 Mold, Olive Amber, Quart .... *Illus* 575.00
Decanter, McK G III-016, Blown, 3 Mold, Deep Olive Amber, Pint 200.00
Decanter, McK G III-016, Blown, 3 Mold, Olive Amber, Pint .... *Illus* 275.00
Decanter, McK G III-019, Keene, Geometric, Amber, Quart 650.00
Decanter, McK G III-031, Blown, Clear, Pint 150.00
Decanter, McK G III-031, Blown, 3 Mold, Clear, Pint 130.00
Decanter, McK G IV-007, Snake & Fern, Flint, Clear 175.00
Decanter, Pittsburgh Riverboat 35.00
Decanter, Pittsburgh, 8 Pillar Mold Riverboat, Stopper, Clear, 11 1/2 In. 50.00
Decanter, 16 Swirls, Teardrop, Pouring Spout, 9 1/4 In. 140.00
Demijohn, Amber, 15 1/2 X 6 In. 18.00
Demijohn, Aqua, 1/2 Gallon 6.75
Demijohn, Avan Hoboken & Co., Rotterdam, Cork, Green, 1/2 Gallon 40.00

Demijohn, Avocado Green, Open Pontil, 1/2 Gallon	44.50
Demijohn, Avocado Green, 1/2 Gallon	18.00
Demijohn, Burnt Orange, 1/2 Gallon	25.00
Demijohn, Cylinder, Refired Pontil, Red Amber	49.50
Demijohn, Deep Golden Amber, 16 In.	26.00
Demijohn, Free-Blown, Deep Aqua, 13 X 8 1/2 In.	190.00
Demijohn, Free-Blown, Open Pontil, Black, 2 1/2 In.	80.00
Demijohn, Kidney, Open Pontil, Green, Large	49.50
Demijohn, Olive Gold, 1/2 Gallon, 12 In.	25.00
Demijohn, Olive Green & Amber Swirl, 15 1/2 X 6 In.	25.00
Demijohn, Open Pontil, Olive, Gallon	19.00

Decanter, Decorated Glass, Green & Gold, 13 In.

Decanter, Cut & Cased, White & Clear, 6 1/2 In.

Decanter, McK G II-006, Blown, 3 Mold, Deep Aqua, Pint

Decanter, McK G III-002, Blown, 3 Mold, Olive Amber, Pint

Decanter, McK G III-016, Blown, 3 Mold, Olive Amber, Pint

Decanter, McK G III-009, Blown, 3 Mold, Olive Amber, Quart

Demijohn, Reddish Amber, Pontil, 16 In.	49.50
Demijohn, Stoddard, N.H., Pontil, Gallon	30.00
Demijohn, Tapered Lip, Bottom Hinge Mold, Yellow Green, 1/2 Gallon	14.50
Demijohn, Yellow Green, 15 7/8 In.	39.50
Demijohn, 2 1/2 Gallon, Emerald Green	44.50
Demijohn, 3 Piece Mold, Open Pontil, Wavy Glass, Olive Green, Gallon	28.00
Dickel, Ceramic Jug	8.00
Dickel, Golf Club, 1967	6.00
Dickel, Powder Horn	7.00
Double Springs, Bentley, Touring, 1972	24.00
Double Springs, Bicentennial, Arizona, 1975	16.00
Double Springs, Bicentennial, California, 1975	35.00
Double Springs, Bicentennial, Colorado, 1975	16.00
Double Springs, Bicentennial, Delaware, 1975	16.00
Double Springs, Bicentennial, Florida, 1975	16.00
Double Springs, Bicentennial, Illinois, 1975	11.00

Double Springs, Bicentennial, Indiana, 1975 .... 16.00
Double Springs, Bicentennial, Iowa, 1975 .... 25.00
Double Springs, Bicentennial, Kentucky, 1975 .... 16.00
Double Springs, Bicentennial, Maryland, 1975 .... 14.00
Double Springs, Bicentennial, Massachusetts, 1975 .... 16.00
Double Springs, Bicentennial, Missouri, 1975 .... 16.00
Double Springs, Bicentennial, New Jersey, 1975 .... 14.00
Double Springs, Bicentennial, New Mexico, 1975 .... 16.00
Double Springs, Bicentennial, New York, 1975 .... 14.00
Double Springs, Bicentennial, Ohio, 1975 .... 11.00
Double Springs, Bicentennial, Rhode Island, 1975 .... 16.00

Drug, Bromo-Seltzer, Emerson Drug Co., Maryland, Blue, 4 In.

Drug, Liq.Ammon.Acct., Cobalt, Paper Label, 8 In.

Double Springs, Bicentennial, Tennessee, 1975 .... 16.00
Double Springs, Bicentennial, Vermont, 1975 .... 14.00
Double Springs, Bicentennial, Washington D.C., 1975 .... 14.00
Double Springs, Bicentennial, Wisconsin, 1975 .... 11.00
Double Springs, Buick, Touring, 1972 .... 54.00
Double Springs, Bull, Red, 1969 .... 18.00
Double Springs, Bull, 1969 .... 18.00
Double Springs, Cadillac, 1913 .... 23.00
Double Springs, Cale Yarborough, 1974 .... 16.00
Double Springs, Chicago Water Tower .... 10.00 To 15.00
Double Springs, Duesenburg S.J., 1931 .... 24.00
Double Springs, Duffer .... 7.95 To 9.00
Double Springs, Excalibur Phaeton, 1975 .... 23.00 To 27.00
Double Springs, Georgia Bulldog, 1971 .... 11.00
Double Springs, Gold Coyote, 1971 .... 10.00 To 12.00
Double Springs, Kentucky Derby, With Glass, 1964 .... 10.00
Double Springs, Matador, 1969 .... 10.00 To 15.00
Double Springs, Mercedes Benz, 1975 .... 24.00 To 26.00
Double Springs, Mercer, 1972 .... 25.00
Double Springs, Milwaukee Buck, 1971 .... 8.00 To 10.00
Double Springs, Model T Ford, 1970 .... 22.00 To 24.00
Double Springs, Owl, Brown, 1968 .... 18.00 To 22.00
Double Springs, Owl, Red, 1968 .... 18.00 To 22.00
Double Springs, Peasant Boy, 1968 .... 6.00 To 9.00
Double Springs, Peasant Girl, 1968 .... 6.00 To 9.00

Double Springs, Pierce Arrow, 1970 .... 31.00
Double Springs, Rolls Royce, 1971 .... 32.00
Double Springs, Stanley Steamer, 1971 .... 33.00
Double Springs, Stutz Bearcat, 1970 .... 22.00 To 29.00
Double Springs, Tiger On Football 11.00
Drioli, African 26.00
Drioli, Cherry Log 8.00
Drioli, Coffeepot 10.00
Drioli, Egyptian Vase, Yellow 12.00
Drioli, Gondola 26.00
Drioli, Mosaic 11.00
Drioli, Swan 18.00
Drug, Alcohol, Stopper, Patent May 1880, Clear 15.00
Drug, Alfred Helgeson, Pharmacist, Vermillion, So.Dak., Clear, 4 In. 9.00
Drug, Alsquith & Co., Pharmacists, Charles Town, W.Va., Clear 6.00
Drug, Bridgham & Son, Druggist, Dexter, Maine, Purple, 6 In. 6.00
Drug, Bromo-Seltzer, Emerson Drug Co., Maryland, Blue, 4 In. ....*Illus* 1.00
Drug, Burnett's Cocaine, Aqua 3.00
Drug, C.T.Dana & Co., Registered Pharmacists, Pawtucket, R.I., Aqua 10.00
Drug, Calcura Solvent, Church Window Panels, Aqua, 8 1/4 In. 15.00
Drug, Callan's Brazilian Gum 5.00
Drug, Caswell & Massey, Chemist & Druggist, N.Y., Glass Stopper, Clear 7.50
Drug, Caswell Hazard & Co., Chemists, Cobalt 15.00
Drug, Cylinder, Free-Blown, Open Pontil, Amethyst, 10 1/2 X 4 1/2 In. 200.00
Drug, Dicky, Pioneer, 1850 Chemist, San Francisco, Blue 12.00
Drug, E.W.Crowther, Druggist, Cincinnati, O., Iron Pontil, Aqua, 8 1/2 In. 90.00
Drug, Earl & Wilkes, Greenville, S.C., 6 1/2 In. 12.00
Drug, Essence, Greenish Aqua, Open Pontil, 4 3/4 In. 9.50
Drug, Foley Cathartic Tablets, Display Jar, Clear 125.00
Drug, Free-Blown, Glass Stoppers, Clear, Pair 10.00
Drug, G.W.Merchant, Chemist, Lockport, Emerald Green, Rectangular, 5 In. 38.50
Drug, George Dart, Druggist, N.Y., Cobalt 7.00
Drug, George Dart, Pharmacist, Tuxedo Park, N.Y., Cobalt, 5 In. 5.00
Drug, Grenfelder & Lauphimer, Druggists, Baltimore, Md., Amber, 10 In. 33.00
Drug, Guth's Fruit Tablets, Baltimore, Display Jar, Stopper, Ice Blue 85.00
Drug, J.J.Reithman, Denver, Clear, 3 In. 12.00
Drug, J.R.Nichols, Chemists, Boston 5.00
Drug, John Phelps, Pharmacist, Blue, BIMAL, 5 In. 10.00
Drug, John Sullivan, Pharmacist, Boston, Milk Glass 10.00
Drug, Keller Drug Co., Fresh Citrate Of Magnesia, Dark Green, 8 In. 35.00
Drug, Liq.Ammon.Acct., Cobalt, Paper Label, 8 In. ....*Illus* 5.00
Drug, Mennen's Liquid Soap, Cobalt, 6 1/2 In. 35.00
Drug, Merriam & Co., Drugs & Books, Pleasant Hill, Mo., C.1880, Flint 7.50
Drug, Miller & Taylor, Drugs & Books, Molden, Mo., C.1880, Flint 7.50
Drug, Nature's Nine American Drug Co., Columbus, Ga., Amber, 8 In. 15.00
Drug, New York Pharmacal Association, Cobalt, BIMAL, 12 In. 25.00
Drug, Nonapah, Nevada, Small 18.00
Drug, O'Rourke & Hurley Druggists, Little Falls, N.Y., Cobalt, 4 1/2 In. 8.00
Drug, Owl Drug Co., Amber, 3 1/4 In. 25.00
Drug, Owl Drug Co., Amber, 4 In. 30.00
Drug, Owl Drug Co., BIMAL, Milk Glass, 5 In. 10.00
Drug, Owl Drug Co., Clear, 4 In. 3.00
Drug, Owl Drug Co., Clear, 4 3/8 In. .... 3.00 To 4.00
Drug, Owl Drug Co., Milk Glass, 4 1/2 In. 25.00
Drug, Owl Drug Co., Milk Glass, 4 7/8 In. 30.00
Drug, Owl Drug Co., Milk Glass, 5 1/2 In. 35.00
Drug, Owl Drug Co., Plaque 50.00
Drug, Owl Drug, Embossed, Milk Glass, 5 In. 35.00
Drug, Owl Drug, Soda, One Winger, Blob Top, Green 30.00
Drug, Owl Drug, Standard Pharmaceuticals, Label, ABM, 8 In. 10.00
Drug, Owl Pharmacy, Pattsburg, N.Y., Clear 5.00
Drug, Owl, Soda, Green 45.00
Drug, Paine Druggist & Apothecary, Windsor, Vt., Milk Glass, 6 1/4 In. 75.00
Drug, Pearl's White Glycerine, Deep Sapphire Blue, 7 In. 20.00
Drug, Perk's Drug Store, Houlton, Maine, Honey Amber, 4 1/4 In. 18.00
Drug, Pitcher, Embossed, Burnham's Wild Cherry Phosphate, Clear 80.00

Drug, Poison, Embossed On Front, Lid & Wire Clamp, Clear, 5 In. 10.00
Drug, Prepared By E.Furman Manfille, West Troy, N.Y., Pontil 45.00
Drug, Prescribed By R.V.Pierce, Buffalo, Oval, Deep Citron 9.00
Drug, R.B.Dacosta, Philadelphia, West Indian Toothwash, Aqua 30.00
Drug, Ralph F.Burnham Mfg., Pharmacist, Auburn, Maine, Amber, 6 1/2 In. 15.00
Drug, Red Cross Pharmacy, Langford, South Dakota, Clear, 5 5/8 In. 5.00
Drug, Reed & Carnrick, Pharmacists, N.Y., Amber, 7 1/2 In. 8.00
Drug, Reseller's Druggist, Pittsburgh, Open Pontil, Aqua, 5 X 1 1/2 In. 30.00
Drug, Rownd Jacob's Pharmacy, Atlanta, Amber, 4 5/8 In. 10.00
Drug, Rushton Clark & Co., Chemists, N.Y., Aqua, 10 In. 45.00
Drug, Rushton Clark, Chemists, N.Y., Open Pontil 13.00
Drug, Sal-Codeia Bell, Hollings Smith Co., Mfg.Chemists, Emerald Green 4.50
Drug, Shampoodle, Cobalt Blue 25.00
Drug, Sherman's Lozenges, Large Opening, Oval 25.00
Drug, Stron, Cobb & Co., Wholesale Druggists, Cleveland, O., Blue, 11 In. 42.00
Drug, Syrup Of Ginger, Nickel Plated Cup Tops, Label 17.50
Drug, Syrup Of Lemon, Nickel Plated Cup Tops, Label 17.50
Drug, Syrup Of Vanilla, Nickel Plated Cup Tops, Label 17.50
Drug, U.S.A. Hospital, Aqua, Pint 75.00
Drug, U.S.A. Hospital, Aqua, Quart 85.00
Drug, U.S.A. Hospital, Blob Top With Ring, Aqua, Pint 150.00
Drug, U.S.A. Hospital, Cobalt, Quart 185.00
Drug, U.S.A. Hospital, Embossed, Olive Green, Quart 85.00
Drug, U.S.A. Hospital, Light Yellow, Quart 125.00
Drug, U.S.A. Hospital, Olive, Quart 85.00
Drug, Weightman Pharmacal Co., N.Y., Honey Amber, 8 In. 12.00
Drug, Wilson, Botanic Druggists, Boston, Open Pontil, Aqua, 4 In. 25.00
Drug, Wing's Corn Remedy 5.00
 Dug Picking, see Dug's West Indies
Dug's West Indies, Canoe .... 14.99 To 15.95
Dug's West Indies, Clipper Ship .... 14.99 To 20.50
Dug's West Indies, Lucky Strike 16.95
Dug's West Indies, Raft, 1975 .... 20.50
Dug's West Indies, Shamrock Cat House .... 14.95 To 15.95
Error, Alwe's, Cincinnati, O., Backward N's, Round, Green 15.00
Error, Drey Mason, Fruit Jar, Backward N, Pint 6.00
Error, Fahnestock's Vermifuge, Backward N 12.00
Error, John Rapp & Son, San Francisco, S's Backward, Amber, Pint 18.00
Error, Montgomery Magnesia Spring Water, G Omitted In Montgomery, Aqua 20.00
Error, Pepsi Cola, Old Dominion, Virginia, Blue Writing, Misprint, Clear 8.00
Error, Pill, Round Bottom, 2 Backward P's, Cobalt Blue, 2 1/2 In. 4.50
Error, Star Spring Mineral Water, Saratoga, Backward S 65.00
Error, Warner's Safe Kidney & Liver Cure, Apostrophe Missing In Warners 35.00
Error, Weiss Beer, St.Louis Brewery, Brewerg Misspelled, Stopper, Amber 35.00

Ezra Brooks fancy bottles were first made in 1964. The Ezra Brooks
Distilling Company is from Frankfort, Kentucky.
Ezra Brooks, Alabama Bicentennial, 1976 .... 9.00 To 25.00
Ezra Brooks, American Legion, Denver, 1977 .... 14.95 To 24.00
Ezra Brooks, American Legion, Hawaii, 1973 .... 6.00 To 30.00
Ezra Brooks, American Legion, Miami Beach, 1974 .... 5.50 To 15.00
Ezra Brooks, American Legion, Texas, 1971 .... 15.00 To 55.00
Ezra Brooks, American Legionnaire, 1972 .... 25.00
Ezra Brooks, Amvets, Dolphin, 1974 .... 20.00
Ezra Brooks, Amvets, 1973 .... 9.00
Ezra Brooks, Antique Cannon, 1969 .... 5.00 To 15.00
Ezra Brooks, Antique Phonograph, 1970 .... 12.00 To 35.00
Ezra Brooks, Arizona Desert Scene, 1969 .... 4.00 To 15.00
Ezra Brooks, Auburn 1932 Classic Car, 1978 .... 25.00 To 30.00
Ezra Brooks, Badger No.1, Boxer, 1973 .... 16.00
Ezra Brooks, Badger No.2, Football, 1974 .... 20.00
Ezra Brooks, Badger No.3, Hockey.1974 .... 20.00
Ezra Brooks, Baltimore Oriole Wild Life, 1979 .... 39.95
Ezra Brooks, Bare Knuckle Fighter, 1972 .... 6.00 To 15.00
Ezra Brooks, Basketball Player, 1974 .... 6.00 To 15.00
Ezra Brooks, Bear, 1968 .... 5.00

Ezra Brooks, Beaver, 1973 .... 5.00 To 15.00
Ezra Brooks, Bengal Tiger Wild Life, 1979 .... 39.95
Ezra Brooks, Betsy Ross, 1975 .... 16.00 To 18.00
Ezra Brooks, Big Bertha Elephant, 1970 .... 7.00 To 20.00
Ezra Brooks, Big Daddy Lounges, Florida, 1969 .... 5.00 To 15.00
Ezra Brooks, Bird Dog, 1971 .... 8.00 To 22.00
Ezra Brooks, Bordertown, 1970 .... 3.00 To 20.00
Ezra Brooks, Bowler, 1973 .... 4.00 To 15.00

Ezra Brooks, Bucking Bronco,
Rough Rider, 1973

Ezra Brooks, Bucky Badger, No.l,
1973, Boxer

Ezra Brooks, Cardinal, 1972
(See Page 56)

(See Page 56)

(See Page 56)

Ezra Brooks, Clown Shrine,
1978

Ezra Brooks, Casey At Bat,
1973

Ezra Brooks, Clown Bust, No.1,
Smiley, 1979

Ezra Brooks, Brahma Bull, 1972 .... 9.00 To 18.00
Ezra Brooks, Bucket Of Blood, 1970 .... 4.00 To 15.00
Ezra Brooks, Bucking Bronco, Rough Rider, 1973 .... *Illus* 14.00
Ezra Brooks, Bucky Badger, Football 25.00
Ezra Brooks, Bucky Badger, Hockey.1975 .... 22.00
Ezra Brooks, Bucky Badger, No.1, 1973, Boxer .... *Illus* 14.00
Ezra Brooks, Buffalo Hunt, 1971 .... 7.00 To 70.00
Ezra Brooks, Bulldog, 1971 .... 14.00 To 25.00
Ezra Brooks, C.B.Convoy Radio, 1976 .... 7.00 To 20.00
Ezra Brooks, Cabin Still, Hillbilly, Papers From Company, Gallon 395.00

Ezra Brooks, Cable Car, Brown, 1968	6.00
Ezra Brooks, Cable Car, Gray, 1968	6.00
Ezra Brooks, Cable Car, Green, 1968	6.00
Ezra Brooks, California Quail, 1970	4.00 To 15.00
Ezra Brooks, Canadian Honker, 1975	17.00 To 25.00
Ezra Brooks, Canadian Loon Wild Life, 1979	39.95
Ezra Brooks, Cardinal, 1972	*Illus* 13.00
Ezra Brooks, Casey At Bat, 1973	*Illus* 6.00
Ezra Brooks, Ceremonial Indian, 1970	17.00 To 30.00
Ezra Brooks, Charolais, 1973	11.00 To 18.00
Ezra Brooks, Cheyenne "Shootout," 1970	4.00 To 22.00
Ezra Brooks, Chicago Fire, 1974	23.00
Ezra Brooks, Chicago Water Tower, 1969	6.00 To 20.00
Ezra Brooks, Christmas Decanter, 1966	6.00
Ezra Brooks, Christmas Tree Musical, 1979	50.00
Ezra Brooks, Cigar Store Indian, 1968	6.00 To 15.00
Ezra Brooks, Clown Bust, No.1, Smiley, 1979	*Illus* 35.00
Ezra Brooks, Clown Bust, No.2, Cowboy, 1979	35.00
Ezra Brooks, Clown Bust, No.3, Pagliacci, 1979	39.95
Ezra Brooks, Clown Shrine, 1978	*Illus* 26.95
Ezra Brooks, Clown With Accordion, 1972	10.00 To 13.00
Ezra Brooks, Clown With Balloon, 1974	13.00 To 18.00
Ezra Brooks, Clown, Imperial Shrine, 1978	*Color* 25.00
Ezra Brooks, Club Bottle, No.2, Birthday Cake, 1972	6.00 To 19.00
Ezra Brooks, Clydesdale, 1974	10.00 To 15.00
Ezra Brooks, Colt Peacemaker, Flask, 1969	3.00
Ezra Brooks, Conquistador's Drum & Bugle, 1972	7.00 To 20.00
Ezra Brooks, Corvette Indy Pace Car, 1978	40.00 To 80.00
Ezra Brooks, Corvette, 1957 Classic, 1977	26.00
Ezra Brooks, Court Jester, 1972	*Illus* 8.00
Ezra Brooks, Creighton Bluejay, 1976	15.00 To 25.00
Ezra Brooks, Dakota Cowboy, 1975	29.95 To 40.00
Ezra Brooks, Dakota Cowgirl, 1976	29.95 To 40.00
Ezra Brooks, Dakota Grain Elevator, 1978	35.00
Ezra Brooks, Dakota Shotgun Express, 1977	25.00
Ezra Brooks, Dead Wagon, 1970	4.00 To 22.00
Ezra Brooks, Delta Belle, 1969	7.00 To 25.00
Ezra Brooks, Democratic Convention, 1976	12.00 To 18.00
Ezra Brooks, Derringer, Flask, 1969	3.00
Ezra Brooks, Distillery, Club Bottle, 1970	7.00 To 40.00
Ezra Brooks, Duesenberg, 1971	12.00 To 20.00
Ezra Brooks, Elephant, Indian, 1973	5.00 To 20.00
Ezra Brooks, Elk, 1973	20.00 To 24.00
Ezra Brooks, Equestrienne, 1974	5.00 To 15.00
Ezra Brooks, Esquire Ceremonial Dancer	12.00
Ezra Brooks, F.O.E.Flying Eagle, 1979	25.00
Ezra Brooks, Farthington Bike, 1972	7.00 To 10.00
Ezra Brooks, Fire Engine, 1971	13.00 To 20.00
Ezra Brooks, Fireman, 1975	18.00
Ezra Brooks, Fisherman, 1974	15.00 To 18.00
Ezra Brooks, Flintlock Pistol, Dueling, 1968	5.00 To 15.00
Ezra Brooks, Flintlock Pistol, Japanese, 1968	22.00 To 75.00
Ezra Brooks, Florida Gator, No.1, 1972, Passing	*Illus* 13.00
Ezra Brooks, Florida Gator, No.2, 1973, Running	19.00 To 25.00
Ezra Brooks, Florida Gator, No.3, 1975, Blocker	21.00 To 30.00
Ezra Brooks, Football Player, 1974	10.00 To 18.00
Ezra Brooks, Ford Thunderbird	20.00 To 26.00
Ezra Brooks, Foremost Astronaut, 1970	5.00 To 15.00
Ezra Brooks, Fresno Grape With Gold	45.00 To 58.00
Ezra Brooks, Fresno Grape, 1970	7.00 To 25.00
Ezra Brooks, Gamecock, South Carolina, 1970	30.00
Ezra Brooks, Go Big Red, No.1, With Football, 1970	25.00 To 50.00
Ezra Brooks, Go Big Red, No.2, With Hat, 1971	15.00 To 30.00
Ezra Brooks, Go Big Red, No.3, With Rooster, 1972	*Illus* 15.00
Ezra Brooks, Go Tiger Go, 1973	15.00 To 17.00
Ezra Brooks, Gold Eagle, 1971	10.00 To 25.00

Ezra Brooks, Gold Horseshoe, 1970	7.00 To 18.00
Ezra Brooks, Gold Prospector, 1970	5.00 To 12.00
Ezra Brooks, Gold Rooster, 1969	35.00 To 75.00
Ezra Brooks, Gold Seal, 1972	10.00 To 18.00
Ezra Brooks, Gold Turkey	45.00
Ezra Brooks, Golden Grizzly Bear, 1968	5.00 To 15.00
Ezra Brooks, Golfer, 1973	*Illus* 21.00
Ezra Brooks, Grandfather's Clock, 1970	5.00 To 25.00
Ezra Brooks, Great White Shark, 1977	8.00 To 25.00
Ezra Brooks, Greater Greensboro Open, 1972, Gold	21.00 To 26.00
Ezra Brooks, Greater Greensboro Open, 1973, Golfer	*Illus* 21.00
Ezra Brooks, Greater Greensboro Open, 1974, Map	40.00 To 45.00
Ezra Brooks, Greater Greensboro Open, 1975, Cup	45.00 To 75.00

Ezra Brooks, Florida Gator,
No.1, 1972, Passing

Ezra Brooks, Go Big Red, No.3,
1972, With Rooter

Ezra Brooks, Golfer, 1973

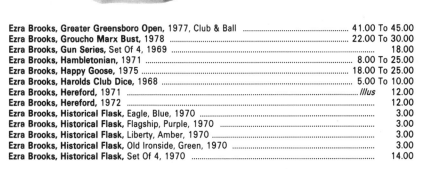

Ezra Brooks, Hereford, 1971

Ezra Brooks, Greater Greensboro Open, 1977, Club & Ball	41.00 To 45.00
Ezra Brooks, Groucho Marx Bust, 1978	22.00 To 30.00
Ezra Brooks, Gun Series, Set Of 4, 1969	18.00
Ezra Brooks, Hambletonian, 1971	8.00 To 25.00
Ezra Brooks, Happy Goose, 1975	18.00 To 25.00
Ezra Brooks, Harolds Club Dice, 1968	5.00 To 10.00
Ezra Brooks, Hereford, 1971	*Illus* 12.00
Ezra Brooks, Hereford, 1972	12.00
Ezra Brooks, Historical Flask, Eagle, Blue, 1970	3.00
Ezra Brooks, Historical Flask, Flagship, Purple, 1970	3.00
Ezra Brooks, Historical Flask, Liberty, Amber, 1970	3.00
Ezra Brooks, Historical Flask, Old Ironside, Green, 1970	3.00
Ezra Brooks, Historical Flask, Set Of 4, 1970	14.00

Ezra Brooks, Hollywood Cops, 1972 .... 11.00
Ezra Brooks, Idaho Potato, 1973 .... 9.00 To 22.00
Ezra Brooks, Indy Racer No.21, 1970 .... 18.00 To 35.00
Ezra Brooks, Iowa Farmer, 1977 .... 59.95 To 75.00
Ezra Brooks, Iowa Grain Elevator, 1978 ....*Color*   35.00
Ezra Brooks, Iron Horse, 1969 .... 6.00 To 15.00
Ezra Brooks, Jack Of Diamonds, 1969 .... 7.00 To 14.00
Ezra Brooks, Jester, 1971 ....*Illus*   8.00
Ezra Brooks, Jug, Old Time, 1.75 Liter 15.00
Ezra Brooks, Kachina Doll, No.1, 1971 .... 100.00 To 195.00
Ezra Brooks, Kachina Doll, No.2, 1973, Hummingbird 45.00
Ezra Brooks, Kachina Doll, No.3, 1974 .... 22.00 To 75.00
Ezra Brooks, Kachina Doll, No.4, 1975 .... 12.00 To 50.00
Ezra Brooks, Kachina Doll, No.5, 1976 ....*Color*   27.00

Ezra Brooks, Keystone Cops, 1971

Ezra Brooks, Keystone Cop, 1979

Ezra Brooks, Jester, 1971

Ezra Brooks, Liquor Square, 1972   Ezra Brooks, Military Tank, 1971

Ezra Brooks, Kachina Doll, No.6, 1977, White Buffalo .... 25.00 To 28.00
Ezra Brooks, Kachina Doll, No.7, 1978, Mud Head 25.00
Ezra Brooks, Kansas Jayhawk, 1969 .... 6.00 To 20.00
Ezra Brooks, Katz Cat, Gray, 1969 .... 12.00 To 20.00
Ezra Brooks, Katz Cat, Philharmonic Conductor, 1970 .... 4.00 To 18.00
Ezra Brooks, Katz Cat, Tan, 1969 .... 10.00 To 12.00
Ezra Brooks, Keystone Cop, 1979 ....*Illus*   35.00
Ezra Brooks, Keystone Cops, 1971 ....*Illus*   11.00
Ezra Brooks, King Of Clubs, 1969 .... 7.00 To 14.00
Ezra Brooks, Kitten On Pillow, 1975 .... 14.00 To 16.00
Ezra Brooks, Liberty Bell, 1970 .... 6.00 To 15.00
Ezra Brooks, Lincoln Continental Mark I, 1941, 1979 .... 30.00
Ezra Brooks, Lion On The Rock, 1971 .... 4.00 To 15.00

Ezra Brooks, Liquor Square, 1972	*Illus* 7.00
Ezra Brooks, M & M Brown Jug, 1975	20.00 To 22.00
Ezra Brooks, Maine Lighthouse, 1971	16.00 To 35.00
Ezra Brooks, Maine Lobster, 1970	15.00 To 40.00
Ezra Brooks, Maine Potato, 1973	7.00 To 18.00
Ezra Brooks, Man O' War, 1969	7.00 To 25.00
Ezra Brooks, Map, U.S.A., Club Bottle, 1973	13.00
Ezra Brooks, Masonic Fez, 1976	8.00 To 19.00
Ezra Brooks, Max, The Hat, Zimmerman, 1976	23.00 To 25.00
Ezra Brooks, Military Tank, 1971	*Illus* 18.00
Ezra Brooks, Minnesota Hockey Player, 1975	25.00
Ezra Brooks, Minuteman, 1975	16.00 To 18.00
Ezra Brooks, Missouri Mule, 1972	9.00 To 18.00
Ezra Brooks, Moose, 1973	25.00
Ezra Brooks, Motorcycle, 1972	7.00 To 18.00
Ezra Brooks, Mr.Foremost, 1969	8.00 To 20.00
Ezra Brooks, Mr.Merchant, 1969	8.00 To 22.00
Ezra Brooks, Mustang Indy Pace Car, 1979	30.00 To 38.00
Ezra Brooks, New Hampshire Statehouse, 1970	5.00 To 25.00
Ezra Brooks, North Carolina Bicentennial, 1975	12.00 To 29.00

Ezra Brooks, Penguin, 1973

Ezra Brooks, Red Fox, Wild Life, 1979
(See Page 60)

Ezra Brooks, Spirit Of '76, 1974
(See Page 60)

Ezra Brooks, Nugget Classic, 1970	7.00 To 25.00
Ezra Brooks, Oil Gusher, 1969	5.00 To 12.00
Ezra Brooks, Old Ez, No.2, Barn Owl, 1977	39.95
Ezra Brooks, Old Ez, No.2, Eagle Owl, 1978	*Color* 45.00
Ezra Brooks, Old Ez, No.3, Snow Owl, 1979	39.95
Ezra Brooks, Old Iowa Capitol, 1971	26.00 To 30.00
Ezra Brooks, Old Man Of The Mountain, 1970	12.00 To 19.00
Ezra Brooks, Oliver Hardy Bust, 1976	12.00 To 23.00
Ezra Brooks, Ontario Race Car, 1970	13.00 To 20.00
Ezra Brooks, Order Of Eagles F.O.E., 1978	*Color* 30.00
Ezra Brooks, Over-Under Flintlock, Flask, 1969	3.00
Ezra Brooks, Overland Express Stagecoach, 1969	5.00 To 25.00
Ezra Brooks, Panda, 1972	9.00 To 18.00
Ezra Brooks, Penguin, 1973	*Illus* 9.00
Ezra Brooks, Penny Farthington, 1973	15.00
Ezra Brooks, Pepperbox, Flask, 1969	3.00
Ezra Brooks, Phoenix Bird, 1971	25.00 To 50.00
Ezra Brooks, Pirate, 1971	4.00 To 15.00

Ezra Brooks, Polish Legion American Vets, 1978 .... 20.00 To 27.50
Ezra Brooks, Potbellied Stove, 1968 .... 6.00 To 18.00
Ezra Brooks, Queen Of Hearts, 1969 .... 6.00 To 14.00
Ezra Brooks, Raccoon Wild Life, 1978 .... 39.95
Ezra Brooks, Ram, 1973 .... 20.00
Ezra Brooks, Razorback Hog, 1969 .... 10.00
Ezra Brooks, Razorback Hog, 1970 .... 9.00 To 14.00
Ezra Brooks, Razorback Hog, 1979 .... 35.00
Ezra Brooks, Red Fox, Wild Life, 1979 .... Illus   42.00
Ezra Brooks, Reno Arch, 1968 .... 4.00 To 10.00
Ezra Brooks, Republican Convention, 1976 .... 9.00 To 18.00
Ezra Brooks, Sailfish, 1971 .... 7.00 To 18.00
Ezra Brooks, Salmon, Washington King, 1971 .... 17.00 To 50.00
Ezra Brooks, San Francisco Cable Car, 1968 .... 12.00
Ezra Brooks, Sea Captain, 1971 .... 9.00 To 15.00
Ezra Brooks, Senator, 1972 .... 12.00 To 25.00
Ezra Brooks, Setter, 1974 .... 8.00 To 25.00
Ezra Brooks, Shrine King Tut Guard, 1979 .... 35.00
Ezra Brooks, Silver Dollar, Black Base, 1970 .... 5.00 To 6.00
Ezra Brooks, Silver Dollar, White Base, 1970 .... 5.00
Ezra Brooks, Silver Saddle, 1973 .... 25.00 To 40.00

Ezra Brooks, Strongman, 1974

Ezra Brooks, Weirton Steel, 1973

Ezra Brooks, Silver Spur, 1971 .... 6.00 To 26.00
Ezra Brooks, Ski Boot, 1972 .... 8.00 To 17.00
Ezra Brooks, Slot Machine, 1971 .... 10.00 To 25.00
Ezra Brooks, Snowmobile, 1972 .... 10.00 To 18.00
Ezra Brooks, South Dakota Air National Guard, 1976 .... 35.00
Ezra Brooks, Spirit Of '76, 1974 .... Illus   7.00
Ezra Brooks, Spirit Of St.Louis, 50th Anniversary, 1977 .... 8.00 To 20.00
Ezra Brooks, Sprint Car, 1971 .... 15.00 To 20.00
Ezra Brooks, Stan Laurel Bust, 1976 .... 12.00 To 23.00
Ezra Brooks, Stonewall Jackson, 1974 .... 25.00 To 30.00
Ezra Brooks, Strongman, 1974 .... Illus   6.00
Ezra Brooks, Sturgeon, 1975 .... 22.00
Ezra Brooks, Tecumseh, 1969 .... 6.00 To 15.00
Ezra Brooks, Telephone, 1971 .... 11.00 To 25.00
Ezra Brooks, Tennis Player, 1973 .... 7.00 To 15.00
Ezra Brooks, Terrapin, Maryland, 1974 .... 14.00 To 25.00
Ezra Brooks, Texas Longhorn Steer, 1971 .... 12.00 To 28.00

Ezra Brooks, Ticker Tape, 1970 .... 5.00 To 15.00
Ezra Brooks, Tonopah, 1972 .... 14.00 To 22.00
Ezra Brooks, Totem Pole, No.1, 1972 .... 5.50 To 25.00
Ezra Brooks, Totem Pole, No.2, 1973 .... 5.50 To 18.00
Ezra Brooks, Tractor, 1971 .... 12.00 To 30.00
Ezra Brooks, Trail Bike, 1973 .... 9.00 To 18.00
Ezra Brooks, Trojan Horse, 1974 .... 7.95 To 18.00
Ezra Brooks, Trout & Fly, 1970 .... 7.00 To 15.00
Ezra Brooks, Truckin & Vannin, 1977 .... 12.00 To 20.00
Ezra Brooks, U.S.C.Trojan, 1973 .... 17.00 To 20.00
Ezra Brooks, V.F.W., Blue, 1973 .... 9.00 To 18.00
Ezra Brooks, V.F.W., White, Gold, 1975 .... 9.00 To 18.00
Ezra Brooks, V.F.W., White, 1974 .... 11.00
Ezra Brooks, Vermont Skier, 1972 .... 13.00 To 27.00
Ezra Brooks, Walgreen Drugs, 1974 .... 8.00 To 25.00
Ezra Brooks, Weirton Steel, 1973 ....*Illus*   16.00
Ezra Brooks, West Virginia Mountain Lady, 1972 .... 12.95 To 30.00
Ezra Brooks, West Virginia Mountaineer, 1971 .... 80.00 To 130.00
Ezra Brooks, Whale, 1972 .... 5.00 To 20.00
Ezra Brooks, Wheat Shocker, 1971 .... 6.00 To 20.00
Ezra Brooks, White Tail Deer, 1974 .... 18.00 To 25.00

Famous Firsts, Honda Motorcycle, 1975
(See Page 62)

Famous Firsts, Phonograph, 1969
(See Page 63)

Ezra Brooks, White Turkey, 1971 .... 16.00 To 35.00
Ezra Brooks, Wichita .... 4.00 To 6.00
Ezra Brooks, Wichita Centennial, 1970 .... 6.00 To 30.00
Ezra Brooks, Winston Churchill, 1969 .... 4.00 To 15.00
Ezra Brooks, Zimmerman, Hat, 1968 .... 6.00 To 18.00
Ezra Brooks, 100th Bottle Award, 1972 .... 10.00 To 16.00
    Face Cream, see Cosmetic, Medicine
Famous Firsts, Alpine Bell, 1970 .... 19.00
Famous Firsts, American Yacht 100, 1970 .... 140.00 To 150.00
Famous Firsts, American Yacht 13, 1970 .... 33.00
Famous Firsts, Balloon, 1971 .... 30.00 To 55.00
Famous Firsts, Bear, 1975 .... 14.00
Famous Firsts, Bennie Bow Wow, 1973 .... 20.00 To 21.00
Famous Firsts, Bersaglieri, 1969 .... 10.00 To 18.00
Famous Firsts, Bugatti Royale Car, 1974 .... 189.00 To 250.00
Famous Firsts, Butterfly, 1971 .... 30.00 To 32.00
Famous Firsts, Cable Car, 1973 .... 45.00 To 55.00

Famous Firsts, Centurion, 1969 .... 10.00 To 18.00
Famous Firsts, Coffee Mill, Blue, 1971 .... 33.00 To 41.00
Famous Firsts, Coffee Mill, Orange, 1971 .... 33.00 To 41.00
Famous Firsts, Corvette Stingray 1963, Red, 1977 .... 100.00
Famous Firsts, Corvette Stingray 1963, White, 1977 .... Color 38.00
Famous Firsts, Corvette 1953, 1975 .... 35.00 To 38.00
Famous Firsts, De Witt Steam Engine, 1969 .... 42.00
Famous Firsts, Dino-Ferrari Car, Green, 1975 .... 19.00
Famous Firsts, Dino-Ferrari Car, White, 1975 .... 19.00
Famous Firsts, Dino-Ferrari Car, Yellow, 1975 .... 19.00
Famous Firsts, Dino-Ferrari Car, Blue, 1975 .... 19.00
Famous Firsts, Don Sympatico, 1973 .... 17.00 To 18.00
Famous Firsts, Egg House, 1975 .... 17.00 To 19.00
Famous Firsts, Filomena Hen, 1973 .... 8.00 To 19.00
Famous Firsts, Floral Telephone, 1973 .... 30.00 To 31.00
Famous Firsts, French Telephone, 1969 .... 33.00

Famous Firsts, Swiss Chalet, 1974
(See Page 64)

Figural, All Scotch, Girl With Dog,
Porcelain, 4 In.
(See Page 64)

Figural, Black Waiter, Frosted & Clear, Mouth Chips, 14 In.
(See Page 64)

Famous Firsts, Garibaldi, 1969 .... 18.00
Famous Firsts, Golden Spirit .... Color 50.00
Famous Firsts, Golden 5000, 1977 .... 65.00
Famous Firsts, Golfer, He, 1973 .... 30.00 To 32.00
Famous Firsts, Golfer, She, 1973 .... 30.00 To 32.00
Famous Firsts, Honda Motorcycle, 1975 .... Illus 31.00
Famous Firsts, Hurdy Gurdy, 1971 .... 28.00
Famous Firsts, Indy Racer, No.11, 1971 .... 28.00 To 35.00
Famous Firsts, Johnny Reb Telephone, 1973 .... Color 33.00
Famous Firsts, Leopard, 1975 .... 14.00
Famous Firsts, Lion, 1975 .... 14.00
Famous Firsts, Lockheed C-131, Hercules, 1979 .... 65.00
Famous Firsts, Locomotive .... 36.00 To 39.00
Famous Firsts, Lombardy Scale, 1970 .... 32.00
Famous Firsts, Lotus, No.2, 1971 .... 34.00 To 75.00
Famous Firsts, Marmon Wasp, No.32, Gold, 1971 .... 16.00 To 18.00
Famous Firsts, Marmon Wasp, No.32, No.1, 1968 .... 42.00
Famous Firsts, Marmon Wasp, No.32, No.2, 1968 .... 32.00 To 39.00

Famous Firsts, Minnie Meow, 1973 .... 21.00
Famous Firsts, Monkey, 1975 .... 14.00
Famous Firsts, Napoleon, 1969 .... 10.00 To 18.00
Famous Firsts, Natchez Mail Pack, 1975 .... 33.00 To 38.00
Famous Firsts, National Racer, No.8, 1972 .... 33.00 To 45.00

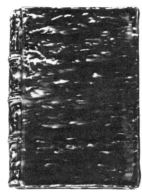

(See Page 64)

Clockwise from upper left: Figural, Bennington Type, Departed Spirits, Glaze, 5 1/2 In.; Figural, Book, Bunt'
... S/companion, Multicolored, 7 5/8 In.; Figural, Book, Departed Spirits, Chip, 5 1/2 In.; Figural, Book,
Rockingham Type Glaze, Marked Kossuth

Famous Firsts, Owl, 1975 .... 14.00
Famous Firsts, P-51 Mustang, 1974 .... 35.00
Famous Firsts, Panther, 1975 .... 14.00
Famous Firsts, Pepper Mill, 1978 .... 35.00
Famous Firsts, Phonograph, 1969 ....*Illus* 32.00
Famous Firsts, Porsche, Targa, 1979 .... 50.00
Famous Firsts, Renault Racer No.3, 1969 .... 36.00 To 45.00
Famous Firsts, Riverboat, Robert E.Lee, 1971 ....*Color* 55.00

Famous Firsts, Roulette Wheel, 1972	31.00 To 33.00
Famous Firsts, Sea Witch Ship, 1976	50.00 To 100.00
Famous Firsts, Sewing Machine, 1970	29.00 To 34.00
Famous Firsts, Ship In Bottle	29.00
Famous Firsts, Skier, He, 1973	17.00
Famous Firsts, Skier, Jack, 1975	34.00
Famous Firsts, Skier, Jill, 1975	34.00
Famous Firsts, Skier, She, 1973	17.00
Famous Firsts, Spirit Of '76	48.00
Famous Firsts, Spirit Of St.Louis, 1969	55.00
Famous Firsts, St.Pol Bell, 1970	19.00
Famous Firsts, Swiss Chalet, 1974 *Illus*	34.00
Famous Firsts, Tennis, 1973	31.00 To 32.00
Famous Firsts, Tiger, 1975	14.00
Famous Firsts, Winnie Mae, 1972	35.00 To 55.00
Famous Firsts, Yankee Clipper, 1975	14.00
Famous Firsts, Yankee Doodle Telephone, 1973 *Color*	33.00
Famous Firsts, Zebra, 1975	14.00

Figural bottles are specially named by the collectors of bottles. Any bottle that is of a recognizable shape, such as a human head, or a pretzel, or a clock, is considered to be a figural. There is no restriction as to date or material.

Figural, see also Bitters, Cologne, Perfume

Figural, Acrobat On Ball, Upside Down, 10 1/2 In.	65.00
Figural, All Scotch, Girl With Dog, Porcelain, 4 In. *Illus*	12.00
Figural, Alle's Galiano, Pontil, Dated	150.00
Figural, Alligator, Wine	9.00
Figural, Alpine Pipe, Wine	8.00
Figural, Arch Of Triumph, Wine	11.00
Figural, Bacchus On Cask, Wine	24.00
Figural, Bagpiper, Wine	8.00
Figural, Banjo, In Holder, Amethyst, Small	27.00
Figural, Bass Fiddle, Pontil, Clear	50.00
Figural, Bather On A Rock, 12 In.	105.00
Figural, Bear, Fenkhousen, Whiskey, Yellow Amber	335.00
Figural, Bear, Kummel, Black Amethyst	40.00 To 60.00
Figural, Bear, Kummel, Cork, See-Through Olive	75.00
Figural, Bear, Kummel, Milk Glass, Cork	100.00
Figural, Bear, Kummel, Screw Cap, Milk Glass	35.00
Figural, Bear, Kummel, Seated, Applied Black Face, Gray Body, Pontil, 11 In.	280.00
Figural, Bear, Olive Amber, 11 In.	25.00
Figural, Bell, Fancy Clear Ground Top, 5 1/2 In.	18.00
Figural, Belle Of Anderson, 6 3/4 In.	85.00
Figural, Belle Of Anderson, 8 1/4 In.	85.00
Figural, Bennington Type, Departed Spirits, Glaze, 5 1/2 In. *Illus*	130.00
Figural, Betty Boop, Perfume, Clear	8.00
Figural, Billiken, Gold	50.00
Figural, Billiken, Original Closure	50.00
Figural, Billy Club, Amber	38.00
Figural, Billy Club, Clear	25.00
Figural, Birdcage, Ink, Bubbles	125.00
Figural, Black Cat, Wine	5.00
Figural, Black Waiter, Frosted & Clear, Mouth Chips, 14 In. *Illus*	180.00
Figural, Black Waiter, Frosted, Covered With Old Paint	300.00
Figural, Book, Bunt'...S/companion, Multicolored, 7 5/8 In. *Illus*	290.00
Figural, Book, Departed Spirits, Chip, 5 1/2 In. *Illus*	100.00
Figural, Book, Rockingham Type Glaze, Marked Kossuth *Illus*	500.00
Figural, Boot, Clear, 11 In.	45.00
Figural, Boot, Polish, Geo.A.Colburnwest, Gardner, Mass., Aqua	35.00
Figural, Boot, 3 1/2 In.	14.00
Figural, Boy Against Tree, Wine	12.00
Figural, Buddha-Like, Bubbly, Light Green, Corker	20.00
Figural, Bulldog, Black, Closure At Bottom, Gold Collar, 4 In.	25.00
Figural, Bust Of Man, Mustache & Medal Around Neck, V.I.T., Clear	20.00

Top row from left: Figural, Cannon Barrel, Amber, Base Marked B. & Co., 3/4 Quart; Figural, Clown, Lymette, Paper Label, 7 1/2 In.; Figural, Dog, Amber, 9 In.; Figural, Flaccus, Catsup, 9 1/2 In. *(See Page 66); Center from left:* Figural, Jester, 7 In.; Figural, Jolly Man, 9 In.; Figural, Lady, Green Interior Painting, 10 1/2 In. *(See Page 67); Bottom from left:* Figural, Lady's Torso, 6 1/2 In.; Figural, Man's Head, 3 In.; Figural, Man Smiling, Van Dunck's Genever, Brown, 9 In.; Figural, Man With Potbelly, 7 In. *(See Page 67).*

Figural, Butterfly, Clear, 12 1/2 In.	40.00
Figural, Cabin, Old Homestead Wild Cherry, Honey Amber	210.00
Figural, California, Bitters	25.00
Figural, Canada Goose, Lord Calvert	125.00
Figural, Canary, Wine	8.00
Figural, Cannon Barrel, Amber, Base Marked B. & Co., 3/4 Quart	*Illus* 325.00
Figural, Cannon, J.T.Gayen, Altoona, Amber	900.00 To 1100.00
Figural, Cannon, J.T.Gayen, Altoona, Blob Top, Red Amber, 13 3/4 In.	1090.00
Figural, Carry Nation	4.00 To 10.00
Figural, Cat, Seated, Light Purple	27.00
Figural, Cat, Smiling, Yellow Green	25.00
Figural, Chicken, 3 Mold, Painted, 9 1/2 In.	*Color* 45.00
Figural, Children Climbing Tree, Frosted & Clear, 14 In.	30.00
Figural, Cigar, Amber, 5 1/4 In.	25.00
Figural, Cigar, Label	25.00
Figural, Clam, Ground Top, Clear	25.00
Figural, Clown, Lymette, Paper Label, 7 1/2 In.	*Illus* 8.00
Figural, Coachman, Van Dunck's, Bitters, Amber	69.00 To 95.00
Figural, Coliseum, Wine	10.00
Figural, Cologne, Bass Fiddle, Pontil	50.00
Figural, Columbine, Wine	8.00
Figural, Crow, Head Is Stopper, Liquid Pours From Beak, Black Pottery, 8 In.	50.00
Figural, Czar & Czarina Of Russia, Milk Glass	200.00
Figural, Dog, Amber, 9 In.	*Illus* 3.00
Figural, Dog, Milk Glass, 3/4 Quart	425.00
Figural, Dog, Seated, Yellow	27.00
Figural, Dog, Sterling Silver Head, 8 In.	*Color* xxxx.xx
Figural, Donkey In Chair, Wine	7.00
Figural, Dutch Shoe, Perfume, Clear	10.00
Figural, Ear Of Corn, Ground Top, Aqua, 6 1/2 In.	40.00
Figural, Ear Of Corn, Metal Cap, Original Paint, Ground Top, 6 1/2 In.	17.00
Figural, Ear Of Corn, National, Patented 1867, Honey Amber	215.00
Figural, Elephant In Chair, Wine	7.00
Figural, Elephant, Bear, Chubby Man, Screw Topped	10.00
Figural, Elephant, Jumbo Peanut Butter	55.00
Figural, Elephant, Old Sol, Amber	9.00
Figural, Elk's Tooth, B.P.O.E., Ceramic	18.50
Figural, Fire Keg, Hazelton's, Barrel With Bail, Amber	90.00
Figural, Fish, Amber, 6 1/4 In.	12.00 To 16.00
Figural, Fish, Cod Liver Oil, Brown, 9 In.	25.00
Figural, Fish, Ground Top, Pewter Cap, Clear, 8 1/2 In.	10.00
Figural, Fish, 4 In.	20.00
Figural, Fish, 7 In.	32.00
Figural, Flaccus, Catsup, 9 1/2 In.	*Illus* 70.00
Figural, Friar John Holding Wine Glass, Wine	12.00
Figural, Frosted Lady With Urn On Shoulder	30.00
Figural, George Washington	5.00
Figural, George Washington, Bust, Corker, Chas.Jacquin, Cobalt	15.00
Figural, Girl Holding Jug, Wine	12.00
Figural, Girl With Muff	15.00 To 25.00
Figural, Globe, Detroit, Barrel, Pat.Oct. 10, 1882, Amber	22.00
Figural, Globe, World's Fair, 1939, Milk Glass, Screw Top	6.00 To 20.00
Figural, Goat, Viarengo, Painted	35.00
Figural, Gold Pig, Good Old Rye In A Hog, Anna Pottery Co.	1000.00
Figural, Goose, Atop Wine Bottle, Alabaster, 15 In.	50.00
Figural, Grandfather Clock, Metal Cap, Ground Lip, Label	15.00
Figural, Grapes, Green Glass, Wine	5.00
Figural, Gun, Ground Top, Clear, Dark Purple	25.00
Figural, Gun, Rifle Shaped, BIMAL, Emerald Green, 16 In.	13.50
Figural, Hammer, German, No.1887, 8 In.	50.00
Figural, Hand Holding Pistol, Frosted & Clear, 13 In.	35.00
Figural, Hand In Flat Clasped Position, Cork, 5 1/4 In.	18.00
Figural, Harlequin, Wine	8.00
Figural, Harvest With Chain Jug, Wine	10.00
Figural, Hat, Geometric, Sandwich Glass, Clear, Flint, 2 1/2 In.	115.00
Figural, Hercules Holding Glass World, Metal	95.00

Figural, **Hessian Soldier,** Cologne, Clear	35.00
Figural, **Hessian Soldier,** 7 1/4 In.	32.00 To 50.00
Figural, **High-Top Shoe,** Clear, 9 In.	35.00
Figural, **High-Top Shoe,** Perfume, Stamp On Bottom	10.00
Figural, **Horn,** Pressed Glass, Clear	29.00
Figural, **Horseshoe,** Ground Top, Amber	18.00
Figural, **Hound Dog,** Seated Lime, Ground Top And Painted Bow, 8 In.	30.00
Figural, **Imperial Cannon,** Wine	24.00
Figural, **Indian,** Standing, Perfume, Open Pontil, Embossed, Aqua, 4 1/8 In.	55.00
Figural, **Ink,** Devil's Head, Ceramic, Rockingham Glaze	90.00
Figural, **Jester,** 7 In. ....*Illus*	55.00
Figural, **Joan Of Arc,** France, 4 1/2 In. ....*Color*	xxxx.xx
Figural, **Joan Of Arc,** Milk Glass, Full Armor	350.00
Figural, **John Bull**	175.00
Figural, **Jolly Man,** 9 In. ....*Illus*	75.00
Figural, **Lady Acrobat,** Frosted & Clear, 13 1/2 In.	40.00
Figural, **Lady In Corset**	18.00
Figural, **Lady,** Green Interior Painting, 10 1/2 In. ....*Illus*	4.00
Figural, **Lady's Boot**	10.00
Figural, **Lady's Leg,** Reed's, Light Amber	175.00
Figural, **Lady's Torso,** 6 1/2 In. ....*Illus*	75.00
Figural, **Leaning Tower Of Pisa,** Wine	7.00
Figural, **Liberty Bell,** Closure At Bottom, Green, 3 1/2 In.	18.00
Figural, **Lighthouse,** Cork, 7 1/2 In.	15.00
Figural, **Lighthouse,** T.T.Morris, Fine Wines & Liquors, Hand-Painted Flowers	1300.00
Figural, **Lighthouse,** Whiskey, Oval, Amber	7.00
Figural, **Log Cabin,** Scalpine	35.00
Figural, **Madonna,** Stopper & Handle, Pontil, Cobalt	20.00
Figural, **Mailbox,** Label, Quart	90.00
Figural, **Mallet,** Spirits, Applied Seal, Dated 1763	1400.00
Figural, **Man Smiling,** Van Dunck's Genever, Brown, 9 In. ....*Illus*	190.00
Figural, **Man With Potbelly,** 7 In. ....*Illus*	65.00
Figural, **Man,** Bowler Hat, Tux, Germany, 10.	15.00
Figural, **Man,** 9 In. ....*Color*	75.00
Figural, **Man's Head,** 3 In. ....*Illus*	350.00
Figural, **Metal Hercules Holding Glass World**	95.00
Figural, **Monks,** Stations Of The Cross, Whiskey Embossed, Amber, 10 In.	65.00
Figural, **Monument,** T.E.A. & Co., 16 In.	60.00
Figural, **Moses,** Green, 1925, 6 In.	475.00
Figural, **Moses,** 7 1/2 In. ....*Color*	xxxx.xx
Figural, **Mount Vernon,** Whiskey, Olive Green	10.00
Figural, **Mrs. Butterworth,** Amber With Original Label And Closure	8.00
Figural, **Mrs.Butterworth Syrup,** Amber	1.00
Figural, **Negro Waiter,** Black-Painted Head, Frosted & Clear, 14 In.	180.00
Figural, **Old Girl In Corset,** Screw, Ground Top, Original Closure, 6 1/2 In.	18.00
Figural, **Oriental Woman**	45.00
Figural, **Owl,** Clear, 9 In.	22.50
Figural, **Owl,** Old Irish Whiskey, Pottery, Quart	28.00
Figural, **Owl,** Pink, 9 In.	27.50
Figural, **Owl,** Standing, Cologne, Clear, C.1890, 5 1/2 In.	36.00
Figural, **Owl,** 4 In.	3.00
Figural, **Palanno,** Wine	12.00
Figural, **Pickle,** Ground Mouth, Green	45.00
Figural, **Pig,** Clear	45.00
Figural, **Pig,** Good Old Rye In A Hog's—, Milk Glass, 8 1/4 In. ....*Illus*	850.00
Figural, **Pig,** Good Ole Bourbon, Clear	55.00
Figural, **Pig,** Jew Pork, Good Old Bourbon In A Hog's—, Kirkpatrick Pottery	2300.00
Figural, **Pig,** Old Bourbon, Amber, 7 In.	225.00
Figural, **Pig,** Pure Old Rye, Tan & Brown	100.00
Figural, **Pig,** Sitting, Clear	42.00
Figural, **Pig,** Something Good In A Hog's Hand, Won't Squeal, Clear, 4 1/2 In.	65.00
Figural, **Pig,** Success Bottling Works	10.00
Figural, **Pig,** Suffolk Bitters, Double Ring Mouth, Light Amber	500.00
Figural, **Pillaza,** Wine	6.00
Figural, **Pistol,** Clear, 7 1/2 In.	11.00
Figural, **Pistol,** Ground Top, Without Cap	9.00

Figural, Ponte Vecchio Bridge, Wine		10.00
Figural, Poodle, Wine		7.00
Figural, Potato, World's Fair, 1893, 5 In.	*Illus*	50.00
Figural, Rebecca At The Well, 8 1/2 In.		35.00
Figural, Robert E.Lee, Southern Comfort	*Illus*	300.00
Figural, Roman Bust, Wine		12.00
Figural, Roman Horse Head, Wine		15.00
Figural, Roman Pitcher, Wine		14.00
Figural, Romeo & Juliet Candleholder, Wine		10.00
Figural, Santa, Husted, Clear		75.00
Figural, Shoe, Glass, Ink		70.00
Figural, Shoe, Old, Bubbles, Thick Heel, 4 X 3 1/2 In.		25.00
Figural, Shoe, 4 3/4 In.		16.00
Figural, Six Shooter Pistol, 8 Sided Barrel, Original Cop, Clear		25.00
Figural, Skull, Poison, Small		315.00
Figural, Soldier Bust, Wine		15.00
Figural, Soldier With Drum, Wine		7.00
Figural, Soldier With Rifle, Wine		7.00
Figural, Soldier, 7 In.	*Illus*	30.00
Figural, Spanish Man, Silveria, 12 In.	*Color*	8.00

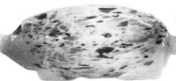

Figural, Pig, Good Old Rye In A Hog's—, Milk Glass, 8 1/4 In.
(See Page 67)

Figural, Potato, World's Fair, 1893, 5 In.

Figural, Robert E.Lee, Southern Comfort

Figural, Soldier, 7 In.

Figural, Spanish Toreador & Senorita, Pair		50.00
Figural, Standing Dog, Milk Glass, Minor Mouth Flakes, 3/4 Qt.	*Illus*	425.00
Figural, Stanley, Pistol, Old Clear Blown, 7 1/4 In.		35.00
Figural, Star Whiskey, W.B.Crowell		500.00
Figural, Statue Of Liberty		400.00

Figural, Steer's Head, Flaccus Bros., Milk Glass	195.00
Figural, Striped Fish, Wine	9.00
Figural, Suffolk Pit, Blob Lip	435.00
Figural, Suitcase With Metal Bottom Slide And Handle	30.00
Figural, Swallow, Wine	14.00
Figural, Teakettle, Whiskey, Olive Amber	215.00
Figural, Teddy Roosevelt, BIMAL, Clear, 6 1/2 In.	75.00
Figural, Tiger Reclining, Wine	7.00

Figural, Standing Dog, Milk Glass,
Minor Mouth Flakes, 3/4 Qt.

Flask, Ain't What She Used To Be, 8 In.

Figural, What A Night, Man In Coat, 5 In.

Figural, Totem Pole & Drum, Wine	9.00
Figural, Turtle, Embossed David's	25.00
Figural, U.S.Mail Box, Rye Whiskey, Dated 1891, Clear, Quart	120.00
Figural, Violin, Amethyst, 10 In.	25.00
Figural, Violin, Bardstown Distillery, Bardstown, Ky., Amber, Pint	10.00
Figural, Violin, BIM, Light Blue	15.00
Figural, Violin, Green, 10 In.	15.00
Figural, Washington, Bust, Cobalt Blue	25.00
Figural, Washington, Standing, Clear	18.00
Figural, What A Night, Man In Coat, 5 In. .... Illus	43.00
Figural, White & Red Speckled Rooster, Wine	13.00
Figural, Woman Holding Urn, Frosted, 14 In.	40.00
Figural, Zimmerman Jug, 1/2 Gallon, Wine	15.00
Fire Grenade, C. & N.W.Ry, Tubular, Clear, Contents, 18 1/2 In.	65.00
Fire Grenade, California Fire Extinguisher, Amber .... Color	xxxx.xx
Fire Grenade, Flagg's, Fire Extinguisher, Golden Amber, 6 1/4 In.	110.00
Fire Grenade, Harden's Hand, Extinguisher, Cobalt Blue, 6 1/4 In.	75.00
Fire Grenade, Harden's Hand, Vertical Ribs, Cobalt Blue, 17 1/4 X 2 1/4 In.	180.00
Fire Grenade, Harden's, Fire Extinguisher, Vertical Ribs, Blue, 8 In.	40.00
Fire Grenade, Harden's, Star, Blue	34.00
Fire Grenade, Hayward's Hand, Bright Yellow Green, 6 In.	55.00
Fire Grenade, Hayward's, Yellow Amber, 6 In.	40.00
Fitzgerald, see Old Fitzgerald	

*Flasks have been made since the 18th century in America. The free-blown,
mold-blown, and decorated flasks are all popular with collectors. The
numbers used in the entries in the form Van R-0 or McK G I-0 refer
to the books "Early American Bottles & Flasks" by Stephen Van
Rensselaer and "American Glass" by George P. and Helen
McKearin.*

Flask, A.Colburn Co., Pumpkin Seed	14.00
Flask, Ain't What She Used To Be, 8 In. .... Illus	12.00

Flask, Alfred Anderson, Minneapolis, Clear	16.00
Flask, Amber, Strap Sided, Pint	15.00
Flask, Americus Club Whiskey, Pocket, Honey Amber	8.00
Flask, Anchor & Rope On Front, Aqua, Pint	8.00
Flask, Anchor, Amber, 7 1/2 In. ....*Color*	6.00
Flask, Anchor, Aqua, Quart	4.00

Flask, Chapman, Baltimore, Md., Dancer & Soldier, Green, Pint

Flask, Double Eagle, Sapphire Blue, Inside Stain, Pint
(See Page 72)

Flask, Anchor, Clear, Pint	22.00
Flask, Anchor, Sheaf Of Wheat, Baltimore Glassworks, Aqua	50.00
Flask, Arctic Explorer, Flag, 1/4 Pint	40.00
Flask, Ashbrook & Co., Picnic	30.00
Flask, B.P.Chapman & Son, Smithfield, Va., Clear, Quart	25.00
Flask, Baltimore Glass Works, Anchor & Resurgam Eagle	50.00
Flask, Baltimore Glass Works, Anchor & Wheat, Aqua, Pint	150.00
Flask, Baltimore Glass Works, Blue Green, Quart	850.00
Flask, Baltimore Glass Works, Olive Yellow, 1/2 Pint	600.00
Flask, Banjo, Amethyst, 7 In.	10.00
Flask, Banjo, Italian Blue, 7 In.	10.00
Flask, Barbee Whiskey, Bottled By J.J.Coleman, Montana, 1/2 Pint	14.00
Flask, Barrel, A Merry Christmas & A Happy New Year, Seated Woman, 1/2 Pint	125.00
Flask, Barrel, Unembossed, 8 Rings, Clear	45.00
Flask, Bartlett & Ostreicher Gem Saloon, Elko, Nev., Coffin, 6 In.	100.00
Flask, Bininger's Night Cap, Broad St., N.Y., Open Pontil, Amber, Pint	285.00
Flask, Blown Cylinder, Pushed-Down Lip, Pontil, C.1790, Olive Green	15.00
Flask, Bonnie Bros., Louisville, Ky., Clear	8.00
Flask, Boston Importers & Bottlers, Strap Sided, Ice Blue, 6 1/2 In.	4.50
Flask, Brande's Brothers, N.Y., Amber, 1/2 Pint	15.00
Flask, Brickwedel, Pint	150.00
Flask, Bristol Flagon, Open Pontil, Handle, Amber	65.00
Flask, Byron Scott, Olive Amber, 1/2 Pint, Pontil	125.00
Flask, C.A.Richards & Co., Boston, Coffin, Bubbles, Deep Aqua	27.00
Flask, C.H.Eddy & Co., Jamaica Ginger, Brattleboro, Vt., Label, Pumpkinseed	20.00
Flask, C.P.Moorman, A.P.Hotaling & Co., Sole Agents	125.00
Flask, C.W.Chesley Importer, Sacramento, Calif., Pumpkin, Pint	30.00
Flask, Calabash, Double Sheaf Of Wheat, Rake, 8 Pointed Star, Push-Up Pontil	80.00
Flask, Calabash, Hunter & Fisherman, Apricot, Quart	450.00
Flask, Calabash, Hunter & Fisherman, Iron Pontil, Quart	215.00
Flask, Calabash, Hunter & Fisherman, Open Pontil, Aqua	65.00
Flask, Calabash, Hunter & Fisherman, Strawberry Puce, Quart	225.00

Flask, Calabash, Hunter & Fishermen, Iron Pontil, Orange Amber 168.00
Flask, Calabash, Jenny Lind, Huffsey Glass Works, Iron Pontil, Aqua 75.00
Flask, Calabash, Jenny Lind, Ravenna, Ohio, Aqua ....*Color* xxxx.xx
Flask, Calabash, Jenny Lind, Ravenna, Ohio, Blue ....*Color* xxxx.xx
Flask, Calabash, Jenny Lind, Ravenna, Ohio, Pale Blue ....*Color* xxxx.xx
Flask, Calabash, Jenny Lind, Ravenna, Ohio, Yellow ....*Color* xxxx.xx
Flask, Calabash, Kossuth & Tree, Deep Aqua 85.00
Flask, Calabash, Sheaf & Star, Applied Handle, Amber 210.00
Flask, Calabash, Sheath, Rake & Fork, Aqua, Large Open Pontil 45.00
Flask, Calabash, Sheath, Rake & Fork, Open Pontil, Aqua, Large 45.00
Flask, Calabash, Soldier & Star, Aqua 85.00
Flask, Centennial, Pewter Screw Cap & Base, Leather Upper Half 18.00
Flask, Chapin & Gore, Barrel, Light Amber 60.00
Flask, Chapman, Baltimore, Md., Dancer & Soldier, Green, Pint ....*Illus* 350.00
Flask, Chapman, Baltimore, Md., Dancing Girl, Open Pontil, Aqua, Pint 110.00
Flask, Chas.Ruger, Wines & Liquors, Houston, Texas, Side Strapped, 1/2 Pint 35.00
Flask, Chestnut Grove Whiskey, Handled, Amber, Quart 100.00
Flask, Chestnut, Handled, Flat, Open Pontil, Golden Amber 32.00
Flask, Chestnut, Handled, Flattened Open Pontil, Amber 22.00
Flask, Chestnut, Handled, Open Pontil, Amber 75.00
Flask, Chestnut, Handled, Wavy Glass, Deep Red Amber, 8 1/2 In. 38.00
Flask, Chestnut, Olive Green, 5 1/2 In. .... 65.00 To 70.00
Flask, Chestnut, Seed Bubbles, Open Pontil, Green, Pint 70.00
Flask, Chestnut, Tooled Lip, Olive Amber, 9 In. .... 70.00 To 650.00
Flask, Chestnut, 14 Diamond, Open Pontil, Deep Aqua, 6 1/2 In. 155.00
Flask, Chestnut, 24 Vertical Ribs, Open Pontil 75.00
Flask, Claremont Hotel, Bernardsville, N.J., Clear, 1/2 Pint 15.00
Flask, Clasped Hands & Eagle With Banner, Aqua, Quart 45.00
Flask, Clasped Hands, Deep Golden Amber, 1/2 Pint 90.00
Flask, Clasped Hands, Eagle, Aqua 60.00
Flask, Clyde Glassworks, Aqua, Quart 25.00
Flask, Coffin, Amber 8.00
Flask, Coffin, Blue Aqua, Pint 17.00
Flask, Coffin, Embossed Key, Aqua, Pint 22.50
Flask, Coffin, Yellow Amber, Quart 8.00
Flask, Cognac Brandy, New Hampshire Glass Co., Double-Ring Top, Label, Oval 55.00
Flask, Collared Lip, Open Pontil, Chestnut, Dark Green 75.00
Flask, Columbia Wine & Liquor Co., Hudson, N.Y., Coffin, Clear, Pint 25.00
Flask, Continental Hotel, New York, Merrifield, Strap Sided, Amber, Pint 35.00
Flask, Corn For The World, Aqua, Open Pontil, Pint 250.00
Flask, Corn For The World, Aqua, Open Pontil, 1/2 Pint 275.00
Flask, Corn For The World, Light Lime Green, Quart 850.00
Flask, Cornucopia & Urn, Olive Amber, Open Pontil, Pint 73.50
Flask, Cornucopia & Urn, Olive Green, Open Pontil, Upward Burst Bubble 53.50
Flask, Cornucopia & Urn, 1/2 Pint 60.00
Flask, Cornucopia, Historical, Greenish Amber, 1/2 Pint 70.00
Flask, Coventry, Conn., Traveler's Companion, Star, Sheaf Of Wheat, Amber, Pt. 125.00
Flask, D.A.Knowlton, Saratoga, N.Y., Deep Green 40.00
Flask, Dalleman & Co., Chicago, Amber 9.00
Flask, Dancer & Musician, Golden Yellow, Base Flake, 1/2 Pint 175.00
Flask, Dancing Soldier, Yellow Green, Pint 350.00
Flask, Diamond Quilted, 1/8 Pint, 4 3/4 In. 3.75
Flask, Double Eagle & Banner, Light Amber, 1/2 Pint 75.00
Flask, Double Eagle & C & I, Aqua, 1/2 Pint 33.50
Flask, Double Eagle & Pittsburgh, Light Blue, Pint 80.00
Flask, Double Eagle Over Oval, Open Pontil 60.00
Flask, Double Eagle, Amber, 1/2 Pint, Open Pontil 70.00
Flask, Double Eagle, Aqua, Pint .... 30.50 To 50.00
Flask, Double Eagle, Aqua, Quart 38.50
Flask, Double Eagle, Aqua, 1/2 Pint 33.50
Flask, Double Eagle, Cunningham Glass Mfgs., Aqua, Pint 55.00
Flask, Double Eagle, Deep Olive Greeen, Pint 135.00
Flask, Double Eagle, Deep Yellow Green, Pint 140.00
Flask, Double Eagle, Eagle Right, Aqua, 1/2 Pint 28.50
Flask, Double Eagle, Geo.A.Berry, Aqua, Quart 125.00
Flask, Double Eagle, Olive Amber, Pint, Pontil 125.00

Flask, Double Eagle, Olive Amber, 1/2 Pint .... 50.00 To 80.00
Flask, Double Eagle, Open Pontil, Aqua, Pint 80.00
Flask, Double Eagle, Pittsburgh, Emerald Green, Quart 175.00
Flask, Double Eagle, Pittsburgh, Light Blue, Pint 85.00
Flask, Double Eagle, Pittsburgh Type, Aqua, Pint 55.00
Flask, Double Eagle, Pittsburgh Type, Deep Yellow Green, Pint 140.00
Flask, Double Eagle, Pittsburgh, Aqua, Quart 55.00
Flask, Double Eagle, Pittsburgh, Pa., Dark Aquamarine 5.00
Flask, Double Eagle, Pittsburgh, Pa., Oval 44.50
Flask, Double Eagle, Red Iron Pontil, Aqua, Pint 50.00
Flask, Double Eagle, Sapphire Blue, Inside Stain, Pint .... Illus 700.00
Flask, Double Eagle, Vertical, Olive Green, 1/2 Pint 125.00
Flask, Double Eagle, Wreath, Aqua, 1/2 Pint 38.50
Flask, Double Union & Clasped Hands, Aqua, Quart 55.00

Flask, Eagle, Prospector To Right, Below For Pike's Peak, Pint

Flask, McK G I-001, Washington & Eagle,
Blue Green, Pint
(See Page 74)

Flask, McK G I-022, Columbia
& Eagle, Clear, Pint
(See Page 75)

Flask, McK G I-018, Washington
& Baltimore Monument, Pint
(See Page 75)

Flask, Dr.Morse's Celebrated Syrup, Strap Sided, Oval, Blue Aqua, 9 In. 11.00
Flask, Dr.W.H.Bull's Herb & Iron, Pat., Oct. 13th, 85, Amber, 9 1/2 In. 14.00
Flask, Dutch Onion, Open Pontil .... 69.50 To 99.50
Flask, Eagle & Cornucopia, Keene Glassworks, Embossed, OP, Olive Green 100.00
Flask, Eagle & Indian, Aqua, Quart 100.00
Flask, Eagle Over Flag, Continental, Indian, Cunningham & Co., Aqua, Quart 118.50
Flask, Eagle, Concentric, Reproduction 65.00
Flask, Eagle, Prospector To Right, Below For Pike's Peak, Pint .... Illus 600.00
Flask, Embossed Hunting Scene, Open Pontil, Clear 170.00
Flask, Embossed Monkey, Chestnut, Clear 40.00
Flask, Embossed Picnic, Amber, Pumpkinseed 20.00
Flask, Engraved, Basket Near Base, Rigaree On Sides, Clear, OP 200.00
Flask, F.B.Robertson & Bros., Richmond, Va, Aqua, Pint 20.00
Flask, Farmville Dispensary, Farmville, Va., Clear, Pint 15.00
Flask, Fell's Point, Monument & Sailboat, Puce, OP, 1/2 Pint 1500.00
Flask, Flora Temple, Applied Handle, Original Label, Puce, Pint 390.00
Flask, For Pike's Peak & Eagle, Aqua, Pint 40.00
Flask, For Pike's Peak & Prospector & Eagle, Light Green, Pint 70.00

Flask, For Pike's Peak & Prospector & Hunter Shooting Deer, Aqua, Pint 110.00
Flask, For Pike's Peak, Prospector, Aqua, 1/2 Pint 50.00
Flask, For Pike's Peak, Prospector, Eagle, Oval, Aqua, Pint 70.00
Flask, For Pike's Peak, Traveler Shooting Deer, Aqua, Quart 140.00
Flask, General MacArthur, Amber, 1/2 Pint 40.00
Flask, George W.Todd, Newport News, Va., Clear, Pint 15.00
Flask, Gilchrist, Pint 25.00
Flask, Grand Army Republic, Embossed U.S. 20.00
Flask, Green, 1/2 Pint 2.50
Flask, Guerin, Fort Smith, Ark., Label, Pint 25.00
Flask, H.Guggenheimer & Sons, Clear 5.00
Flask, Half Barrel, Amethyst, 7 1/4 In. 12.00
Flask, Hip, Curved, 10 1/2 In. 10.00
Flask, Historical, Cornucopia, Olive Green, Pint 40.00

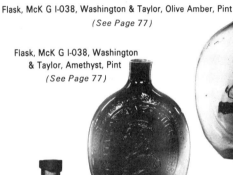

Flask, McK G I-038, Washington & Taylor, Olive Amber, Pint
(See Page 77)

Flask, McK G I-038, Washington
& Taylor, Amethyst, Pint
(See Page 77)

Flask, McK G I-023,
Washington & Taylor
Puce, Quart
(See Page 76)

Flask, McK G I-037, Washington
& Taylor, Yellow, Stain, Quart
(See Page 77)

Flask, Hobnail, Deep Ice Blue, 1/2 Pint 210.00
Flask, Horseshoe, Hand-Threaded Top, Pewter Filigree, 1/2 Pint 15.00
Flask, Hotel Statler, Buffalo, Detroit, Cleveland, Pumpkinseed 10.00
Flask, Hound Pictorial, Aqua, Pint, C-4 .... 320.00
Flask, Hunter & Fisherman, Calabash, Pontil, Aqua, Quart 75.00
Flask, Hunter, Fisherman, Blue Green 350.00
Flask, Hunter, Fisherman, Iron Pontil, Calabash, Puce 275.00
Flask, Hunter, Fisherman, Large Tree, Aqua 75.00
Flask, Initialed D.F., Open Pontil, 1/2 Pint 20.00
Flask, Irish Whiskey, Oval, Aqua, Pint 5.00
Flask, Isaac Well & Sons, Minneapolis, Clear 16.00
Flask, Jenny Lind, Fisherville Glass Works, Aqua, Calabash 53.50
Flask, Jockey & Hound, Aqua, Quart 85.00
Flask, Jockey & Hound, Golden Amber, Pint 350.00
Flask, John J.Murphy, Utica, Strap Sided, Aqua, 9 3/4 In. 25.00
Flask, Jos.Magnus & Co., Amber 4.00
Flask, L.Eppinger, Portland, Coffin, Clear, 1/2 Pint 35.00
Flask, L.G.Co., Cognac Brandy, Amber, Pint 20.00

Flask, **Lady Pictured Under Glass,** 5 1/2 In. ....*Color*   40.00
Flask, **Lafayette & Liberty Cap,** Olive Amber, 1/2 Pint 50.00
Flask, **Lafayette,** Liberty Cap On Pole, Light Amber, 1/2 Pint 485.00
Flask, **Lilienthal,** Amber 175.00
Flask, **Lilienthal,** Amber, Pint 150.00

Flask, McK G I-039, Washington
& Taylor, Base Stain, Quart

(See Page 77)

Flask, McK G I-060, Washington
& Taylor, Ice Blue, Quart

Flask, McK G I-044, Washington
& Taylor, Yellow, Stain, Pint

(See Page 78)

Flask, McK G I-054, Washington
& Taylor, Yellow Green, Quart

Flask, McK G I-073, Gen'l Taylor
& Baltimore Monument, Pint

Flask, **Log Cabin,** Embossed, Spring Garden Glass Works, Aquamarine, Pint 135.00
Flask, **Louisville,** Ribbed, Aqua, Pint 115.00
Flask, **Louisville,** Vertical Rib, Hand-Applied Ring, Blue Green 70.00
Flask, **Masonic,** Open Pontil, Pint 100.00
Flask, **May You Live Long & Prosper,** Quilted Pattern, Clear 30.00
Flask, **McK G I-001,** Washington & Eagle, Blue Green, Pint ....*Illus* 700.00
Flask, **McK G I-002,** General Washington & Eagle, Light Green 400.00

Flask, McK G I-002, Washington & Eagle, Aqua, Pint .... 250.00 To 395.00
Flask, McK G I-007, Aqua 125.00
Flask, McK G I-014, Washington & Eagle & T.W.D., Aqua, Pint .... 260.00 To 295.00
Flask, McK G I-014, Washington & Eagle, Aqua, Pint 225.00
Flask, McK G I-014, Washington, Eagle, Open Pontil, Dark Green 300.00

Flask, McK G I-081, Lafayette
& Dewitt Clinton, 1/2 Pint

Flask, McK G I-074, Zachary Taylor
& Cornstalk, Aqua, Pint

Flask, McK G I-080, Lafayette
& Dewitt Clinton, Green, Pint

(See Page 78)

Flask, McK G I-085, Lafayette
& Liberty Cap, Amber, Pint

Flask, McK G I-087, Lafayette
& Liberty Cap, Amber, 1/2 Pint

Flask, McK G I-084, Lafayette
& Masonic, Amber, 1/2 Pint

Flask, McK G I-016, Washington & Eagle, Aqua, Pint 200.00
Flask, McK G I-018, Tree In Leaf, Pale Yellow Green, Quart 300.00
Flask, McK G I-018, Washington & Baltimore Monument, Pint .... *Illus* 2900.00
Flask, McK G I-020, Washington & Baltimore Monument, Aqua, Pint 140.00
Flask, McK G I-021, Columbia & Eagle, Aqua, Pint 350.00
Flask, McK G I-021, Washington & Baltimore, Pale Amethystine, Quart 650.00
Flask, McK G I-022, Columbia & Eagle, Clear, Pint .... *Illus* 2000.00

Flask, McK G I-023, Washington & Baltimore Glass Works, Aqua, Quart 175.00
Flask, McK G I-023, Washington & Baltimore Glass Works, Deep Puce, Quart 1800.00
Flask, McK G I-023, Washington & Taylor, Puce, Quart ....*Illus* 1400.00
Flask, McK G I-024, Washington, Bridgeton, Taylor, Aqua, Pint .... 165.00 To 200.00
Flask, McK G I-026, Washington & Eagle & 12 Star, Emerald Green, Pint 350.00
Flask, McK G I-026, Washington & Eagle, Aqua, Quart .... 120.00 To 145.00
Flask, McK G I-026, Washington & Eagle, Bright Yellow Green, Quart 250.00
Flask, McK G I-031, Washington & Jackson, Dark Olive Green, Pint 185.00

Flask, McK G I-089, Lafayette
& Masonic, Amber, 1/2 Pint

Flask, McK G I-099, Calabash,
Jenny Lind & Huffsey, Quart

(See Page 78)

(See Page 79)

Flask, McK G I-089, Lafayette
& Masonic, Green, 1/2 Pint
(See Page 78)

Flask, McK G I-105, Jenny Lind,
Stain, Aqua, Quart

(See Page 79)

(See Page 79)

(See Page 79)

Flask, McK G I-104, Jenny Lind
& Factory, Sapphire, Quart

Flask, McK G I-108, Jenny Lind
& Lyre, Aqua, Pint

Flask, McK G I-031, Washington & Jackson, Olive Amber, Pint 110.00
Flask, McK G I-032, Washington, Jackson, Embossed, Amber, Pint 250.00
Flask, McK G I-032, Washington, Jackson, Olive Amber 150.00
Flask, McK G I-032, Washington, Jackson, Pale Olive Amber 140.00
Flask, McK G I-033, Washington & Jackson, Olive Amber 135.00
Flask, McK G I-034, Masonic & Franklin, Aqua, Pint 240.00
Flask, McK G I-034, Washington & Jackson, Light Olive Amber, 1/2 Pint 190.00
Flask, McK G I-037, Washington & Taylor & Dyottville, Light Blue, Quart 325.00
Flask, McK G I-037, Washington & Taylor, Aqua, Quart 50.00

Flask, McK G I-037, Washington & Taylor, Deep Pontil, Aqua, Quart 390.00
Flask, McK G I-037, Washington & Taylor, Doyttsville, Clear, Quart 65.00
Flask, McK G I-037, Washington & Taylor, Golden Yellow, Quart 475.00
Flask, McK G I-037, Washington & Taylor, Open Pontil, Aqua, Large 45.00
Flask, McK G I-037, Washington & Taylor, Yellow, Stain, Quart .... *Illus* 475.00
Flask, McK G I-038, Washington & Taylor, Amethyst, Pint .... *Illus* 1425.00
Flask, McK G I-038, Washington & Taylor, Aqua, Pint .... 65.00 To 70.00
Flask, McK G I-038, Washington & Taylor, Light Aqua, Pint 39.00

Flask, McK G I-113, Kossuth
& Tree In Leaf, Calabash, Quart

Flask, McK G I-118, Columbia
& Eagle, Yellow Green, 1/2 Pint

(See Page 79)

Flask, McK G II-007, Eagle
& Sunburst, Clear, Pint

Flask, McK G II-009, Eagle
& Serpent Of Corruption, Pint

Flask, McK G II-011, Eagle
& Cornucopia, Aqua, 1/2 Pint

Flask, McK G II-011, Eagle
& Cornucopia, Clear, 1/2 Pint

Flask, McK G I-038, Washington & Taylor, Olive Amber, Pint .... *Illus* 375.00
Flask, McK G I-039, Washington & Taylor, Base Stain, Quart .... *Illus* 400.00
Flask, McK G I-039, Washington & Taylor, Blue Green, Quart 275.00
Flask, McK G I-039, Washington & Taylor, Light Yellow Green, Quart 125.00
Flask, McK G I-040, Washington & Taylor, Sapphire Blue, Pint 220.00
Flask, McK G I-041, Washington & Taylor, Aqua 100.00
Flask, McK G I-041, Washington & Taylor, Aqua, 1/2 Pint 65.00
Flask, McK G I-042, Washington & Taylor, Aqua, Quart 70.00
Flask, McK G I-043, Washington & Taylor, Aqua, Quart 80.00
Flask, McK G I-043, Washington & Taylor, Lime Green 95.00

Flask, McK G I-044, Washington & Taylor, Yellow, Stain, Pint ....*Illus* 625.00
Flask, McK G I-045, Washington & Taylor, Light Yellow Green, Quart 90.00
Flask, McK G I-047, Washington, Blue Green, Quart 350.00
Flask, McK G I-047, Washington, Open Pontil, Medium Green 150.00
Flask, McK G I-048, Washington, Clear Blue Green, Pint 350.00
Flask, McK G I-048, Washington, Light Green, Pint 600.00
Flask, McK G I-051, Washington & Taylor, Pale Yellow Green, Quart 90.00
Flask, McK G I-051, Washington, Taylor, Iron Pontil, Pale Green, Quart 105.00
Flask, McK G I-054, Washington & Taylor, Aqua, Quart 80.00
Flask, McK G I-054, Washington & Taylor, Emerald Green, Open Pontil 300.00

Flask, McK G II-012, W.C. Eagle
& Cornucopia, Olive, 1/2 Pt.

Flask, McK G II-021, For Pike's
Peak & Eagle, Green, Pint

(See Page 80)

Flask, McK G II-011, Eagle
& Cornucopia, Green, 1/2 Pint

Flask, McK G II-013,
Eagle & Cornucopia,
Aqua, 1/2 Pint

Flask, McK G I-054, Washington & Taylor, Yellow Green, Quart ....*Illus* 400.00
Flask, McK G I-057, Washington & Sheaf Of Rye, Aqua, Quart 60.00
Flask, McK G I-058, Sloping Collar, Open Pontil, Aqua, Pint .... 60.00 To 85.00
Flask, McK G I-059, Washington & Sheaf Of Wheat, 1/2 Pint 74.00
Flask, McK G I-059, Washington & Sheaf, Aqua, 1/2 Pint .... 55.00 To 95.00
Flask, McK G I-059, Washington, Sheaf, Aqua, Amber Striations, 1/2 Pint 78.00
Flask, McK G I-060, Washington & Taylor, Ice Blue, Quart ....*Illus* 1850.00
Flask, McK G I-068, Jackson & Floral Medallion, Aqua, Pint 600.00
Flask, McK G I-071, Taylor & Ringgold, Blue Green, Pint 800.00
Flask, McK G I-073, Gen'l Taylor & Baltimore Monument, Pint ....*Illus* 2100.00
Flask, McK G I-074, Taylor & Corn For The World, Aqua, Pint 550.00
Flask, McK G I-074, Taylor & Cornstalk, Amethyst, Pint 1000.00
Flask, McK G I-074, Zachary Taylor & Cornstalk, Aqua, Pint ....*Illus* 650.00
Flask, McK G I-080, Clinton Collar, Olive Green 300.00
Flask, McK G I-080, Lafayette & DeWitt Clinton, Green, Pint ....*Illus* 400.00
Flask, McK G I-080, Lafayette & DeWitt Clinton, Light Olive Amber 725.00
Flask, McK G I-080, Lafayette & DeWitt Clinton, Olive Amber, Pint 250.00
Flask, McK G I-080, Lafayette, Clinton, OP, Olive, Pint .... 500.00 To 700.00
Flask, McK G I-081, Lafayette & DeWitt Clinton, 1/2 Pint ....*Illus* 475.00
Flask, McK G I-084, Lafayette & Masonic, Amber, 1/2 Pint ....*Illus* 3750.00
Flask, McK G I-085, Lafayette & Liberty Cap, Amber, Pint ....*Illus* 575.00
Flask, McK G I-086, Lafayette & Liberty Cap, Amber, 1/2 Pint ....*Illus* 375.00
Flask, McK G I-086, Lafayette & Liberty, Olive Amber, 1/2 Pt. .... 240.00 To 525.00
Flask, McK G I-086, Layfayette, Open Pontil, Amber 550.00
Flask, McK G I-087, Lafayette & Liberty Cap, Amber, 1/2 Pint ....*Illus* 4100.00
Flask, McK G I-089, Lafayette & Masonic, Amber, 1/2 Pint ....*Illus* 2150.00

Flask, McK G I-089, Lafayette & Masonic, Green, 1/2 Pint .... *Illus* 400.00
Flask, McK G I-090, Lafayette & Eagle, Aqua, Pint 100.00
Flask, McK G I-094, Franklin & Dyott, Aqua, Pint .... 130.00 To 310.00
Flask, McK G I-097, Double Franklin, Aqua, Quart .... 260.00 To 275.00
Flask, McK G I-099, Calabash, Jenny Lind & Huffsey, Aqua, Quart 50.00
Flask, McK G I-099, Calabash, Jenny Lind & Huffsey, Quart .... *Illus* 925.00
Flask, McK G I-099, Calabash, Jenny Lind, Aqua, Quart 80.00
Flask, McK G I-099, Calabash, Jenny Lind, Teal Green 350.00
Flask, McK G I-099, Jenny Lind, Light Yellow Green, Quart 150.00
Flask, McK G I-100, Jenny Lind & Kossuth, Calabash, Open Pontil, Aqua 190.00

Flask, McK G II-058, Eagle
& Cornucopia, Olive, 1/2 Pint

Flask, McK G II-068,
New London Glass,
Anchor & Eagle, Pint

Flask, McK G II-069, Eagle
& Cornucopia, Aqua, 1/2 Pint

(See Page 80)

Flask, McK G II-075, Eagle
& Cornucopia, Amber, Pint

Flask, McK G I-101, Calabash, Jenny Lind & Millfora, Aqua, Quart 90.00
Flask, McK G I-102, Jenny Lind, Blue Green, Quart 575.00
Flask, McK G I-104, Jenny Lind & Factory, Sapphire, Quart .... *Illus* 1700.00
Flask, McK G I-104, Jenny Lind, Calabash, Ravenna, Iron Pontil, Deep Aqua 100.00
Flask, McK G I-105, Jenny Lind, Stain, Aqua, Quart .... *Illus* 250.00
Flask, McK G I-107, Jenny Lind, Reproduction, Clear 10.00
Flask, McK G I-108, Jenny Lind & Lyre, Aqua, Pint .... *Illus* 1125.00
Flask, McK G I-109, Double Jenny Lind & Lyre, Violin, Aqua 1450.00
Flask, McK G I-112, Kossuth, Mississippi, Calabash, Aqua, Quart 190.00
Flask, McK G I-113, Kossuth & Tree In Leaf, Calabash, Quart .... *Illus* 625.00
Flask, McK G I-113, Kossuth & Tree, Calabash, Aqua 105.00
Flask, McK G I-113, Kossuth & Tree, Calabash, Light Olive Yellow, Quart 625.00
Flask, McK G I-114, Byron & Scott, Golden Amber, 1/2 Pint 140.00
Flask, McK G I-114, Byron & Scott, Light Olive Amber, 1/2 Pint 140.00
Flask, McK G I-114, Byron & Scott, Olive Amber, 1/2 Pint .... 130.00 To 190.00
Flask, McK G I-114, Byron & Scott, Open Pontil, Yellow Amber, 1/2 Pint 185.00
Flask, McK G I-114, Byron, Scott, Light Amber, 1/2 Pint 160.00
Flask, McK G I-117, Columbia & Eagle, Aqua, Pint 875.00
Flask, McK G I-118, Columbia & Eagle, Yellow Green, 1/2 Pint .... *Illus* 3400.00
Flask, McK G I-121, Columbia & Eagle, Aqua .... 325.00 To 365.00
Flask, McK G II-002, Double Eagle, Aqua, Pint 50.00
Flask, McK G II-007, Eagle & Sunburst, Clear, Pint .... *Illus* 300.00
Flask, McK G II-007, Eagle With Ribbons, Calabash, Soda Green 95.00
Flask, McK G II-009, Eagle & Serpent Of Corruption, Pint .... *Illus* 5250.00
Flask, McK G II-011, Eagle & Cornucopia, Aqua, 1/2 Pint .... *Illus* 160.00
Flask, McK G II-011, Eagle & Cornucopia, Clear, 1/2 Pint .... *Illus* 825.00

Flask, McK G II-011, Eagle & Cornucopia, Green, 1/2 Pint ....*Illus* 2900.00
Flask, McK G II-012, Eagle & Cornucopia, Aqua, 1/2 Pint 800.00
Flask, McK G II-012, W.C.Eagle & Cornucopia, Olive, 1/2 Pt. ....*Illus* 6900.00
Flask, McK G II-013, Eagle & Cornucopia, Aqua, 1/2 Pint ....*Illus* 2200.00
Flask, McK G II-016, Eagle & Cornucopia, Aqua, 1/2 Pint 250.00
Flask, McK G II-017, Cornucopia & Urn, Open Pontil, Aqua 100.00
Flask, McK G II-021, For Pike's Peak & Eagle, Green, Pint ....*Illus* 410.00
Flask, McK G II-022, Eagle & Lyre, Aqua, Pint 800.00
Flask, McK G II-024, Aqua 130.00
Flask, McK G II-024, Double Eagle, Bright Yellow Green, Pint 500.00
Flask, McK G II-024, Louisville Double Eagle, Aqua, Pint 150.00
Flask, McK G II-026, Double Eagle, Aqua, Quart .... 145.00 To 285.00
Flask, McK G II-031, Lafayette & Eagle, Ice Blue, Quart 190.00
Flask, McK G II-033, Louisville Glass Works 143.50
Flask, McK G II-036, Chestnut, 24 Vertical Rib, Amber, 1/2 Pint 300.00
Flask, McK G II-036, Eagle & Banner & Louisville, Ribbed, Aqua, Pint 155.00
Flask, McK G II-037, Eagle & Ravenna & Anchor, Ice Blue, Pint 325.00
Flask, McK G II-041, Eagle Above Panel & Tree, Aqua, Pint .... 125.00 To 140.00
Flask, McK G II-042, Eagle & Franklin & Frigate, Aqua, Pint .... 100.00 To 130.00
Flask, McK G II-044, Eagle & Cornucopia, Aqua, 1/2 Pint 210.00
Flask, McK G II-048, Eagle, Flag, Quart 175.00
Flask, McK G II-049, Eagle & Stag, Aqua, Pint 400.00
Flask, McK G II-050, Eagle & Coffin, Aqua, 1/2 Pint 375.00
Flask, McK G II-052, Aqua, Pint 60.00
Flask, McK G II-053, Eable & Flag, For Our Country, Aqua, Pint 145.00
Flask, McK G II-053, Eagle & Flag, Aqua, Pint .... 110.00 To 140.00
Flask, McK G II-054, Eagle & Flag, For Our Country, Aqua, Pint 125.00
Flask, McK G II-055, Bunch Of Grapes & Eagle, Aqua, Quart .... 100.00 To 150.00
Flask, McK G II-055, Byron, Scott, Amber, 1/2 Pint 175.00
Flask, McK G II-056, Eagle & Grapes, Aqua, 1/2 Pint 200.00
Flask, McK G II-058, Eagle & Cornucopia, Olive, 1/2 Pint ....*Illus* 2750.00
Flask, McK G II-060, Eagle & Eagle & Oak Tree, Yellow Green, 1/2 Pint 1900.00
Flask, McK G II-060, Eagle & Oak Tree, Aqua, 1/2 Pint 425.00
Flask, McK G II-060, Eagle & Oak Tree, Green, 1/2 Pint 1900.00
Flask, McK G II-061, Eagle & Wreath, Amber, Quart 100.00
Flask, McK G II-061, Eagle & Wreath, Olive Amber .... 80.00 To 110.00
Flask, McK G II-061, Eagle & Wreath, Olive Green 155.00
Flask, McK G II-062, Eagle & Willington Glass Co., Olive Amber, Pint 60.00
Flask, McK G II-063, Eagle & Willington Glass, Olive Green, 1/2 Pint 70.00
Flask, McK G II-063, Eagle & Willington, Olive Amber, 1/2 Pint 100.00
Flask, McK G II-064, Eagle & Willington Glass Co., Bright Green, Pint 80.00
Flask, McK G II-064, Eagle & Willington Glass Co., Olive Amber, Pint 85.00
Flask, McK G II-064, Willington & Eagle, Olive Green, Pint 90.00
Flask, McK G II-065, Eagle & Westford Glass, Amber, 1/2 Pint 130.00
Flask, McK G II-065, Eagle & Westford Glass Co., Olive Amber, 1/2 Pint 70.00
Flask, McK G II-065, Eagle & Westford, Amber, 1/2 Pint 85.00
Flask, McK G II-065, Eagle & Westford, Dark Golden Amber, 1/2 Pint 125.00
Flask, McK G II-066, Eagle & General Jackson, Pontil, Aqua, Pint 500.00
Flask, McK G II-067, Eagle, New London & Anchor, Blue-Green, 1/2 Pint 175.00
Flask, McK G II-067, Eagle, New London & Anchor, Yellow Green, 1/2 Pint 325.00
Flask, McK G II-067, Eagle, New London, Light Blue Green, 1/2 Pint 225.00
Flask, McK G II-068, New London Glass Works, Golden Amber, Pint 520.00
Flask, McK G II-068, New London Glass, Anchor & Eagle, Pint ....*Illus* 400.00
Flask, McK G II-069, Eagle & Cornucopia, Aqua, 1/2 Pint ....*Illus* 1225.00
Flask, McK G II-071, Double Eagle, Olive Amber, 1/2 Pint .... 80.00 To 110.00
Flask, McK G II-071, Eagle On Panel, Pontil, Olive Green, 1/2 Pint 190.00
Flask, McK G II-072, Double Eagle, Olive Amber, 1/2 Pint 90.00
Flask, McK G II-073, Cornucopia & Urn, Aqua, Bubbles 198.50
Flask, McK G II-073, Eagle & Cornucopia, Honey Amber, Pint 135.00
Flask, McK G II-073, Eagle & Cornucopia, Olive Amber, Pt. .... 50.00 To 105.00
Flask, McK G II-074, Eagle & Cornucopia, Aqua, Pint .... 50.00 To 60.00
Flask, McK G II-074, Golden Amber, Pint 75.00
Flask, McK G II-075, Eagle & Cornucopia, Amber, Pint ....*Illus* 2300.00
Flask, McK G II-076, Concentric Ring & Eagle, Green, Pint ....*Illus* 4000.00
Flask, McK G II-126, Double Eagle, Rose Amethyst 600.00
Flask, McK G III-001, Cornucopia & Star, Green, 1/2 Pint ....*Illus* 3050.00

Flask, McK G III-002, Cornucopia & Star, Light Blue Green, 1/2 Pint 3050.00
Flask, McK G III-002, Cornucopia, Aqua 110.00
Flask, McK G III-004, Deep Olive Green 75.00
Flask, McK G III-004, Masonic & S.K.B., Clear, Pint .... Illus 1500.00
Flask, McK G III-007, Cornucopia & Urn, Olive Amber, 1/2 Pint 57.00
Flask, McK G III-007, Cornucopia, Yellow Green, 1/2 Pint 75.00
Flask, McK G III-013, Cornucopia & Urn, Deep Olive, 1/2 Pint 350.00
Flask, McK G III-015, Cornucopia Urn, Rolled Lip, Teal 135.00
Flask, McK G III-015, Yellow Green 400.00
Flask, McK G III-017, Cornucopia & Urn, Deep Blue Green 225.00
Flask, McK G III-017, Cornucopia, Urn, Blue Green, Seed Bubbles 195.00
Flask, McK G IV-001, Double Success To The Railroad, Italian Green 275.00
Flask, McK G IV-001, Masonic & Eagle, Light Blue Green, Pt. .... 200.00 To 230.00
Flask, McK G IV-001, Masonic, Eagle, Green, Pint 325.00
Flask, McK G IV-005, Masonic & Eagle, Yellow Green, Pint 250.00
Flask, McK G IV-005, Railroad, Dark Green, Pint 175.00
Flask, McK G IV-009, Masonic & Eagle, Yellow Green, Pint 700.00
Flask, McK G IV-009, Railroad, Eagle & Cart, Amber, Pint 165.00
Flask, McK G IV-014, Masonic & Eagle, Green, 1/2 Pint .... Illus 375.00
Flask, McK G IV-014, Masonic Eagle, Inside Stain, Yellow Green 575.00
Flask, McK G IV-015, Masonic & Eagle, Greenish Cast, Pint .... Illus 8000.00
Flask, McK G IV-016, Masonic & Eagle, Deep Olive Amber, Pint 3600.00
Flask, McK G IV-016, Masonic & Eagle, Olive Amber, Pint .... Illus 3600.00
Flask, McK G IV-017, Masonic & Eagle & Keene, Olive Amber, Pint 175.00
Flask, McK G IV-018, Eagle & Masonic, Olive Amber, Pint 110.00
Flask, McK G IV-018, Italian Amber, Pint 150.00
Flask, McK G IV-018, Masonic & Eagle, Light Olive Amber 140.00
Flask, McK G IV-019, Masonic & Eagle, Dark Olive Amber, Pint 120.00
Flask, McK G IV-019, Masonic & Eagle, Olive Amber, Pint 120.00
Flask, McK G IV-020, Masonic & Eagle, Olive Amber, Pint .... 100.00 To 155.00
Flask, McK G IV-024, Masonic & Eagle, Olive Amber, 1/2 Pint .... 140.00 To 180.00
Flask, McK G IV-024, Olive Green 150.00
Flask, McK G IV-027, Masonic & Eagle, Aqua, Pint 375.00
Flask, McK G IV-028, Double Masonic, Green, 1/2 Pint .... Illus 1250.00
Flask, McK G IV-028, Light Emerald Green 335.00
Flask, McK G IV-028, Masonic & Arch, Green Aqua, 1/2 Pint 400.00
Flask, McK G IV-028, Masonic, Embossed, Open Pontil, Green, Pint 450.00
Flask, McK G IV-028, Masonic, Pimple Head, Clear Green, 1/2 Pint 440.00
Flask, McK G IV-029, Hourglass Masonic, Yellow, 1/2 Pint .... Illus 7000.00
Flask, McK G IV-032, Masonic & Eagle, Ice Blue, Pint 350.00
Flask, McK G IV-032, Masonic, Zanesville, Deep Aqua 325.00
Flask, McK G IV-032, Yellow 650.00
Flask, McK G IV-034, Masonic, Franklin, Kensington, Aqua, Pt. .... 145.00 To 250.00
Flask, McK G IV-039, Aqua, Pint 55.00
Flask, McK G IV-042, Union Clasped Hands, Calabash, Aqua 55.00
Flask, McK G V-001, Success To The Railroad, Aqua, Pint 300.00
Flask, McK G V-003, Success To The Railroad, Golden Amber, Pint 180.00
Flask, McK G V-003, Success To The Railroad, Honey Colored, Pint 158.50
Flask, McK G V-003, Success To The Railroad, Olive Amber, Pint 110.00
Flask, McK G V-003, Success To The Railroad, Olive Green, Pint 160.00
Flask, McK G V-004, Double Railroad, Olive Green, Pint 150.00
Flask, McK G V-005, Double Railroad, Emerald, Moss Green 295.00
Flask, McK G V-005, Double Success To The Railroad, Olive Green, Pint 260.00
Flask, McK G V-005, Double Success To The Railroad, Yellow Olive, Pint 160.00
Flask, McK G V-005, Success To The Railroad, Aqua, Pint 400.00
Flask, McK G V-005, Success To The Railroad, Olive Amber, Pint 120.00
Flask, McK G V-006, Success To The Railroad, Olive Amber, Pint 110.00
Flask, McK G V-008, Success To The Railroad, Olive Amber, Pint 80.00
Flask, McK G V-009, Cart, Eagle, Yellow Amber, Green Tint 140.00
Flask, McK G V-009, Railroad, Olive Amber 150.00
Flask, McK G V-010, Lowell Railroad, Olive Green, Clear, 1/2 Pint 185.00
Flask, McK G V-014, Corn For The World, Amber 450.00
Flask, McK G V-020, Lowell Railroad & Eagle, Olive Amber, 1/2 Pint 160.00
Flask, McK G V-054, Washington & Taylor, Yellow Green, Quart 275.00
Flask, McK G V-101, Lowell Railroad & Eagle, Olive Amber, 1/2 Pint 75.00
Flask, McK G VI-002, Baltimore & Sloop, Green, 1/2 Pint .... Illus 650.00

Flask, McK G VI-002, Baltimore Monument & Sloop, Yellow Green, 1/2 Pint 650.00
Flask, McK G VI-003, Baltimore & Liberty & Union, Aqua, Pint 425.00
Flask, McK G VI-003, Baltimore & Liberty, Brilliant Yellow Olive, Pint 3600.00
Flask, McK G VI-003, Baltimore Monument & Liberty, Pint .... *Illus* 3600.00
Flask, McK G VI-004, Baltimore & Corn For The World, Amber, Quart 375.00
Flask, McK G VI-004, Baltimore & Corn For The World, Deep Aqua, Quart 175.00

Flask, McK G II-076, Concentric
Ring & Eagle, Green, Pint

(See Page 80)

Flask, McK G III-004,
Masonic & S.K.B., Clear, Pint

(See Page 81)

Flask, McK G III-001, Cornucopia
& Star, Green, 1/2 Pint
(See Page 80)

Flask, McK G IV-015, Masonic
& Eagle, Greenish Cast, Pint

(See Page 81)

(See Page 81)

Flask, McK G IV-014, Masonic
& Eagle, Green, 1/2 Pint

Flask, McK G IV-016, Masonic
& Eagle, Olive Amber, Pint

Flask, McK G VI-004, Baltimore Monument & Corn, Golden Yellow, Quart 400.00
Flask, McK G VI-004, Corn For The World & Baltimore, Olive Amber, Quart 275.00
Flask, McK G VI-004, Corn For The World, Baltimore, Quart .... *Illus* 400.00
Flask, McK G VI-004, Corn For The World, Deep Aqua, Quart 170.00
Flask, McK G VI-006, Corn For The World & Baltimore, Aqua, Pint 325.00
Flask, McK G VII-003, Sunburst, Olive Amber, Pint 325.00
Flask, McK G VII-009, Sunburst, Blue Green, 1/2 Pint 330.00
Flask, McK G VIII-002, Keene Sunburst, Open Pontil, Light Green 490.00
Flask, McK G VIII-002, Sunburst, Bright Yellow Green, Pint 85.00
Flask, McK G VIII-005, Sunburst, Olive Amber, Pint 475.00
Flask, McK G VIII-009, Sunburst, Keene, Olive Amber, 1/2 Pt. .... 225.00 To 250.00
Flask, McK G VIII-010, Sunburst, Olive Amber, 1/2 Pint 395.00

Flask, McK G VIII-016, Sunburst & Coventry, Olive Green, 1/2 Pint 325.00
Flask, McK G VIII-016, Sunburst, Medium Olive Amber, 1/2 Pint 329.00
Flask, McK G VIII-016, Sunburst, Olive Amber, 1/2 Pint .... 300.00 To 325.00
Flask, McK G VIII-016, Sunburst, Olive Green, 1/2 Pint 390.00
Flask, McK G VIII-018, Olive Green 325.00
Flask, McK G VIII-018, Sunburst, Olive Amber, 1/2 Pint .... 275.00 To 350.00

Flask, McK G IV-028, Double
Masonic, Green, 1/2 Pint

Flask, McK G VI-002, Baltimore
& Sloop, Green, 1/2 Pint

Flask, McK G IV-029, Hourglass
Masonic, Yellow, 1/2 Pint

(See Page 81)

Flask, McK G VI-004, Corn For
The World, Balitmore, Quart

Flask, McK G VI-003, Balitmore
Monument & Liberty, Pint

Flask, McK G VIII-023,
Sunburst, Apricot, Pint

Flask, McK G VIII-020, Sunburst, Aqua, Pint 325.00
Flask, McK G VIII-020, Sunburst, Deep Golden Amber, Pint 175.00
Flask, McK G VIII-021, Sunburst, Aqua, Pint 325.00
Flask, McK G VIII-016, Sunburst, Olive Green, 1/2 Pint 390.00
Flask, McK G VIII-023, Sunburst, Apricot, Pint .... *Illus* 1800.00
Flask, McK G VIII-026, Sunburst, Clear, Pint 300.00
Flask, McK G VIII-027, Sunburst, Aqua, 1/2 Pint 225.00
Flask, McK G VIII-028, Sunburst, Clear, 1/2 Pint 325.00
Flask, McK G IX-001, Scroll, Golden Amber, Pint 380.00
Flask, McK G IX-002, Scroll, Deep Sapphire Blue, Quart 2300.00
Flask, McK G IX-002, Scroll, Double Star, Open Pontil, Quart 50.00
Flask, McK G IX-002, Scroll, Green, Mouth Roughness, Quart .... *Illus* 550.00

Flask, McK G IX-002, Scroll, Iron Pontil, Aqua, Pint 45.00
Flask, McK G IX-003, Scroll, Aqua, Quart 65.00
Flask, McK G IX-007, Scroll & Louisville Glass, Aqua, Quart 200.00
Flask, McK G IX-008, Scroll, Louisville, Ky., Glass Works, Aqua, Pint 110.00
Flask, McK G IX-010, Double 8 Pointed Stars, Pontil, Ice Blue, 1/2 Pint 1600.00
Flask, McK G IX-010, Scroll, Amber 425.00
Flask, McK G IX-010, Scroll, Aqua, Pint .... 56.00 To 65.00
Flask, McK G IX-010, Scroll, Blue, Mouth Roughness, Pint .... Illus 850.00
Flask, McK G IX-010, Scroll, Deep Yellow Green, Pint 550.00

Flask, McK G IX-010, Scroll,
Blue, Mouth Roughness, Pint

Flask, McK G IX-002, Scroll,
Green, Mouth Roughness, Quart
(See Page 83)

Flask, McK G IX-011, Scroll,
Blue Green, Pint

Flask, McK G IX-011, Scroll,
Golden Amber, Pint

Flask, McK G IX-029, Scroll,
Stain, Aqua, 2 1/2 Quarts

Flask, McK G IX-010, Scroll, Olive Yellow, Pint 450.00
Flask, McK G IX-011, Scroll, Aqua, Pint 49.50
Flask, McK G IX-011, Scroll, Blue Green, Pint .... Illus 900.00
Flask, McK G IX-011, Scroll, Deep Aqua, Pint 65.00
Flask, McK G IX-011, Scroll, Deep Golden Amber, Pint .... 380.00 To 390.00
Flask, McK G IX-011, Scroll, Golden Amber 375.00
Flask, McK G IX-011, Scroll, Golden Amber, Pint .... Illus 380.00
Flask, McK G IX-011A, Scroll, Brilliant Citron, Pint 425.00
Flask, McK G IX-011A, Scroll, Deep Golden Amber, Pint 325.00
Flask, McK G IX-012, Scroll, Dark Yellow Olive, Pint 350.00
Flask, McK G IX-014, Scroll, Ice Blue, Pint 50.00
Flask, McK G IX-014, Scroll, Sapphire Blue, Pint 140.00
Flask, McK G IX-025, Scroll, Aqua, Pint 175.00
Flask, McK G IX-029, Scroll, Stain, Aqua, 2 1/2 Quarts .... Illus 275.00

Flask, McK G IX-029, Sunburst, Light Blue Green, 1/2 Pint 170.00
Flask, McK G IX-031, Scroll, Deep Green Aqua, 1/2 Pint .... 55.00 To 85.00
Flask, McK G IX-033, Scroll, Open Pontil, Aqua, 1/2 Pint 75.00
Flask, McK G IX-034, Scroll, Bright Yellow Green, 1/2 Pint .... *Illus* 550.00
Flask, McK G IX-034, Scroll, Deep Burgundy, 1/2 Pint .... *Illus* 1000.00
Flask, McK G IX-036, Scroll, Aqua, 1/2 Pint 75.00
Flask, McK G IX-037, Scroll, Double Star, Yellow Green, 1/2 Pint 325.00
Flask, McK G IX-038, B P & B Scroll, Aqua, 1/2 Pint 225.00
Flask, McK G IX-039, Cornflower Blue 75.00
Flask, McK G IX-048, M'Carty & Torreyson, Sunburst, Pint .... *Illus* 1350.00
Flask, McK G X-003, Sheaf Of Wheat & Grapes, Aqua, 1/2 Pint .... 160.00 To 180.00

Flask, McK G IX-034, Scroll,
Bright Yellow Green, 1/2 Pint

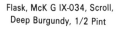

Flask, McK G IX-034, Scroll,
Deep Burgundy, 1/2 Pint

Flask, McK G IX-048, M'Carty
& Torreyson, Sunburst, Pint

Flask, McK G X-006, Cannon &
Captain Bragg, Apricot, 1/2 Pint

Flask, McK G X-015, Summer
& Winter, Yellow Green, Pint

Flask, McK G X-006, Cannon & Captain Bragg, Apricot, 1/2 Pint .... *Illus* 1600.00
Flask, McK G X-008, Sail Boat & Sunflower, Aqua, 1/2 Pint 125.00
Flask, McK G X-008, Sailboat & Sunflower, Aqua, 1/2 Pint 125.00
Flask, McK G X-008, Sloop & Star, Aqua, 1/2 Pint .... 90.00 To 145.00
Flask, McK G X-008, Sloop & Star, Light Yellow Green, 1/2 Pint 350.00
Flask, McK G X-008, Sloop & Star, Pontil, Aqua, Pint 125.00
Flask, McK G X-015, Summer & Winter, Aqua, Pint .... 30.00 To 40.00
Flask, McK G X-015, Summer & Winter, Double Collar, OP, Green Mint, Pint 250.00
Flask, McK G X-015, Summer & Winter, Yellow Green, Pint .... *Illus* 225.00
Flask, McK G X-015, Summer, Winter, Embossed, Aqua 55.00
Flask, McK G X-018, Collared Mouth, Extruded Pontil, Light Green, Quart 350.00
Flask, McK G X-018, Open Pontil, Teal 200.00

Flask, McK G X-018, Tree In Leaf, Light Yellow Green, Quart 250.00
Flask, McK G X-027, Stoddard & Flag, Olive Amber, Pint .... *Illus* 2400.00
Flask, McK G X-030, The Great Western & Female & Stag, Aqua, Pint 400.00
Flask, McK G XII-029, Union, Clasped Hands, Yellow Green, 1/2 Pint 150.00
Flask, McK G XIII-054, Resurgam, Aqua, Pint 75.00
Flask, McK G XIV-6, Traveler's Companion, Lockport, Pint .... *Illus* 1500.00
Flask, Merry Christmas, Birds, Label, Colorful 110.00
Flask, Merry Xmas & Happy New Year, Pumpkinseed 10.00
Flask, Miller's Extra Old Bourbon, Single Rolled Collar, Green Amber 125.00

Flask, McK G X-027, Stoddard
& Flag, Olive Amber, Pint

Flask, Pike's Peak, Eagle, Prospector
To Right Below, Amber, Pt.

Flask, Pitkin Type,
Ribs Swirled To Right,
Olive Yellow, Pint

Flask, Pitkin Type, Ribs Swirled
To Right, Yellow Green, 5 In.

Flask, Pitkin Type, 26 Ribs Swirled
To Right, Amber, 1/2 Pint

Flask, Moore & Alexander, Fort Smith, Ark., 1/2 Pint 35.00
Flask, Moore's Revealed Remedy, M.R.R., Inside Union Shield, Amber, Pint 35.00
Flask, Morris Fink, Wines & Liquors, St.Paul, Minn., Coffin 30.00
Flask, Mounted Soldier & Hound, Citron, Quart 375.00
Flask, Musician & Dancer, Aqua, Pint 100.00
Flask, Nailsea Type, Multicolored, Pint 60.00
Flask, Nailsea Type, White Loops, Open Pontil, Clear, Pint .... 38.00 To 50.00
Flask, Old Rey, A. & D.H.C., Pittsburgh, Medium Citron 225.00
Flask, Oval, Embossed Star In Circle, Ice Blue 15.00
Flask, P.Wiedman, Claremont, Va., Clear, Pint 15.00
Flask, Paul Jones, Label, Amber, 1/2 Pint 10.00
Flask, Phoenix Saloon, Natchitoches, La., Clear, Pint 50.00
Flask, Picnic, Dark Aqua 12.00
Flask, Picnic, Label, Cork Type 15.00

Flask, Picnic, 5 Pointed Star, Clear, 3 1/2 In. 4.50
Flask, Picnic, 6 1/2 In. 24.00
Flask, Pike's Peak, Eagle, Old Rye, Pittsburgh, Aqua, Pint 50.00
Flask, Pike's Peak, Eagle, Prospector To Right Below, Amber, Pt. .... *Illus* 600.00
Flask, Pike's Peak, Pittsburgh Old Rye, Aqua, 1/2 Pint 40.00
Flask, Pike's Peak, Prospector Shooting Deer, Aqua, Pint 70.00
Flask, Pike's Peak, Prospector, Hunter & Deer, Amber, Pint 495.00
Flask, Pitkin Type, Olive Green, 1 1/2 X 2 5/8 In. 275.00
Flask, Pitkin Type, Ribs Swirled To Left, Light Olive Amber, Pint 120.00
Flask, Pitkin Type, Ribs Swirled To Left, Light Olive Amber, 1/2 Pint 110.00
Flask, Pitkin Type, Ribs Swirled To Left, Olive Amber, Pint .... 110.00 To 150.00

Flask, McK G XIV-6, Traveler's
Companion, Lockport, Pint

Flask, Scroll, Dark Olive Green,
Mouth Flakes, Pint
(See Page 88)

Flask, Scroll, Yellow Green,
Large Medial Rib Bubble, Pint
(See Page 88)

Flask, Pitkin Type, Ribs Swirled To Left, Olive Yellow, Pint 150.00
Flask, Pitkin Type, Ribs Swirled To Right, Deep Golden Amber, Pint 225.00
Flask, Pitkin Type, Ribs Swirled To Right, Deep Yellow Green, Pint 170.00
Flask, Pitkin Type, Ribs Swirled To Right, Light Olive Amber, 1/2 Pint 125.00
Flask, Pitkin Type, Ribs Swirled To Right, Light Yellow Green, Pint 130.00
Flask, Pitkin Type, Ribs Swirled To Right, Light Yellow Olive, 1/2 Pint 110.00
Flask, Pitkin Type, Ribs Swirled To Right, Olive Amber, 1 7/8 X 2 In. 190.00
Flask, Pitkin Type, Ribs Swirled To Right, Olive Green, Pint 150.00
Flask, Pitkin Type, Ribs Swirled To Right, Olive Yellow, Pint .... *Illus* 220.00
Flask, Pitkin Type, Ribs Swirled To Right, Pale Green, Pint 110.00
Flask, Pitkin Type, Ribs Swirled To Right, Pale Yellow Green, Pint 160.00
Flask, Pitkin Type, Ribs Swirled To Right, Pale Yellow Green, 1/2 Pint 270.00
Flask, Pitkin Type, Ribs Swirled To Right, Yellow Green, 5 In. .... *Illus* 285.00
Flask, Pitkin Type, Sunburst, Double Post, Swirled Right, Green, 7 In. 325.00
Flask, Pitkin Type, Vertical Ribs, Yellow Olive, Pint 210.00
Flask, Pitkin Type, 26 Ribs Swirled To Right, Amber, 1/2 Pint .... *Illus* 725.00
Flask, Pitkin, Miniature Chestnut, Swirl Left, Pontil, Olive Amber 500.00
Flask, Pitkin, Vertical & Swirled Ribbing, Forest Green, 1/2 Pint 75.00
Flask, Pocket, Americus Club Whiskey, Honey Amber 8.00

Flask, Quaker Maid, Dark Amber, 1/2 Pint	8.00
Flask, Ravenna Glass Co. & Traveler's Companion ....*Color*	xxxx.xx
Flask, Resurgam, Baltimore Glass Works, Aqua, Pint	55.00
Flask, Richard Knoll Wholesale Liquors, Portland, Or., Coffin	50.00
Flask, S.C.Dispensary, Jo Jo	10.00
Flask, S.O.Dunbar, Taunton, Mass., Aqua, 8 Sided, 2 1/2 In.	130.00
Flask, Saddle, Persian, Pontil, Green	60.00
Flask, Screw Cap, Ground Top, Amber, Pint	10.00
Flask, Scroll, Aqua, Iron Pontil, Pint	43.50
Flask, Scroll, Aqua, Open Pontil, Quart	43.50
Flask, Scroll, Dark Olive Green, Mouth Flakes, Pint ....*Illus*	400.00
Flask, Scroll, Open Pontil, Aqua, Pint	43.50
Flask, Scroll, Rolled Lip, Iron Pontil, Aqua	65.00
Flask, Scroll, Yellow Green, Large Medial Rib Bubble, Pint ....*Illus*	145.00
Flask, Seeing Eye, Olive Amber, Pint	130.00
Flask, Sheaf Of Rye & Tools, Westford Glass Co., Westford, Conn., Amber	85.00
Flask, Sheaf Of Wheat & Fork & Traveler's Companion, Amber, Quart	110.00
Flask, Sheaf Of Wheat & Fork & Westford Glass Co., Amber, Pint	135.00
Flask, Sheaf Of Wheat & Westford Glass Co., Olive Amber, Pint	70.00
Flask, Sheaf Of Wheat & Westford Glass Co., Olive Amber, 1/2 Pint	70.00
Flask, Sheaf Of Wheat & Westford, Olive Amber, Pint	70.00
Flask, Sheaf Of Wheat & Westford, Olive Amber, 1/2 Pint	50.00
Flask, Sheaf Of Wheat, Fork & Rake & 8 Pointed Star, Olive Amber, Quart	125.00
Flask, Sheaf Of Wheat, Westford Glassworks, 1/2 Pint	75.00
Flask, Sheaf, Rake & Fork Under Vine, Open Pontil, Aqua	49.00
Flask, Sheaf, Star, Calabash, Light Aqua	50.00
Flask, Shoo-Fly, Diamond Quilting, Purple, 5 In.	10.00
Flask, Shoo-Fly, P.U.Benjamine & Co., Natchez, Miss., 1/2 Pint	55.00
Flask, Smithfield Dispensary, Smithfield, N.C., Strap Side, Clear, 1/2 Pint	28.00
Flask, Soldier & Baltimore & Dancer, Golden Amber, Pint	400.00
Flask, South Carolina Dispensary, Embossed Palm Tree, E.P.Jr. & Co.	15.00
Flask, South Caroline Dispensary, Palm Tree, Aqua, 9 In.	75.00
Flask, Spring Garden Glass Works & Cabin & Tree, Aqua, Pint	75.00
Flask, Spring Garden Glass Works, Yellow Amber, Pint	450.00
Flask, Spring Garden Glass Works, Yellow Olive, Pint	350.00
Flask, Spring Garden Glassworks, Yellow, Pint	550.00
Flask, Standard Club Whiskey, Full Label, Clear, 4 1/2 In.	10.00
Flask, Star & Ravenna Glass Co., Aqua With Amber Striation, Pint	170.00
Flask, Stickland's, Amber	38.50
Flask, Stoddard Type, Bubbly, Citron, Quart	19.00
Flask, Stoddard Type, Deep Amber, 1/2 Pint	25.00
Flask, Stoddard Type, Honey Amber, Quart	22.00
Flask, Stoddard Type, Red Amber, Pint	14.00
Flask, Stoddard Type, 1/2 Pint, Honey Amber	10.00
Flask, Stoddard, Amber, Quart	18.00
Flask, Stoddard, Applied Top, Strap Sided, Amber, Pint	8.00
Flask, Stoddard, Bubbly, Amber, Pint	10.00
Flask, Stoddard, Double Eagle, Open Pontil, Yellow Amber, 1/2 Pint	79.50
Flask, Stoddard, Unembossed, Red Amber, 1/2 Pint	17.50
Flask, Strap Sided, Amber, Quart	7.00
Flask, Success To The Railroad, Double, Open Pontil, Olive Green, Pint	235.00
Flask, Success To The Railroad, Open Pontil, Horse Pulling Cart, Green	150.00
Flask, Sunburst Diamond, Clear, Pumpkinseed	5.00
Flask, Texas Whiskey, J.A.Miller, Houston, Texas, Clear	7.00
Flask, Theo.Gier Co., Oakland, Amber, Quart	8.00
Flask, Thixton & Slaughter, Owens, Ky., Clear, Pumpkinseed	53.00
Flask, Try It, Amber	40.00
Flask, Try It, Amber, Pumpkinseed, 4 3/4 In.	37.00
Flask, U.S.Warship Maine, Dated 1898, Screw-On Cap, Round Top, 1/2 Pint	150.00
Flask, Udolpho Wolfe's Schiedam Aromatic Schnapps, Bubbles, Yellow	55.00
Flask, Union Pacific Tea Co., Elephant & Rider, Pumpkinseed	78.00
Flask, Union, Aqua, Pint, 7 3/4 In.	4.00
Flask, Union, Clasped Hands Both Sides, Aqua, Quart	43.50
Flask, Union, Clasped Hands, Aqua, 1/2 Pint	34.50
Flask, Union, Clasped Hands, Eagle & L.F.& Co., Pale Blue, Quart	39.50
Flask, Union, Clasped Hands, Eagle & L.F.& Co., Pittsburgh, Aqua, Quart	55.00

**Cosmetic, White Clover Cream, 5 In.;
Cosmetic, Hind's Honey & Almond Cream,
5½ In.**

**Medicine, Catarrh Cure,
Paper Label, 2½ In.**

**Household, Win-Shine,
Paper Label, 6½ In.**

**Figural, Cyrano De Bergerac,
Ceramic, 11 In.**

Medicine, Lydia Pinkham, Paper Label, 9 In.

Flask, Anchor, Amber, 7½ In.

Whiskey, Old Kentucky Valley, Amber, Paper Label, 11½ In.

Whiskey, Driving Club Rye, Amber, 12 In.

Cologne, Cathedral, Open Pontil,
5¾ In.

Fruit Jar, Petal, Blue, Quart; Fruit Jar, Petal,
Green, Quart

Fruit Jar, Hartell, Black Amethyst,
Quart

Bitters, Dr. Lion's, Amber, Paper Label, 11½ In.

**Medicine, Moore's Revealed
Remedy, Amber, 10 In.**

Ink, Pottery, C. 1850, 2½ In.

**Figural, Spanish Man,
Silveria, 12 In.**

Figural, Man, 9 In.

**Soda, P.D.F., Ferguson's Carbonated Water
(Back And Front), Obliterated Design, Aqua,
Iron Pontil, 7 In.**

Perfume, Red Roses,
Paper Label, 4½ In.

Fruit Jar, Ludlow's Infallible,
Deep Aqua, Pint

Fruit Jar, Leader, Amber,
Quart

Perfume, Watkins' Rose, Box, 5 In.

Whiskey, Meredith's Diamond Club, 8 In.

**Beer, Charles Hobleman (Backward S),
Green, Iron Pontil**

**Bitters, Dr. Loew's Celebrated Stomach
Bitters, Green, 10 In.**

Bitters, Pineapple, Green, 9 In.

**Whiskey, P. Schille, Columbus, Ohio, Blue,
10 In.**

Coca-Cola, 75th Anniversary, 1974, Printed,
7 In.; Coca-Cola, Aqua, Paper Label, 7 In.;
Coca-Cola, Root Reproduction, 1965, 7 In.;
Coca-Cola, Miniature, 2½ In.

Beer, Anheuser-Busch, Quart   Food, Mudry's Horseradish,   Bitters, Hops & Malt, Sample,
                                     Aqua, 6 In.   Amber, 4 In., W-176

Figural, Joan Of Arc, France, 4½ In.

Household, Morgan's Ammonia, Aqua, 8½ In.

Pickle, H. J. Heinz Gherkins, 8 In.

Soda, Hires Raspberry Ade, Aqua, 9½ In.

Flask, Union, Clasped Hands, Eagle & S.A.& Co., Aqua, Pint 25.00
Flask, Union, Clasped Hands, Eagle, Aqua, 1/2 Pint .... 43.00 To 45.00
Flask, Union, Clasped Hands, Eagle, Calabash, Amber, Iron Pontil .... 168.50 To 175.00
Flask, Union, Clasped Hands, Eagle, Red Amber, Pontil 150.00
Flask, Union, Clasped Hands, Frank & Sons, Pittsburgh, Cannon, Aqua, Quart 70.00

Flask, Van R VI-045, Hunter & Fisherman, Calabash, Quart

Flask, Van R VI-116, Sheaf Of
Wheat & Tree In Leaf, Quart

Flask, Van R VI-086, Sheaf Of Wheat,
Calabash, Amber, Quart

Flask, Wooden Boat Inside, 7 In.
(See Page 90)

Flask, Union, Clasped Hands, S.A. & Co., Cannon, Aquamarine, Pint 450.00
Flask, Union, Clasped Hands, Wm.Frank, Pittsburgh, Oval, Aqua, Pint 55.00
Flask, Union, Clasped Hands, 13 Stars, Dove With Ribbon, Ice Blue, 1/2 Pint 165.00
Flask, Union, Clasped Hands, 13 Stars, Eagle With Ribbon, Aqua, Pint 45.00
Flask, Union, Clasped Hands, 13 Stars, Eagle, Amber, 1/2 Pint 82.00
Flask, Union, Eagle & Old Rye & D.H.C., Aqua, Quart 25.00
Flask, Union, Eagle, A. & Co., Aqua, Pint 50.00
Flask, Union, Eagle, Amber, 1/2 Pint 60.00
Flask, Union, Eagle, 11 Stars, Aqua, Pint 55.00
Flask, Urn & Cornucopia, 1/2 Pint 70.00
Flask, Urn & Cornucopia, 7 Ribbed, Open Pontil, Olive Amber, 1/2 Pint 90.00
Flask, Van R VI-045, Hunter & Fisherman, Calabash, Quart ....*Illus* 225.00
Flask, Van R VI-086, Sheaf Of Wheat, Calabash, Amber, Quart ....*Illus* 350.00
Flask, Van R VI-116, Sheaf Of Wheat & Tree In Leaf, Quart ....*Illus* 1000.00
    Flask, Violin, see also Flask, Scroll
Flask, Washington & Taylor, Aqua, Pint 43.50
Flask, Washington & Taylor, Aqua, Quart 53.50
Flask, Washington & Taylor, Open Pontil, Aqua, Pint 75.00
Flask, Washington, Shock Of Grain, Open Pontil, Aqua 70.00
Flask, Westford Glass Co., Conn., Liberty Eagle, Olive Amber, 1/2 Pint 88.50
Flask, Westford Glass Co., Conn., Sheaf Of Wheat, Amber, Pint 98.50
Flask, Westford Glass Co., Conn., Wheat, Fork & Rake, Red Amber 89.50
Flask, Whitney Glass Works, Red Amber, Pint 65.00
Flask, Williams, Seattle, Wa., Clear, Pumpkinseed, 1/2 Pint 50.00
Flask, Willington Glass Co., Conn., Eagle, Green, 1/2 Pint 90.00

Flask, Willington Glass Co., Conn., Eagle, Olive Green, 1/2 Pint 65.00
Flask, Willington Glass Co., Conn., Liberty Eagle, Green, Pint 120.00
Flask, Willington Glass Co., Conn., Ring Lip, Honey Amber, Pint 155.00
Flask, Wooden Boat Inside, 7 In. ....*Illus* 100.00
    Flask, Zanesville, see also Flask, Chestnut, Zanesville
Flask, Zanesville, Swirled To Right, Deep Aqua, 8 3/4 In. 260.00

*Food bottles include all of the many grocery store containers, such as those
for catsup, horseradish, jelly, and other foodstuffs. A few special bottles,
such as those for vinegar, are listed under their own headings.*
Food, A. & H.Premium Catsup, C.T.Ammon's, Richmond, Va, BIMAL, Aqua 22.00
Food, Apple Butter, Jumbo, 8 In. ....*Illus* 20.00
Food, Baking Powder, Brookmont Brand, 5 1/2 In. ....*Illus* 15.00

Food, Apple Butter, Jumbo, 8 In.

Food, Catsup, Beech-Nut Brand,
Paper Label, 10 In.

Food, Baking Powder,
Brookmont Brand, 5 1/2 In.

Food, Chili Sauce, Cru Bro,
Paper Label, 7 In.

Food, Gherkins, Frank Vogel,
Paper Label, 7 1/2 In.

Food, Heinz, Apple Butter,
Pittsburgh

Food, Ketchup, Down
On The Farm, 10 In.

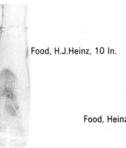

Food, H.J.Heinz, 10 In.

Food, Heinz, Horseradish, 1880s

Food, My Wife's Salad
Dressing, Chicago, 8 In.

Food, Pure Maple Syrup,
J.Zachary, Pottery, 4 1/2 In.
(See Page 92)

Food, Salad Dressing, Chef, Paper Label, 8 In.
(See Page 92)

Food, **Baking Powder,** Mason Jar, Pint ....*Color*	5.50
Food, **Beef Peptonoids,** Arlington Chemical Co., Yonkers, N.Y., Amber	1.50
Food, **Boerscherdt's Malt Soup Extract,** BIMAL	4.00
Food, **Butler's Ketchup,** 8 In. ....*Color*	xxxx.xx
Food, **California Perfume Co.,** see Avon, California Perfume Co.	
Food, **Capers,** Crude, 6 1/2 In.	3.50
Food, **Capers,** Emerald Green, 8 In.	7.00
Food, **Catsup,** Beech-Nut Brand, Paper Label, 10 In. ....*Illus*	3.50
Food, **Catsup,** John Getz & Son, York, Penna., Picture Of Tomato, Amber	20.00
Food, **Challenge Ketchup,** Cincinnati, BIMAL, Clear	15.00
Food, **Chili Sauce,** Cru Bro, Paper Label, 7 In. ....*Illus*	3.00
Food, **Cider,** Eastern Co., Amber	65.00
Food, **Cider,** Green & Clark, Missouri, Amber	37.00
Food, **Cleveland Fruit Juice Co.,** Clear, 1/2 Gallon	5.00
Food, **Crandall & Godley Co.,** Perfect Fruit Juice	8.00
Food, **Croft's Swiss Milk Cocoa,** Ground Top ....8.00 To 10.00	
Food, **Curtice Bros.Co.,** Preserves, C.B.Monogram, Sample Size, 4 3/4 In.	2.50
Food, **Eyer's Sarsaparilla Compound Extract,** Lowell, Mass., U.S.A., Aqua	3.00
Food, **Gherkins,** Frank Vogel, Paper Label, 7 1/2 In. ....*Illus*	4.00
Food, **Gibson's Syrup,** Teal Green, Quart	30.00
Food, **Giessen's Union Mustard,** N.Y., Eagle	69.50
Food, **H.J.Heinz & Co.,** 8 Sided Neck, Bulbous, Clear, 6 3/8 In.	3.00
Food, **H.J.Heinz Co.,** 14 Side Panels, Patented Base	10.00
Food, **H.J.Heinz,** 10 In. ....*Illus*	14.00
Food, **Heinz,** Apple Butter, Pittsburgh ....*Illus*	25.00
Food, **Heinz,** Horseradish, 1880s ....*Illus*	3.00
Food, **Hellmann,** Crock, 8 In. ....*Color*	xxxx.xx
Food, **J.T.Morton,** Mustard, London, Beveled Corners, Deep Aqua, 9 In.	5.00
Food, **Jumbo Peanut Butter,** Embossed Elephant, Clear, Pint ....50 To 2.50	
Food, **Ketchup,** Down On The Farm, 10 In. ....*Illus*	9.00
Food, **L.Rose & Co.,** Lime Juice, Wines & Fruit, Aqua, 7 3/4 In.	9.00
Food, **M.T.Quinan,** Savannah, Ga., Cider	20.00
Food, **Mellins,** Aqua, BIMAL	1.50
Food, **Mitchell's Flavoring Extracts,** Rochester, N.Y., 4 7/8 In.	20.00
Food, **Mrs.Chapin's Salad Dressing,** 4 1/4 In.	4.00
Food, **Mudry's Horseradish,** Aqua, 6 In. ....*Color*	xxxx.xx
Food, **Mustard,** Moutarde Diaphane Louit Freres, Barrel, Open Pontil	9.00
Food, **Mustard,** U.S.Navy, Open Pontil	23.00
Food, **My Own Catsup,** 7 In. ....*Color*	xxxx.xx
Food, **My Wife's Salad Dressing,** Chicago, 8 In. ....*Illus*	2.50

Food, Nubian Tea, Embossed Man's Head, Large & Small, Pair	25.00
Food, Old Virginia, Dayton Spice Mills, Black Mammy On Label	6.00
Food, Parisian Sage, Embossed, Label, Stopper	5.00
Food, Paskola, The Pre-Digested Food Co., Embossed Pineapple, Amber	7.00
Food, Peacock's OK Sauce, Shield Panel, Tapered Neck, Dark Amber	6.75
Food, Pepper Sauce, see Pepper Sauce	
Food, Pickle, see Pickle	
Food, Premium Coffefille, Amethyst	25.00
Food, Pure Maple Syrup, J.Zachary, Pottery, 4 1/2 In. ....*Illus*	4.50
Food, R.T.French Mustard, Atlantic, 5 In. ....*Color*	xxxx.xx
Food, Rumford Baking Powder, Cork Top, Round, Clear	1.00
Food, Salad Dressing, Chef, Paper Label, 8 In. ....*Illus*	.25
Food, Salad Dressing, Macrisco, Paper Label, 7 In. ....*Illus*	4.00
Food, Sandford's Jamaica Ginger, The Quintessence, Boston, Mass., Aqua	3.50
Food, Sar-A-Lee, Salad Dressing, Quart	2.00
Food, Schenk's Syrup, Philada., 8 Sided, Aqua, 6 3/4 In.	7.50
Food, Tomato Sauce, Cylinder, Deep Purple, 9 1/2 In.	35.00
Food, Valentine's Meat Juice, 1871 Label, Ham Shaped, Cork, Amber	10.00
Food, Vinegar, White House, 6 In. ....*Illus*	3.00
Food, Weideman Quality First, 8 1/2 In. ....*Illus*	.50

Fruit jars made of glass have been used in the United States since the 1850s. Over one thousand different jars have been found with varieties of closures, embossing, and colors. The date 1858 on many jars refers to a patent, not the age of the bottle. Be sure to look in this listing under any name or initial that appears on your jar. If not otherwise indicated the jar is clear glass, quart size. The numbers used in the entries in the form T-0 refer to the book "A Collectors' Manual of Fruit Jars" by Julian Harrison Toulouse.

Fruit Jar, A R & S, Aqua, 8 1/2 In. ....*Illus*	60.00
Fruit Jar, A. & D.H.Chambers, Base Embossed, Aqua, 1/2 Gallon	7.00
Fruit Jar, A.Stone & Co., Graphite Pontil, Wax Sealer, Aqua, 1/2 Gallon	450.00
Fruit Jar, Amazon Swift Seal, 1/2 Gallon	8.00
Fruit Jar, Anchor, Pint	250.00
Fruit Jar, Arnold Patent, Yellowware	200.00
Fruit Jar, Atlas E-Z Seal, Amber, Quart	13.00 To 28.00
Fruit Jar, Atlas E-Z Seal, Blue, 1/2 Gallon	6.00
Fruit Jar, Atlas E-Z Seal, Blue, 1/2 Pint	6.00
Fruit Jar, Atlas E-Z Seal, Clear, 1/2 Gallon	1.00
Fruit Jar, Atlas E-Z Seal, Milk Glass Lid, Amber, Quart	35.00
Fruit Jar, Atlas Special, Aqua, Pint	2.50
Fruit Jar, Atlas, Good Luck, With Clover, Quart	8.50
Fruit Jar, Atlas, Good Luck, 1/2 Pint	11.00
Fruit Jar, Ball Ideal, Ball Building On Reverse, Blue, Pint	75.00
Fruit Jar, Ball Ideal, Bicentennial, Blue, 1/2 Pint	5.00
Fruit Jar, Ball Ideal, Bicentennial, Signed Edmund, Blue, Quart	75.00
Fruit Jar, Ball Ideal, Blue Aqua, 1/2 Pint	20.00
Fruit Jar, Ball Ideal, Dated 1908, Aqua, Pint	2.75
Fruit Jar, Ball Ideal, Dated 1908, Aqua, Quart	2.00
Fruit Jar, Ball Perfect Mason, Amber, 1/2 Gallon	18.00 To 20.00
Fruit Jar, Ball Perfect Mason, Blue Aqua, 1 1/2 Quart	16.00
Fruit Jar, Ball Perfect Mason, Blue, 1/2 Pint	20.00
Fruit Jar, Ball Perfect Mason, Italian Green	10.00
Fruit Jar, Ball Perfect Mason, Screw Top, Square, Clear, 2 1/2 In.	3.00
Fruit Jar, Ball Sure Seal, Banner In Circle, 1/2 Pint	10.00
Fruit Jar, Banner 1864, Complete, Aqua, 1/2 Gallon	65.00
Fruit Jar, Banner, Wide Mouth, Aqua, Quart	10.00
Fruit Jar, Beaver Midget, Pint	65.00
Fruit Jar, Beaver, Aqua, Quart	15.00
Fruit Jar, Best Fruit Keeper, The, Repro Clamp, Aqua, 1/2 Gallon	35.00
Fruit Jar, Bloeser, Aqua, Quart	75.00
Fruit Jar, Boldt Mason, 1/2 Gallon	20.00
Fruit Jar, Bomberger's Mason, Aqua, Pint	7.00
Fruit Jar, Brighton, Fisher Crack On Lid, Quart	50.00
Fruit Jar, Brockway Clear Vu Mason, Clear	1.50
Fruit Jar, C F J Co., Mason's Improved, Aqua, Quart	10.00

Fruit Jar, **C F J Co.,** Mason's Improved, Light Blue, Quart 12.00
Fruit Jar, **C.F.Spencer's,** Pat. 1868, Repro Closure, 1/2 Gallon 210.00
Fruit Jar, **Canton Domestic,** Quart .... 30.00 To 53.00
Fruit Jar, **Canton Domestic,** 1/2 Gallon 65.00
Fruit Jar, **Canton,** Domestic, Pint 45.00
Fruit Jar, **Chef,** Bergan & Co., 5 In. .... *Illus*   6.00

Food, Salad Dressing,
Macrisco, Paper Label, 7 In.

Food, Weideman Quality First, 8 1/2 In.

Food, Vinegar, White House, 6 In.

Fruit Jar, Cohansey,
Aqua, 6 1/2 In.
(See Page 94)

Fruit Jar, A R & S,
Aqua, 8 1/2 In.

Fruit Jar, Chef,
Bergan & Co., 5 In.

Fruit Jar, Doolittle, 4 In.
(See Page 94)

Fruit Jar, Franklin,
Aqua, 6 In.
(See Page 94)

Fruit Jar, Green, 8 In.
(See Page 94)

Fruit Jar, Mason Drey
Square, 9 1/2 In.
(See Page 96)

Fruit Jar, Handy Jar,
Smalley Kivlan, 8 In.
(See Page 95)

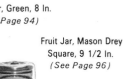

Fruit Jar, Lighting, Trademark,
Copper, Bronze, 8 In.
(See Page 95)

Fruit Jar, Choice Leaf, Lard, Boston, Mass, Top, Clear 22.00
Fruit Jar, Christmas Mason, Aqua, Pint 45.00
Fruit Jar, Clark's Peerless, Aqua, Pint 9.00
Fruit Jar, Clark's Peerless, Glass Lid, Quart 10.00
Fruit Jar, Clark's Peerless, Pale Green, Quart 8.00
Fruit Jar, Clarke, Cleveland, Ohio, Pint 95.00
Fruit Jar, Cohansey, Amber, Pint 65.00
Fruit Jar, Cohansey, Aqua, Quart .... 16.00 To 20.00
Fruit Jar, Cohansey, Aqua, 6 1/2 In. ....Illus 150.00
Fruit Jar, Cohansey, Barrel, Aqua, Quart 90.00
Fruit Jar, Columbia, Repro Clamp, Aqua, Quart 22.00
Fruit Jar, Conserve, Embossed, Clear, Quart 5.00
Fruit Jar, Crown, Amethyst, Midget 12.00
Fruit Jar, Crown, Imperial 1/2 Pint 8.50
Fruit Jar, Crown, Maple Leaf On Bottom, Lid, Imperial 1/2 Gallon 225.00
Fruit Jar, Crown, Quart 11.00
Fruit Jar, Crystal, 1/2 Gallon 19.50
Fruit Jar, Cunningham & Ihmsen, Pgh., Pa. 15.00
Fruit Jar, Cunningham's & Ihmsen, Pitts., Pa., 1/2 Gallon 15.00
Fruit Jar, Curtis & Moore, Trade Mark, Boston, Mass. 15.00
Fruit Jar, Dandy, The Trademark, Amber, Pint 285.00
Fruit Jar, Dandy, The, Embossed, Amber, 1/2 Gallon 125.00
Fruit Jar, Diamond Of Nova Scotia, The, 2 Quart 225.00
Fruit Jar, Doolittle, 4 In. ....Illus 45.00
Fruit Jar, Double Safety, 1/2 Pint 5.50
Fruit Jar, Drey Square Mason, Embossed, Clear, Pint 4.00
Fruit Jar, Easy Vacuum Jar, Aqua, Quart 12.00
Fruit Jar, Eclipse, The, Aqua, 1/2 Gallon 70.00
Fruit Jar, Economy Sealer 15.00
Fruit Jar, Electric, Salem, N.J., Aqua 11.00
Fruit Jar, Everlasting, Amethyst, Quart 18.00
Fruit Jar, Everlasting, Aqua, Quart 18.00
Fruit Jar, Excels Iron, Quart 50.00
Fruit Jar, Excelsior Improved, 1/2 Gallon 30.00
Fruit Jar, Fahnstock & Albree, Aqua, Quart 55.00
Fruit Jar, Fahnstock, Albree & Co., Blue Aqua, 1/2 Gallon 65.00
Fruit Jar, Flaccus Bros.Steershead, Milk Glass 160.00
Fruit Jar, Flaccus Co., E.C.Steershead, Lid, Amber .... 260.00 To 445.00
Fruit Jar, Flaccus Co., E.C.Steershead, Milk Glass 160.00
Fruit Jar, Flaccus Co., E.C.Steershead, Pint 45.00
        Fruit Jar, Foster, see Fruit Jar, Sealfast, Foster
Fruit Jar, Foster Sealfast, 1/2 Pint 5.50
Fruit Jar, Franklin Dexter, Aqua, Quart 25.00
Fruit Jar, Franklin, Aqua, Quart 40.00
Fruit Jar, Franklin, Aqua, 6 In. ....Illus 99.00
Fruit Jar, Fruit Growers' Trade, Aqua, Quart 30.00
Fruit Jar, Fruit Keeper, Aqua, Quart .... 25.00 To 30.00
Fruit Jar, G.J. Co., Aqua, Quart 25.00
Fruit Jar, G.J. Co., Milk Glass Immerser Lid, Quart 14.00
Fruit Jar, Gayner Glass Top, The, Clear, Quart 5.00
Fruit Jar, Gem, The, Aqua, Quart 5.00
Fruit Jar, Gem, The, Aqua, 1/2 Gallon 4.00
Fruit Jar, Gem, The, Green, Quart 18.00
Fruit Jar, Gem, The, 1/2 Gallon 8.50
Fruit Jar, Genuine Mason, Light Vaseline, Pint 8.00
Fruit Jar, Gilberd's Improved, Aqua, Quart 95.00
        Fruit Jar, Gilchrist, see Fruit Jar, G J Co.
Fruit Jar, Glassboro, Pint 25.00
Fruit Jar, Globe, Amber, Pint .... 50.00 To 65.00
Fruit Jar, Globe, Amber, Quart 40.00
Fruit Jar, Globe, Amber, 1/2 Gallon 60.00
Fruit Jar, Globe, Aqua .... 10.00 To 22.00
Fruit Jar, Gold Medal Mockingbird, Amethyst 15.00
Fruit Jar, Golden State Mason, No Lid, Pint 2.50
Fruit Jar, Good Housekeepers, Clear, 1/2 Gallon 5.00
Fruit Jar, Green, 8 In. ....Illus 28.50

Fruit Jar, Haine's Improved, March 1st, 1870, Aqua 75.00
Fruit Jar, Handy Jar, Smalley Kivlan, 8 In. ....*Illus* 59.00
 Fruit Jar, Hansee's, see Fruit Jar, Palace Home, Hansee's
Fruit Jar, Hartell, Aqua, Quart 18.00
Fruit Jar, Hartell, Black Amethyst, Quart ....*Color* xxxx.xx
Fruit Jar, Haserot Co., Cleveland, Mason Patent 9.50
 Fruit Jar, Helme's, see Fruit Jar, Rail Road Mills, Helme's
Fruit Jar, Hemingray, Tin Lid, Ears, Patent Cin., O., June 9, 1863, Aqua, Quart 80.00
Fruit Jar, Hero Cross Mason's, 1858, Amber, Quart 90.00
Fruit Jar, Hero, The, Quart 10.00
Fruit Jar, Heroine, The, Aqua, Quart 30.00
Fruit Jar, Heroine, The, Aqua, 1/2 Gallon 21.00
Fruit Jar, Honsee's Home Palace, Canada 25.00

Fruit Jar, Mason's Patent,
Nov.30, 1958, 7 1/2 In.

(See Page 96)

Fruit Jar, Mason's Patent,
Nov.30, 1858, 7 1/2 In.

Fruit Jar, Ne Plus Ultra, Airtight, Aqua, Quart

Fruit Jar, Howe Jar, The, Clear 52.00
Fruit Jar, Howe Jar, The, Star, Aqua, Quart 45.00
Fruit Jar, Howe, The, Scranton, Aqua, Pint 40.00
Fruit Jar, Imperial, The, Crown, 1/2 Gallon 12.00
Fruit Jar, Improved Jam, L.G.Co., Aqua, Pint .... 70.00 To 85.00
Fruit Jar, J.& B., 1/2 Gallon 50.00
Fruit Jar, J.P.Smith & Co., Philadelphia, Green, 1/2 Gallon ....*Color* xxxx.xx
Fruit Jar, J.P.Smith & Son Co., Embossed Wax Sealer Face, Quart 25.00
Fruit Jar, K.H. & G.Z.O., Aqua, Quart 10.00
Fruit Jar, Kerr Self Sealing Mason, Amber, Quart 9.50
Fruit Jar, Kerr Self Sealing Mason, 1915, 1/2 Pint 4.50
Fruit Jar, Kerr Self Sealing, Mason, Blue, Quart 20.00
Fruit Jar, Keystone, Aqua, Quart 10.00
Fruit Jar, Keystone, Bail Top, Clear, Quart 7.50
Fruit Jar, Keystone, Mason, Pat., Nov.30th, 1858, Aqua 10.00
Fruit Jar, King Oval, Crown Above King, Clear, Quart 10.00
Fruit Jar, King, Crown & Flags, Pint 10.00
Fruit Jar, Knowlton Vacuum, Light Blue, Quart 25.00
Fruit Jar, Knowlton Vacuum, Pint .... 18.00 To 25.00
Fruit Jar, Knowlton, Free-Blown Tear Drop, Laid On Ring, Green 80.00
Fruit Jar, Knowlton, Vacuum, Star, Quart 12.50
Fruit Jar, Knox Keystone Mason, K In Keystone, 1/2 Pint 7.50
Fruit Jar, Knox Mason, Square, Clear, Pint 3.00
Fruit Jar, Knox Mason, Square, Clear, Quart 3.00
Fruit Jar, L. & W., Rice & Burnett, Cleveland, Ohio, Stopper 50.00
Fruit Jar, L. & W., Stopper, Aqua, Quart 30.00
Fruit Jar, La Lorraine, Milk Bottle Shape, French, Aqua 40.00
Fruit Jar, Lafayette, Clear, Quart 85.00
Fruit Jar, Leader, Amber, Quart ....*Color* 120.00
Fruit Jar, Leotric, Aqua, Pint 8.00
Fruit Jar, Lighting, Trademark, Copper, Bronze, 8 In. ....*Illus* 48.00
Fruit Jar, Lightning, Amber, Pint .... 43.00 To 60.00
Fruit Jar, Lightning, Amber, Quart .... 25.00 To 30.00
Fruit Jar, Lightning, Amber, 1/2 Gallon .... 30.00 To 55.00
Fruit Jar, Lightning, Apple Green, Pint 60.00
Fruit Jar, Lightning, Apple Green, Quart 50.00
Fruit Jar, Lightning, Clear, Pint 7.00

Fruit Jar, Lightning, Clear, Quart	5.00
Fruit Jar, Lightning, Honey Amber, Pint	65.00
Fruit Jar, Lightning, Trademark, Aqua, Quart	2.50
Fruit Jar, Lightning, Trademark, Aqua, 1/2 Pint	67.00
Fruit Jar, Lightning, Yellow-Green Amber, 1/2 Gallon	40.00
Fruit Jar, Lockport, Mason, 1/2 Gallon	5.00
Fruit Jar, Longlife, Mason, Clear, Pint	1.00
Fruit Jar, Ludlow's Infallible, Deep Aqua, Pint ....Color	xxxx.xx
Fruit Jar, Lynchburg Standard Mason, Aqua, Quart	15.00
Fruit Jar, M.G.Co., Yellow Green, Quart	75.00
Fruit Jar, Magic, The, Star, Aqua, Pint	235.00
Fruit Jar, Magic, TM, Mason, Clear, Pint	1.00
Fruit Jar, Marion Jar, The, Embossing, Deep Aqua, Quart	16.00
Fruit Jar, Marion Jar, The, Mason's Patent, Nov.30th, 1858, Aqua, 1/2 Gallon	10.00
Fruit Jar, Mascot Improved, The, Disk Immerser Insert, Clear, 1/2 Gallon	50.00
Fruit Jar, Mason Drey Square, 9 1/2 In. ....Illus	5.00
Fruit Jar, Mason Red Patent, Nov.30, 1958, 7 1/2 In. ....Illus	12.00
Fruit Jar, Mason 1858, Snowflake Zinc Lid, Clear, Quart	43.00
Fruit Jar, Mason, Patent, Nov. 30, 1858, Christmas	45.00
Fruit Jar, Mason's C F J Co., see Fruit Jar, C F J Co.	
Fruit Jar, Mason's Cross, see Fruit Jar, Hero Cross	
Fruit Jar, Mason's Cross, Pat., Nov.30th, 1858, Midget	10.00
Fruit Jar, Mason's Cross, Patent Nov.30th, 1858, Aqua, Quart	4.00
Fruit Jar, Mason's Crystal Jar, Embossed, Clear, Midget	75.00
Fruit Jar, Mason's Hero Cross, 1858, Ambossed, Amber, Quart	90.00
Fruit Jar, Mason's Improved, Clyde, N.Y.	12.00
Fruit Jar, Mason's Improved, Amber, 1/2 Gallon	68.00
Fruit Jar, Mason's Improved, Clyde, N.Y., Midget, Aqua	9.00
Fruit Jar, Mason's Improved, 3 Gallon	310.00
Fruit Jar, Mason's Patent Nov.30, 1858, Amethyst, 1/2 Gallon ....Color	xxxx.xx
Fruit Jar, Mason's Patent Nov.30th, 1858, Amber, 1/2 Gallon	90.00
Fruit Jar, Mason's Patent Nov.30th, 1858, Aqua, Quart	8.00
Fruit Jar, Mason's Patent 1858, Snowflake Zinc Lid, Clear, Quart	43.00
Fruit Jar, Mason's Patent 1872, Aqua, Quart	20.00
Fruit Jar, Mason's Patent, Nov.30, 1858, 7 1/2 In. ....Illus	8.00
Fruit Jar, Mason's Patent, Nov.30th, 1858, Aqua, Pint	1.50
Fruit Jar, Mason's Patent, Nov.30th, 1880, Protector Lid, 1/2 Gallon	85.00
Fruit Jar, Mason's S Co., 1858, Embossing, Quart	50.00
Fruit Jar, Mason's Union, Shield, Aqua, 1/2 Gallon	135.00
Fruit Jar, Mason's, C.F.J.Co., Improved, Bubbles, Amber, 1/2 Gallon	100.00
Fruit Jar, Mason's, C.G.Co., Patent Nov.30th, 1858, Aqua, Pint	7.00
Fruit Jar, McDonald Perfect Seal, Dated, Aqua, Quart	2.75
Fruit Jar, Millville Atmospheric Fruit Jar, Lid & Clamp, Quart	25.00
Fruit Jar, Millville Atmospheric, Lid & Clamp, 1 1/2 Pint	45.00
Fruit Jar, Millville Atmospheric, Pint	50.00
Fruit Jar, Millville, CWT Co., Improved, Quart	46.50
Fruit Jar, Mission Mason's Bell, Clear, Quart	5.00
Fruit Jar, Moore's, Patent Dec. 3, 1861, 1/2 Gallon	73.00
Fruit Jar, Mrs.G.E.Haller, Syrup Stopple, Aqua	175.00
Fruit Jar, Myer's Test Jar, Original Tin Lid & Brass Clamp, Aqua, Quart	135.00
Fruit Jar, Ne Plus Ultra, Airtight, Aqua, Quart ....Illus	475.00
Fruit Jar, New Gem, Clear, Pint	5.00
Fruit Jar, Ohio Quality, Mason, Pint	7.00
Fruit Jar, Pail, Boston, Mass, Collar & Bail, Clear	35.00
Fruit Jar, Palace Home, Hanses's, Aqua, Quart	45.50
Fruit Jar, Pansy, Canadian, Wide Mouth	585.00
Fruit Jar, Patented, 5 In. ....Illus	8.50
Fruit Jar, Peerless, Aqua	55.00
Fruit Jar, Peerless, Quart	80.00
Fruit Jar, Petal 10, 4 Mold, Iron Pontil, Aqua, Quart	200.00
Fruit Jar, Petal 10, 4 Mold, Iron Pontil, Emerald Green, Quart	800.00
Fruit Jar, Petal, Aqua, 9 1/2 In. ....Illus	135.00
Fruit Jar, Petal, Blue, Quart ....Color	xxxx.xx
Fruit Jar, Petal, Green, Quart ....Color	xxxx.xx
Fruit Jar, Petal, Tin Top, Blue ....Color	xxxx.xx
Fruit Jar, Petal, 10 Panel, Graphite, Pontil, Aqua, 8 1/2 In.	150.00

Fruit Jar, **Porcelain Lined,** Patent Dates, Aqua	15.00
Fruit Jar, **Porcelain Lined,** Quart	9.50
Fruit Jar, **Pottery,** Gray With Blue Glaze, Quart	100.00
Fruit Jar, **Premium,** Coffeyville, Kas., Clear, Pint	25.00
Fruit Jar, **Presto Glass Top,** Illinois Glass, 1/2 Pint	8.50
Fruit Jar, **Presto Supreme Mason,** Pint	1.00
Fruit Jar, **Presto Supreme Mason,** 1/2 Pint	5.00

Fruit Jar, Patented, 5 In.

Fruit Jar, Petal, Aqua, 9 1/2 In.

Fruit Jar, Stark, Patented 1923, Quart

Fruit Jar, **Presto,** Glass Lid, Wire Bale, 1/2 Pint	6.00
Fruit Jar, **Protector,** Round, Repro.Lid, 1/2 Gallon	24.00
Fruit Jar, **Putnam Glassworks,** Zanesville, O.	20.00
Fruit Jar, **Putnam,** Lid & Bail Wire, Apple Green	35.00
Fruit Jar, **Queen,** SKO, Smalley, Clear, 1/2 Pint	7.50
Fruit Jar, **Queen,** The, C.F.J.Lettered Zinc Band, Green, Quart	29.00
Fruit Jar, **Railroad Malls,** Helme's, Amber, Snuff	15.00
Fruit Jar, **Ravenna Glass Works,** Airtight, C.1857 ....*Color*	xxxx.xx
Fruit Jar, **Red Key Mason,** Aqua, Quart	6.00
Fruit Jar, **Root Mason,** Aqua, Quart	4.00
Fruit Jar, **Rose,** The, Clear, Quart	42.50
Fruit Jar, **Safety Valve,** Greek Key, Aqua	25.00
Fruit Jar, **Safety,** Amber, Pint	200.00
Fruit Jar, **Safety,** Bail, Amber, Quart	75.00
Fruit Jar, **Schaffer Jar,** The, Aqua	175.00
Fruit Jar, **Schram Automatic Sealer,** Aluminum Lid, Aqua, Quart	20.00
Fruit Jar, **Schram,** B, Clear, 1/2 Gallon	6.00
Fruit Jar, **Scranton Jar,** The, No Top	300.00
Fruit Jar, **Sealfast,** Clear, Quart	1.00
Fruit Jar, **Sealfast,** Foster, 1/2 Pint	5.50
Fruit Jar, **Simplex,** In Diamond, Paper Label	15.00
Fruit Jar, **Smalley Full Measure,** AGS, Aqua, Quart	9.00
Fruit Jar, **Smalley Nu-Seal,** Logo In Diamond	4.00
Fruit Jar, **Smalley Self Sealer,** The, Pint	5.00
Fruit Jar, **Standard,** Quart ....*Color*	xxxx.xx
Fruit Jar, **Star,** Clear, 1/2 Gallon	39.00
Fruit Jar, **Stark,** Patented 1923, Quart ....*Illus*	65.00
Fruit Jar, **Steer's Head,** see Fruit Jar, Flaccus	
Fruit Jar, **Steven's Tin Top,** Pat.July 27, 1875	120.00
Fruit Jar, **Sun,** Aqua, Quart	25.00
Fruit Jar, **Sun,** Pint	50.00
Fruit Jar, **Sun,** Quart	25.00 To 50.00
Fruit Jar, **Swayzee's Improved Mason,** Blue	8.00
Fruit Jar, **Swayzee's Improved Mason,** Quart	2.50
Fruit Jar, **Swazee's Improved,** Mason, Olive, 1/2 Gallon	15.00
Fruit Jar, **Telephone,** Buckley & Woodlief, New Orleans, Aqua	25.00
Fruit Jar, **Telephone,** The, Whitney Glass Works, Aqua, Pint	8.00
Fruit Jar, **Telephone,** The, Widemouth, Aqua, Quart	5.00 To 10.00
Fruit Jar, **Texas Mason,** Pint	10.00
Fruit Jar, **Texas Mason,** Quart	8.00 To 10.00
Fruit Jar, **Union Fruit,** Pittsburgh, Pa., Wax Sealer Embossed On Base	11.00

Fruit Jar, **Vacuum Fruit Jar**, The, Detroit, Embossed, Clear, Quart	45.00
Fruit Jar, **Valve Jar**, The, Aqua, Quart	140.00
Fruit Jar, **W.McC. & Co.**, Standard	15.00
Fruit Jar, **W.McCully**, Standard	20.00
Fruit Jar, **W.W.Lyman**, Original Lid & Gasket, 1/2 Gallon	55.00
Fruit Jar, **W.W.Lyman**, Quart	20.00
Fruit Jar, **W.W.Lyman**, 1864, Aqua, Quart	29.00
Fruit Jar, **Wan-Eta**, Label, Amber	10.00
Fruit Jar, **Wax Sealer**, Blackberry Label, Amber ....*Color*	110.00
Fruit Jar, **Weideman Boy Brand**, Clear, Quart	5.00
Fruit Jar, **Western Pride**, No Lid, Repro Clamp	110.00
Fruit Jar, **Whitall's Patent**, Millville Atmospheric, Lid & Clamp	18.00
Fruit Jar, **Whitney Mason**, Quart	6.00
Fruit Jar, **Winslow**, Repro Clamp, Aqua, 1/2 Gallon	20.00
Fruit Jar, **Wm.McCully & Co.**, Patented June 6th, 1866	650.00
Fruit Jar, **Woodbury Improved**, 1/2 Gallon	17.50
Fruit Jar, **Woodbury**, Monogram, Aqua, Quart	27.50
Fruit Jar, **Woodbury**, Quart	39.00
Fruit Jar, **Yeoman's**, Aqua, Quart	35.00 To 38.00
Galliano, Gallon Guard	155.00
Galliano, Gold Award Guard	100.00
Galliano, Guard, 10th	10.00 To 12.00
Galliano, Guard, 19 In.	9.00
Galliano, Guard, 5th	10.00

Garnier bottles were first made in 1899 to hold Garnier Liqueurs. The firm was founded in 1859 in France. Figurals have been made through the twentieth century, except for the years of prohibition and World War II.

Garnier, **Aladdin's Lamp**, Silver, 1963	43.00
Garnier, **Alfa Romeo Racer**, 1969	9.60
Garnier, **Alfa Romeo 1913**, 1970	16.00
Garnier, **Alfa Romeo 1929**, 1969	16.00
Garnier, **Antique Coach**, No.276, 1970	20.00
Garnier, **Apollo**, 1969	16.00
Garnier, **Aztec Vase**, 1965	11.00
Garnier, **Baby Foot**, No. 200, 1963	12.00 To 13.00
Garnier, **Bacchus**, 1967	12.00
Garnier, **Bahamas**, Black Policeman, 1970	27.00 To 30.50
Garnier, **Bedroom Candlestick**, 1967	15.00 To 18.00
Garnier, **Bellows**, 1969	17.00
Garnier, **Bluebird**, 1976	16.00
Garnier, **Bouquet**, White Basket, Multicolor Flowers, 1966	10.00 To 16.00
Garnier, **Bullfighter**	14.00 To 18.00
Garnier, **Burmese Man**, Vase, 1965	17.00
Garnier, **Canada Mountie**, 1970	14.95
Garnier, **Candlestick**, Glass, No.216, 1965	19.00
Garnier, **Candlestick**, No.134, 1955	38.00
Garnier, **Cannon**, 1964	53.00
Garnier, **Cardinal State Bird**, Illinois, 1969	12.00
Garnier, **Cat**, Black, 1962	15.00
Garnier, **Cat**, Gray, 1972	15.00
Garnier, **Cat**, No.52, 1930	75.00
Garnier, **Chalet**, 1955	45.00
Garnier, **Chimney**, 1956	58.00
Garnier, **Chinese Dog**, 1965	15.00
Garnier, **Chinese Statuette**, Man, 1970	20.00
Garnier, **Chinese Statuette**, Woman, 1970	20.00
Garnier, **Christmas Tree**, 1956	63.00
Garnier, **Citroen 1922**, 1970	16.00
Garnier, **Clock**, 1958	23.00
Garnier, **Clown Holding Tuba**, 1955	18.00
Garnier, **Clown**, No.20, 1910	42.00
Garnier, **Clown's Head**, No.53, 1931	75.00
Garnier, **Coffee Mill**, 1966	27.00
Garnier, **Coffeepot**, No.192, 1962	33.00
Garnier, **Country Jug**, 1937	31.00

Garnier, Diamond Bottle, No.234, 1969	13.00
Garnier, Drunkard, Drunk On Lamppost	17.00
Garnier, Duck, No.21, 1910	13.00 To 20.00
Garnier, Duckling, 1956	38.00
Garnier, Egg, White Egg-Shaped House, 1956	73.00
Garnier, Eiffel Tower, 1951	17.00
Garnier, Elephant, No.183, 1961	22.00
Garnier, Elephant, No.66, 1932	75.00
Garnier, Empire Vase, 1962	13.00
Garnier, Faceless Soldier, 1949	60.00
Garnier, Fiat Nuevo, 1913, 1970	9.60
Garnier, Ford 1913, 1970	9.60 To 16.00
Garnier, Fountain, No.204, 1964	27.00
Garnier, Giraffe, No.184, 1961	17.00
Garnier, Goddess, No.196, 1963	43.00
Garnier, Goldfinch, 1970	15.00
Garnier, Goose, No.141, 1955	17.00
Garnier, Greyhound, No.51, 1930	75.00
Garnier, Harlequin, No.166, 1958	35.00
Garnier, Horse Pistol, 1964	14.00
Garnier, Hula Hoop, 1959	28.00
Garnier, Hunting Vase, 1964	28.00
Garnier, Inca, 1969	16.00
Garnier, Indian, 1958	14.00 To 15.00
Garnier, Jockey, 1961	18.00
Garnier, La Dona, 1963	43.00
Garnier, Lafayette, 1949	19.00
Garnier, Laurel Crown, 1963	21.00
Garnier, Locomotive, 1969	13.00
Garnier, Loon, 1970	14.00
Garnier, Maharajah, 1958	73.00
Garnier, Marquis, No.54, 1931	73.00
Garnier, Marquise, No.55, 1931	78.00
Garnier, Marseillaise, 1970	19.00
Garnier, MG 1933, 1970	16.00
Garnier, Mocking Bird, 1970	14.00
Garnier, Montmartre Jug, 1960	15.00
Garnier, Napoleon, 1969	19.00 To 21.00
Garnier, New York Policeman, 1970	14.95
Garnier, Oacjard 1830, 1970	16.00
Garnier, Oasis, 1959	20.00
Garnier, Old Watch, 1966	18.00 To 25.00
Garnier, Painting, 1961	25.00
Garnier, Paris Monument, 1966	14.00 To 17.00
Garnier, Paris Taxi, 1960	26.00
Garnier, Parrot, 1910	23.00
Garnier, Partridge, No.177, 1961	35.00
Garnier, Partridge, No.254, 1969	14.00
Garnier, Pegasus, 1958	42.00
Garnier, Penguin, 1930	75.00
Garnier, Petanque, Pair Of Balls, 1966	34.00
Garnier, Pheasant, State Bird, South Dakota, 1969	16.00 To 25.00
Garnier, Pony, 1961	17.00
Garnier, Poodle, Black, 1954	14.00
Garnier, Poodle, No.139, 1954	12.00
Garnier, Quarter Log, 1958	28.00
Garnier, Rainbow, No.133, 1952	28.00 To 29.00
Garnier, Renault 1911, 1969	9.60 To 16.00
Garnier, Road Runner, State Bird, New Mexico, 1969	13.00 To 14.00
Garnier, Robin, 1970	15.00
Garnier, Rolls Royce 1908, 1970	16.00
Garnier, Rooster, Black, 1952	14.00
Garnier, Rooster, Maroon, 1952	21.00
Garnier, Rouen Vase, 1962	24.00
Garnier, Round Log, 1958	23.00
Garnier, Saint Tropez Jug, 1961	15.00

Garnier, Scarecrow, 1960	14.00
Garnier, Sheriff, 1958	14.00
Garnier, Sheriff, 2 Guns, Badge, Cowboy Hat, 1958	14.00
Garnier, Snail, 1950	39.00
Garnier, Soccer Shoe, No.193, 1962	35.00
Garnier, SS France, No.191, 1962	115.00
Garnier, SS Queen Mary, 1970	21.00 To 22.00
Garnier, Stanley Steamer 1907, 1970	16.00
Garnier, Tam Tam, 1961	50.00
Garnier, Teapot, No.180, 1961	18.00
Garnier, Tierce, Musical, 1965	30.00
Garnier, Trio, 1955	15.00
Garnier, Trout, 1967	10.00 To 13.00
Garnier, Valley Quail, State Bird, California, 1969	8.00
Garnier, Violin, 1966	18.00
Garnier, Water Pitcher, 1965	15.00
Garnier, Watering Can, 1958	15.00
Garnier, Woman With Jug, 1930	50.00
Garnier, Young Deer, 1964	28.00
Garnier, 4 Compartment, 1970	19.00
Garnier, 5-Handled Jug, 1959	21.00
Gilbey, Barrel, Cognac	35.00
Gilbey, Barrel, Scotch	30.00
Gilbey, Barrel, Sherry	33.00

Gin was first made in the 1600s and gin bottles have been made ever since. Gin has always been an inexpensive drink. That is why so many of these bottles were made. Many were of a type called case bottles today.

Gin, Bininger, see Bininger

Gin, Blankenheym & Nolet, 9 1/2 In.	6.00
Gin, Blown, Open Pontil, Flanged Lip, Case, Olive Green	35.00
Gin, Boll & Dunlop, Rotterdam, Applied Lip, 8 3/4 In.	30.00
Gin, Booth & Sedgwick, London Cordial Gin, Applied Lip, Quart	70.00
Gin, Bouvier Bucner	5.00
Gin, C.W.Herwig, Schiedam, Embossed Corkscrew, Sea Green, Quart	75.00
Gin, Case, Applied Seal, Blankenhym & Nolet, Amber, 9 1/4 In.	18.00 To 25.00
Gin, Case, Applied Seal, Daniel Visser & Zonen, 11 In.	60.00
Gin, Case, Applied Seal, Emerald Green, 10 1/2 In.	65.00
Gin, Case, Applied Seal, Olive Green, 10 1/2 In.	75.00
Gin, Case, Applied Seal, Van Dynken Weiland & Co., 9 1/4 In.	85.00
Gin, Case, Applied Seal, 6 1/4 In.	80.00
Gin, Case, Black, 10 In.	19.00
Gin, Case, Dark Emerald, Quart	19.00
Gin, Case, Free-Blown, Open Pontil, Olive Green	50.00
Gin, Case, Holland's Genever, Full Label	12.00
Gin, Case, O.G.Seal On Shoulder, W.H.& Co.	55.00
Gin, Case, Paddle Sides, Olive Green, 9 In.	12.00
Gin, Case, Risley & Co., Importers, Buffalo, Amber	55.00
Gin, Cosmopoliet, Schiedam, Square Shoulder, Applied Lip, Deep Green	125.00
Gin, Daniel Visser & Zonen Schiedam, Applied Seal, Case, 11 1/4 In.	55.00
Gin, Daniel Visser, Case, Set Of 6	50.00
Gin, E.Kiderlin, Aqua, 10 1/2 In.	50.00
Gin, E.Kiderlin, Black Glass	25.00
Gin, E.Kiderlin, Olive Emerald, 7 1/2 In.	30.00
Gin, Fairchild's Excelsior, Applied Lip, Aqua, Quart	15.00
Gin, Flankenheim & Nolet, Black Glass	25.00
Gin, Free-Blown, Emerald	9.50
Gin, Genuine Holland's Geneva, Dip Mold, Case	22.00
Gin, Ginter & Co., Importers, Boston, Mass, Emerald Green, 8 1/2 In.	70.00
Gin, Hasenkamp, Hoyetema, Marken, Africa, Case	15.00
Gin, J.J.W.Peter's, Embossed Dog With Bird, Oval, Amber, Quart	55.00
Gin, J.J.W.Peters, Medium Green, Case, 10 In.	15.00
Gin, J.T.Beuker's, Schiedam, Applied Lip	35.00
Gin, London Charles Cordial, Open Pontil, Quart	105.00
Gin, London Jockey Clubhouse, Embossed Horse & Jockey, Teal Green	210.00
Gin, London Jockey Clubhouse, Embossed Horse & Rider, IP, Green	250.00

Gin, London Jockey Clubhouse, Embossed Jockey & Horse, IP, Olive	230.00
Gin, London Royal Tiger, Aqua, 9 1/2 In.Square	30.00
Gin, London, Royal, Imperial Gin, Embossed 3 Sides, Blue, 10 In.	245.00
Gin, Melcher's Finest Canadian, Geneva Distillers, Stamp Date 1917, Blue	29.00
Gin, Melcher's, Sharp Taper, Amber, 1/ 1/2 In.	125.00
Gin, Mercer, Agnew & Co., London, Swan Gin, Label, Aqua, Quart	20.00
Gin, Paul Jones Red Star, Aqua, Quart	35.00
Gin, Tapered, Olive Green, 6 1/2 In.	12.00
Gin, V.Houtema, Rolled Lip	20.00
Gin, Vandenberg & Co., Open Pontil, Case	39.50
Gin, Vandenberg, Shoulder Seal, Case, Olive Green	30.00
Gin, W.M.A.Gin, Wicker Basket, Pewter Cap, Reverse Painting, 12 In.	100.00
Globular, Midwest, Aqua, 7 1/2 In.	55.00
Globular, Pitkin, 16 Vertical & 16 Swirled Ribs, Grass Green, 7 In.	320.00
Globular, 24 Swirled Ribs To Right, Light Golden Amber, 8 In.	375.00

*Glue bottles are often included with information about ink bottles. The
numbers in the form C-0 refer to the book "Ink Bottles and Inkwells" by
William E. Covill, Jr.*

Glue, Carter's Mucilage, Clear, C-33	12.00
Glue, Spalding's, Round, Pontil, Aqua, 3 1/4 In.	10.00 To 15.00
Glue, U.S.Treasury Mucilage	7.00

Grenadier, Fray Junipero Serra, 1974

Hoffman, Big, Big Trouble On The Trail
(See Page 103)

Glue, Upton's Refined Liquid, Open Pontil, Aqua	20.00
Grant's, Drummond	16.00
Grant's, Flask, Covered	8.00
Grenadier, Bicentennial, Set Of 12, 1976	231.00
Grenadier, Fray Junipero Serra, 1974	*Illus* 31.00
Grenadier, Frosty The Snowman, 1978	36.95 To 40.00
Grenadier, Here Comes Santa, Green	28.50 To 35.00
Grenadier, Horse, American Saddlebred, 1978	30.00 To 32.95
Grenadier, Horse, American Thoroughbred, 1978	30.00 To 32.95
Grenadier, Horse, Appaloosa, 1978	30.00 To 32.95
Grenadier, Horse, Arabian, 1978	30.00 To 34.50
Grenadier, Mission Carmel, 1977	30.00
Grenadier, Mission San Carlos	30.00
Grenadier, Mission San Gabriel, 1978	30.00
Grenadier, Mission Santa Clara, 1978	30.00
Grenadier, Molly Pitcher	19.25
Grenadier, Moose Lodge, 1970	18.00
Grenadier, Nancy Hart	19.25
Grenadier, Shriner's Jester, 1977	27.00 To 40.00
Grenadier, Soldier, Baron General Von Steuben, 1978	30.00 To 34.95
Grenadier, Soldier, Baron Johann De Kalb	31.00 To 34.95
Grenadier, Soldier, Baylor's 3rd, 1969	16.00 To 40.00
Grenadier, Soldier, British Officer	18.00
Grenadier, Soldier, Brunswick Dragoons, 1976	19.25

Grenadier, Soldier, Bud Moore Ford Thunderbird .... 39.50 To 43.95
Grenadier, Soldier, Captain, Confederate, 1970 .... 16.00 To 25.00
Grenadier, Soldier, Captain, Union Army, 1970 .... 21.00 To 24.50
Grenadier, Soldier, Comte De Rochambeau .... 30.00 To 34.95
Grenadier, Soldier, Connecticut Foot Guards .... 16.00 To 19.95
Grenadier, Soldier, Continental Marines, 1969 .... 30.00 To 85.00
Grenadier, Soldier, Corporal Grenadier, 1970 .... 14.00 To 25.00
Grenadier, Soldier, Count Pulaski .... 31.50 To 36.00
Grenadier, Soldier, Dragoon 17th Regiment, 1970 .... 14.00 To 25.00
Grenadier, Soldier, Eugene, 1969 .... 16.00 To 35.00
Grenadier, Soldier, Fire Chief, 1973 .... 22.00 To 35.00
Grenadier, Soldier, Fireman Statue, Coit, 1974 .... 50.00 To 52.00
Grenadier, Soldier, Ford T-Bird, No.15 .... 46.00
Grenadier, Soldier, General Billy Mitchell, 1975 .... 22.00 To 45.00
Grenadier, Soldier, General Douglas MacArthur, 1975 .... 22.00 To 30.00
Grenadier, Soldier, General George Washington, 1973 .... 20.00 To 35.00
Grenadier, Soldier, General Lafayette, 1978 .... 30.00
Grenadier, Soldier, General Robert E.Lee, 1974 .... 20.00 To 30.00
Grenadier, Soldier, General Robert E.Lee, 1977 .... 30.00
Grenadier, Soldier, General Thaddeus Kosciuszko, 1978 .... 28.00 To 34.95
Grenadier, Soldier, General Ulysses S. Grant, 1975 .... 20.00 To 30.00
Grenadier, Soldier, George S.Custer, 1970 .... 16.00 To 25.00
Grenadier, Soldier, Hesse-Cassel 19.25
Grenadier, Soldier, Jeanne D'arc .... 75.00 To 125.00
Grenadier, Soldier, Jeb Stuart, 1970 .... 16.00 To 30.00
Grenadier, Soldier, John Paul Jones .... 18.00 To 25.00
Grenadier, Soldier, King's African Rifle Corps, 1971 .... 12.00 To 30.00
Grenadier, Soldier, Lannes, 1970 .... 17.00 To 40.00
Grenadier, Soldier, Lassal, 1969 .... 30.00 To 75.00
Grenadier, Soldier, Lucky Strike 23.00
Grenadier, Soldier, Marquis De Lafayette .... 30.00 To 34.95
Grenadier, Soldier, Minute Man 19.25
Grenadier, Soldier, Murat, 1970 .... 17.00 To 35.00
Grenadier, Soldier, Napoleon, 1969 .... 35.00 To 100.00
Grenadier, Soldier, Ney, 1969 .... 24.50 To 35.00
Grenadier, Soldier, Officer Scots Fusileer, 1971 .... 12.00 To 28.00
Grenadier, Soldier, Officer 3rd Guard, 1971 .... 12.00 To 28.00
Grenadier, Soldier, Pancho Villa & Carranza, 1977 .... 30.00
Grenadier, Soldier, Pancho Villa & Fierro .... 35.00 To 40.00
Grenadier, Soldier, Pancho Villa & Maytorena, 1977 .... 30.00
Grenadier, Soldier, Pancho Villa & Obregon, 1977 .... 30.00
Grenadier, Soldier, Pancho Villa & Zapata, 1977 .... 30.00
Grenadier, Soldier, Pancho Villa At Palacio, 1977 .... 30.00
Grenadier, Soldier, Pancho Villa Historical, Set Of 4 .... 159.95
Grenadier, Soldier, Pancho Villa Historical, Set Of 6 .... 110.00
Grenadier, Soldier, Pancho Villa Into Battle, 1977 .... 30.00
Grenadier, Soldier, Pancho Villa On Horseback .... 25.00 To 35.50
Grenadier, Soldier, Pancho Villa On Horseback, Gallon 154.95
Grenadier, Soldier, San Fernando Electric Co., 1977 .... 35.00
Grenadier, Soldier, San Francisco, 1978 .... 30.00
Grenadier, Soldier, Sgt.Major, Coldstream Guards, 1971 .... 12.00 To 28.00
Grenadier, Soldier, Stonewall Jackson, 1976 .... 36.50 To 55.00
Grenadier, Soldier, Teddy Roosevelt, 1977 .... 27.00 To 35.00
Grenadier, Soldier, Texas Ranger, 1977 .... 26.00 To 35.00
Grenadier, Soldier, 1st Georgia Regiment 19.25
Grenadier, Soldier, 1st Officer Guard, 1970 .... 19.00 To 25.00
Grenadier, Soldier, 1st Pennsylvania, 1970 .... 54.95 To 70.00
Grenadier, Soldier, 18th Continental, 1970 .... 16.00 To 35.00
Grenadier, Soldier, 1821 Officer Grenadier, 1970 .... 14.00 To 28.00
Grenadier, Soldier, 2nd Maryland, 1969 .... 30.00 To 75.00
Grenadier, Soldier, 3rd New York, 1969 .... 16.00 To 35.00
Grenadier, Tennessee Walking Horse, 1978 .... 30.00 To 32.95
    Hair Products, see Cosmetic, Medicine
Hamm, Bear No.1, 1972 .... 14.00
Hamm, Bear No.2, Bartender, 1973 .... 10.50 To 12.00
Hamm, Burgieman, , 1971 .... 50.00

Hamm, Burgieman, 1974		15.00
Hand Lotion, see Cosmetic, Medicine		
Heisey, Bottle, Banjo, Amethyst		22.50
Hoffman, Accordion Player, 1978	Color	19.95
Hoffman, Alaska Pipeline, 1975		26.00
Hoffman, Androcles And The Lion, 1978		28.00 To 30.00
Hoffman, Appaloosa Yearling, 1978		20.00
Hoffman, Bareback Rider, 1978		41.00 To 43.00
Hoffman, Bear And Cubs		49.00 To 55.00
Hoffman, Bear, 1978		40.00
Hoffman, Betsy Ross, Musical Decanter, 1974		45.00 To 55.00
Hoffman, Big Red Machine, 1973		27.00 To 34.95
Hoffman, Big, Big Trouble On The Trail	Illus	200.00
Hoffman, Blue Wing Teal, 1978		37.95
Hoffman, Bobbie Bassett, 1978	Color	19.95
Hoffman, Bobcat And Pheasant		53.00
Hoffman, Boy And Wolf		34.95
Hoffman, Buffalo Hunter, 1978		26.00 To 32.00
Hoffman, Buffalo Man, 1976		24.00 To 30.00
Hoffman, Buffalo, 1970		46.00
Hoffman, Bull Riding, 1978		40.00 To 42.00
Hoffman, Calf Roping, 1978		40.00 To 41.00
Hoffman, Canada Goose, Duck Decoy		17.00
Hoffman, Civil War Colt, Pistol, 1978		12.95
Hoffman, Clarinet Player, 1979	Color	19.95
Hoffman, Clown, 1978		40.00
Hoffman, Concord Set, Soldiers, 1973		28.00
Hoffman, Cowboy And Puma		250.00 To 300.00
Hoffman, Cowboy, 1978		26.00 To 33.00
Hoffman, Dallas Cheerleader		31.00
Hoffman, Dallas Cheerleader, Topless		150.00
Hoffman, Doe And Fawn, Musical Decanter, 1975		41.50 To 58.00
Hoffman, Dog And The Shadow, 1970		27.00 To 34.95
Hoffman, Dog Series No.1, Set Of 6		85.00
Hoffman, Donahue		25.00
Hoffman, Drummer, 1978	Color	26.00
Hoffman, Eagle, 1976		41.50 To 100.00
Hoffman, Eagle, 1977		51.00
Hoffman, Ellie Elephant, 1978	Color	19.95
Hoffman, Falcon And Rabbit		52.00
Hoffman, Family, 1977		50.00
Hoffman, Fighting Rams, Set Of 4, 1977		185.00
Hoffman, Flathead Squaw, 1976		24.00 To 30.00
Hoffman, Fox And The Grapes, 1978		27.00 To 30.00
Hoffman, Foyter, No.2, Racer, 1973		36.00
Hoffman, France, Children Of The World Series, 1978		34.00
Hoffman, Freddie Frog, 1978	Color	19.95
Hoffman, Goose With Golden Egg, 1978		28.00 To 34.95
Hoffman, Half-Breed Trader, 1978		24.00 To 32.00
Hoffman, Hare And The Tortoise, 1978		27.00 To 34.95
Hoffman, I Rode Him, C.M.Russell, 1978, Pair		60.00 To 100.00
Hoffman, Jack The Ripper	Illus	49.95
Hoffman, Jaguar, 1978		40.00
Hoffman, Jamaica, Children Of The World Series, 1978		34.00
Hoffman, Johncock Commemorative, 1978		23.00
Hoffman, Johncock, No.20, Racer, 1974		23.00
Hoffman, Kangaroo, 1978		40.00
Hoffman, Kentucky Flintlock, 1975		28.00 To 30.00
Hoffman, Lady Godiva		37.00
Hoffman, Last Of The 5000, 1975		24.00 To 35.00
Hoffman, Leo Lion, 1978	Color	19.95
Hoffman, Leprechaun Set No.2, Set Of 6		59.95
Hoffman, Leprechaun Set No.3, Set Of 6		74.95
Hoffman, Leprechaun Set No.4, Set Of 6		74.95
Hoffman, Lion & Dall Sheep, Set Of 3, 1977		152.00 To 175.00
Hoffman, Loon, 1978		37.95

Hoffman, **Marty Mouse,** 1978 ....*Color*   19.95
Hoffman, **Merganzer,** 1978 ....*Color*   39.95
Hoffman, **Mexico,** Children Of The World Series, 1978 .... 34.00
   Hoffman, **Miniature, see Miniature, Hoffman**
Hoffman, **Mr.Baker,** Musical Decanter, 1978 M .... 31.00 To 40.95
Hoffman, **Mr.Bartender,** Musical Decanter, 1975 .... 25.00 To 29.00
Hoffman, **Mr.Blacksmith,** Musical Decanter, 1976 .... 25.00 To 31.00
Hoffman, **Mr.Butcher,** Musical Decanter, 1978 .... 35.00 To 40.95
Hoffman, **Mr.Carpenter,** Musical Decanter, 1970 .... 25.00 To 35.95
Hoffman, **Mr.Charmer,** Musical Decanter, 1974 .... 24.00 To 30.95

(See Page 103)

Hoffman, Jack The Ripper

Hoffman, Puma, Mountain Goat & Kid

Hoffman, **Mr.Cobbler,** Musical Decanter, 1973 .... 23.00 To 32.95
Hoffman, **Mr.Dancer,** Musical Decanter, 1974 .... 25.00 To 32.95
Hoffman, **Mr.Doctor,** Musical Decanter, 1974 .... 25.00 To 32.95
Hoffman, **Mr.Electrician,** 1978 .... 35.00 To 38.00
Hoffman, **Mr.Fiddler,** Musical Decanter, 1974 .... *Color*   30.00
Hoffman, **Mr.Fireman,** Musical Decanter, 1976 .... 25.00 To 30.00
Hoffman, **Mr.Guitarist,** Musical Decanter, 1975 .... *Color*   32.95
Hoffman, **Mr.Harpist,** Musical Decanter, 1974 .... 25.00 To 30.00
Hoffman, **Mr.Lucky Retired,** Musical Decanter, 1978 .... 40.95
Hoffman, **Mr.Lucky,** Musical Decanter, 1973 .... 27.00 To 45.00
Hoffman, **Mr.Mailman,** Musical Decanter, 1976 .... 25.00 To 30.00
Hoffman, **Mr.Mechanic,** Musical Decanter, 1978 .... 35.00 To 41.00
Hoffman, **Mr.Plumber,** Musical Decanter, 1978 .... 35.00 To 41.00
Hoffman, **Mr.Policeman,** Musical Decanter, 1975 .... 25.00 To 30.95
Hoffman, **Mr.Sandman,** Musical Decanter, 1974 .... 24.00 To 32.95
Hoffman, **Mr.Saxaphonist,** Musical Decanter, 1975 .... 25.00 To 32.95
Hoffman, **Mr.Schoolteacher,** Musical Decanter, 1976 .... 25.00 To 30.00
Hoffman, **Mr.Stockbroker,** Musical Decanter, 1976 .... 25.00 To 31.00
Hoffman, **Mr.Tailor,** Musical Decanter, 1978 .... 35.00 To 38.00
Hoffman, **Mrs.Lucky,** Musical Decanter, 1974 .... 24.00 To 30.00
Hoffman, **Musk Ox,** Pair .... 91.00 To 104.95
Hoffman, **Northern Cree,** 1978 .... 24.95 To 32.00
Hoffman, **Panama,** Children Of The World Series, 1978 .... 34.00
Hoffman, **Panda,** Musical Decanter .... 43.95 To 55.00
Hoffman, **Porky Pig,** 1978 .... *Color*   19.95
Hoffman, **Pot Of Gold** 25.00
Hoffman, **Prospector,** 1976 .... 24.00 To 30.00
Hoffman, **Puma,** Mountain Goat & Kid .... *Illus*   100.00
Hoffman, **Ram,** Set Of 4 .... 150.00 To 195.00
Hoffman, **Red River Breed,** 1976 .... 24.00 To 30.00
Hoffman, **Rodeo Saddle,** 1978 .... 43.00
Hoffman, **Rutherford,** No.3, Racer 39.00
Hoffman, **Saddle Bronc,** 1978 .... 40.00 To 43.00
Hoffman, **Scout,** 1978 .... 24.95 To 32.00
Hoffman, **Shepherd's Bow,** 1978 .... 27.00 To 30.00
Hoffman, **Shoe Cobbler,** Musical Decanter .... 24.00 To 32.95
Hoffman, **Spain,** Children Of The World Series, 1978 .... 34.00
Hoffman, **Stage Robber,** 1978 .... 24.95 To 32.00
Hoffman, **Stagecoach Driver,** 1976 .... 24.00 To 31.00
Hoffman, **Steer Wrestling,** 1978 .... 40.00 To 43.00
Hoffman, **Stranger,** This Land Is Mine .... *Color*   200.00

Hoffman, Sunoco, No.66, Racer, 1972 .... 25.00
Hoffman, Swan, White, 1978 .... 37.95 To 41.95
Hoffman, Tower Flintlock, Pistol, 1975 .... 27.00 To 30.00
Hoffman, Trapper, 1976 .... 24.00 To 30.00
Hoffman, Tuba Player, 1978 ....*Color* 19.95
Hoffman, Vanquished, Ram, 1977 .... 50.00
Hoffman, Victor, Ram, 1977 .... 50.00
Hoffman, Widgeon, 1978 .... 37.95 To 42.50
Hoffman, Wild Life No.1, Set Of 6 .... 82.50
Hoffman, Wolf And Raccoon 55.00
Hoffman, Wood Duck, 1978 .... 37.95 To 43.95
Hoffman, Yugoslavia, Children Of The World Series, 1978 .... 34.00
    Holly City, see Millville Art Glass
Household, Aromatic Furniture Polish, Square, Grape Violet, 5 In. 65.00
Household, Confer's Remedies & Fine Housing Extracts, 6 In. ....*Illus* 8.00
Household, Favorite Sewing Machine Oil, 4 1/2 In. ....*Illus* 1.00

Household, Confer's Remedies
& Fine Housing Extracts, 6 In.

Household, Mufti Dry
Cleaner, Cincinnati, 6 In.

Household, Favorite Sewing
Machine Oil, 4 1/2 In.

Household, Nu-Air Delight,
Paper Label, 6 1/2 In.

Household, Gaslight Ammonia, Aqua 5.00
Household, Gate's Slate Cleaner, Worcester, Mass. 8.00
Household, Gordon's Chafola Furniture Polish, Embossed, Open Pontil 150.00
Household, Kil-Ol Bug Killer 5.00
Household, Morgan's Ammonia, Aqua, 8 1/2 In. ....*Color* xxxx.xx
Household, Mufti Dry Cleaner, Cincinnati, 6 In. ....*Illus* .25
Household, Nu-Air Delight, Paper Label, 6 1/2 In. ....*Illus* ' 1.00
Household, Osborn's Liquid Polish, Open Pontil, Olive Green, 3 5/8 In. 450.00
Household, Race & Sheldon's Polish, Emerald Green, Open Pontil 140.00
    Household, Shoe Polish, see Shoe Polish
Household, Stove Polish, Black Silk, 5 1/2 In. ....*Color* xxxx.xx
Household, Wavenlock For Hair, Glass Label, 8 1/2 In. ....*Color* xxxx.xx
Household, Win-Shine, Paper Label, 6 1/2 In. ....*Color* xxxx.xx
    Hudson Bay, Miniature, see Miniature, Hudson Bay
I.W.Harper, Barrel 11.00
I.W.Harper, Croquet Players 20.00
I.W.Harper, Flags Of Nations, 1966 .... 7.00
I.W.Harper, Grand Prize, 1960 .... 9.00
I.W.Harper, Harper Man, Blue, 1968 .... 10.00
I.W.Harper, Harper Man, Grey, 1968 .... 10.00
I.W.Harper, Harper Man, White 50.00
I.W.Harper, Roman Coins 8.00
I.W.Harper, Tip Bottle 15.00

*Ink bottles were first used in the United States in 1819. Early ink
bottles were of ceramic and were often imported. Inks can be identified by
their shape. They were made to be hard to tip over. The numbers used in
entries in the form C-0 or Mc Kearin G I-0 refer to the books
"Ink Bottles and Inkwells" by William E. Covill, Jr., and
"American Glass" by George P. and Helen Mc Kearin.*

Ink, Alling, 3 Cornered, Green	60.00
Ink, Barrel, Aqua, 5 1/8 In.	90.00
Ink, Barrel, Teakettle, Cobalt Blue, 2 1/4 X 3 1/4 In. ....*Illus*	550.00
Ink, Beehive Teakettle, Yellow, Green & Gold, 2 1/4 X 3 1/4 In. ...*Illus*	500.00
Ink, Beehive, Aqua, 1 X 2 1/8 In.	90.00
Ink, Bertinguiot, Olive Amber, 2 X 2 1/4 In., C-575	110.00 To 150.00
Ink, Billing's, Mauve Ink, Aqua	16.00
Ink, Blown, Deep Olive Amber, 2 1/4 X 2 7/8 In., C-1026	425.00
Ink, Blown, 3 Mold, Clear, 1 5/8 X 2 In., C-1192	625.00

Ink, Barrel, Teakettle,
Cobalt Blue, 2 1/4 X 3 1/4 In.

Ink, Cabin, Clear,
3 1/4 X 2 1/2 In., C-677

Ink, Beehive Teakettle, Yellow,
Green & Gold, 2 1/4 X 3 1/4 In.

Ink, Carter's, Cathedral,
Label, Cobalt, 8 In.

Ink, Carter's, Writing Fluid

Ink, Carter's, 1916

Ink, C.Boynton & Co., Troy, Crossed Feathers,
1 1/2 X 3 3/4 In.

Ink, Blown, 3 Mold, Golden Amber, 1 1/2 X 2 1/8 In., C-1221	90.00
Ink, Bristol Recorder Ink, Amber, ABM	8.00
Ink, C.Boynton & Co., Troy, Crossed Feathers, 1 1/2 X 3 3/4 In. .....*Illus*	950.00
Ink, C.Crolius, Manhattan, Wells, N.Y., Gray & Blue, 3 1/4 In. ....*Illus*	1600.00
Ink, Cabin, Aqua, C-682	160.00
Ink, Cabin, Clear, 3 1/4 X 2 1/2 In., C-677 ....*Illus*	100.00
Ink, Cabin, Shear Top, Green	7.00
Ink, Cabin, 3 1/4 X 2 1/2 X 1 7/8 In., C-677	110.00
Ink, Canadian Grand Trunk System, Rippled	50.00
Ink, Cardinal, Aqua	40.00
Ink, Carter's Crimson Fluid, Label	7.50
Ink, Carter's Master, Bright Green, 5 1/8 X 1 7/8 In., C-804	45.00
Ink, Carter's Spanish Mixture, Open Pontil, Olive Green	125.00
Ink, Carter's, Aqua, 9 3/4 In., Quart	15.00
Ink, Carter's, Blue Green, Pint	15.00

Ink, Carter's, Cathedral, ABM, Quart	38.00 To 65.00
Ink, Carter's, Cathedral, Label, Cobalt, 8 In. ....*Illus*	115.00
Ink, Carter's, Cathedral, 1/2 Pint	90.00
Ink, Carter's, Cathedral, 6 Sided, Blue, Label	40.00
Ink, Carter's, Cone, Amber	5.00 To 10.00
Ink, Carter's, Cone, Embossed Name On Neck Ring, Emerald Green	35.00
Ink, Carter's, Cone, Full Label, Peacock Green	17.00
Ink, Carter's, Cone, Light Amber	6.00
Ink, Carter's, Cone, Olive Green	15.00
Ink, Carter's, Cone, On Base, Emerald Green	12.00
Ink, Carter's, Cone, Yellow	15.00
Ink, Carter's, Cylinder, 1/4 Pint	5.00
Ink, Carter's, Enterprise Pottery Co., Newbrighton, Pa, Pint	5.00
Ink, Carter's, Georgetown, Mass., Embossed, Aqua, 5 1/16 In.	3.00
Ink, Carter's, Italian Green, Pint	10.00
Ink, Carter's, Ma & Pa Carter	75.00
Ink, Carter's, Made In U.S.A., Cone, Amber	6.00

Ink, C.Crolius, Manhattan, Wells, N.Y.,
Gray & Blue, 3 1/4 In.

Ink, Cone, Wood's Black Ink,
Portland, Aqua, 2 1/2 X 2 In.
(See Page 108)

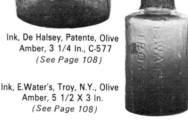

Ink, David Br'stol Troy, Gray & Blue,
1 1/2 X 4 1/2 In., C-1573
(See Page 108)

Ink, De Halsey, Patente, Olive Amber,
3 X 3 1/2 In., C-577
(See Page 108)

Ink, De Halsey, Patente, Olive
Amber, 3 1/4 In., C-577
(See Page 108)

Ink, E.Water's, Troy, N.Y., Olive
Amber, 5 1/2 X 3 In.
(See Page 108)

Ink, Carter's, Nickel Mucilage, Cylinder, Aqua, 2 3/4 In.	5.50
Ink, Carter's, Patent On Base, Feb. 14, 1899, Quart	15.00
Ink, Carter's, Spanish Mixture, Graphite Pontil, Green	85.00
Ink, Carter's, Spanish Mixture, Iron Pontil, Olive, Bubbles	85.00
Ink, Carter's, Writing Fluid ....*Illus*	.
Ink, Carter's, 1916 ....*Illus*	6.00
Ink, Carter's, 3-Piece Mold, Pouring Spout, Orange Amber, 10 In.	25.00
Ink, Carter's, 6-Panel, Clover Leaf On Base, Cobalt	48.00
Ink, Caw's Black Fluid, Pouring Spout, 8 In.	30.00
Ink, Ceramic, C-983	4.00
Ink, Clear, 2 X 3 3/4 In., C-1313	15.00
Ink, Cone, Amber	3.00 To 6.00
Ink, Cone, Aqua, 2 1/2 X 2 1/4 In., C-12	130.00
Ink, Cone, Bright Green, 2 3/8 X 2 1/4 In., C-lo	55.00
Ink, Cone, Dark Cobalt	10.00

Ink, Cone, Emerald Green	15.00
Ink, Cone, Green	12.00
Ink, Cone, Light Cobalt	7.00
Ink, Cone, Olive Amber, 2 1/4 X 2 In.	90.00
Ink, Cone, Olive Green	10.00
Ink, Cone, Pottery, Pint	29.50
Ink, Cone, Teal Green	5.00
Ink, Cone, Wood's Black Ink, Portland, Aqua, 2 1/2 X 2 In. *Illus*	130.00
Ink, Cone, Yellow Green, 2 1/2 X 2 1/4 In.	60.00
Ink, Confederate, Hand Made Pottery Cone	20.00
Ink, Continental Inks & Mucilage, Embossed, Dome, Aqua, 3 In.	7.00
Ink, Cottage, Pale Blue	250.00

Ink, Farley's, Multi-Sided, Olive Amber, 1 7/8 X 1 3/4 In.

Ink, Farley's, Octagonal, Olive Amber, 3 3/4 X 1 7/8 In.

Ink, Gray & Blue, Top Marked In Blue, Rim Chips, 1 1/2 X 4 In.

Ink, Gleich's Writing Fluid, Cobalt Blue, 10 In.

Ink, Harrison's Columbian, Cobalt Blue, 4 1/8 X 1 3/4 In.

Ink, Harrison's Columbian, Cobalt Blue, 7 1/8 X 3 1/2 In.

Ink, Harrison's Columbian, Sapphire Blue, 2 1/8 X 2 1/2 In.

Ink, Cottage, Water Butt, Aqua	100.00
Ink, Coventry, Geometric, Olive Green, 2 1/2 X 2 5/8 In.	145.00
Ink, Cylinder, Open Pontil, Light Emerald, Small, C-199	25.00
Ink, Cylinder, Spout, Open Pontil, Light Emerald	32.50
Ink, Cylinder, Tooled Pouring Lip, Blue Green, 9 In.	30.00
Ink, David Br'stol Troy, Gray & Blue, 1 1/2 X 4 1/2 In., C-1573 *Illus*	675.00
Ink, David's & Black, N.Y., Open Pontil, Green, C-753	98.00
Ink, David's & Black, Teal-Green, Open Pontil, C-205	95.00
Ink, David's, N.Y., Pottery, Pint	5.00
Ink, De Halsey, Patente, Olive Amber, 3 X 3 1/2 In., C-577 *Illus*	250.00
Ink, De Halsey, Patente, Olive Amber, 3 1/4 X 3 In., C-577 *Illus*	175.00
Ink, Diamond, Original Label, Stopper, Clear, 1 1/2 Oz.	4.50
Ink, Diamond, Red, Label, ABM	2.00
Ink, Domed, Olive Amber, 2 X 2 1/2 In., C-573	80.00
Ink, Dunbar, Taunton, Mass., Pontil, 2 1/2 In.	135.00
Ink, E.S.Curtis, Blue Black, Eagle Banner, Pouring Spout, Green, 1/2 Pint	110.00
Ink, E.Water's B Plus, 2 3/4 X 1 3/16 In., C-384, Pair	150.00
Ink, E.Water's, Green, C-208	175.00
Ink, E.Water's, Troy, N.Y., Aqua, 6 7/8 X 4 5/8 In., C-774	90.00
Ink, E.Water's, Troy, N.Y., Olive Amber, 5 1/2 X 3 In. *Illus*	375.00

Ink, English, Bust-Off Top, Green, 2 In. ....*Color* xxxx.xx
Ink, F.Kidder, Embossed, C-481 .... 90.00
Ink, Farley's, C-528 .... 375.00
Ink, Farley's, Multi-Sided, Olive Amber, 1 7/8 X 1 3/4 In. ....*Illus* 215.00
Ink, Farley's, Octagonal, Olive Amber, 3 3/4 X 1 7/8 In. ....*Illus* 340.00
Ink, Farley's, 1 7/8 X 1 3/4 In., C-526 .... 200.00
Ink, Figural, Bonney Barrell, Open Pontil 95.00
Ink, Figural, Stump, Green, Amber Swirls, C-1422 .... 245.00
Ink, Fountain Pattern, Light Yellow Green, 2 3/4 X 2 3/4 In. 250.00
Ink, Fountain, Stoneware, Tiger Eye Glaze, 1 5/8 X 3 3/8 In. 25.00
Ink, Geometric, McK G II-015, Dark Amber, C-1177 .... 175.00
Ink, Ger's & Millman, Cincinnati, O., Drip Lip, Refired Pontil, Aqua, C-59 .... 100.00
Ink, Gleich's Writing Fluid, Cobalt Blue, 10 In. ....*Illus* 15.00
Ink, Globe, Aqua, 3 X 2 1/2 In. 20.00

Ink, Igloo, Sapphire Blue,
Faint Inside Spots,
1 1/8 X 2 In.

Ink, Ithemac Conkey,
Amherst, Mass, 1835,
1 1/2 X 6 1/2 In.
(See Page 110)

Ink, J & I.E.M., Turtle, Cobalt Blue,
2 1/8 In., C-628
(See Page 110)

Ink, J.Gundry, Umbrella,
12 Sided, Embossed
Lettering, 3 In.
(See Page 110)

Ink, J.S.Dunham, Umbrella,
Aqua, 2 1/2 X 2 1/8 In.
(See Page 110)

Ink, J.Bourne & Son,
Derby Pottery, Stoneware, 7 1/4 In.
(See Page 110)

Ink, Gray & Blue, Top Marked In Blue, Rim Chips, 1 1/2 X 4 In. ....*Illus* 200.00
Ink, Ground Lip, Sun Colored Amethyst, C-605 .... 15.00
Ink, Harrison's Columbian, Aqua, 1 3/4 X 1 3/4 In., C-530 .... 45.00 To 52.00
Ink, Harrison's Columbian, Aqua, 2 X 2 In. 35.00
Ink, Harrison's Columbian, Aqua, 2 5/8 X 1 1/8 In., C-535 .... 35.00
Ink, Harrison's Columbian, Aqua, 6 7/8 X 4 1/8 In. 85.00
Ink, Harrison's Columbian, Aqua, 8 Sided, 3 1/8 In. 50.00
Ink, Harrison's Columbian, Cobalt Blue, 4 1/8 X 1 3/4 In. ....*Illus* 350.00
Ink, Harrison's Columbian, Cobalt Blue, 7 1/8 X 3 1/2 In. ....*Illus* 500.00
Ink, Harrison's Columbian, Light Yellow Green, 2 1/8 X 2 1/8 In., C-531 .... 195.00
Ink, Harrison's Columbian, Medium Green 325.00
Ink, Harrison's Columbian, Multi-Sided, Open Pontil, Green, 1 1/4 In. 150.00
Ink, Harrison's Columbian, Octagonal, Aqua, 3 1/8 X 1 1/2 In. 50.00
Ink, Harrison's Columbian, Open Pontil, Aqua, Pint, 6 In. 185.00
Ink, Harrison's Columbian, Open Pontil, Aqua, 1/2 Pint 90.00
Ink, Harrison's Columbian, Open Pontil, Cobalt Blue, Pint 250.00
Ink, Harrison's Columbian, Open Pontil, Cobalt Blue, 5 In. 145.00
Ink, Harrison's Columbian, Open Pontil, Cylinder, Cobalt Blue, 4 1/2 In. 175.00
Ink, Harrison's Columbian, Sapphire Blue, 2 1/8 X 2 1/2 In. ....*Illus* 225.00

Ink, Harrison's Columbian, 8 Sided, Open Pontil, Aqua, 4 In.	35.00
Ink, Harrison's Columbian, 12 Sided Panel, Pouring Spout, Open Pontil, Pint	125.00
Ink, Harrison's Columbian, 16 Sided, Emerald Green	250.00
Ink, Harrison's, Clear, C-538	125.00
Ink, Harrison's, Medium Green, C-530	250.00
Ink, Hover, Phila., Green, C-118	200.00
Ink, Hover, Phila., 12 Sided, C-119	129.50
Ink, Howe's Unchangeable Ink, Boston, 4 Flags, OP, Apple Green, 1/2 Pint	90.00
Ink, Igloo, Amber, 2 X 2 In.	50.00

Ink, John Holland, Cincinnati, 3 In.

Ink, Locomotive, Aqua,
Mouth Bruise, 2 X 1 1/2 In.

Ink, Josiah Jonson's, Fountain,
Brown Glaze, 2 1/2 X 2 1/4 In.

Ink, McK G II-015, 3 Mold,
Yellow Green, 1 3/4 X 2 1/4 In.

Ink, McK G II-015, 3 Mold,
Sapphire Blue, 1 3/4 X 2 1/4 In.

Ink, Igloo, Amethyst, 2 X 1 3/4 In.		45.00
Ink, Igloo, Blown, Pat., Oct.1, 1867, Metal Cap, Clear		125.00
Ink, Igloo, Deep Sapphire Blue, 2 X 1 3/4 In.		190.00
Ink, Igloo, Sapphire Blue, Faint Inside Spots, 1 1/8 X 2 In.	*Illus*	170.00
Ink, Igloo, Sapphire Blue, 2 X 1 7/8 In., C-647		110.00
Ink, Indian Sagwa, Embossed, Aqua		7.00
Ink, Ithemac Conkey, Amherst, Mass, 1835, 1 1/2 X 6 1/2 In.	*Illus*	475.00
Ink, J & I.E.M., Turtle, Amber, 1 1/2 X 2 1/8 In., C-628		55.00
Ink, J & I.E.M., Turtle, Cobalt Blue, 2 1/8 In., C-628	*Illus*	350.00
Ink, J & I.E.M., Turtle, Golden Amber, 1 3/4 X 2 1/8 In.		110.00
Ink, J.& I.E.M., Patent Oct.31, 1865		14.75
Ink, J.& I.E.M., Turtle, Aqua		15.00
Ink, J.Bourne & Son, Derby Pottery, Stoneware, 7 1/4 In.	*Illus*	7.00
Ink, J.Bourne & Sons, London, Pottery, Brown		8.00
Ink, J.Gundry, Umbrella, 12 Sided, Embossed Lettering, 3 In.	*Illus*	340.00
Ink, J.J.Butler Mercantile Writing Fluid, Cone		125.00
Ink, J.M. & S., Domed Igloo, Aqua		25.00
Ink, J.M. & S., Domed Offset Spout, Embossed, Aqua, C-633		17.50
Ink, J.S.Dunham, Umbrella, Aqua, 2 1/2 X 2 1/8 In.	*Illus*	225.00
Ink, James S.Mason & Co., Umbrella, Open Pontil, Aqua		55.00
Ink, John Holland, Cincinnati, 3 In.	*Illus*	30.00
Ink, Josiah Jonson's, Fountain, Brown Glaze, 2 1/2 X 2 1/4 In.	*Illus*	160.00
Ink, Joy's, Round, Clear, C-289		15.00

Ink, Keene, Geometric, Amber, 1 1/2 X 2 1/4 In.	125.00
Ink, Kosmian, Crossed Anchors, Square, Amber	38.00
Ink, Laughlin & Bushfield, Aqua, Open Pontil, 2 5/8 In.	250.00
Ink, Laughlin & Bushfield, Wheeling, Va., Open Pontil, 8 Sided, Green	225.00
Ink, Lockport-Saratoga, Bubbles, Pour Spout, Open Pontil, Green	55.00
Ink, Lockport, Open Pontil, Green, 8 3/4 In.	74.50
Ink, Locomotive, Aqua, Mouth Bruise, 2 X 1 1/2 In. *Illus*	550.00
Ink, Lyon's, On Base, 3 Ribbed Sides, Pen Rests	15.00
Ink, M.Tyler & Co., N.Y., Gray & Blue Glaze, 1 7/8 X 4 In. *Illus*	525.00

Ink, McK G III-020, 3 Mold, Black,
Amethyst, 2 1/4 X 3 In.

Ink, Ohr, Cabin, Green Glaze,
Base Marked, 2 3/8 X 2 1/2 In.
(See Page 112)

Ink, M.Tyler & Co., N.Y.,
Gray & Blue Glaze, 1 7/8 X 4 In.

Ink, Pitkin Type, 5 Ring,
Olive Green, 1 1/2 X 2 5/8 In.
(See Page 112)

Ink, McK G II-015, 3 Mold,
Yellow Olive , 1 3/4 X 2 1/4 In.

Ink, Marked GWR, Gray & Brown, English, 2 3/4 X 4 1/2 In.	60.00
Ink, Master, Cobalt, Label	64.50
Ink, Master, Oatmeal, 9 1/4 In.	14.75
Ink, Master, Open Pontil, Emerald Green, Quart	32.50
Ink, Master, Pour Spout, Whittled Saratoga Green, 8 1/4 In.	55.00
Ink, McK G II-015, Blown, 3 Mold, Olive Green, 1 5/8 X 2 1/8 In.	160.00
Ink, McK G II-015, Geometric, Ringed Base, Large	105.00
Ink, McK G II-015, 3 Mold, Sapphire Blue, 1 3/4 X 2 1/4 In. *Illus*	2650.00
Ink, McK G II-015, 3 Mold, Yellow Green, 1 3/4 X 2 1/4 In. *Illus*	375.00
Ink, McK G II-015, 3 Mold, Yellow Olive, 1 3/4 X 2 1/4 In. *Illus*	100.00
Ink, McK G II-016, Blown, 3 Mold, Deep Olive Amber, 1 1/2 X 2 1/4 In.	70.00
Ink, McK G II-016, Blown, 3 Mold, Deep Olive Amber, 2 X 2 1/2 In.	70.00
Ink, McK G II-018, Blown, 3 Mold, Deep Olive Amber, 1 1/2 X 2 1/4 In.	70.00
Ink, McK G II-018, Blown, 3 Mold, Deep Olive Amber, 1 3/4 X 1 3/4 In.	35.00
Ink, McK G II-018, Blown, 3 Mold, Deep Olive Amber, 1 3/4 X 2 1/2 In.	35.00
Ink, McK G II-018, Blown, 3 Mold, Deep Olive Amber, 1 5/8 X 1 3/4 In.	70.00
Ink, McK G II-018, Blown, 3 Mold, Deep Olive Amber, 1 7/8 X 1 7/8 In.	45.00
Ink, McK G II-018, Keene, Geometric, Open Pontil	95.00
Ink, McK G II-018f, Geometric, Open Pontil, Olive Green	95.00
Ink, McK G III-016, Blown, 3 Mold, Deep Olive Amber, 1 5/8 X 2 1/4 In.	40.00
Ink, McK G III-020, 3 Mold, Black, Amethyst, 2 1/4 X 3 In. *Illus*	1350.00
Ink, McK G III-029, Blown, 3 Mold, Deep Olive Amber, 1 1/2 X 2 1/8 In.	90.00
Ink, Moore Bros., Umbrella, Aqua, 2 1/4 X 2 1/4 In.	12.00

Ink, **Multisided,** Deep Olive Amber, Pontil Flake, 2 X 2 In.	35.00
Ink, **Multisided,** Light Green, 2 X 2 In., C-550	30.00
Ink, **Munyon's Paw Paw,** Large	10.00
Ink, **New England,** Pouring Spout, Olive Green, Pint	40.00
Ink, **Ohr,** Cabin, Green Glaze, Base Marked, 2 3/8 X 2 1/2 In. *Illus*	325.00
Ink, **Opdyke,** Aqua, 2 1/2 X 2 1/4 In., C-664	100.00
Ink, **P.J.Arnold,** Pottery	4.50
Ink, **Paul's,** Cobalt, Pint, Label	40.00
Ink, **Penn Mfg.Works,** Octagonal, 3 X 3 In., C-563	60.00
Ink, **Pewter Screwcap,** Clear, 1 1/2 In., C-1488	50.00
Ink, **Pitkin Type,** Deep Olive Amber, 1 5/8 X 2 3/8 In., C-1134	350.00

Ink, Pitkin Type, 6 Annular Rings,
Olive Green, 1 1/4 X 2 In.

Ink, Pottery, Ohr, Tiger's Head,
Blue Glaze, 3 1/2 In.

Ink, Pottery, Ohr, A Biloxi Welcome,
Yellow, Green, 1 1/2 X 5 In.

Ink, S.O.Dunbar, Taunton,
Mass, Umbrella, Aqua,
2 1/2 X 2 In.

Ink, Teakettle, Cobalt Blue,
Lid Missing, 2 X 3 1/2 In.
(See Page 114)

Ink, T.D.Park & Sons,
Cincinnati, Ohio, 3 In.

Ink, **Pitkin Type,** Deep Olive Green, 1 1/2 X 2 1/4 In., C-1169	250.00
Ink, **Pitkin Type,** Deep Olive Green, 1 3/4 X 2 1/4 In., C-1133	210.00
Ink, **Pitkin Type,** Olive Amber, 1 3/4 X 2 1/8 In., C-1140	160.00
Ink, **Pitkin Type,** Ribs Swirled To Left, Olive Amber	460.00
Ink, **Pitkin Type,** 5 Ring, Olive Green, 1 1/2 X 2 5/8 In. *Illus*	275.00
Ink, **Pitkin Type,** 6 Annular Rings, Olive Green, 1 1/4 X 2 In. *Illus*	475.00
Ink, **Pitkin,** Melon, Olive Green	1300.00
Ink, **Pottery,** Brown, Pouring Spout	10.00
Ink, **Pottery,** Brown, Quart	15.00
Ink, **Pottery,** C.1850, 2 1/2 In. *Color*	xxxx.xx
Ink, **Pottery,** Cone, Hilton Head Island, S.C., Civil War	8.00
Ink, **Pottery,** Ohr, A Biloxi Welcome, Yellow, Green, 1 1/2 X 5 In. *Illus*	150.00
Ink, **Pottery,** Ohr, Tiger's Head, Blue Glaze, 3 1/2 In. *Illus*	300.00
Ink, **Pottery,** Reclining Girl, 3 1/4 X 4 1/4 In, Rockingham Glaze	45.00
Ink, **Pottery,** Round, Gray Glaze, 1 5/8 X 3 In.	70.00
Ink, **Pottery,** Round, Tan Glaze, 1 3/8 X 3 3/4 In., C-1571	30.00
Ink, **Pourer,** Copper, C-1744	75.00
Ink, **Red-Amber,** Open Pontil, C-145	85.00
Ink, **Redware Pattern,** Reddish Brown Glaze, 1 3/4 X 3 3/4 In.	90.00
Ink, **Redware,** Crimped, Green & Black Mottled Glazes, 1 3/4 X 3 In.	200.00
Ink, **Redware,** Light & Dark Brown Mottled Glazes, 1 1/4 X 2 1/2 In.	100.00
Ink, **S.Fine Black,** Amber, C-192	310.00
Ink, **S.O.Dunbar,** Taunton, C-115	64.50
Ink, **S.O.Dunbar,** Taunton, Mass, Aqua, C-735	45.00
Ink, **S.O.Dunbar,** Taunton, Mass, Umbrella, Aqua, 2 1/2 X 2 In. *Illus*	120.00

Ink, Sanford's Fountain Pen, Clear	6.00
Ink, Sanford's Ink & Library Paste, BIM, Amber	5.00
Ink, Sanford's, Amber, 7 In.	3.50
Ink, Sanford's, Chimney Shape	14.00
Ink, Saratoga, Master, Vertical Pour Spout, Green, 8 In.	35.00
Ink, Schoolhouse, Diamond & Onyx, Amber	35.00
Ink, Shaw's Inks Are The Best, 8 Sided, Sheared Top, Aqua	25.00
Ink, Sheared Top, Yellow, Square	20.00
Ink, Signet, Cobalt, 9 In. ....*Color*	xxxx.xx
Ink, Snail Form Fountain, Clear, 1 3/4 X 3 1/2 In., C-1292	160.00
Ink, Square, Cobalt	4.00

Ink, Teakettle, Green, Minor Rib Flake,
2 3/8 X 3 1/2 In.
(See Page 114)

Ink, Umbrella, Sapphire Blue,
Stain, 2 1/4 X 2 In., C-129
(See Page 114)

Ink, Water's Troy, N.Y., Umbrella,
Aqua, 2 3/4 X 2 In.
(See Page 115)

Ink, Umbrella, Green,
2 1/8 X 2 1/4 In., C-118
(See Page 114)

Ink, Stafford, Pouring Lip, Deep Teal, Pint	28.00
Ink, Stafford's, Aqua, 2 3/8 In.	7.50
Ink, Stafford's, Cobalt, Pint	30.00
Ink, Stafford's, Cobalt, Quart	30.00
Ink, Stafford's, Cobalt, 1/2 Pint	8.00
Ink, Stafford's, Embossed, Kelly Green, 7 3/4 In.	30.00
Ink, Stafford's, Master, Ice Blue	17.00
Ink, Stafford's, Pouring Spout, Cobalt, 1/2 Pint	12.00
Ink, Stoddard, Cone, Embossed X On Base, Olive Yellow	90.00
Ink, Stoddard, Long Neck, Flared Lip, Open Pontil, Reddish Amber, C-145	110.00
Ink, Stoddard, Olive Amber, Open Pontil, 6 In.	35.00
Ink, Stoddard, Open Pontil, Olive Green, 4 In.	100.00
Ink, Stoddard, Open Pontil, 12 Sided ....*Color*	45.00
Ink, Stoddard, Rolled Lip, Funnel Pontil, Orange-Amber	89.50
Ink, Stoddard, Umbrella, Emerald Green	39.50
Ink, Stoddard, Umbrella, Octagonal, Orange To Reddish Amber	99.50
Ink, Stoddard, 3 Piece Mold, Amber, Pint	25.00
Ink, Stoddard, 3 Piece Mold, Green, Pint	25.00
Ink, Stoddard, 3 Piece Mold, Red Amber, Pint	25.00
Ink, Stoneware, C.Crolius, 2 3/8 X 3 1/4 In., Gray With Blue Glaze	1600.00
Ink, Stoneware, Cream Colored Glaze, 1 1/2 X 6 1/2 In., C-1574	475.00
Ink, Stoneware, Gray Glaze, 1 X 2 1/4 In., C-1555	60.00
Ink, Stoneware, Smith & Day, Gray Glaze, 2 X 3 3/8 In.	190.00
Ink, Stoneware, Tan Glaze, 1 1/2 X 3 1/4 In., C-1551	110.00
Ink, Superior Jet Black Ink, Open Pontil, Green	35.00
Ink, T. & M., Bottom Hinge Mold, Aqua, C-486	22.50
Ink, T.D.Park & Sons, Cincinnati, Ohio, 3 In. ....*Illus*	30.00
Ink, Teakettle, Barrel, Cobalt Blue, 2 1/4 X 3 1/4 In., C-1286	550.00
Ink, Teakettle, Blue Green, 2 X 3 1/4 In., C-1235	100.00

Ink, Teakettle, Clear, 1 1/2 X 2 1/8 In., Brass Cover, C-1248	80.00
Ink, Teakettle, Cobalt Blue, Lid Missing, 2 X 3 1/2 In. *Illus*	210.00
Ink, Teakettle, Cobalt Blue, 1 1/2 X 2 1/4 In., C-1268	200.00
Ink, Teakettle, Cobalt Blue, 2 X 3 1/4 In., C-1257	130.00
Ink, Teakettle, Electric Blue, 2 3/4 X 3 3/4 In., C-1237	320.00
Ink, Teakettle, Fiery Opalescent, 2 1/2 X 3 1/2 In., C-1239	180.00
Ink, Teakettle, Green, Minor Rib Flake, 2 3/8 X 3 1/2 In. *Illus*	525.00
Ink, Teakettle, Light Amethyst, 2 X 3 1/2 In., C-1257	50.00
Ink, Teakettle, Opalescent, 2 X 3 1/4 In., C-1266	80.00 To 185.00
Ink, Teakettle, Upright Barrel, Black Amethyst	600.00
Ink, Teakettle, Violet, Cobalt, Flip Brass On Spout, 7 Sided	350.00
Ink, Teakettle, Yellow Amber, 2 X 3 In., C-1235	120.00
Ink, Traveler's, Encased In Rosewood Tube, 1 X 2 1/4 In.	25.00
Ink, Traveling, Civil War Period, Wood, Encased, Spring Action	29.50
Ink, Turtle, David's Beauty, Aqua	30.00
Ink, Turtle, Embossed Bird, Green	135.00
Ink, Turtle, Light Blue Green, 1 1/2 X 2 In.	40.00
Ink, Turtle, Paneled At Base, Aqua	16.00
Ink, Umbrella, Aqua, Open Pontil	6.00 To 20.00
Ink, Umbrella, Aqua, 2 1/2 X 2 In., C-115	120.00
Ink, Umbrella, Aqua, 2 3/4 X 2 In., C-132	185.00
Ink, Umbrella, Base Embossed, Olive Green, 4 X 4 In.	125.00
Ink, Umbrella, Bright Green, 2 1/2 X 2 1/4 In., C-129	35.00
Ink, Umbrella, Cadmium Steel, Pontil, Aqua, 2 1/2 In. *Color*	xxxx.xx
Ink, Umbrella, Cobalt Blue, Open Pontil	290.00
Ink, Umbrella, Dark Aqua, Open Pontil	8.00 To 29.50
Ink, Umbrella, Deep Olive Yellow, 2 1/4 X 2 1/8 In., C-129	80.00
Ink, Umbrella, Deep Reddish Amber, 2 3/8 X 2 1/4 In.	80.00
Ink, Umbrella, Dense Amber, 2 3/4 X 2 1/2 In.	70.00
Ink, Umbrella, Funnel Pontil, Cobalt	250.00
Ink, Umbrella, Golden Amber, Open Pontil, C-133	80.00
Ink, Umbrella, Golden Amber, 2 1/2 X 2 1/2 In., C-183	50.00
Ink, Umbrella, Green, Open Pontil	29.00
Ink, Umbrella, Green, 2 1/8 X 2 1/4 In., C-118 *Illus*	250.00
Ink, Umbrella, Greenish Blue	20.00
Ink, Umbrella, Ice Blue, Open Pontil	8.00
Ink, Umbrella, Infolded Lip, Open Pontil, Medium Green	35.00
Ink, Umbrella, Light Green, 2 3/8 X 2 1/8 In.	30.00
Ink, Umbrella, Medium Amber, Open Pontil	85.00
Ink, Umbrella, Medium Green, 2 1/2 X 2 1/4 In.	40.00
Ink, Umbrella, Octagon, Cobalt	250.00
Ink, Umbrella, Octagonal, Olive Amber, 2 1/2 X 2 1/4 In.	45.00
Ink, Umbrella, Olive Amber, 2 1/4 X 2 1/8 In., C-133	65.00
Ink, Umbrella, Open Pontil, Aqua	14.75 To 24.50
Ink, Umbrella, Open Pontil, Cobalt Blue	325.00
Ink, Umbrella, Open Pontil, Deep Aqua, 2 1/4 X 2 3/4 In.	15.00
Ink, Umbrella, Open Pontil, Embossed Base, Olive Green, 4 X 4 In.	125.00
Ink, Umbrella, Open Pontil, Flat Shoulders, Emerald Green, 2 1/4 In.	32.50
Ink, Umbrella, Open Pontil, Light Green	20.00
Ink, Umbrella, Open Pontil, Olive Amber, 2 1/4 X 2 3/4 In.	65.00
Ink, Umbrella, Open Pontil, Reddish Amber	100.00
Ink, Umbrella, Open Pontil, Teal Green	50.00
Ink, Umbrella, Pontil, Embossed Base, Deep Olive, 4 X 4 In.	125.00
Ink, Umbrella, Pontil, Emerald Green	55.00 To 75.00
Ink, Umbrella, Pontil, Golden Yellow	125.00
Ink, Umbrella, Pontil, Medium Green	35.00
Ink, Umbrella, Pontil, Olive Green	45.00 To 80.00
Ink, Umbrella, Pontil, Puce	195.00
Ink, Umbrella, Pontil, Yellow Olive	80.00 To 125.00
Ink, Umbrella, Reverse 4 On Base, C-141	85.00
Ink, Umbrella, S.O.Dunbar, Taunton, Embossed Label, OP, Aqua	95.00 To 165.00
Ink, Umbrella, Sapphire Blue, Stain, 2 1/4 X 2 In., C-129 *Illus*	225.00
Ink, Umbrella, Sea Green, C-151	195.00
Ink, Umbrella, Stoddard Type, Amber	155.00
Ink, Umbrella, 6 Sided, Clear Olive Green	78.00
Ink, Umbrella, 8 Sided, Blue Green	7.00

Ink, Umbrella, 8 Sided, Open Pontil, Emerald Green, 2 1/4 In. 49.50
Ink, Umbrella, 8 Sided, Pontil, Aqua 22.00
Ink, Umbrella, 12 Sided, Bright Green, 1 7/8 X 1 3/4 In., C-182 .... 120.00
Ink, Umbrella, 12 Sided, Green, 2 1/8 In. 69.50
Ink, Umbrella, 12 Sided, Open Pontil, Aqua 39.50
Ink, Umbrella, 16 Sided, Olive Amber, 2 1/4 X 2 3/8 In. 150.00
Ink, Underwood, Embossed, Cobalt, 1/2 Pint 30.00
Ink, Underwood, Round, 2 Pen Slots, Aqua 15.00
Ink, Underwood, 8 Panel 7.00
Ink, W.E.Bonney, Barrel, Aqua, 2 5/8 X 1 3/4 In. 95.00

Ink, 3 Mold, Clear,
1 5/8 X 2 In.

Jack Daniel, Old Time
Whiskey Distillery

Jack Daniel, Old Time
Distillery Sour Mash

Jack Daniel, Pure Lincoln
County Corn Whiskey

Jack Daniel, Topaz Sour
Mash Corn Whiskey

Jack Daniel, The Finest
& Purest Of Liquors

Ink, W.E.Bonney, Barrel, Aqua, 6 X 3 In., C-660 .... 70.00
Ink, W.E.Bonney, Round, Aqua 20.00
Ink, W.E.Bonney, S.Hanover, Mass, Cone, Aqua, C-39 .... 35.00
Ink, W.W. Trademark, Teal 25.00
Ink, Ward's, Boston, Pouring Spout, 3 Piece Mold, Green, Pint 65.00
Ink, Ward's, Boston, Pouring Spout, 3 Piece Mold, Green, 9 1/4 In. 95.00
Ink, Water's, Troy N.Y., Umbrella, Aqua, 2 3/4 X 2 In. .... Illus 185.00
Ink, Wood's Black, Portland, Open Pontil, Cone, Aqua 150.00
Ink, Wordens, Metal Screw Top, Patented July 28, 1885 .... 9.00
Ink, 3 Mold, Clear, 1 5/8 X 2 In. .... Illus 625.00
Ink, 36 Rib Mold, Polished Pontil, Clear, C-1083 .... 90.00
Ink, 8 Sided, Iron Pontil, Civil War Era 24.50
Ink, 12 Sided, Open Pontil, Aqua, 2 1/8 In. 39.50
Ink, 18 Sided, Pouring Lip, Cobalt, 6 In. 30.00
Irish Mist, Decanter, Wade China 12.00
Irish Mist, Guard 5th 11.00
Jack Daniel, Old Time Distillery Sour Mash .... Illus 9.00
Jack Daniel, Old Time Whiskey Distillery .... Illus 5.00
Jack Daniel, Pure Lincoln County Corn Whiskey .... Illus 10.00
Jack Daniel, The Finest & Purest Of Liquors .... Illus 9.00
Jack Daniel, Topaz Sour Mash Corn Whiskey .... Illus 8.00

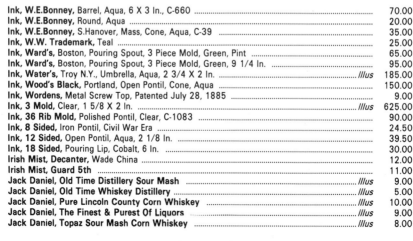

Jack Daniels, Old No.7, Gold Lettering	25.00
Jar, Baltimore Glass Works, Aqua, Quart	225.00
Jar, Baltimore Glass Works, Aqua, 1/2 Gallon	250.00
Jar, Dutch Boy Picture, Milk Glass, 6 In.	7.50
Jar, Food, Wide Tooled Lip, Hinge Mold, Funnel Pontil, Yellowish Aqua	7.00
Jar, Horlick's Malted Milk, Racine, Wis., Clear, Gallon	6.00
Jar, Kohr's, Davenport, Iowa, Glass Lid, Clear, Quart	7.50
Jar, Snuff, Hand-Painted Flowers, Wayman & Bro., Pittsburgh, Pa., Pottery	18.00
Jon-Sol, see Wisconsin Wildlife	
Jon-Sol, Slyvester Cat	12.95
Jon-Sol, Speedy Gonzales	12.95
Jon-Sol, Totem Pole	5.00
Jon-Sol, Tweety	12.95
Jug, A.P.Hotaling Co., Portland, Or., Clear, 1/5 Quart	10.00
Jug, Chestnut, Grove Whiskey, Handled, Amber	98.33
Jug, Detrick Distilling Co., Dayton, O., Eat, Drink & Be Merry, Brown	40.00
Jug, Detrick Distilling Co., Dayton, O., If You Try Me Once, Brown	37.50
Jug, Detrick Distilling Co., Dayton, O., Motto, Brown & Tan, Small	24.00
Jug, E.J.Miller, Bell Shape, 19th Century, Gray, 2 Gallon	125.00
Jug, Gilmour Thomson's Royal Stag Whiskey, Stag Trade Mark, Glasgow	65.00
Jug, Hanson's Cider Mill, Hot Springs, Ark., Tan, Blue Rim On Shoulder, 4 In.	30.00
Jug, Hayner, Dayton, Ohio, 1 Gallon	18.00
Jug, Hyman LeVine, Pueblo, Colo., 1 Gallon	30.00
Jug, J.Berkelhamer, Newburgh, N.Y., Stenciled, 1/2 Gallon	25.00
Jug, J.F.T. & Co., Handled, Golden Amber, 3/4 Quart	260.00
Jug, Jas.Durkin, Spokane, Wash., Label, Embossed, Amber, Pint	40.00
Jug, Meredith's Diamond Club Whiskey, China, Quart	40.00
Jug, Meredith's Diamond Club, Pure Rye, China, K.T.& K.On Bottom, Quart	39.00
Jug, Nock & Snyder, Louisville, Ky., 2 Gallon	16.00
Jug, O'Keefe's Pure Malt Whiskey, Oswego, N.Y., Black Print, Flowers	50.00
Jug, Our Little Pet Jug, Embossed, Applied Handle, Amber, 2 3/4 In.	45.00
Jug, R.B.Cutter's, Handled, Red Amber, Pint	120.00
Jug, R.P.Webb, Monroe, La., 1/2 Gallon	25.00
Jug, Star Whiskey, Molded Seal, Handled, Open Pontil, Amber	465.00
Jug, Star Whiskey, W.B.Crowell, Jr., N.Y., Glass Handled	375.00
Jug, Tapered Cylinder, Applied Handle & Lip, Red Amber	60.00
Jug, W.J.Van Schuyver & Co., Inc., Portland, Stopper, Amber	15.00
Jug, Whiskey, Iron Pontil, Handled, Puce	75.00
Jug, Ye Olden Time, Clay Pipe On Shoulder, Handled, Brown & Tan Design	15.00
Kentucky Gentleman, Confederate Soldier, 1969	9.00 To 11.00
Kentucky Gentleman, Frontiersman, 1969	14.00 To 17.00
Kentucky Gentleman, Gentleman With Cane, 1969	14.00 To 16.00
Kentucky Gentleman, Pink Lady, 1969	19.00
Kentucky Gentleman, Revolutionary Soldier, 1969	9.00 To 11.00
Kentucky Gentleman, Union Soldier, 1969	9.00 To 11.00
Kentucky Tavern, Captain's Quart, Gold, 1968	12.00
Kentucky Tavern, Country Scene	9.00
Kentucky Tavern, Decanter, 1952	20.00
Kentucky Tavern, Dresser, 1978	40.00
Kentucky Tavern, Shriner, 1976	20.00
Kentucky Tavern, Treasure Island	9.00
Kontinental Classics, Car, Billy Vukovich Sugarripe Special	35.00
Kontinental Classics, Car, Bobby Unser Olsonite Eagle	35.00
Kontinental Classics, Car, Corvette, 1963, Split Window	35.00
Kontinental Classics, Car, Corvette, 1978	35.00
Kontinental Classics, Dock Worker, 1978	29.95 To 35.95
Kontinental Classics, Editor, 1976	29.95 To 36.95
Kontinental Classics, Gandy Dancer, 1976	30.00 To 32.95
Kontinental Classics, Gunsmith, 1977	29.95 To 36.95
Kontinental Classics, Homesteader, 1978	29.95 To 33.95
Kontinental Classics, Innkeeper, 1978	30.00 To 35.95
Kontinental Classics, Land Surveyor, 1978	34.00 To 35.95
Kontinental Classics, Lumberjack, 1978	30.00 To 32.50
Kontinental Classics, Medicine Man, 1977	30.00 To 33.95
Kontinental Classics, Pioneer Dentist, 1978	29.95 To 35.95
Kontinental Classics, Prospector & Burro, 1977	30.00 To 40.00

Kontinental Classics, Saddlemaker, 1977 .... 30.00 To 38.00
Kontinental Classics, Santa Claus, 1973 .... 15.00
Kontinental Classics, School Marm, 1977 .... 29.95 To 34.00
Kontinental Classics, Statue Of Liberty, 1976 .... 30.00 To 32.00
Kontinental Classics, Stephen Foster, White Coat, Striped Pants, 1976 .... 100.00
Kontinental Classics, Stephen Foster, 1975 .... 30.00 To 32.50
Kontinental Classics, Village Pharmacist .... 29.95 To 34.00
Kord, Coach 38.00
Kord, Country Scene 39.00
Kord, Dancing Scene 39.00
Kord, Dolphin 12.00
Kord, Horsehead 14.00
Kord, Milk Glass 9.00
Kord, Sleigh 38.00
    Kummel Bear, see Figural
    W.A. Lacey, see Cyrus Noble
Lady's Leg, Iron Pontil, Olive Green 60.00

Lionstone, Annie Oakley, 1919
(See Page 118)

Lionstone, Camp Cook, 1969
(See Page 118)

Lady's Leg, Olive Green 45.00
Lady's Leg, Stained, Honey Amber, 12 In. 24.00
Lady's Leg, U.A.H., Red Amber, Quart 9.00
Laird's, Heritage Vase 14.00
Laird's, Jug, 1 Handle 9.00
Laird's, Jug, 2 Handle 40.00
Laird's, New Jersey Blue Soldier 24.00
Larsen, Viking Ship, China, 1969 .... 32.00
Larsen, Viking Ship, Glass 17.00
Last Chance, Banker, 1972 .... 14.00
Last Chance, Bar Scene, 1971 .... 85.00
Last Chance, Wyoming Stockgrowers 95.00
Laurel & Hardy, Hardy 16.00
Laurel & Hardy, In Car 16.00
Laurel & Hardy, Laurel 16.00
Lewis & Clark, Charbonneau, 1972 .... 46.00 To 48.00
Lewis & Clark, Clark, 1971 .... 79.00
Lewis & Clark, Cook .... 44.00 To 46.50
Lewis & Clark, Cowboy .... 44.00 To 46.50
Lewis & Clark, Frontier Family, Parents, Son, Daughter, 1978 .... 86.00 To 94.95
Lewis & Clark, General Custer, 1974 .... 32.00 To 36.00
Lewis & Clark, Indian Bust, 1978 .... 42.00
Lewis & Clark, Indian Scout, 1974 .... 32.00 To 47.95
Lewis & Clark, Lewis, 1971 .... 87.00
Lewis & Clark, Major Rend, 1975 .... 33.50 To 36.00
Lewis & Clark, Montana State, 1976 .... 48.00
Lewis & Clark, Sacajawea, 1972 .... 68.00
Lewis & Clark, Sitting Bull, 1976 .... 33.50 To 36.00
Lewis & Clark, Sun Of A Gun Stew, 1977 .... 80.00

Lewis & Clark, Trader .... 42.00 To 47.50
Lewis & Clark, Trooper, 1975 .... 33.50 To 36.00
Lewis & Clark, York, 1972 .... 48.00
Lionstone, Afgan Hound 13.95
Lionstone, Al Unser No.1 .... 15.00 To 30.00
Lionstone, Alaskan Malamute, 1977 .... 14.00
Lionstone, Annie Christmas, 1969 .... 19.00 To 23.00
Lionstone, Annie Oakley, 1919 ....*Illus*   27.00
Lionstone, Antique Car, Set Of 4 .... 59.95
Lionstone, Bar Scene No.1, 1970 .... 95.00
Lionstone, Bar Scene No.2, With Nude, 1970 .... 117.00
Lionstone, Bar Scene No.2, 1970 .... 95.00
Lionstone, Bar Scene No.3, 1970 .... 95.00
Lionstone, Bar Scene No.4, 1970 .... 95.00
Lionstone, Bar Scene, Nude Painting, Set Of 4, 1970 .... 325.00 To 750.00
Lionstone, Barber, 1976 .... 13.95 To 40.00
Lionstone, Bartender, 1969 .... 10.95 To 39.00
Lionstone, Baseball Players, 1974 .... 22.50 To 33.95
Lionstone, Basket Weaver, 1974 .... 34.95 To 55.00
Lionstone, Basketball Players, 1974 .... 23.00 To 31.95
Lionstone, Beagle 13.95
Lionstone, Belly Robber, 1969 .... 10.00 To 55.00
Lionstone, Betsy Ross, 1974 .... 15.00 To 34.00
Lionstone, Bird Set, Cardinal, Dove, Robin & Woodpecker 44.95
Lionstone, Blacksmith, 1973 .... 31.00 To 37.00
Lionstone, Blue Jay, 1971 .... 20.00 To 26.00
Lionstone, Bluebird, Eastern, 1972 .... 18.00 To 24.00
Lionstone, Bluebird, Western, 1972 .... 28.00 To 30.00
Lionstone, Boxers, 1974 .... 24.00 To 31.95
Lionstone, British Pointer, 1975 .... 11.95 To 15.00
Lionstone, British Rough Collie, 1975 .... 11.95 To 15.00
Lionstone, Bronco Buster 28.00
Lionstone, Buccaneer, 1973 .... 27.50 To 50.00
Lionstone, Buffalo Hunter, 1973 .... 35.00 To 42.00
Lionstone, Calamity Jane, 1973 .... 25.00 To 35.00
Lionstone, Camp Cook, 1969 ....*Illus*   27.00
Lionstone, Camp Follower, 1969 .... 20.00 To 28.00
Lionstone, Cannonade .... 35.00 To 49.95
Lionstone, Cardinal, 1972 .... 13.95 To 32.00
Lionstone, Casual Indian .... 5.00 To 14.00
Lionstone, Cavalry Scout, 1969 .... 5.00 To 36.00
Lionstone, Cherry Valley Club, Silver, 1971 .... 31.00
Lionstone, Cherry Valley Club, 1971 .... 19.00 To 28.00
Lionstone, Chinese Laundryman, 1969 .... 15.00 To 20.00
Lionstone, Circuit Riding Judge, 1969 .... 15.00 To 18.00
Lionstone, Circus Palomino 22.95
Lionstone, Clown, No.1, Monkey Business .... 31.00 To 43.95
Lionstone, Clown, No.2, Sad Sam .... 31.00 To 43.95
Lionstone, Clown, No.3, Say It With Music .... 31.00 To 40.00
Lionstone, Cocker Spaniel .... 11.95 To 15.00
Lionstone, Country Doctor, 1969 .... 16.00 To 37.00
Lionstone, Cowboy, 1969 .... 5.00 To 28.00
Lionstone, Cowgirl, 1973 .... 25.00 To 35.00
Lionstone, Custer's Last Stand .... 265.00 To 329.95
Lionstone, Dancehall Girl, 1973 .... 10.95 To 61.00
Lionstone, Delta Queen 50.00
Lionstone, Doberman Pinscher 13.95
Lionstone, Dove 44.00
Lionstone, Doves Of Peace, 1977 .... 35.00 To 59.95
Lionstone, Egg Merchant, 1974 .... 34.95 To 55.00
Lionstone, Elephants, 1977 .... 13.50
Lionstone, Elvis Bust .... 52.95 To 55.00
Lionstone, Elvis, No.1 .... 79.95 To 95.00
Lionstone, European Workers, Set Of 6, 1974 .... 175.00 To 198.00
Lionstone, Falcon, 1973 .... 25.00 To 30.00
Lionstone, Fireman, No.1, Yellow Hat, 1972 .... 85.00 To 95.00

Lionstone, Fireman, No.2, With Child, 1974 .... 61.00 To 89.00
Lionstone, Fireman, No.3, Down Pole, 1975 .... 37.00 To 44.00
Lionstone, Fireman, No.4, Emblem, 1977 .... 42.00
Lionstone, Fireman, No.5 .... 45.00
Lionstone, Fireman, No.7, Red Hat, 1972 .... 45.00 To 83.00
Lionstone, Football Players, 1974 .... 22.50 To 31.00
Lionstone, French Poodle, 1975 .... 11.95 To 15.00
Lionstone, Frontiersman, 1969 .... 10.00 To 55.00
Lionstone, Gambel's Quail 12.00
Lionstone, Gambler, 1969 .... 5.00 To 17.00
Lionstone, Gardener, 1974 .... 34.95
Lionstone, George Washington, 1975 .... 20.00 To 35.00
Lionstone, German Boxer, 1975 .... 15.00

Lionstone, Madame, 1969

Lionstone, German Dachshund, 1977 .... 11.95 To 14.00
Lionstone, German Shepherd, 1975 .... 11.95 To 15.00
Lionstone, Giraffes, 1977 .... 13.50
Lionstone, God Of War, 1978 .... 23.00 To 42.95
Lionstone, Goddess Of Love, 1978 .... 23.00 To 41.00
Lionstone, Gold Panner, 1969 .... 10.95 To 81.00
Lionstone, Golden Retriever, 1977 .... 11.95 To 14.00
Lionstone, Goldfinch, 1972 .... 18.00 To 24.00
Lionstone, Golfer, 1974 .... 24.00 To 34.95
Lionstone, Great Dane 13.95
Lionstone, Highway Robber, 1969 .... 13.00 To 17.00
Lionstone, Hippos, 1977 .... 13.50
Lionstone, Hockey Players, 1974 .... 22.50 To 33.95
Lionstone, Indian Squaw, 1973 .... 25.00 To 35.00
Lionstone, Indian Tribal Chief, 1973 .... 35.00 To 43.00
Lionstone, Indian Weaver, 1976 .... 25.00 To 40.00
Lionstone, Irish Setter, 1972 .... 11.95 To 14.00
Lionstone, Jesse James, 1969 .... 14.00 To 18.00
Lionstone, Johnnie Lightning, No.1, 1972 .... 44.00
Lionstone, Johnnie Lightning, No.2, 1973 .... 38.00 To 41.00
Lionstone, Judge Roy Bean, 1973 .... 25.00 To 37.00
Lionstone, Koala Bears, 1977 .... 13.50
Lionstone, Labrador Retriever, 1977 .... 14.00
Lionstone, Lion & Cub, 1977 .... 13.50 To 43.95
Lionstone, Lonely Luke, 1974 .... 10.95 To 45.00
Lionstone, Lucky Buck, 1974 .... 10.95 To 55.00
Lionstone, Madame, 1969 .... *Illus*   62.00
Lionstone, Mailman, 1974 .... 25.00 To 33.95
Lionstone, Meadowlark, 1969 .... 19.00 To 33.00
Lionstone, Mecklenburg, 1975 .... 30.00 To 50.00
Lionstone, Mecklenburg, 1975, Set Of 4 .... 100.00
    Lionstone, Miniature, see Miniature, Lionstone
Lionstone, Molly Brown, 1973 .... 29.00 To 35.00
Lionstone, Molly Pitcher, 1975 .... 23.00 To 32.00

Lionstone, Mountain Man, 1969 .... 17.00 To 48.00
Lionstone, Old Commonwealth Coal Miner, Pick 30.00
Lionstone, Olsonite Eagle, No.6 .... 26.00
Lionstone, Oriental Workers, Set Of 6, 1974 .... 185.00
Lionstone, Owls, 1973 .... 34.00
Lionstone, Paul Revere, 1975 .... 20.00 To 33.00
Lionstone, Pheasant, 1977 .... 13.95 To 45.00
Lionstone, Photographer, 1976 .... 13.95 To 41.00
Lionstone, Policeman .... 41.95 To 42.00
Lionstone, Primadonna Club Set, 1978 .... 275.00
Lionstone, Professor, 1973 .... 10.95 To 83.00
Lionstone, Proud Indian, 1969 .... 5.00 To 14.00
Lionstone, Quail, 1969 .... 13.00 To 17.00
Lionstone, Railroad Engineer, 1969 .... 13.00 To 20.00
Lionstone, Rain Maker .... 13.95 To 40.00

Lionstone, Turbo Car, STP, Red, 1972

Lionstone, Squawman, 1973

Lionstone, Sahara Golf Invitational, 1973

Lionstone, Renegade Trader, 1969 .... 25.00 To 35.00
Lionstone, Riverboat Captain, 1969 .... 10.00 To 20.00
Lionstone, Roadrunner, 1969 .... 13.95 To 30.00
Lionstone, Robin, 1975 .... 13.95 To 45.00
Lionstone, Rose Parade .... 18.00 To 35.00
Lionstone, Safari Set, No.1, 1977, Set Of 7 .... 69.95
Lionstone, Safari Set, No.2, Set Of 6 .... 69.95
Lionstone, Sahara Golf Invitational, 1973 .... Illus 40.00
Lionstone, Saturday Night Bath .... 13.95 To 41.00
Lionstone, Schnauzer 13.95
Lionstone, Sculptor, 1974 .... 34.95 To 55.00
Lionstone, Secretariat, 1977 .... 38.00 To 53.00
Lionstone, Sheepherder, 1969 .... 10.95 To 100.00
Lionstone, Sheriff, 1969 .... 5.00 To 13.00
Lionstone, Shootout At O.K.Corral, 1971, Set Of 3 .... 74.95 To 300.00
Lionstone, Sodbuster, 1969 .... 10.00 To 18.00
Lionstone, Sons Of Freedom, 1975 .... 35.00 To 43.00
Lionstone, Squawman, 1973 .... Illus 36.00
Lionstone, St.Bernard, 1977 .... 11.95 To 14.00
Lionstone, Stage Driver, 1969 .... 10.00 To 28.00
Lionstone, Swallow, Gold Bell .... 20.00 To 28.00
Lionstone, Swallow, Silver Bell 51.00

Lionstone, Tea Vendor, 1974 .... 34.95 To 55.00
Lionstone, Telegrapher, 1969 .... 19.00 To 23.00
Lionstone, Timekeeper, 1974 .... 34.95 To 55.00
Lionstone, Tinker, 1974 .... 29.00 To 37.00
Lionstone, Trapper, 1976 .... 25.00 To 40.00
Lionstone, Turbo Car, STP, Gold, 1972 .... 56.00
Lionstone, Turbo Car, STP, Platinum, 1972 .... 56.00
Lionstone, Turbo Car, STP, Red, 1972 .... *Illus*   19.00
Lionstone, Valley Forge, 1975 .... 25.00 To 35.00
Lionstone, Vigilante, 1969 .... 15.00 To 20.00
Lionstone, Wells Fargo Man, 1969 .... 10.00 To 30.00
Lionstone, Woodhawk .... 20.00 To 57.00
Lionstone, Woodpecker, 1975 .... 13.95 To 45.00
Lionstone, Zebra, 1972 .... 13.50
Liqueur, Fine Champagne Cognac, 1850, Christopher & Co., London, Black Glass 175.00

Liquor, Orange Bitters, Field, Son & Co., 6 In.

Luxardo, Clock, Cherry Ardo
(See Page 122)

Luxardo, Alabaster Fish, 1960

Liquor, Orange Bitters, Field, Son & Co., 6 In. .... *Illus*   5.00
Liquor, Osgood's India Cholacogue, Open Pontil 11.00
Lord Calvert, Canada Goose 105.00
Lord Calvert, Canadian Goose, 1977 .... 120.00 To 150.00
Lord Calvert, Wood Duck .... 55.00 To 75.00

    Luxardo bottles were first used in the 1930s to bottle the Italian liqueurs.
    The firm was founded in 1821. Most of the Luxardo bottles found today
    date after 1943. The dates given are the first year the bottle was made.
Luxardo, Alabaster Fish, 1960 .... *Illus*   35.00
Luxardo, Ampulla, 1959 .... 28.00
Luxardo, Apothecary Jar, 1960 .... 11.00
Luxardo, Apple Figural, 1960 .... 20.00
Luxardo, Assyrian Ashtray, 1961 .... 25.00
Luxardo, Autumn Leaves, Majolica, 1952 .... 60.00
Luxardo, Bablyon, 1960 ....   7.00
Luxardo, Baby Amphoras, 1956 .... 25.00
Luxardo, Bacchus .... 17.00 To 18.00
Luxardo, Bantu, 1962 .... 15.00
Luxardo, Barrel, Ceramic, 1968 .... 12.00
Luxardo, Bizantina, 1959 .... 32.00
Luxardo, Blue Fiammetta, 1957 .... 25.00
Luxardo, Bottle, Clock, 1960 .... 15.00
Luxardo, Bottle, Wobble, 1957 .... 11.00
Luxardo, Buddha Goddess, 1961 .... 25.00 To 30.00
Luxardo, Calypso Girl, 1962 .... 13.00 To 20.00
Luxardo, Cellini, 1952 .... 39.00

Luxardo, Cellini, 1968 .... 15.00
Luxardo, Cherry Basket, 1960 .... 20.00
Luxardo, Cherry Este, 1959 .... 10.00
Luxardo, Chess Horse, Quartz, 1959 .... 40.00
Luxardo, Classical Fragment, 1961 .... 20.00
Luxardo, Clock, Cherry Ardo .... *Illus* 11.00
Luxardo, Cocktail Shaker, 1957 .... 20.00
Luxardo, Coffee Carafe, 1962 .... *Illus* 25.00
Luxardo, Congo, 1960 .... 25.00
Luxardo, Curva Vaso, 1961 .... 33.00
Luxardo, Deruta Amphora, 1956 .... 25.00
Luxardo, Deruta Cameo Amphora, 1959 .... 28.00
Luxardo, Diana, 1956 .... 20.00
Luxardo, Dinosaur 13.00
Luxardo, Dinosaurs, Set Of 6 .... 54.95

Luxardo, Nubian, 1959

Luxardo, Coffee Carafe, 1962

Luxardo, Gambia, 1961

Luxardo, Dogal, Silver & Green, 1952 .... 25.00
Luxardo, Dolphin, 1959 .... 44.00
Luxardo, Dragon Amphoria, 1953 .... 25.00
Luxardo, Duck, Green, 1960 .... 34.00 To 35.00
Luxardo, Eagle, Onyx, 1970 .... 49.00
Luxardo, Egyptian, 1960 .... 20.00
Luxardo, Etrusca, 1959 .... 25.00
Luxardo, Euganean Bronze, 1952 .... 35.00
Luxardo, Euganean, Coppered, 1952 .... 25.00
Luxardo, Faenza, 1972 .... 8.00
Luxardo, Fakir, 1960 .... 31.00 To 40.00
Luxardo, Fighting Cocks, 1962 .... 25.00
Luxardo, Fish, Alabaster, 1960 .... 35.00
Luxardo, Fish, Green & Gold, 1960 .... 35.00
Luxardo, Fish, Quartz 37.00
Luxardo, Fish, Ruby, 1961 .... 30.00
Luxardo, Florentine, 1956 .... 30.00
Luxardo, Gambia, 1961 .... *Illus* 25.00
Luxardo, Golden Fakir, 1961 .... 40.00
Luxardo, Gondola, 1960 .... 16.00 To 18.00
Luxardo, Goose, Alabaster, 1960 .... 30.00
Luxardo, Mayan, 1960 .... 20.00
Luxardo, Mazzo Amphora, 1954 .... 25.00
Luxardo, Medieval Palace, 1952 .... 34.00
Luxardo, Medieval Palace, 1970 .... 8.00
    Luxardo, Miniature, see Miniature, Luxardo
Luxardo, Miss Luxardo 16.00
Luxardo, Nubian, 1959 .... *Illus* 15.00
Luxardo, Opal Majolica, 1952 .... 30.00
Luxardo, Owl, Onyx 42.00
Luxardo, Paestum, 1959 .... 19.00

Luxardo, Pagliaccio, 1959	18.00
Luxardo, Penguin, On Base, 1968	33.00
Luxardo, Pheasant, Black O.Kasis	175.00
Luxardo, Pheasant, Quartz	42.00
Luxardo, Pierrot, 1959	53.00
Luxardo, Primavera Amphora, 1958	25.00
Luxardo, Puppy, Cucciola, 1961	25.00 To 40.00
Luxardo, Puppy, On Base, 1960	32.00
Luxardo, Rhino	7.00
Luxardo, Safari, 1960	25.00
Luxardo, Santa Maria Ship	14.00
Luxardo, Silver Blue Decanter, 1952	25.00
Luxardo, Silver Brown Decanter, 1952	30.00
Luxardo, Sir Lancelot, 1962	25.00
Luxardo, Sphinx, 1961	13.00

Luxardo, Zodiac, Onyx, 1970

McCormick, Train Jupiter 60, Mail & Passenger Car
(See Page 126)

McCormick, Air Race Pylon, 1970

Luxardo, Spring Box Amphora, 1952	25.00
Luxardo, Squirrel, 1968	32.00 To 35.00
Luxardo, Sudan, 1960	25.00
Luxardo, Tamburello, 1959	24.00
Luxardo, Topa Print, 1970	8.00
Luxardo, Torre Azzurn, 1961	20.00
Luxardo, Torre Bianca, 1962	19.00
Luxardo, Torre Tinta, 1962	17.00
Luxardo, Tower Of Flowers, 1968	14.00
Luxardo, Tower Of Fruit, 1968	15.00
Luxardo, Turkey	34.00
Luxardo, Venetian Gold Rosy, 1952	23.00
Luxardo, Venetian Merletto, 1957	26.00
Luxardo, Venus Di Milo, 1959	15.00 To 25.00
Luxardo, Zodiac, Onyx, 1970	*Illus* 15.00
MBC, see Miniature, MBC	
McCormick, Abraham Lincoln, 1976	26.00 To 32.95
McCormick, Air Race Propeller, 1971	16.00 To 17.00
McCormick, Air Race Pylon, 1970	*Illus* 12.00
McCormick, Alabama Bama	10.00
McCormick, Alexander Graham Bell, 1977	26.00 To 31.00
McCormick, Arizona State Sun Devil	24.00
McCormick, Arizona Wildcat	18.00 To 22.00
McCormick, Arkansas Hog, 1972	27.00
McCormick, Auburn War Eagle	10.00
McCormick, Barrel, With Stand & Shot Glasses, 1958	30.00
McCormick, Barrel, With Stand, Gold Hoops, 1968	21.00
McCormick, Barrel, With Stand, Plain Hoops, 1968	12.00
McCormick, Bat Masterson, 1972	22.00 To 25.00
McCormick, Baylor Bears, 1972	25.00 To 26.00
McCormick, Benjamin Franklin, 1975	*Illus* 35.00
McCormick, Betsy Ross, 1975	*Illus* 37.50

McCormick, Billy Mitchell 35.00
McCormick, Billy The Kid, 1973 .... 22.00 To 25.00
McCormick, Black Bart, 1974 .... 22.00 To 25.00
McCormick, Blue Bird, 1971 .... 14.00
McCormick, Blue Jay, 1971 .... 25.00
McCormick, Brahma, 1972 .... 40.00
McCormick, C.I.A.O.Baby .... 35.00 To 38.00
McCormick, Calamity Jane, 1974 .... 22.00 To 24.00
McCormick, California Bears 10.00
McCormick, Captain John Smith, 1977 .... 26.00 To 35.50
McCormick, Charles Lindbergh, 1977 .... 16.95 To 29.00
McCormick, Charolais, 1972 .... 31.00
McCormick, Confederate, 1976, Set Of 4 .... 65.00
McCormick, Daniel Boone, 1975 .... 22.00 To 27.00
McCormick, Davy Crockett, 1975 .... 22.00 To 27.00
McCormick, Doc Holiday, 1972 .... 22.00 To 25.00
McCormick, Drake University Bulldog, 1975 .... 18.00 To 26.00

McCormick, Missouri Sesquicentennial, China, 1970

McCormick, Patrick Henry, Ben Franklin, George Washington,
Betsy Ross, Thomas Jefferson, Paul Revere, 1975

McCormick, Dune Buggy, 1976 .... 30.00 To 40.95
McCormick, Eleanor Roosevelt, 1977 .... 26.00 To 30.00
McCormick, Elvis Bust, 1978 .... 59.95 To 60.00
McCormick, Elvis Presley No.1, 1978 ....*Color* 150.00
McCormick, George Washington Carver, 1977 .... 26.00 To 30.00
McCormick, George Washington, 1975 ....*Illus* 38.00
McCormick, Georgia Bulldog .... 9.00 To 15.00
McCormick, Georgia Tech .... 9.00 To 18.00
McCormick, Gunfighter, Set Of 8 ....*Color* 100.00
McCormick, Henry Ford, 1977 .... 16.95 To 29.00
McCormick, Hereford, 1972 .... 42.00
McCormick, Houston Cougars, 1972 .... 24.00 To 30.00
McCormick, Hutchinson Kansas Centennial, 1972 .... 13.00
McCormick, Indiana Hoosiers, 1975 .... 12.00 To 18.00
McCormick, Iowa Cyclone, 1975 .... 10.00
McCormick, Iowa Hawkeye, 1975 .... 43.00
McCormick, Iowa Northern University Purple Panther 10.00
McCormick, Iowa, No Panther 34.00
McCormick, Jeb Stuart, 1976 .... 22.00 To 30.00
McCormick, Jefferson Davis, 1976 .... 22.00 To 30.00
McCormick, Jesse James, 1973 .... 22.00 To 25.00
McCormick, Jester, Mirth King, 1920 .... 25.00 To 49.50
McCormick, Jim Bowie, 1975 .... 22.00 To 27.00
McCormick, John Hancock, 1975 .... 25.00 To 35.00
McCormick, John Paul Jones, 1975 .... 25.00 To 35.00
McCormick, John Smith, 1977 .... 26.50
McCormick, Joplin Miner, 1972 .... 23.00 To 25.00

McCormick, Julia Bulette, 1974 .... 85.00
McCormick, Kansas City Chief, 1969 .... 25.00 To 41.00
McCormick, Kansas City Royals, 1971 .... 8.00 To 15.00
McCormick, King Arthur, 1979 .... 42.50 To 44.00
McCormick, Kit Carson, 1975 .... 22.00 To 27.00
McCormick, Lady Guinevere, 1979 .... 44.00
McCormick, Louisiana State Tigers, 1975 .... 12.00 To 18.00
McCormick, Mark Twain, 1977 .... 16.95 To 35.95
McCormick, McCormick Centennial, 1956 .... 175.00
McCormick, Meriwether Lewis .... 26.00 To 35.50
McCormick, Merlin, 1979 .... 44.00
McCormick, Mexican Fighting Bull, 1972 .... 32.00
McCormick, Michigan State Spartans .... 9.00 To 18.00
McCormick, Michigan Wolverines, 1975 .... 9.00 To 18.00
    McCormick, Miniature, see Miniature, McCormick
McCormick, Minnesota Gophers, 1975 .... 9.00 To 18.00
McCormick, Mississippi Rebels, 1975 .... 10.00 To 15.00
McCormick, Mississippi State Bulldog, 1975 .... 9.00 To 12.00
McCormick, Missouri Sesquicentennial, China, 1970 .... Illus 15.00
McCormick, Missouri Sesquicentennial, Glass, 1971 .... 8.00 To 12.00
McCormick, Missouri University Tiger, 1972 .... 20.00
McCormick, Nebraska Cornhusker, 1975 .... 13.00 To 18.00
McCormick, Nebraska Football Player, 1972 .... 25.00
McCormick, New Mexico Lobo, 1973 .... 33.00
McCormick, Oklahoma Sooner Wagon, 1974 .... 15.00 To 30.00
McCormick, Oklahoma Southern Cowboy, 1975 .... 12.00 To 18.00
McCormick, Oregon Beaver, 1975 .... 12.00 To 18.00
McCormick, Oregon Duck, 1975 .... 10.00 To 15.00
McCormick, Patrick Henry, 1975 .... Illus 35.00
McCormick, Patriot, Set Of 8, 1975 .... 262.50
McCormick, Paul Revere, 1975 .... Illus 52.50
McCormick, Pioneer Theater Auditorium, Reno, 1972 .... 9.95 To 8.00
McCormick, Pirate No.1, 1972 .... 10.00
McCormick, Pirate No.2, 1972 .... 10.00
McCormick, Pirate No.3, 1972 .... 10.00
McCormick, Pirate No.4, 1972 .... 10.00
McCormick, Pirate No.5, 1972 .... 10.00
McCormick, Pirate No.6, 1972 .... 10.00
McCormick, Pirate No.7, 1972 .... 10.00
McCormick, Pirate No.8, 1972 .... 10.00
McCormick, Pirate No.9, 1972 .... 10.00
McCormick, Pirate No.10, 1972 .... 10.00
McCormick, Pirate No.11, 1972 .... 10.00
McCormick, Pirate No.12, 1972 .... 10.00
McCormick, Platte Valley, Jug, Fifth 5.00
McCormick, Platte Valley, Jug, Pint 3.00
McCormick, Platte Valley, Jug, 2 Handles, Fifth, 1953 .... 10.00
McCormick, Pocahontas, 1977 .... 26.00 To 35.50
McCormick, Pony Express, 1978 .... 49.95 To 55.95
McCormick, Purdue Boilermaker .... 10.00 To 15.00
McCormick, Rice Owls, 1972 .... 25.00 To 26.00
McCormick, Robert E.Lee, 1976 .... 22.00 To 30.00
McCormick, Robert E.Peary, 1977 .... 26.00 To 31.00
McCormick, S.M.U.Mustangs, 1972 .... 25.00 To 26.00
McCormick, Sam Houston, 1977 .... 25.50 To 30.00
McCormick, Shriner, The Noble, 1976 .... 16.95 To 26.00
McCormick, Sir Lancelot, 1979 .... 44.00
McCormick, Skibob Commemorative, 1971 .... Illus 15.00
McCormick, Spirit Of '76, 1976 .... 21.95 To 75.00
McCormick, Stephen F.Austin, 1977 .... 26.00 To 33.00
McCormick, Stonewall Jackson, 1976 .... 22.00 To 30.00
McCormick, T.C.U.Horned Frog, 1972 .... 25.00
McCormick, Tennessee Volunteer, 1975 .... 9.00 To 18.00
McCormick, Texas A & M Aggies, 1972 .... 25.00 To 26.00
McCormick, Texas Longhorn, 1972 .... 25.00 To 34.00
McCormick, Texas Tech Raiders, 1972 .... 25.00 To 30.00

McCormick, Thomas Edison, 1977 .... 26.00 To 32.00
McCormick, Thomas Jefferson, 1975 .... *Illus* 35.00
McCormick, Train Engine, 1969 .... 35.00
McCormick, Train Jupiter 60, Mail & Passenger Car .... *Illus* 55.95
McCormick, Train, Mail Car, 1976 .... 35.00 To 37.50
McCormick, Train, Passenger Car, 1970 .... 32.00 To 45.00
McCormick, Train, Wood Tender, 1969 .... 24.00 To 35.00
McCormick, Ulysses S.Grant, 1976 .... 26.50 To 32.95
McCormick, Washington Cougars, 1975 .... 10.00 To 15.00
McCormick, Washington Huskies, 1975 .... 10.00 To 15.00

McCormick, Skibob
Commemorative, 1971
(See Page 125)

Medicine, Alexander's Silameau,
Bell Shape, Blue, 6 1/8 In.

Medicine, Arthur's
Renovating Syrup, A. & A.

McCormick, Wild Bill Hickok, 1973 .... 22.00 To 25.00
McCormick, Will Rogers, 1977 .... 16.95 To 35.95
McCormick, William Clark .... 26.00 To 35.50
McCormick, Wisconsin Badgers, 1975 .... 9.00 To 18.00
McCormick, Wyatt Earp, 1972 .... 22.00 To 25.00

Medicine bottles held all of the many types of medications used in past
centuries. Most of those collected today date from the 1850-1930 period.
Bitters, sarsaparilla, poison, and a few other types of medicine are listed
under their own headings.

Medicine, A.McEckron's R.B.Liniment, N.Y. 30.00
Medicine, A.Trask's Magnetic Ointment, Aqua, Square, BIMAL 1.00
Medicine, Acid Iron Earth, Nature's Own Remedy, Mobile Ala, Amber, 6 5/8 In. 45.00
Medicine, Acker Remedy For Throat & Lungs, Milk Glass 8.00
Medicine, Adamson's Botanic Cough Balsam, BIMAL 10.00
Medicine, Alaska Blood Purifier, Aqua, 9 In. 50.00
Medicine, Alexander's Silameau, Bell Shape, Blue, 6 1/8 In. .... *Illus* 400.00
Medicine, Alexander's Silameau, Light Sapphire Blue, 6 1/8 In. 400.00
Medicine, Alexander's Sure Cure For Malaria, Amber, Label .... 15.00 To 30.00
Medicine, Alexander's Sure Cure For Malaria, Liver & Kidney Tonic, Amber 12.00
Medicine, Alexander's Tricobaphe R. & G.A.Wright, Flint, Clear, 3 In. 50.00
Medicine, Alexander's Tricobaphe, R. & G.A.Wright, Flint, Aqua, 2 1/2 In. 40.00
Medicine, Allen's Lung Balsam, J.N.Harris & Co., Aqua .... 5.75 To 12.50
Medicine, Altenheim Medical Dispensary, The, Clear, 8 In. 4.00
Medicine, American Therapeutic Co., Shape Of Squat Beer, Green, 7 1/2 In. 8.00
Medicine, Anchor Pain Expeller, BIMAL 3.00
Medicine, Anderson's Dermador, Open Pontil 45.00
Medicine, Angell's Rheumatic Gum, Label 8.00
Medicine, Arabian Tonic Blood Purifier, BIMAL 25.00
Medicine, Arctic Frost Bite Cure, Box & Label, Aqua, 2 1/2 In. .... 5.00 To 8.00
Medicine, Arnica & Oil Liniment, 4 1/2 In. 3.00
Medicine, Arnold's Cough Killer, BIMAL 1.50
Medicine, Arnold's Vegetable Hair Balsam 12.00
Medicine, Arthur's Renovating Syrup, A. & A. .... *Illus* 100.00
Medicine, Asker's English Remedy, Cobalt .... 6.50 To 8.00

Medicine, Astol Hair Color Restorer, Amber	15.00
Medicine, Atlas Baby Syrup For Teething, Bowels, Griping, Label, Boxed	4.50
Medicine, Atlas Celery Phosphate Vitalizer, Manhood Hysterics, 6 In.	6.00
Medicine, Atlas Diarrhea Curative, Cures & Directions On Label, Boxed	12.00
Medicine, Atlas Liver Pellets For Dyspepsia, Amber, 5 3/4 In.	2.75
Medicine, Atlas Worm Killer, Aqua, 6 In.	4.50
Medicine, Ayer's Cherry Pectoral	2.00 To 5.00
Medicine, Ayer's Cherry Pectoral, Lowell, Mass, Open Pontil, 7 1/4 In.	40.00
Medicine, Ayer's Cherry Pectoral, Rectangular, OP, Aqua, 7 In.	12.00 To 30.00
Medicine, Ayer's Hair Vigor, Cobalt	15.00
Medicine, Ayer's Hair Vigor, Rectangular, Deep Peacock Blue	16.00
Medicine, Ayer's Senopos, Contents	5.00
Medicine, B.W.Hair's Asthma Cure, Cincinnati, Ohio, Clear	15.00
Medicine, B.W.Hair's Asthma Cure, Hamilton, Ohio, C.1878, Aqua	19.00
Medicine, Baker's Pain Panacea, Open Pontil	45.00
Medicine, Baker's Vegetable Blood & Liver Cure	200.00
Medicine, Baker's Vegetable Blood & Liver Cure, Amber, 9 1/2 In.	250.00
Medicine, Baldwin's Celery Pepsin & Dandelion Tonic, Amber	20.00
Medicine, Balm Of Thousand Flowers, Fetridge & Co., Beveled, OP	50.00
Medicine, Balm Of Thousand Flowers, Fetridge & Co., N.Y.	23.00
Medicine, Balm, Of Thousand Flowers, N.Y., 8 Sided, Rectangular, OP	60.00
Medicine, Balsam Of Honey, Open Pontil, Aqua	30.00
Medicine, Bancroft's Instant Relief & Liniment, BIMAL	8.50
Medicine, Barry's Triopherous For Skin & Hair, Open Pontil	12.00 To 25.00
Medicine, Batchelor's Hair Dye, Open Pontil	15.00
Medicine, Bauer's Cough Cure, Aqua	3.50
Medicine, Bauer's Cough Cure, Clear, 3 In.	4.50
Medicine, Bauer's Cough, Label, Sample Size	5.00
Medicine, Beck's Sprudel Vichi Cures Headache, Clear, 2 1/2 In.	10.00
Medicine, Begg's Cherry Cough Syrup, Aqua	5.00
Medicine, Bell's Vegetable Pectoral Balsam, Cylinder, Cobalt, 5 In.	20.00
Medicine, Berry's Canker Cure	3.00
Medicine, Billington's Lightning Liniment	5.00
Medicine, Bird's Lung Cure	15.00
Medicine, Bishop's Citrate Of Lithia For Gout, Blue	9.00
Medicine, Bitterwitch, San Francisco, Amber	160.00
Medicine, Blasser's Hemlock Liniment, Open Pontil	20.00
Medicine, Blood & Liver Syrup, Light Green	12.00
Medicine, Bonpland's Fever & Ague Remedy, New York, Open Pontil	45.00
Medicine, Boston Cough Balm, Dayton, O., BIMAL, Aqua	10.00
Medicine, Brandreth's Vegetable Antidote For Ague, Piqua, Ohio, 7 1/2 In.	15.00
Medicine, Brant's Indian Pulmonary Balsam	32.00 To 45.00
Medicine, Brant's Indian Pulmonary Balsam, Open Pontil	46.00 To 50.00
Medicine, Brant's Indian Purifying Extract	45.00
Medicine, Brinckerhoff's Health Restorative, Iron Pontil	245.00
Medicine, Brinckerhoff's Health Restorative, Price One Dollar, Green	250.00
Medicine, Bristol Pills, Aqua	6.00
Medicine, Bromo Caffeine, Cobalt	1.00
Medicine, Bromo Caffeine, Light Blue, 3 1/4 In.	2.00
Medicine, Brooking's American Life Drops	3.00
Medicine, Brother Benjamin Herbalo Compound For The Stomach, Blood, Aqua	12.00
Medicine, Buchan's Hungarian Balm Of Life, Aqua, Open Pontil, 6 In.	55.00
Medicine, Buchu Remedy, Log Cabin Hops, Dark Amber	120.00
Medicine, Budwell's Emulsion Cod Liver Oil, Lynchburg, Va., Cobalt, Pint	44.50
Medicine, Bull's Cough Syrup	1.00
Medicine, Burk's White Pine Balsam Cough Cure, Quincy, Ill.	4.50
Medicine, Burke's Bone & Nerve Liniment	5.00
Medicine, Burlington's Vegetable Cough Syrup, Aqua, Open Pontil	30.00
Medicine, Burnside's Purifico, Clear	6.00
Medicine, C.Goddard Pain Extracting Lotion, Baltimore, OP, Aqua	60.00
Medicine, C.Heimstreet & Co., Troy, N.Y., Open Pontil, Cobalt Blue	100.00
Medicine, C.Sine's Tar Wild Cherry & Hoarhound, Phil., Cloudy	22.00
Medicine, Caldwell's Syrup Pepsin	2.00
Medicine, California Fig Syrup	1.00
Medicine, Calvert's Derby Cure For Influenza & Colds, Aqua	35.00
Medicine, Cann's Kidney Cure	20.00

Medicine, Carson's Blood Purifier, Jamestown, N.Y., Aqua, 7 5/8 In. 25.00
Medicine, Carter's Spanish Mixture, Amber, 3/4 Quart 200.00
Medicine, Carter's Spanish Mixture, Olive Green, Open Pontil 135.00
Medicine, Castor Oil, Cobalt Blue, 8 1/2 In. 6.00
Medicine, Castor Oil, Paper Label 3.00
Medicine, Caswell Hazard & Co., Chemists, BIMAL, Cobalt Blue 35.00
Medicine, Catarrh Cure, Paper Label, 2 1/2 In. ....Color xxxx.xx
Medicine, Celery Compound, BIMAL 12.00
Medicine, Celery Nerve Tonic, Toledo, Amber 15.00
Medicine, Certain Group Cure 4.00
Medicine, Chamberlain's Cough Remedy, Contents & Label, 5 In. 5.00
Medicine, Chamberlain's Pain Balm, Des Moines, Iowa, Aqua, 5 1/4 In. 3.00
Medicine, Chamerlain's Colic Cholera & Diarrhoea Remedy, Milk Glass 4.00
Medicine, Chas.Bachman's, Holland & Genever Cordial, Olive Amber, 3/4 Quart 150.00
Medicine, Chase's Dyspepsia Cure 10.00
Medicine, Checini's Indian Sebago, The Great Blood Purifier, Aqua 15.00
Medicine, Checker's Makes People New All Over, Winston-Salem, Amber 20.00
Medicine, Christie's Aqua Balsam, Chicago 4.00
Medicine, Christie's Magnetic Fluid Cure, Aqua 50.00
Medicine, Clark's Peruvian Syrup, Aqua 5.00
Medicine, Clemets Tonic, Amber, 7 3/4 In. 12.75
Medicine, Clewley's Miraculous Cure For Rheumatism, Aqua, 7 1/4 In. 125.00
Medicine, Clewley's Miraculous Cure, Embossed Nun's Head, Aqua, 6 1/2 In. 99.50
Medicine, Clewley's Miraculous Cure, Small 55.00
Medicine, Clifton's Balsamic Cough Mixture 8.75
Medicine, Clinic Blood Purifier, The, Amber, 9 In. 15.00
Medicine, Clirehugh's Tricopherous For Hair & Skin, Open Pontil, Aqua 30.00
Medicine, Cod Liver Oil, Reddish Amber 25.00
Medicine, Coe's Dyspepsia Cure, Aqua 16.00
Medicine, Coffeen's, Liniment, No.2, 4 1/4 In. 50.00
Medicine, Collier's Celery Compound, Contents & Label 6.00
Medicine, Collin's Cough Elixir 7.75
Medicine, Compound Asiatic Balsam, Open Pontil 35.00
Medicine, Compound Seneka Balsam, Lambertville, N.J. 5.00
Medicine, Congreve's Celebrated Balsamic Elixir, Clear, 5 In. 7.50
Medicine, Connell's Brahminical Moonplant, Embossed Feet & Star, Amber 115.00
Medicine, Conner's Blood Remedy, Amber, 9 7/8 In. 15.00
Medicine, Conner's Blood Remedy, Embossed On Crock, Tan, 6 1/2 In. 20.00
Medicine, Constitution Life Syrup, BIMAL 35.00
Medicine, Cough Cold Fever Drops 2.00
Medicine, Craemer's Certain Cure, St.Louis, Flask Shape, Amber 75.00
Medicine, Craft's Distemper & Cough Remedy, Amber 6.00
Medicine, Craig Kidney Cure Co., Oval Sides, Amber, 9 1/2 In. 175.00
Medicine, Craig Kidney Cure Co., Slug For Label, Light Amber, 9 1/2 In. 175.00
Medicine, Craig's Kidney & Liver Cure 135.00
Medicine, Craig's Kidney & Liver Cure Co., Amber 125.00
Medicine, Cramer's Cough Cure, Label 8.00
Medicine, Cramer's Kidney & Liver Cure .... 6.00 To 8.00
Medicine, Cramer's Kidney & Liver Cure, Label, BIMAL, Clear 20.00
Medicine, Cramer's Kidney Cure, Aqua, 4 1/4 In. 5.00
Medicine, Crosby's Balsamic Cough Elixir 11.50
Medicine, Cure-Schiline, Cures Cattle Diseases, Aqua, 7 1/4 In. 60.00
Medicine, Cuticura System Of Curing Constitutional Humors, Aqua 10.00
Medicine, Cuticura System Of Curing Constitutional Humors, Green 10.00
Medicine, Cutler Bros., Vegetable Pulmonary Balsam 5.00
Medicine, D.F.Owen's Wood's Liniment, Rockville, Md., Aqua 15.00
Medicine, D.Howe's Arabian Milk Cure, Aqua, 7 5/8 In. 30.00
Medicine, DaCosta's Radical Cure, Aqua, Small 18.00
Medicine, DaCosta's Radical Cure, Morris & Heritage, Philadelphia 45.00
Medicine, Dale's Remedy For Epilepsy, Imperative, Register, Blue, 6 1/2 In. 31.00
Medicine, Davis Pain Killer, Aqua, 4 1/4 In. 15.00
Medicine, Davis Pain Killer, Aqua, 6 In. 2.50
Medicine, Davis Vegetable Pain Killer, Open Pontil, Aqua, 4 1/2 In. 25.00
Medicine, Davis Vegetable Pain Killer, Open Pontil, BIMAL 28.00
Medicine, Davis' Indian Remedy Sure Cure, Triangular Shape, Aqua 275.00
Medicine, Diabetes Cure, Dark Amber 45.00

Medicine, Dill's Balm Of Life	3.00
Medicine, Dill's Cough Syrup, Rectangular	1.00
Medicine, Dinsmore Croup Balsam	2.00
Medicine, Doctor Crumb's Union Ointment	4.00
Medicine, Doctor Harrison's Chalybeate Tonic, 3 Panel, Green, 9 1/8 In.	75.00
Medicine, Dodol's Dyspepsia Cure, Sample Size, Clear	5.00
Medicine, Double Strength Life Balsam, Lockport, Green, Quart	35.00
Medicine, Down's Balsamic Elixir, 4 1/2 In.	2.50
Medicine, Dr.A.C.Daniel's Liniment	2.50
Medicine, Dr.A.P.Sawyer's Family Cure, Chicago, Contents, Seal, Aqua, 7 In.	35.00
Medicine, Dr.Armistead's Famous Ague Tonic	7.00
Medicine, Dr.B.W.Hair's Asthma Cure, Hamilton, Ohio, Square, Clear	8.00
Medicine, Dr.Baker's Pain Panacea, Open Pontil, Greenish Aqua	40.00
Medicine, Dr.Ball's Hustena, Greatest Of All Cough Cures, Clear Amethyst	8.00
Medicine, Dr.Bauer's Cough Cure	4.00
Medicine, Dr.Bell's Universal Blood Purifier, Clear, 9 In.	15.00
Medicine, Dr.Birney's Catarrhal Powder, 2 1/2 In.	3.00
Medicine, Dr.Blackman's Genuine Healing Balsam, Open Pontil	40.00
Medicine, Dr.Bock's Restorative, Paducah	20.00
Medicine, Dr.Boshee's German Syrup, 7 In.	2.00
Medicine, Dr.Broga's Blood & Liver Syrup, Clear, 8 3/4 In.	30.00
Medicine, Dr.Browder's Syrup Of Indian Turnip, Open Pontil, Aqua	90.00
Medicine, Dr.Buck's Cough Remedy	12.00
Medicine, Dr.Buker's Kidney Pills Cure, BIMAL	10.00
Medicine, Dr.Bull's Cough Syrup, Aqua, Rectangular	1.00
Medicine, Dr.Bull's Cough Syrup, Milk Glass	4.00
Medicine, Dr.Burham's San-Jak Kidney Cure, Label, Box & Contents	35.00
Medicine, Dr.Ceeson's Tiger Oil, Lung Cotus & Elephant Of The Blood, Aqua	50.00
Medicine, Dr.Chapman's Cholera Syrup	10.00
Medicine, Dr.Chase's Liquid Menthol, BIMAL	5.00
Medicine, Dr.Cole's Catarrh, Aqua, Small	10.00
Medicine, Dr.Craig's Kidney Cure	200.00
Medicine, Dr.Cumming's Vegetine, Aqua, 9 3/4 In.	3.50
Medicine, Dr.Dadirrian's Zoolak	4.00
Medicine, Dr.Daniel's Colic Cure, Milk Glass	4.00
Medicine, Dr.Daniel's Veterinary Colic Drops	1.00
Medicine, Dr.Davis Compound Syrup Of Wild Cherry & Tar, Aqua	22.00
Medicine, Dr.Denig's Worm Syrup, Open Pontil	10.00
Medicine, Dr.Dewitt's Liver, Blood & Kidney Cure, Parker Co., Amber, 8 In.	25.00
Medicine, Dr.Drake's Croup Remedy	1.75
Medicine, Dr.Drake's German Group Remedy, Milk Glass	5.00
Medicine, Dr.E.C.'s Balm, Aqua	5.00
Medicine, Dr.E.G.Gould's Pin Worm Syrup, Open Pontil, Aqua	30.00
Medicine, Dr.E.S.Johnson Blood Syrup, Farmington, Me., Aqua, 10 1/4 In.	35.00
Medicine, Dr.Edward's Tar, Wild Cherry & Naphtha Cough Syrup, Aqua	30.00
Medicine, Dr.Elliot's Speedy Cure, Aqua	16.00
Medicine, Dr.Elmore's Rheumatine Coutaline, Amber, Pint, Label	25.00
Medicine, Dr.Evan's Camomile Pills, Open Pontil, Aqua	15.00
Medicine, Dr.Faloon's R.W.Balsam	8.00
Medicine, Dr.Flint's Remedy, Amber	20.00
Medicine, Dr.Flower's Scientific Remedies, Amber, BIMAL	20.00
Medicine, Dr.Forsha's Alterative Balm	75.00
Medicine, Dr.Frost's Dyspepsia Cure, Label, Pills, Box	1.25
Medicine, Dr.Geo.Clayton Dog Remedies, 4 1/2 In.	4.00
Medicine, Dr.Goss, Rheumatic Remedy & Blood Purifier, Aqua, 9 1/4 In.	20.00
Medicine, Dr.Goudy's Magic Liniment	5.00 To 12.00
Medicine, Dr.Graydon, Diseases Of The Lung, Cincinnati, O., Amber, 7 In.	30.00
Medicine, Dr.Green's Blood Purifier & Nerve Tonic, Label, 9 In.	7.00
Medicine, Dr.Guertin's Nervine Syrup, For Epilepsy, BIMAL	12.00
Medicine, Dr.H.A.Ingham's Nervine Pain Cural, Label, Blue Aqua, 5 7/8 In.	15.00
Medicine, Dr.H.A.Ingham's Nervine Pain Extract, Pontil, 4 1/4 In.	18.00
Medicine, Dr.H.G.Boot, Elipizone, Cure For Fits & Epilepsy, Aqua, 8 1/2 In.	37.00
Medicine, Dr.H.Swayne's Compound Syrup Of Wild Cherry, 4 Panels, 6 In.	35.00
Medicine, Dr.Haingham's Nervine Pain Cural, Label, Blue Aqua, 5 7/8 In.	15.00
Medicine, Dr.Hale's Household Cough Cure, 6 In.	6.00
Medicine, Dr.Hart's King Of Remedies For The Blood, Aqua, 8 7/8 In.	20.00

Medicine, Dr.Hart's King Of Remedies, Southington, Conn., BIMAL, Aqua	5.00
Medicine, Dr.Hart's Rheumatic Remedy, Milk Glass	8.00
Medicine, Dr.Harter's Dixie Tonic, Half-Moon, Word Trademark, Oval, Amber	200.00
Medicine, Dr.Harter's Iron Tonic, Amber, 6 In.	26.00
Medicine, Dr.Harter's Iron Tonic, Amber, 9 In.	4.00 To 20.00
Medicine, Dr.Harter's Lung Balm, Label	27.00
Medicine, Dr.Hartshorn's Family Medicines, Aqua, 7 In.	8.00
Medicine, Dr.Hartshorn's Family, Oval, Aqua, 7 In.	24.00
Medicine, Dr.Hawk's Universal Stimulant, Aqua, 3 1/2 In.	4.00
Medicine, Dr.Hay's Hair Health, Amber, 6 1/2 In.	5.00
Medicine, Dr.Hayne's Arabian Balsam	3.00
Medicine, Dr.Henley's Celery, Beef & Iron, San Francisco, Amber	40.00

Medicine, Dr.Herrick's German Horse Liniment, 6 1/2 In.

Medicine, Dr.Herrick's German Horse Liniment, 6 1/2 In. *Illus*	4.00
Medicine, Dr.Hess' Distemper, Fever & Cough Remedy, BIMAL	8.50
Medicine, Dr.Higgins' Great Antalgica, Label	13.00
Medicine, Dr.Hooker's Cough & Croup Syrup	8.00 To 35.00
Medicine, Dr.Hooker's Cough & Croup Syrup, Aqua, 5 3/4 In.	5.50
Medicine, Dr.Ira Hatch's Febrifuge Mixture	10.00
Medicine, Dr.J.A.McArthur Syrup Of Hypophosphates, Clear, Square, Bimal	2.00
Medicine, Dr.J.Blackman's Genuine Healing Balsam, 8 Sided, Flint, OP	35.00
Medicine, Dr.J.H.McLean's Balm, BIMAL	14.00
Medicine, Dr.J.H.McLean's Strengthening Cordial, Blood Purifier, BIMAL	12.00
Medicine, Dr.J.J.McBride, King Of Pain, Sunken Panels, Aqua, 6 1/8 In.	10.00
Medicine, Dr.J.Kauffman's Angline Rheumatism Cure, Hamilton, Ohio, Clear	12.00
Medicine, Dr.J.Pettit's Canker Balsam, Aqua, 3 In.	6.50
Medicine, Dr.Jackson's Rheumatic Liniment, Phila., Open Pontil	65.00
Medicine, Dr.Jayne's Alterative, Open Pontil	20.00 To 25.00
Medicine, Dr.Jayne's Alterative, Open Pontil, Aqua	15.00
Medicine, Dr.Jayne's Alterative, Open Pontil, 6 3/4 In.	9.75
Medicine, Dr.Jayne's Carminative Balsam, Philadelphia, Open Pontil	25.00
Medicine, Dr.Jayne's Expectorant, Philadelphia, Open Pontil, Aqua	22.00
Medicine, Dr.Jayne's Liniment, Open Pontil	45.00
Medicine, Dr.Jayne's Tonic Vermifuge, Open Pontil	13.00
Medicine, Dr.Jones' Liniment, Aqua, 6 1/2 In.	5.00
Medicine, Dr.Jones' Red Clover Tonic, Amber	25.00 To 55.00
Medicine, Dr.Jones' Sanguin, A Blood & Nerve Remedy, Aqua, 9 In.	10.00
Medicine, Dr.Josephus' Great Shoshone Remedy, Aqua	45.00
Medicine, Dr.Keeley's, Cure For Drunkenness, 1881	35.00 To 75.00
Medicine, Dr.Kennedy's Favorite Remedy	2.00
Medicine, Dr.Kennedy's Medical Discovery, Aqua, 9 In.	8.00
Medicine, Dr.Kennedy's Medical Discovery, Deep Aqua, 9 In.	35.00
Medicine, Dr.Kennedy's Medical Discovery, Roxbury, Mass.	50.00
Medicine, Dr.Kennedy's Prairie Weed	26.00
Medicine, Dr.Kennedy's Prairie Weed, Roxbury, Mass., Aqua	12.00
Medicine, Dr.Kennedy's Rheumatic Liniment	3.50 To 8.00
Medicine, Dr.Kennedy's Salt Rheum Ointment, Aqua, Pontil	75.00
Medicine, Dr.Kilmer's Autumn Leaf Extract Of Uterine Injection, Aqua	35.00
Medicine, Dr.Kilmer's Cough Cure, Aqua, 5 3/4 In.	18.00
Medicine, Dr.Kilmer's Cough Cure, Aqua, 7 1/4 In.	25.00

Medicine, Dr.Kilmer's Female Remedy, Aqua, 9 In.	25.00
Medicine, Dr.Kilmer's Heart Remedy	25.00
Medicine, Dr.Kilmer's Herbal Extract For Uterine Injection	65.00
Medicine, Dr.Kilmer's Indian Cough Cure Consumption Oil, Aqua, 7 In.	18.00
Medicine, Dr.Kilmer's Indian Cough Remedy Consumption Oil, Aqua, 5 3/4 In.	15.00
Medicine, Dr.Kilmer's Ocean Weed Heart Remedy, Embossed, Aqua, 8 1/2 In.	25.00
Medicine, Dr.Kilmer's Ocean Weed Heart Remedy, Small	12.00
Medicine, Dr.Kilmer's Swamp Root & Kidney Cure, Aqua	15.00
Medicine, Dr.Kilmer's Swamp Root Cure, London	10.00
Medicine, Dr.Kilmer's Swamp Root, Kidney, Liver & Bladder Remedy, Aqua	3.50
Medicine, Dr.King's Liver, Kidney & Blood Cleanser, Clear, 9 In.	20.00
Medicine, Dr.King's New Discovery For Consumption, Aqua, 6 1/4 In., BIMAL	4.00
Medicine, Dr.King's New Life Pills, Square, BIMAL	1.00
Medicine, Dr.L.E.Keeley's Cure For The Tobacco Habit, Pouring Lip, Clear	99.50
Medicine, Dr.Larivieri's Female Health Regulator, Aqua	12.00
Medicine, Dr.Larookah's Indian Vegetable Pulmonic Syrup	25.00
Medicine, Dr.Lawrence's Cough Balsam	1.75
Medicine, Dr.Lekeeley's Gold Cure For Drunkenness, Lip Chip	28.00
Medicine, Dr.Lemke's Family Medicines	3.00
Medicine, Dr.Lesure's Liniment, Keene, N.H., Clear, 6 1/4 In.	4.00
Medicine, Dr.Lesure's Veterinary Colic Cure, Clear	3.00
Medicine, Dr.M.F.Margle's Blood Syrup, Gardiner, Me., Aqua, 7 5/8 In.	20.00
Medicine, Dr.M.G. Kerr & Bertolet Compound, Asiatic Balsam, Norristown, Pa.	50.00
Medicine, Dr.M.M.Fenner's Blood & Liver Pills, Paper Box	5.00
Medicine, Dr.M.M.Fenner's Cure, Glop Top, Amber	20.00
Medicine, Dr.M.M.Fenner's Kidney And Backache Cure, Amber	27.50
Medicine, Dr.M.M.Fenner's Peoples Remedies, Kidney & Backache, Amber	15.00
Medicine, Dr.M.M.Fenning's Fever Cure, Aqua, 6 1/4 In.	4.00 To 7.00
Medicine, Dr.M.M.Townsend's Remedy For Hay Fever, BIMAL	15.00
Medicine, Dr.McMunn's Elixer Of Opium	8.00
Medicine, Dr.McMunn's Elixir Of Opium, Cylindrical, Open Pontil	20.00
Medicine, Dr.Miles Nervine, Aqua, 8 In. ....Color	1.00
Medicine, Dr.Miles New Heart Cure, Aqua	5.00
Medicine, Dr.Miles New Heart Cure, BIMAL, 8 In.	10.00
Medicine, Dr.Miles Restorative Nervine	2.00
Medicine, Dr.Miles Restorative Nervine, Lime Green, 8 In.	15.00
Medicine, Dr.Morse's Indian Root Pills, 1901, Indian On Horse	10.00
Medicine, Dr.Morse's Invigorating Cordial, Aqua, Open Pontil, 7 1/2 In.	50.00
Medicine, Dr.N.C.White's Poly Elixir, Aqua, 4 1/2 In.	4.00
Medicine, Dr.Nywall's Family Medicine, 7 1/2 In.	9.00
Medicine, Dr.O.Phelp's Acacian Balsam, BIMAL	19.50
Medicine, Dr.O.Phelp's Brown, Jersey City, N.J., Square, Aqua	1.00
Medicine, Dr.Park's Wyandoke Indian Liniment, Label	8.00
Medicine, Dr.Parke's Sure Cure For Headache, Clear	9.00
Medicine, Dr.Perer's Blood Vitalizer, 1780-1880 Trademark, Amethyst, 10 In.	8.00
Medicine, Dr.Peter Fahrney's Blood Cleanser, Amber, 9 1/2 In.	50.00
Medicine, Dr.Philip Thorpe's Laxative, Pumpkinseed	30.00
Medicine, Dr.Pierce's Anuric Tablets For Kidney & Backache, Aqua, BIMAL	2.50
Medicine, Dr.Pierce's Golden Medical Discovery, Aqua	2.00 To 8.00
Medicine, Dr.Pinkham's Emmenagogue, Dark Aqua	65.00
Medicine, Dr.Poland's White Pine Compound, Aqua	6.00
Medicine, Dr.Porter's, N.Y., Open Pontil, Aqua	19.50 To 25.00
Medicine, Dr.Puscheck's Pushkuro, Chicago, Ill., Round, Amber, 8 3/4 In.	25.00
Medicine, Dr.Pyle's Azoturia, Box, 8 1/2 In. ....Color	xxxx.xx
Medicine, Dr.R.A.Ingham's Nervine Paincural, Aqua, 4 3/4 In.	4.50
Medicine, Dr.R.W.Lougee Vitalizing Compound, BIMAL	27.00
Medicine, Dr.Richmond's Samaritan Nervine, 1880s, Embossed Man, Flint	5.00
Medicine, Dr.Roback's Swedish Remedy, Internal Haze, Small	85.00
Medicine, Dr.Robbins' Tecumseh Rheumatic Drops, Blue, 4 In. ....Illus	650.00
Medicine, Dr.Robert B.Folger's Olosaonian, N.Y., Long Neck, Aqua, 7 3/8 In.	75.00
Medicine, Dr.Roger's Liverwort, Tar, Canchalagua	75.00
Medicine, Dr.Roger's Vegi-Medica Syrup, Aqua, 9 In.	9.00
Medicine, Dr.Rooke's Rheumatic Lixile, Cobalt, 5 1/8 In.	15.00 To 21.75
Medicine, Dr.Rookis' Golden Ointment, Pottery, Pot	20.00
Medicine, Dr.S.A.Tuttle, Boston, Mass, Aqua	2.50
Medicine, Dr.S.A.Weaver's Canker & Salt Rheum Syrup, Aqua, 9 1/2 In.	75.00

Medicine, Dr.S.A.Weaver's Canker & Salt Rheum Syrup, Oval, GP, Aqua, 9 In. 35.00
Medicine, Dr.S.J.Engrey's Blood Purifier, Lexington, Tenn., Aqua, 9 5/8 In. 50.00
Medicine, Dr.S.M.Gidding's Preparation, N.Y., Embossed, Oval, 7 1/8 In. 30.00
Medicine, Dr.S.S.Fitch, Broadway, N.Y., Open Pontil 18.00
Medicine, Dr.Sanford's Liver Invigorator, N.Y., Open Pontil, Aqua, 7 1/2 In. 55.00
Medicine, Dr.Sawen's Cough Balsam, Aqua, Open Pontil 40.00
Medicine, Dr.Sawyer's Family Cure, Chicago, Label 45.00
Medicine, Dr.Seth Arnold's Cough Killer 4.00
Medicine, Dr.Shiloh's System Vitalizer, Aqua 10.00
Medicine, Dr.Shoop's Family Medicine, Racine, Wis. 4.00
Medicine, Dr.Shoop's Rheumatic Remedy, BIMAL 18.00
Medicine, Dr.Shoop's Twenty Minute Croup Remedy, Label, BIMAL 6.00
Medicine, Dr.Stowe's Ambrosial Nectar, Bubbles, Amber 34.00
Medicine, Dr.Stowe's Ambrosial Nectar, Lime Green 16.00
Medicine, Dr.Sweet's Celebrated Sprain Liniment 7.00
Medicine, Dr.Syke's Sure Cure For Catarrh, 3 Piece Mold, Aqua, 7 In. 10.00
Medicine, Dr.Syke's Sure Cure For Catarrh, 4 Piece Mold, Cylinder, Aqua 25.00
Medicine, Dr.Thacher's Liver & Blood Syrup, BIMAL 15.00
Medicine, Dr.Thenard Gold Lion Iron Tonic, Embossed Lion, Amber, 8 3/4 In. 20.00
Medicine, Dr.Thompson's Eye Water, New London, Conn., Open Pontil 25.00
Medicine, Dr.Tibbald's Blood Tonic, Cobalt 30.00
Medicine, Dr.Tobias Venetian Horse Liniment, Aqua, 8 In. 60.00
Medicine, Dr.Tobias Venetian Horse Liniment, N.Y., Light Aqua 8.00
Medicine, Dr.Tobias Venetian Horse Liniment, Pontil, 6 In. 22.50
Medicine, Dr.Tobias Venetian Liniment, Aqua, Open Pontil 18.00
Medicine, Dr.Townsend's Aromatic Holland Tonic, Amber, Square 75.00
Medicine, Dr.True's Elixir Worm Expeller, BIMAL, 6 In. 8.00
Medicine, Dr.V.G., Dyspepsia Remedy, Blue Aqua, 6 1/2 In. 5.50
Medicine, Dr.Vanderpool's Cough & Consumption Cure, Aqua, 6 In. 25.00
Medicine, Dr.W.B. Caldwell, see Medicine Caldwell's
Medicine, Dr.W.H.Long's Vegetable Blood Purifier, Phila., Aqua, 9 1/2 In. 15.00
Medicine, Dr.W.Towns' Epilepsy Cure, Fond Du Lac, Wis., Amber, 7 3/4 In. 50.00
Medicine, Dr.Warren's Tonic Cordial, Aqua, 8 1/2 In. 22.00

Medicine, Dr.Robbins' Tecumseh Rheumatic Drops, Blue, 4 In.
(See Page 131)

Medicine, Dr.Weaver's Cerate, Open Pontil, Aqua, 2 3/4 In. 25.00
Medicine, Dr.White's Specialty For Diphtheria 3.00
Medicine, Dr.William's Antidyspeptic Elixir, Aqua 13.00
Medicine, Dr.Wistar's Balsam Of Wild Cherry, Aqua, Open Pontil 40.00
Medicine, Dr.Wistar's Balsam Of Wild Cherry, Aqua, 5 In. 4.00
Medicine, Dr.Wistar's Balsam Of Wild Cherry, Green, 4 1/2 In. 3.00
Medicine, Dr.Wistar's Balsam Of Wild Cherry, Philadelphia, OP, Aqua 25.00
Medicine, Dr.Wistar's Balsam Of Wild Cherry, Pint, Pontil 40.00
Medicine, Dr.Wistar's Balsam Of Wild Cherry, 8 Sided, Open Pontil, Aqua 35.00
Medicine, Dr.Wistar's Balsam Wild Cherry, Cinn., Ohio, Open Pontil, Aqua 50.00
Medicine, Dr.Zimmerman's Easy To Take Castor Oil, Johnstown, Pa., 6 In. 20.00
Medicine, Drs.M.G.Kerr & Gertolet Compound, Asiatic Balsam, Norristown, Pa. 45.00
Medicine, Dubin's Lung Cure, Amber 3.00
Medicine, Duff's Formula, BIMAL, Amber, 9 3/4 In. 20.00
Medicine, Dyer's Healing Embrocation, Aqua, Pontil, 5 1/4 In. 75.00
Medicine, Dyer's Healing Embrocation, Providence, R.I. 60.00
Medicine, E.A.Buckhout's Dutch Liniment, Mechanicville, N.Y., OP 300.00
Medicine, E.I.Barnett Magic Cure Liniment, Easton, Pa. 20.00

Medicine, E.Lyon's & Sons, Jan., 1859, St.Helens, Snap Case, 2 Mold, Green 450.00
Medicine, E.M.Parmelee, Dansville, N.Y., Indented Panels, Olive Yellow 23.00
Medicine, E.S.Reed's Apothecary, Label, Amber 4.00
Medicine, Egyptian Vegetable Compound, Amethyst, 8 7/8 In. 12.00
Medicine, Eilert's Extract Of Tar & Wild Cherry, Aqua 4.00
Medicine, Electric Liniment Cure, Label 8.50
Medicine, Elipizone, A Certain Cure For Fits & Epilepsy, H.G.Root, Aqua 55.00

Medicine, Germ, Bacteria Or Fungus Destroyer, 10 1/2 In.
(See Page 134)

Medicine, Ely's Cream Balm, 3 In.

Medicine, G.W.Stone's Liquid Cathartic,
Lowell, Mass., 9 In.

Medicine, Elixir Babek For Malaria, Chills & Fevers, Washington, D.C. 8.00
Medicine, Ellman's Royal Embrocation For Horses, Green 10.00
Medicine, Ellman's Royal Embrocation For Horses, Label 14.00
Medicine, Ely's Cream Balm, 3 In. .... Illus 2.00
Medicine, Emerson's Rheumatic Cure, Amber 30.00
Medicine, Epping's Buchu, Mfg., L.Pierce, Columbus, Ga., Aqua, 9 In. 60.00
Medicine, Erso Anti Bilious, Label, Contents, Clear 14.00
Medicine, Esco Distinctive Embalming Fluid, 8 In. 4.00
Medicine, Excelsior Mustard, Mills, N.Y., Shape Of Early Pint Milk Bottle 18.00
Medicine, Extract Valerian, Shaker Fluid, Open Pontil, Full Label 80.00
Medicine, F.Sterns & Co., Detroit, Mich, Sample, Amber, 4 1/2 In. 5.00
Medicine, Fahnestock's Vermifuge, Open Pontil 15.00
      Medicine, Fahrney's, see Medicine, Dr. Peter Fahrney's
Medicine, Farr's Gray Hair Restorer, Amber 5.00
Medicine, Fellow's Syrup Of Hypophosphates, Aqua 1.00
      Medicine, Fenner's, see Dr.M.M.Fenner's
Medicine, Fenner's Cure, Glop Top, Amber 20.00
Medicine, Five Minute Cough Cure, Price 25 Cents, Aqua 3.00
Medicine, Foley's Honey & Tar, Label, Boxed 5.00
Medicine, Foley's Kidney & Bladder Cure, Amber, 7 1/4 In. .... 8.00 To 14.00
Medicine, Foley's Kidney & Bladder Cure, Amber, 9 1/2 In. .... 10.00 To 12.00
Medicine, Foley's Kidney & Bladder Cure, Chicago, Amber, 7 1/4 In. 10.00
Medicine, Foley's Kidney & Bladder Remedy, Amber, 9 1/2 In. 15.00
Medicine, Foley's Kidney Cure, Cylinder Shape, Sample, 4 1/4 In. 8.00
Medicine, Foley's Safe Diarrhea & Colic Cure, 4 1/2 In., Label 15.00
Medicine, Folger's Olosaonian, N.Y., Open Pontil, Aqua 18.00
Medicine, Four Cities Safe Cure, Pint 80.00
Medicine, Frey's Vermifuge, Baltimore, Label & Contents, 4 1/2 In. 8.00
      Medicine, Friedenwald's, see Medicine, Buchu Remedy
Medicine, Frisco Cough Syrup, Sherburn, Minn., Label 6.00
Medicine, G.Lomax, Blue 55.00
Medicine, G.W.Davis, Inflammatory Expirator & Cleanser, Label, Aqua 55.00
Medicine, G.W.Merchant's, Chemists, Lockport, N.Y., Iron Pontil, Green 75.00
Medicine, G.W.Merchant's, Lockport, N.Y., Open Pontil, Aqua 110.00
Medicine, G.W.Stone's Liquid Cathartic, Lowell, Mass., 9 In. .... Illus 1900.00
Medicine, Gargling Oil, Amber 2.00

Medicine, Gargling Oil, Cobalt, 7 1/2 In. 45.00
Medicine, Gargling Oil, Emerald Green, 5 5/8 X 2 1/2 X 1 1/2 In. 10.00
Medicine, Gargling Oil, Lockport, N.Y., Emerald Green, 5 1/2 In. 11.00
Medicine, Gate's Acadian Liniment 10.00
Medicine, Gauvin's Syrup For Babies, Aqua, 5 In. 2.50
Medicine, Geller's Hair Producer, Amber, 10 In. 175.00
Medicine, Genuine Essence, Open Pontil, 4 3/4 In. 9.50
Medicine, Germ, Bacteria Or Fungus Destroyer, 10 1/2 In. .... Illus 55.00
Medicine, Gibson's Syrup, Deep Green Blue 40.00
Medicine, Gin, see Gin
Medicine, Ginseng Panacea, Open Pontil, Rectangular, Aqua, 4 1/2 In. 110.00
Medicine, Glover's Imperial Distemper Cure, Amber 5.00
Medicine, Glover's Imperial Distemper Remedy, N.Y., Light Olive 18.00
Medicine, Glover's Imperial Distemper Remedy, N.Y., Teal 18.00
Medicine, Glover's Imperial Mange Cure, Amber 8.00
Medicine, Goff's Indian Vegetable Cough Syrup, Blood Purifier .... 6.00 To 20.00
Medicine, Goff's Magic Oil Liniment, BIMAL 5.00
Medicine, Gold Dandruff Cure, BIMAL 12.50
Medicine, Gooch's Mexican Quick Relief, BIMAL 16.00
Medicine, Grady Vegetable Remedies 12.00
Medicine, Graham's Dyspepsia Cure, Clear 4.00
Medicine, Gralfenberg Co., Dysentery Syrup, Pontil, Aqua, 4 3/4 In. 21.00
Medicine, Grand Pa's Liniment, Rectangle, BIMAL, Aqua 10.00
Medicine, Grant's Indian Pulmonary Balsam, M.T.Wallace, Prop, 8 Sided 60.00
Medicine, Gray's Balsam Best Cough Cure, BIMAL 16.00
Medicine, Gray's Balsam Best Cough Cure, 6 1/2 In., Label 15.00
Medicine, Gray's Glycerine Tonic, BIMAL 4.00
Medicine, Great Blood & Rheumatism Cure, Aqua, 9 In. 12.00
Medicine, Great Blood & Rheumatism Cure, 9 In. 3.00
Medicine, Great English Sweeny 6.00
Medicine, Green's Gargling Oil, Lockport, N.Y. 4.50
Medicine, Green's Lung Restorer, Oroville, Cal., Aqua, 7 1/2 In. .... 12.00 To 15.00
Medicine, Griscom's Bone Marrow Liniment 12.00
Medicine, Grove's Tasteless Chill Tonic, Label 4.00
Medicine, Grover Graham's Dyspepsia Cure, Milk Glass 4.00
Medicine, Guild's Green Mountain Asthma Cure 35.00
Medicine, Guinn's Pioneer Blood Renewer, Macon, Ga., Amber, 9 In. 30.00
Medicine, Gwllym Evan's Quinine, Rectangular, Star On Shoulder, Aqua 25.00
Medicine, H.H.H. Horse Medicine, Cornflower Blue 50.00
Medicine, H.H.Warner & Co., Ltd., Melbourne, ABM, Amber, 5 1/2 In. 15.00
Medicine, H.H.Warner's, see Medicine, Warner's
Medicine, Hadlock's Vegetable Syrup, Pontil, Aqua 110.00
Medicine, Hagan's Magnolia Balm, Milk Glass .... 6.00 To 10.00
Medicine, Hall's Balsam For Lungs, Rectangular, Deep Aqua 6.00
Medicine, Hall's Balsam For The Lungs, Green 12.50
Medicine, Hall's Catarrh Cure, Aqua, Round, 4 1/2 In. .... 1.00 To 4.00
Medicine, Hall's Hair Renewer, Teal Blue 18.00
Medicine, Hall's Painless Corn Cure, Clear, 2 In. 10.00
Medicine, Hampton's V.Tincture, Mortimer & Mowbray, Balto., Puce 220.00
Medicine, Hampton's V.Tincture, Open Pontil, Yellow 325.00
Medicine, Harper's Cuforhedake Brain Food, Washington, D.C., Aqua, 5 In. 8.00
Medicine, Harper's Headache Remedy, BIMAL, 5 In. 4.00
Medicine, Hart's Honey & Horehound Cure, Label 20.00
Medicine, Hartshorn's Cough Balsam, Label 7.50
Medicine, Hawker's Dyspepsia Cure, Clear, 4 1/2 In. 12.00
Medicine, Healey & Bigelow Indian Sagwa 6.00
Medicine, Healey & Bigelow Kickapoo Indian Cough Cure, 6 1/4 In. 5.00
Medicine, Healey & Bigelow Kickapoo Indian Oil, BIMAL 5.00
Medicine, Healy & Bigelow Indian Sagwa, Embossed Indian, Aqua 18.00
Medicine, Healy & Bigelow Indian Sagwa, 9 In. .... Illus 20.00
Medicine, Healy & Bigelow Kickapoo Sage Hair Tonic, Cobalt 65.00
Medicine, Healy & Bigelow's Kickapoo Indian Cough Cure, Aqua 7.00
Medicine, Helmbold's Genuine Fluid Extract, Aqua 5.00
Medicine, Henry Wampole's Stimulant Tonic, Label, Box, BIMAL 2.00
Medicine, Herballa, Double Ring Lip, Light Amber 75.00
Medicine, Hermanus Cure, Embossed Roman Soldier, Amber, 8 1/2 In. 100.00

Medicine, Hermanus Germaney's Infallible Cure, Sample Size 15.00
Medicine, Hermanus Germany's Infallible Dyspepsia Cure, Amber, 8 1/2 In. 65.00
Medicine, Hernia Cure Co., Rupturing Cures Ruptures, Clear, 6 In. 50.00
Medicine, Hibbard's Rheumatic Syrup, Amber, 9 1/4 In. 3.00
Medicine, Hick's Capudine For Headaches, Amber, 3 3/8 In. 2.00
Medicine, Hill's Cys-Pep-Cu, St.Louis, Reddish Amber, 8 1/2 In. 55.00
Medicine, Hill's Dyspepsia Remedy, Embossed Snake, 1906 Label, Clear 30.00
Medicine, Himalaya, The Kola Compound, Nature's Cure For Asthma, Amber 12.00
Medicine, Hindoo Pain Conqueror, Aqua, 6 In. ....*Illus* 12.00

Medicine, Hindoo Pain Conqueror, Aqua, 6 In.

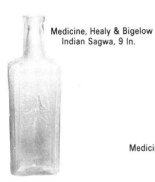

Medicine, Healy & Bigelow
Indian Sagwa, 9 In.

Medicine, Kobolo Tonic Medicine Co., Milk Glass, 9 In.
(See Page 136)

Medicine, Hire's Cough Cure 8.50
Medicine, Hire's Cough Cure, Aqua 22.00
Medicine, Hobensack's Medicated Worm Syrup, Open Pontil 30.00
Medicine, Hobensack's Medicated Worm Syrup, Philadelphia, Aqua 32.00
Medicine, Hoff's German Liniment, Aqua, 12 Sided 1.00
Medicine, Holloway's Worm Confections 5.00
Medicine, Holmes Sure Cure Mouthwash 47.50
Medicine, Hood's Tooth Powder 3.00
Medicine, Hooker & Co., For Throat & Lungs, Cobalt 5.00
Medicine, Hop-Cel Nerve, Blood & Brain Tonic, 11 In. 35.00
Medicine, Hopkin's Chalybeate, Green 35.00
Medicine, Howard's Tonic Mixture, Philada., 6 Sided, Open Pontil, Aqua 30.00
Medicine, Howe's Arabian Tonic Blood Purifier, Aqua 16.00
Medicine, Hull Ouridge's Lung Tonic, Aqua, 5 In. 4.00
Medicine, Humphrey's Homeopathic Veterinary Specific, Clear, 3 1/2 In. 2.50
Medicine, Hunnewell Universal Cough Remedy, Open Pontil, Aqua 33.00
Medicine, Hunnicutt's Rheumatic Cure, Deep Aquamarine 35.00
Medicine, Hunt's Liniment, Label, Apple Green, Open Pontil 45.00
Medicine, Hunt's Liniment, Open Pontil 30.00
Medicine, Hunt's Liniment, Pontil, Aqua 25.00
Medicine, Hunt's Liniment, Sing Sing, N.Y. .... 6.00 To 31.00
Medicine, Hunt's Liniment, Sing Sing, N.Y., Open Pontil, Aqua 25.00
Medicine, Hunter's Pulmonic Balsam Cough Syrup, Bangor, Me., Contents 44.50
Medicine, Hurd's Cough Balsam 45.00
Medicine, Hyatt's Infallible Life Balsam, Aqua, 9 1/2 In. .... 18.00 To 23.00
Medicine, Hyatt's Infallible Life Balsam, Bright Medium Green, 10 1/4 In. 45.00
Medicine, Hyatt's Infallible Life Balsam, Olive Green, Quart 45.00
Medicine, Hyatt's Infallible Life Balsam, Teal Blue 75.00
     Medicine, Indian Sagwa, see Medicine, Healy & Bigelow
Medicine, Indian Cough Syrup, Warm Springs, Oregon, Clear 13.00
Medicine, J.& C.Maguire's Family Medicines, Amber, 8 1/4 In. 12.00
Medicine, J.A.Melvin's Rheumatic & Dyspepsia Cure, BIMAL 12.50
Medicine, J.B.Wheatley's Compound Syrup, Dallasburg, Ky., OP, Aqua 65.00
Medicine, J.E.Gombault's Caustic Balsam, Aqua, 6 1/4 In. 6.00
Medicine, J.H.Fisher's, Wildfire Rheumatic, Liniment 90.00
Medicine, J.J.Butler, Cincinnati, O. 14.00

Medicine, J.R.Burdsall's Arnica Liniment, Aqua, 5 1/2 In., Pontil	32.50
Medicine, J.R.Stafford's Olive Tar, Aqua	25.00
Medicine, J.T.Forrest, Opera House Pharmacy, Cleveland, Ohio, Amber	7.00
Medicine, J.T.Rowand, Philadelphia, 6 Sided, Open Pontil	15.00
Medicine, J.W.Bull's Cough Syrup, Baltimore, Md.	10.00
Medicine, J.W.Hunnewell & Co., Universal Cough Remedy, OP, 6 1/2 In.	25.00
Medicine, Jacob's Cholera & Dysentery Cordial, Pontil	75.00
Medicine, Jacquot's One Night Cough Cure, Green Bay, Wisc., Label	14.00
Medicine, Jadwin's Subduing Liniment, Honesdale, Pa., Aqua	25.00
Medicine, Jadwin's Subduing Liniment, 8 1/2 In.	3.00
Medicine, Jaffe's Electric Pain Expeller, San Jose, Aqua, 5 1/2 In.	6.00
Medicine, Joan Of Arc Smelling Salt, Art Deco, Amber	22.00
Medicine, John Madina, Rico Balm, Boston, Mass, Clear, 6 3/4 In.	3.50
Medicine, John Wyeth & Bros., Dosage Cap, Cobalt Blue, 6 1/2 In.	7.00
Medicine, John Wyeth, Beef Juice, BIMAL, 4 In.	5.00
Medicine, Johnson's American Anodyne Liniment	3.00
Medicine, Johnson's American Anodyne Liniment, Pontil	15.00
Medicine, Johnson's Chill & Fever Tonic, Amethyst, 5 3/4 In.Square	9.00
Medicine, Johnson's Pure Herb Tonic, Deep Amber	40.00
Medicine, Jones & Primley Iron & Wahoo Tonic, Elkhart, Ind.	18.00
Medicine, K.K.Cures Bright's Disease, BIMAL, 7 In.	20.00
Medicine, K.K.Cures Bright's Disease & Cystitis, K.K.Medicine Co., Aqua	25.00
Medicine, K.K.K., Kay's Kentucky Kure	12.00
Medicine, Keeley's Cure Tobacco Habit, Light Amethyst	95.00
Medicine, Keller's Catarrh Remedy & Blood Purifier, Embossed Cat, Aqua	30.00
Medicine, Kemp's Balsam For Throat & Lungs, Aqua, 5 1/4 In.	2.00
Medicine, Kemp's Balsam, Throat & Lungs, BIMAL, 1 In.	4.00
Medicine, Kendall's Spavin Cure For Human Flesh, Label	3.50
Medicine, Kendall's Spavin Cure For Human Flesh, 10 Panels, Aqua, 5 1/2 In.	5.00
Medicine, Kendall's Spavin Cure For Human Flesh, 12 Sided, Amber, 5 1/2 In.	6.00
Medicine, Kennedy's Medical Discovery, Aqua, BIMAL	1.50
Medicine, Kennedy's Rheumatic Dissolvent, BIMAL	6.00
Medicine, Kennedy's Salt Rheum Ointment, Onion Shaped, OP, Aqua, 2 In.	50.00
Medicine, Keough's Foul Remedy, Aqua, 7 In.	75.00
Medicine, Kerr & Bertolet Asiatic Balsam	25.00
Medicine, Kickapoo Oil, see Medicine, Healy & Bigelow	
Medicine, King Of Blood, Aqua	9.00
Medicine, Kobolo Tonic Medicine Co., Milk Glass, 9 In. _Illus_	135.00
Medicine, Kodol Dyspepsia Cure, E.C.Dewitt & Co., Sunken Panels, Aqua, 6 In.	12.00
Medicine, Kodol Dyspepsia Cure, Front Embossed, Small	6.00

Medicine, Laxol, Cobalt Blue, 7 In.

Medicine, Kodol Dyspepsia Cure, Side Embossed, Large	8.00
Medicine, Lactopeptine For Digestive Ailments, Blue Green, 2 1/2 In.	7.50
Medicine, Lactopeptine, Remedial For Digestive Disorders, Cobalt	8.00
Medicine, Lady Hill, Hobnail, Open Pontil, Aqua	20.00
Medicine, Langenbach's Dysentery Cure, BIMAL	18.50
Medicine, Lanman & Kemp Cod Liver Oil	3.00
Medicine, Laxol, Cobalt Blue, 7 In. _Illus_	8.00
Medicine, Lediard's Morning Call, Cylinder, Black Glass, Quart	75.00
Medicine, Lediard's Morning Call, Round, Olive Green, Quart	90.00
Medicine, Lengfeld's, San Francisco, Amber	3.00

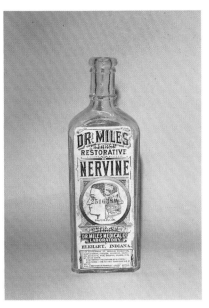

Ink, Umbrella, Cadmium Steel, Pontil, Aqua, 2½ In.; Ink, English, Bust-Off Top, Green, 2 In.

Medicine, Dr. Miles Nervine, Aqua, 8 In.

Pepper Sauce, Gothic, Aqua, Paper Label, 8½ In.

Ink, Carter's, Pencraft Office And Fountain Pen Ink, 10½ In.

Pickle, Aqua, Paper Label, 6 In.

Ezra Brooks, Iowa Grain Elevator,
1978

Famous Firsts, Yankee Doodle Telephone,
1973; Johnny Reb Telephone, 1973

Famous Firsts, Riverboat, Robert E. Lee,
1971

Ezra Brooks, Order Of Eagles
F.O.E., 1978

Hoffman, Merganser, 1978

Famous Firsts, Golden Spirit

Famous Firsts, Corvette Stingray 1963,
White, 1977

Fruit Jar, Standard, Quart

Hoffman Animal Band: Marty Mouse, 1978;
Ellie Elephant, 1978; Porky Pig, 1978;
Bobbie Bassett, 1978; Leo Lion, 1978;
Freddie Frog, 1978

Soda, Moxie, Glass Label, 12½ In.;
Soda, Moxie, Printed Label

Hoffman, Stranger, This Land Is Mine

Ski Country, Lady of Leadville, Blue And Brown

Cyrus Noble, Blacksmith, 1974; Gambler, 1974; Miner's Daughter, 1975

Michter's, Penn State Nittany Lion

Millville Art Glass, "Good Buddy"/Beaver Breaker CBer, Blue

Beam, Model A Ford, Red, 1978

Ski Country, Blue Jay

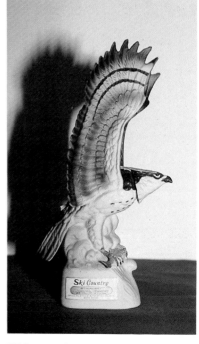

Ski Country, Osprey Hawk

Beam, Coho Salmon, 1976, Trophy

Ezra Brooks, Clown, Imperial Shrine, 1978

Beam, Madama Butterfly, 1977, Opera Series

Beam, Commemorative Plate, 1976, George Washington

McCormick, Gunfighters

Millville Art Glass, 1878 Silver Dollar, Amethyst

Millville Art Glass, Hawaii, Captain Cook Bicentennial, Amber

McCormick, Elvis Presley 1978

Medicine, Lengley's Red Bottle Elixir Of Life, Square Panel, Aqua	20.00
Medicine, Leonard's Cough	7.00
Medicine, Lesure's Colic Cure	1.50
Medicine, Light's Celery Nerve Compound, Labels, Panels, Amber, 9 1/2 In.	40.00
Medicine, Lightning Kidney & Liver Cure, Aqua	45.00 To 75.00
Medicine, Lightning Liniment, BIMAL	13.50
Medicine, Lillybeck's Chill & Fever Tonic, BIMAL	6.50
Medicine, Limcrick's Great Mast Of Pain, Rodney, Miss., IP, Aqua	250.00
Medicine, Lindsey's Blood Searcher, Purple	7.50
Medicine, Liqufruta Cough Cure, Green	35.00
Medicine, Little Bears Oil, Crooked Neck, Open Pontil, Aqua	30.00
Medicine, Lockport Gargling Oil, Cobalt Blue	10.00
Medicine, Longley's Panacea, Rectangular, 6 1/4 In.	115.00
Medicine, Lord's Opodeldoc, Embossed Man With Crutches, Aqua	10.00
Medicine, Louden & Co's, Carminative Balsam, Flared Lip, Aqua, 5 1/4 In.	55.00
Medicine, Lung & Cough Syrup, Honey Amber	55.00
Medicine, Lydia Pinkham, Paper Label, 9 In. ....Color	xxxx.xx
Medicine, Lydia Pinkham's Blood Purifier	6.00
Medicine, Lydia Pinkham's Vegetable Compound, Label	1.00
Medicine, Lyon's Kathairon For Hair	32.00
Medicine, Lyon's Powder, B. & P., N.Y., Open Pontil, Puce	80.00
Medicine, Lyon's Powder, N.Y., Open Pontil, Puce, 4 1/4 In.Diameter	65.00
Medicine, M.Calm, Laxol, Emerald Green	32.00
Medicine, Macassar Oil, Pontil, Rectangular, Aqua, 3 1/2 In.	19.00
Medicine, Madame M.Yale's Fruitcura, Aqua	12.00
Medicine, Magic Cure Liniment	15.00
Medicine, Magic Mosquito Bite Cure & Insect Exterminator	8.00
Medicine, Makrauer's Hair & Dandruff Cure	5.00
Medicine, Marine Hospital Service, Insignia, Dated, 1791-1871, Clear, 1/2 Pt.	8.00
Medicine, Marine Hospital Service, Insignia, Square, Clear, 1/4 Pint	5.00
Medicine, Matchett's Liniment	2.00
Medicine, May's Cod Liver Extract, Label, Amber	3.00
Medicine, May's Wonderful Stomach Remedy, ABM, Caseline	2.00
Medicine, McClellan's Diphtheria Remedy, San Francisco, Aqua, 8 In.	12.00
Medicine, McCormick Chill Tonic	12.00
Medicine, McCreedy's Corn Solvent, Ballston Spa, N.Y.	3.00
Medicine, McLean's Strengthening Cordial, Aqua, 9 In.	20.00
Medicine, McMunn Elixir, Open Pontil	18.00
Medicine, McPike & Fox, Kansas, Peruvian Strengthening Elixir, Amber	6.00
Medicine, Meade & Baker, Carbolic Mouth Wash, Richmond, Va.	5.00
Medicine, Merchant's Gargling Oil, Dark Green, Label	20.00
Medicine, Metzger's African Catarrh Cure	12.00
Medicine, Mexican Hair Renewer, Cobalt	34.50
Medicine, Mexican Mustang Liniment	2.00 To 12.00
Medicine, Mexican Mustang Liniment, Open Pontil	25.00
Medicine, Meyer's Oil Of Gladness, 7 In.	4.00
Medicine, Mikado Tonic, The Japanese Remedy, Square, Amber	45.00
Medicine, Modoc Indian Oil, Full Label	14.00
Medicine, Modoc Indian Oil, 6 1/2 In.	5.00
Medicine, Moore's Revealed Remedy, Amber, 10 In. ....Color	xxxx.xx
Medicine, Morley's Hair Restorer	18.00
Medicine, Morley's Liver & Kidney Cordial, Golden Amber, Square	15.00
Medicine, Morris DaCosta's Radical Cure, Small	30.00
Medicine, Morse's Celebrated Syrup, Providence, R.I., Iron Pontil	75.00
Medicine, Morse's Indian Root Pills, Amber, 2 1/2 In.	2.00
Medicine, Mortimore's Bitter Cordial & Blood Purifer, OP, Aqua, 7 7/8 In.	125.00
Medicine, Mother Bailey's Quieting Syrup	2.75
Medicine, Moxie Nerve Food, BIMAL, Aqua	10.00
Medicine, Moxie Nerve Food, Lowell, Mass.	4.00
Medicine, Mrs.Allen's Hair Restorer, Amber, Label	23.00
Medicine, Mrs.Allen's World Hair Balsam, Aqua, Open Pontil	35.00
Medicine, Mrs.Dinsmore's Cough & Croup Balsam, Aqua, 6 3/8 In.	6.00 To 10.00
Medicine, Mrs.Dinsmore's Cough & Croup Balsam, Milk Glass	4.00
Medicine, Mrs.E.Kidder's Dysentery Cordial, Boston, Open Pontil, Aqua	65.00
Medicine, Mrs.Matteson Clairvoyant Psychic Remedies, 8 In.	9.00
Medicine, Mrs.Potter's Hygenic Supply, Amber	1.00

Medicine, Mrs.Wheeler's Nursing Syrup 8.00
Medicine, Mrs.Winslow's Soothing Syrup, Curtis & Perkins .... 12.50 To 15.00
Medicine, Mrs.Winslow's Soothing Syrup, Open Pontil .... 11.00 To 15.00
Medicine, Mrs.Winslow's Soothing Syrup, Pontil, Aqua, 5 In. 8.00
Medicine, Mulford's Digestive Malt Extract, Amber, 8 3/4 In. 5.00
Medicine, Mull's Grape Tonic 16.00
Medicine, Munyon's Catarrh Cure, Olive Green 13.00
Medicine, Munyon's Homeopathic Home Remedies, Clear, 3 1/2 In. 2.50
Medicine, Munyon's Inhaler, Cures Colds, Emerald Green .... 10.00 To 22.00
Medicine, Murine Eye Remedy, Milk Glass 30.00
Medicine, Murine For Your Eyes, Embossed, ABM 9.00
Medicine, Muxton's Rheumatic Cure, Aqua 10.00
Medicine, N.E.Well's, Pulmonary Syrup, Philada., Blue Aqua, 7 1/2 In. 8.00
Medicine, N.Wood & Son, Portland, Me., Castor Oil, Aqua, 4 1/2 In. 6.00
Medicine, N.Y.College Of Medicine & Pharmacy, Oval, Open Pontil, Aqua 65.00
Medicine, N.Y.College Of Medicine & Pharmacy, Oval, Aqua 80.00
Medicine, Nash's Rheumatic & Kidney Cure, Honey Amber, 3 1/2 In. 7.00
Medicine, National Kidney & Liver Cure, Contents, Square, Amber, 9 In. 45.00
Medicine, National Remedy Co., Aqua 1.00
Medicine, National Remedy, Tonic Elixir Of Cod Liver Oil, 8 Sided, Amber 17.00
Medicine, Nature No.9, American Drug Co., Columbus, Ga., Amber 15.00
Medicine, Nature's Herbal Remedies, BIMAL, 7 In. 14.00
Medicine, Nau's Dyspepsia Remedy, Label, Contents, Amber 8.00
Medicine, Nerve & Bone Liniment, Aqua, Open Pontil .... 16.00 To 25.00
Medicine, Nerve, Blood & Brain Tonic, San Francisco, Cal., Amber, 8 7/8 In. 80.00
Medicine, New England Cough Syrup, Daniel Goddard, N.Y., Aqua, 4 3/4 In. 60.00
Medicine, No.3919, Rheumatism, Clear 12.00
Medicine, Nowill's Pect-Oral Hone Of Liverwort, OP, Aqua, 4 1/2 In. 35.00
Medicine, Odol, Milk Glass, BIMAL, 4 In. 5.00
Medicine, Ointment Cup Cure For Gout & Rheumatism 21.00
Medicine, One Minute Cough Cure, Aqua, 5 1/2 In. 10.00
Medicine, One Minute Cough Cure, 4 1/4 In. 2.00
Medicine, One Minute Cough Cure, 5 1/2 In. 5.00
Medicine, Opodeldoc Liquid, Bu-Mold, Aqua 8.00
Medicine, Opodeldoc Liquid, Cylinder Shape, Pontil, Aqua, 4 1/2 In. 8.00
Medicine, Oregon Blood Purifier, Amber 20.00
Medicine, Osgood's, India Cholagogue, Aqua 30.00
Medicine, Otto's Cure For Throat & Lungs .... 3.00 To 5.00
Medicine, Otto's Cure For Throat & Lungs, Rochester, N.Y., Aqua, 7 1/4 In. 12.00
Medicine, Owbridges Lung Tonic 3.75
Medicine, Owl Drug, San Francisco, Amethyst, 8 1/2 In. 9.00
Medicine, Ozard Eye Strengthener 8.00
Medicine, P.P.Prickley Ash, Poke Root, The Great Blood Purifier, Amber 10.00
Medicine, Pages Vegetable Syrup For Females, BIMAL 34.00
Medicine, Paine's Celery Compound 4.00
Medicine, Paine's Celery Compound, Honey Amber 15.00
Medicine, Parisian Safe Hair Tonic 3.00
Medicine, Parker's Ginger Tonic, Amber, Milk Glass 4.00
Medicine, Parker's Hair Balsam, Amber, 6 1/2 In. 3.00
Medicine, Pawnee Indian Too-Re, Rectangular, Aqua, 7 3/4 In. 4.00
Medicine, Pearl's White Glycerine, Cobalt 20.00
Medicine, Peptenzyme, Reed & Carnick, Cobalt Blue, 3 In. 3.50
Medicine, Pepto Mongon Gude, 6 Sided Heart On Base, Aqua 3.50
Medicine, Perry Davis Pain Killer, Open Pontil, Aqua, 5 In. 26.00
Medicine, Peruvian Strengthening Elixir 25.00
Medicine, Peruvian Syrup, 8 1/2 In. 3.75
Medicine, Phelp's Rheumatic Elixir, Scranton, Pa., Aqua, 5 1/2 In. 3.50
Medicine, Phillips' Milk Of Magnesia, Cobalt 1.00
Medicine, Pierce's Golden Medical Discovery 5.00
Medicine, Pine Tree Tar Cordial, see Medicine, Wishart's
Medicine, Pinkham's Emmenagogue, Open Pontil 45.00
Medicine, Piso's Cure For Consumption, Hazeltine & Co., Green 8.00
Medicine, Piso's Cure For Consumption, Hazeltine & Co., Olive Green, 5 In. 5.00
Medicine, Places Pectoral Balsam, Emerald Green 24.50
Medicine, Polar Star Cough Cure 4.00
Medicine, Polar Star Cough Cure, Aqua 10.00

Medicine, Polar Star Cough Cure, Sample Size, 4 In.	3.50
Medicine, Polar Star Diarrhea Cure	7.00
Medicine, Pond's Extract Catarrh Remedy, Cobalt Blue, 6 In.	20.00
Medicine, Pond's Extract, Aqua	1.00
Medicine, Porter's Cure Of Pain, Aqua, 7 In.	75.00
Medicine, Porter's Cure Of Pain, Cleveland, O., Sunken Panels, Aqua, 6 In.	12.00
Medicine, Pratt's Distemper & Pink Eye Box, Label	40.00
Medicine, Pratt's Distemper & Pink Eye Cure, Amber, 6 3/4 In.	20.00
Medicine, Pratt's Distemper & Pink Eye Cure, Label	21.00
Medicine, Preston's Hed-Ake Cures You, Lip Flake	12.00
Medicine, Primley's Iron & Wahoo Tonic, Square Amber, 8 1/2 In.	16.00
Medicine, Primley's Speedy Cure For Coughs & Colds, Indiana, 6 1/2 In.	18.00
Medicine, Pritchard's Teething Powder	6.75
Medicine, Prof.Callon's Brazilian Gum	3.00
Medicine, Prof.Peeke's Remedy, N.Y., 5 1/2 In.	4.00
Medicine, Prof.W.Peeke's Remedy, New York, Square, Large, Amber	20.00
Medicine, Professor De Grath's Electric Oil, Philadelphia, Aqua, 3 3/4 In.	18.00

Medicine, Rosewood Dandruff Remedy, J.R.Reeves Co., 6 1/2 In.
(See Page 140)

Medicine, RRR, Radway & Co., New York, 6 1/2 In.
(See Page 140)

Medicine, Professor Wood's Restorative Cordial & Blood Renovator, Aqua	25.00
Medicine, Pure Cod Liver Oil, Embossed Fish, Sapphire Blue, 9 1/2 In.	135.00
Medicine, Purifying Extract, Aqua	65.00
Medicine, R.F.Kinsell, Pontil, Yellow Green, 9 1/2 In.	200.00
Medicine, Race's Indian Blood Renovator, Aqua, 9 1/4 In.	30.00
Medicine, Radam's Microbe Killer Cure, Amber	60.00
Medicine, Radam's Microbe Killer Cure, Embossed	65.00
Medicine, Radam's Microbe Killer No.2, Jug	32.50
Medicine, Radam's Microbe Killer, Amber	22.00
Medicine, Radam's Microbe Killer, Amber, Quart	50.00
Medicine, Radam's Microbe Killer, Dark Amber	60.00
Medicine, Radam's Microbe Killer, Embossed, Pottery	35.00
Medicine, Radam's Microbe Killer, Golden Amber	40.00
Medicine, Radical Cure, Cobalt	25.00
Medicine, Rainey Vitality Tablets, Amber, 3 1/4 In.	2.00
Medicine, Ransom's Hive Syrup & Tolu, Aqua, Square 4 In., BIMAL	8.00
Medicine, Red Star Cough, Deep Aqua	8.00
Medicine, Red Thyme Pain Cure	13.00
Medicine, Reed's Carnick Cod Liver Oil With Fish, Cobalt	125.00
Medicine, Reed's Gilt Edge Tonic, Amber	10.00 To 25.00
Medicine, Reid's German Cough & Kidney Cure, Clear, 7 In.	9.00
Medicine, Rennes Pain Killing Magic Oil	1.50
Medicine, Retham Pain Killer, Emerald Green	25.00
Medicine, Rev.T.Hill's Vegetable Remedy, Aqua, 5 3/4 In.	65.00
Medicine, Rheumatic Syrup, Amber	75.00
Medicine, Rhode's Fever & Ague Cure, OP, Label, Green Aqua, Pint	74.50
Medicine, Rhode's Fever & Ague Cure, OP, Wrapper & Circular	130.00
Medicine, Rhodes' Fever & Ague Cure, Label & Wrapper, Aqua	25.00

Medicine, Richmond's Samaritan Nervine, Rectangular	8.00
Medicine, Rickett's, Patent Shoulder, 3 Piece Mold	22.00
Medicine, Ridgway's Acme Liniment, Hydetown, Pa., Honey Amber	10.00
Medicine, Robert Turlington, Balsam Of Life, Applied Collar	6.00
Medicine, Robert's Tasteless Chill Tonic, Green	3.00
Medicine, Robert's Vegetable Embrocation, Amber	25.00
Medicine, Robert's Vegetable Embrocation, Teal, Open Pontil	100.00
Medicine, Roche's Embrocation, Whooping Cough, BIMAL, 5 In.	10.00
Medicine, Rock's Cough & Cold Cure, Aqua, 5 5/8 In.	4.00 To 10.00
Medicine, Rock's Cough & Cold Cure, New York, Sunken Panels, Aqua, 5 5/8 In.	8.00
Medicine, Roderic's Wild Cherry Cough Balsam, 5 1/4 In.	3.50
Medicine, Roehl's Hair Restorer, Amber, Rectangular	5.00
Medicine, Rohrer's Expectoral Wild Cherry Tonic, Amber, IP, 3/4 Quart	140.00
Medicine, Rohrer's Expectoral Wild Cherry Tonic, Lancaster, Pa, Amber	155.00
Medicine, Rohrer's Wild Cherry Expectoral Tonic, Golden Amber	100.00
Medicine, Rosewood Dandruff Remedy, J.R.Reeves Co., 6 1/2 In. *Illus*	10.00
Medicine, Royal Cough Cure, 6 3/4 In., Label	25.00
Medicine, RRR Radway & Co., N.Y., Aqua	16.00
Medicine, RRR, Radway & Co., New York, 6 1/2 In. *Illus*	6.00
Medicine, Rub-My-Tism, Box, 5 1/2 In. *Color*	xxxx.xx
Medicine, Rubifoam For The Teeth, BIMAL	1.50
Medicine, Ruby Remedy That Cures, Graduated Numbers	10.00
Medicine, Rupturine Cures Rupture, Westbrook, Maine, Amethyst, 6 1/8 In.	45.00
Medicine, Rupturine Cures Ruptures, 6 In.	40.00
Medicine, Rush's Lung Balm, A.H.Flanders, M.D., Aqua, 7 In.	8.00
Medicine, S.A.Richmond, M.D., St.Joseph, Mo., Clear	10.00
Medicine, S.B.Kitchel's Liniment, Square, Aqua, 8 1/2 In.	6.00
Medicine, S.D.Howe's Arabian Milk-Cure, Burst Bubble, Aqua	26.00
Medicine, S.Grover Graham's Dyspepsia Cure, Newburgh, N.Y., Clear, 6 5/8 In.	10.00
Medicine, S.M.Kier Petroleum, Pittsburgh, Open Pontil, Lime Green	150.00
Medicine, S.Smith, Green Mountain Renovator, Vermont, Aqua, 7 1/2 In.	75.00
Medicine, Safe Nervine, Amber, 7 1/2 In.	10.00
Medicine, Safe Nervine, Amber, 9 1/2 In.	35.00
Medicine, Sallade Mosquito Bite Cure, Milk Glass	6.00
Medicine, Sanborn's Kidney & Liver Vegetable Laxative	38.00
Medicine, Sanford's Cure, Cobalt Blue	20.00
Medicine, Sanford's Extract Of Hammemalis Or Witch Hazel, Cobalt, 8 In.	35.00
Medicine, Sanford's Radical Cure, Blue	10.00 To 28.00
Medicine, Sanford's Radical Cure, Rectangular, Italian Cobalt, 8 In.	18.00
Medicine, Sanitol For The Teeth, Milk Glass	6.00
Medicine, Sanitol For The Teeth, Milk Glass, 5 In.	5.00
Medicine, Sano Rheumatic Cure	8.00
Medicine, Save The Horse, Spavin Remedy, Binghamton, N.Y., Aqua	7.00 To 10.00
Medicine, Sayman's Cure, Clear, 6 1/2 In.	10.00
Medicine, Sayman's Vegetable Liniment, Cures Catarrh	15.00 To 18.00
Medicine, Schenck's Pulmonic Syrup, Philad., Aqua, 7 In.	8.00 To 18.00
Medicine, Schenck's Pulmonic Syrup, 8 Sided, Open Pontil	25.00
Medicine, Schenck's Seaweed Tonic, Aqua	6.00 To 15.00
Medicine, Scovill's Blood & Liver Syrup, Aqua	12.00
Medicine, Scovill's Blood & Liver Syrup, Cincinnati & N.Y.	16.00
Medicine, Scovill's Blood & Liver Syrup, Cincinnati, Aqua, 9 1/2 In.	11.00
Medicine, Seng Sultan Drug Co., St.Louis, BIMAL	4.00
Medicine, Shaker Cherry Pectoral Syrup, Open Pontil, Aqua	72.00
Medicine, Shaker Extract Of Roots, Clear, 5 1/2 In. *Color*	xxxx.xx
Medicine, Shaker Syrup No.1, Canterbury, N.H., Aqua, 7 In.	75.00
Medicine, Shaker Syrup No.1, Canterbury, N.H., Indented Panels, 7 3/4 In.	75.00
Medicine, Shaker Syrup No.1, Canterbury, N.H., Open Pontil	48.00
Medicine, Shaker, Tilden & Co., New Lebanon, N.Y., Cobalt Blue	25.00
Medicine, Shiloh's Consumption Cure, Label, Contents	6.00 To 12.00
Medicine, Shiloh's Consumption Cure, S.C., Rectangular, Aqua, 7 7/8 In.	12.00
Medicine, Shiloh's For Coughs & Colds, BIMAL	11.00
Medicine, Shriner's Cough Syrup, Open Pontil, Aqua	32.00
Medicine, Silver Pine Healing Oil, Aqua	8.00
Medicine, Simmon's Liver Regulator, Brass Horseshoe	27.00
Medicine, Sloan's Liniment, Sample Size, 4 X 1 1/4 X 1/2 In.	12.00
Medicine, Sloan's Sure Colic Cure, Clear, 2 1/2 In.	8.00

Medicine, Smith's Green Mountain Renovator, Amber .... 5.00 To 9.50
Medicine, Smith's Green Mountain Renovator, St.Albans, Vt., Label, Amber 22.00
Medicine, Smolander's Preparations, Embossed Horse In Diamond, Aqua 6.00
Medicine, South American Nervine 50.00
Medicine, Spark's Kidney & Liver Cure, Amber 18.00
Medicine, Speicher Dandruff Cure 6.00
Medicine, Sperry's Rheumatic & Nerve Liniment, Open Pontil, Aqua 42.50
Medicine, St.Clair's Hair Lotion, Deep Cobalt Blue, 7 1/2 In. 35.00
Medicine, Standard Liver Pills, Amber, 2 1/2 In. .... 2.00 To 4.50
Medicine, Stanley's Celery Malt, Golden Yellow 30.00
Medicine, Stanley's Celery Malt, Indented Panels, Yellow 75.00
Medicine, Stanley's Snake Oil Liniment 5.00
Medicine, Stephen Sweet's Infallible Liniment, Open Pontil 24.50
Medicine, Stephen Sweet's Infallible Liniment, Pontil, Aqua, 5 In. 32.50
Medicine, Stomach, Liver & Kidney Renovator, Aqua, 8 1/2 In., BIMAL 12.50
Medicine, Strickland's Diarrhea Dysentery Mixture 32.00
Medicine, Strickland's Wine Of Life, 3 Piece Mold, Cylinder, Amber, Fifth 30.00
Medicine, Sun Liniment 7.00
Medicine, Sunderland Sisters' Hair Grower 2.50
Medicine, Sutherland's Rheumatine, 1881 .... 10.00
Medicine, Swaim's Panacea, Apple Green 85.00
Medicine, Swaim's Panacea, Olive Amber, 7 5/8 In. 240.00
Medicine, Swaim's Panacea, Open Pontil, Aqua 200.00
Medicine, Swaim's Panacea, Phila., Olive Green 118.00
Medicine, Swaim's Vermifuge Dysentery, Cholera, Morbus, Dyspepsia, Aqua 30.00
Medicine, Swamp Chill, Fever Tonic 4.50
Medicine, Swayne's Sure Safe Cure, C.1875, Contents, Aqua 25.00
Medicine, Sweet Oil, Phila., Rectangular, Open Pontil, Aqua 10.00
Medicine, Swift's Syphilitic Specific, Strap Sided, Oval, Cobalt 95.00
Medicine, Swift's Syphilitic Specific, Strap Sided, 1870s, Cobalt, 9 In. 75.00
Medicine, Swift's Syphilitic Specific, Applied Lip, Cobalt Blue 325.00
Medicine, Syrup Squill & Honey, F.A.Barker Druggist, 2 Piece Mold, 5 In. 95.00
Medicine, Teardrops, Threaded Top, Milk Glass 50.00

Medicine, Tilden & Co., New Lebanon, N.Y., Yellow Olive, Pint

Medicine, Temple Of Health, Aqua 12.50
Medicine, Thompson's Eye Water 15.00
Medicine, Thorn's Hop & Burdock Tonic, Brattleboro, Vt., Yellow Amber 8.00
Medicine, Three Cities Warner's Safe Cure 25.00
Medicine, Tilden & Co., New Lebanon, N.Y., Electric Blue 65.00
Medicine, Tilden & Co., New Lebanon, N.Y., Yellow Olive, Pint .... *Illus* 285.00
Medicine, Todd's, ABM 20.00
Medicine, Tonic, BIMAL, Amber, Paper Label, 9 In. ....*Color* xxxx.xx
Medicine, Toothpowder Jar, Curved Neck, Embossed Odol, Milk Glass 4.00
Medicine, Trask's Magnetic Ointment, BIMAL 1.50
Medicine, Troup & Fickardt's Black Liniment, Aqua 6.00
Medicine, True's Worm Elixir For Horses 12.00
Medicine, True's Worm Elixir For Horses, Amber, 9 In. .... 17.00 To 25.00
Medicine, Turner's Balsam, 8 Sided 25.00
Medicine, Tuttle's Elixir, Boston, Mass., 12 Sided, Aqua, 6 1/4 In. 3.00
Medicine, U.S.A.Hospital Dept., Amber, 9 1/2 In. 58.00

Medicine, U.S.A.Hospital Dept., Aqua, Pint 75.00
Medicine, U.S.A.Hospital Dept., Aqua, Quart 85.00
Medicine, U.S.A.Hospital Dept., Blob Top, Aqua, Pint 150.00
Medicine, U.S.A.Hospital Dept., Cobalt, Quart 185.00
Medicine, U.S.A.Hospital Dept., Cornflower Blue 69.50
Medicine, U.S.A.Hospital Dept., Embossed, Clear, 4 In. 5.00
Medicine, U.S.A.Hospital Dept., Embossed, Olive Green, Quart, 9 In. 85.00
Medicine, U.S.A.Hospital Dept., Light Yellow, Quart 125.00
Medicine, U.S.A.Hospital Dept., Olive Amber, Quart 65.00
Medicine, U.S.A.Hospital Dept., Oval, Cobalt Blue 90.00
Medicine, U.S.A.Hospital Dept., Yellow, 10 In. 65.00
Medicine, Urinal, Free-Blown, Open Pontil 5.00
Medicine, V.P.D.Townsend's Liniment 7.00
Medicine, Van Buskirk's Fragrant Sozodont For Teeth & Breath, 6 1/4 In. 3.50
Medicine, Vaughn's Lithontripic Mixture 25.00
Medicine, Vege-Tonic, Square, Amber, Quart 5.00
Medicine, Vegetable Pulmonary Balsam, Flared Lip, Cylinder, Aqua, 5 In. 5.00
Medicine, Vegetable Tonic Syrup, BIMAL 5.00
Medicine, Veno's Lightning Cough Cure, Aqua, 5 1/4 In. .... 5.00 To 25.00
Medicine, Veno's Lightning Cough Cure, Rectangular, Blue Aqua, 5 1/4 In. 4.00
Medicine, Veronica Medicinal Water, Amber 4.00
Medicine, Vetter's Dyspepsia Remedy, Cleveland, Ohio, Clear 12.00
Medicine, Victor Gail Remedy, Amber, 7 1/2 In. 3.00
Medicine, Vigor Of Life 11.00
    Medicine, W.B. Caldwell's, see Medicine, Caldwell's
Medicine, W.Edward's & Son, Embrocation For Whooping Cough .... 6.75 To 12.00
Medicine, W.F.Lawrence's Genuine Preparations, Epping, N.Y., 3 Panels, Aqua 35.00
Medicine, W.Radam's Microbe Killer, Amber, 10 In. 49.00
Medicine, W.W.Clarke's, Worm Syrup, Aqua 35.00
Medicine, Wagner's Dandruff, Clear 20.00
Medicine, Wakefield's Blackberry Balsam, Label, Contents, Box 7.50
Medicine, Walt's Wild Cherry Tonic, Amber 9.00
Medicine, Wampole's Stimulant Tonic 1.00
Medicine, Warner's Diabetes Cure 20.00
Medicine, Warner's Kidney & Liver Cure, Medium Amber 10.00
Medicine, Warner's Log Cabin Extract, Small 85.00
Medicine, Warner's Log Cabin, Pills, Complete, Pamphlet 5.00
Medicine, Warner's Nervine, Large 20.00
Medicine, Warner's Nervine, Small 20.00
Medicine, Warner's Remedy, 8 Oz. 16.00
Medicine, Warner's Rheumatic Cure, London, Amber, Pint 80.00
Medicine, Warner's Safe & Liver Kidney Cure, Light Amber 10.00
Medicine, Warner's Safe Cure Co., Rochester, N.Y., Free Sample 15.00
Medicine, Warner's Safe Cure, Amber, 7 In. 25.00
Medicine, Warner's Safe Cure, Golden Amber, 7 1/4 In. 26.00
Medicine, Warner's Safe Cure, London, Amber 100.00
Medicine, Warner's Safe Cure, London, Grass Green & Olive Green, Print 75.00
Medicine, Warner's Safe Cure, London, Green 100.00
Medicine, Warner's Safe Cure, London, Green, Miniature 150.00
Medicine, Warner's Safe Cure, London, Green, 1/2 Pint .... 85.00 To 95.00
Medicine, Warner's Safe Cure, London, Honey Amber, 1/2 Pint 60.00
Medicine, Warner's Safe Cure, London, Orange Amber, 9 1/4 In. 45.00
Medicine, Warner's Safe Cure, London, Toronto, Rochester, Light Amber 50.00
Medicine, Warner's Safe Cure, Melbourne, Red Amber 40.00
Medicine, Warner's Safe Cure, Melbourne, Red Amber, Pint, 9 1/4 In. 35.00
Medicine, Warner's Safe Cure, 3 City 33.00
Medicine, Warner's Safe Cure, 4 Cities, Amber, 9 1/4 In. 65.00
Medicine, Warner's Safe Diabetes Cure, Amber .... 35.00 To 38.00
Medicine, Warner's Safe Diabetes Cure, Label & Contents, Amber 70.00
Medicine, Warner's Safe Diabetes Cure, Rochester, N.Y., Amber .... 36.00 To 40.00
Medicine, Warner's Safe Kidney & Liver Cure .... 10.00 To 55.00
Medicine, Warner's Safe Kidney & Liver Cure, Amber .... 10.00 To 70.00
Medicine, Warner's Safe Kidney & Liver Cure, Amber, 9 1/2 In. 150.00
Medicine, Warner's Safe Kidney & Liver Cure, Dark Amber, 9 1/2 In. 12.00
Medicine, Warner's Safe Kidney & Liver Cure, Light Olive Amber 50.00
Medicine, Warner's Safe Kidney & Liver Cure, Reverse Left Hinge 55.00

Medicine, Warner's Safe Kidney & Liver Cure, Rochester, N.Y., 9 1/4 In.	75.00
Medicine, Warner's Safe Kidney & Liver Remedy, Clear, Large	50.00
Medicine, Warner's Safe Medicines, Melbourne, Red Amber, 9 1/4 In.	35.00
Medicine, Warner's Safe Nervine, Amber	30.00
Medicine, Warner's Safe Nervine, Amber, Small	22.00
Medicine, Warner's Safe Nervine, Medium Amber, 7 1/2 In.	35.00
Medicine, Warner's Safe Nervine, Rochester, Honey Amber, Pint	24.00
Medicine, Warner's Safe Nervine, Rochester, N.Y., Light Amber, Small	20.00
Medicine, Warner's Safe Nervine, Rochester, Small	50.00

Michter's, Automobile, York Pullman, 1977

Medicine, Warner's Safe Nervine, 1/2 Pint	24.50
Medicine, Warner's Safe Rheumatic Cure, Amber	38.00 To 40.00
Medicine, Warner's Safe Rheumatic Cure, Dark Amber	55.00
Medicine, Warner's Safe Rheumatic Cure, Light Yellow Amber	250.00
Medicine, Warner's White Wine & Tar Syrup, Reading, Mich.	4.00
Medicine, Warner's, Melbourne, ABM, Amber, 5 1/2 In.	15.00
Medicine, Wayne's Diuretic Elixir, Light Amber, Square, 8 In.	25.00
Medicine, Web's A No.I Cathartic Tonic, Embossing, Amber, 9 1/4 In.	40.00
Medicine, Web's Anol Cathartic Tonic, Amber	48.00
Medicine, Weedon & Dent's Green Bottle Remedy, Eufaula, Ala., Bright Green	15.00
Medicine, Wheatley's Compound Syrup, Aqua, Open Pontil	62.00
Medicine, Wheeler & Bolton Improved Citrate Of Magnesia, Cobalt, 7 In.	43.00
Medicine, Wheeler's Tissue Phosphate	5.00
Medicine, White Pine Balsam, Gem Cough Anodyne, Open Pontil, Label	25.00
Medicine, White's Curative Syrup, Aqua	3.00
Medicine, Willard Wright, Druggist, BIMAL, 5 In.	6.00
Medicine, Willson's Monarch Remedies, Aqua, 7 1/2 In.	4.00
Medicine, Winan's Bros., Indian Cure, Aqua, 3/4 Quart	65.00
Medicine, Winan's Bros., Indian Cure, Indian Queen On Front, Aqua, 9 1/4 In.	205.00
Medicine, Winan's Indian Cure, Embossed Indian, Aqua	110.00
Medicine, Wishart's Balsam Wild Cherry, Large Pontil, Thin Neck, Aqua	34.50
Medicine, Wishart's Pine Tree Tar Cordial, Green	35.00
Medicine, Wishart's Pine Tree Tar Cordial, Green, Large Size	65.00
Medicine, Wistar's Balsam Wild Cherry, Large Pontil, Thin Neck, Aqua	34.50
Medicine, Wm.Radam's Fungus Destroyer, 1/2 Gallon _____Color_	xxxx.xx
Medicine, Wm.Radam's Germ Bacteria Or Fungus Destroyer, Amber, 10 1/4 In.	48.00
Medicine, Wm.Radam's Microbe Killer, Embossed Man Beating Skeleton, Amber	70.00
Medicine, Wm.Radam's Microbe Killer, Square, Sheer Top, Bubbly, Amber	65.00
Medicine, Wolfstirns Rheumatic & Gout Remedy, Aqua, 5 In.	1.75
Medicine, Wonderful Wintergreen Rheumatic Remedy, J.L.Filkin, Aqua	12.00
Medicine, Wood's Great Peppermint Cure For Cough & Colds, Aqua, 5 In.	9.00
Medicine, World Famed Blood Mixture, Clarke's, Cobalt Blue, 7 1/4 In.	7.50
Medicine, Wright's Indian Cough Balsam	10.00
Medicine, Wright's Indian Vegetable Syrup	6.00
Medicine, Wyanoke Indian Liniment	3.00
Medicine, Wyeth's Eye Bath, Cobalt, BIMAL, 7 In.	18.00
Medicine, Wyeth's Sage & Sulphur, Label, 12 Oz.	10.00
Medicine, Zoa-Phora, Woman's Friend, Kalamazoo, Mich., Aqua	15.00
Metaxa, Crescent Decanter	7.00
Metaxa, Floral Decanter	12.00
Metaxa, Greek Girl	23.00
Metaxa, Greek Man	23.00
Metaxa, White Vase	28.00
Michter's, Automobile, York Pullman, 1977 _____Illus_	112.00
Michter's, Christmas Tree, 1978	50.00

Michter's, Conestoga Wagon, 1976 ....*Illus*	150.00
Michter's, Daniel Boone Homestead Barn, 1977 .... 35.00 To	46.00
Michter's, Death Mask Of King Tut, 1978, 1.75 Liter .... 36.00 To	58.00
Michter's, Fleetwood Packard, 1979	28.90
Michter's, Jug, 5 Color, 1978, Pint	9.50
Michter's, Jug, 5 Color, 1978, Quart	16.00
Michter's, Jug, 5 Color, 1978, 1/2 Gallon	28.00
Michter's, Liberty Bell, Bisque, 1976 .... 52.00 To	60.00
Michter's, Liberty Bell, Brown, 1976 .... 28.00 To	35.00
Michter's, Penn State Nittany Lion, 1978 ....*Color*	72.00
Michter's, Pennslyvania Dutch Hex, 1977	20.00
Michter's, Pittsburgh University Gold Panther, 1977 ....*Illus*	35.00
Michter's, Reading Pagoda, 1977 ....*Illus*	40.00
Michter's, Stagecoach, Wells Fargo, 1978 .... 25.00 To	62.00

Michter's, Reading Pagoda, 1977

Michter's, Conestoga Wagon, 1976

Michter's, Pittsburgh University Gold Panther, 1977

Michter's, Union Canal Boat, 1976	35.00
Midland, Eagle, 1971	15.00
Midland, Moonwalk, Gray, 1970	12.00
Midland, Moonwalk, Yellow, 1970	12.00
Midland, Spirit Of '76	17.00

Milk Glass, see also Cologne, Cosmetic, Drug, Ink, Medicine

*Milk bottles were first used in the 1880s. The characteristic shape and
printed or embossed wording identify these bottles for collectors. Pyro is
the shortened form of pyroglaze, an enameled lettering used on milk bottles.*

Milk, A.B.Chapin, Allegany, N.Y., Embossed 1/4 Pint .... 4.00 To	5.00
Milk, Alex Bolin & Son, Bradford, Pennsylvania, Embossed, Pint	2.00
Milk, Alta Crest Farms, Spencer, Mass., Green 210.00	275.00
Milk, Anderson's Dairy, Auburn, California, White Pyro, Quart	4.00
Milk, B.& O.Railroad, Cone Paper, Picture Of Train, 1/2 Pint	4.00
Milk, Bee Gardens & Dairy Farm, Embossed, Round, Pint	3.50
Milk, Bell Dairy, Norwalk, Ohio, Cottage Cheese At It's Best, Green Pyro	2.50
Milk, Bell Of Anderson	63.50
Milk, Belle Vernon, Cream Top, Pat., March 3, 1925	25.00
Milk, Bellevue Dairy Inc., Jar, 1/2 Pint	2.75
Milk, Bellview Dairy, Syracuse, N.Y., 1/3 Pint	1.50
Milk, Bellview Dairy, Syracuse, N.Y., 1/3 Quart	1.50
Milk, Big Elm, Green, Quart	225.00
Milk, Borden's, Eagle, Clear, 1/2 Pint	3.00
Milk, Brighton Place, Green, Quart	230.00
Milk, Broadacre Dairies, Poewell Sta., Tenn., Pint	4.00
Milk, Brookfield Dairy, Single Baby Face, Embossed, 1/2 Pint	7.50

Milk, Brookfield, Double Baby Face, Quart .... *Illus*   12.00
Milk, Burbank Creamery, Reg., Cal., Round, Embossed, Amber 3.00
Milk, Buttermilk, Amber, Quart 125.00
Milk, Capitol Dairy, Embossed Capitol Building Dome, Pint 4.00
Milk, Chestnut Farms, Chevy Chase Dairy, Wash., D.C., 1/4 Pint 1.50
Milk, City Sanitary Milk Co., Chicago, Ill., Embossed Clasped Hands, Pint 8.00
Milk, Cream Top, Embossed, Round, 1/2 Pint 4.50
Milk, Dairy Industry Division, Davis, California, Blue Pyro, Quart 8.50
Milk, Dean's Sunshine Dairy, Ridge Crest, Calif., Round, 1/2 Gallon 7.50
Milk, Dingley Dell Goat Dairy, Embossed, 1/2 Pint 7.00
Milk, Double Baby Face, Pyro, Red, Painted Square, Quart 12.00
Milk, E.F.Mayer, 289 Hollenbeck St., Embossed, Amber 35.00
Milk, Edwin Hartsock Dairy, DuQuoin, Ill., Pint 2.50
Milk, EzE Beverages, Embossed, 1/2 Pint 4.50
Milk, F.A.Neurogic And Sons, Salamanca, New York, Orange Pyro, 1/3 Quart 1.00
Milk, Fair Oaks Milk Co., Pyro, Gallon 15.00
Milk, Fair Oaks Milk Co., Wire Bail, Round, Gallon 12.00
Milk, Ft.Smith Pure Milk Co., Ft.Smith, Ark., Pint 6.00
Milk, Gettysburg, 1/2 Pint 3.50
Milk, Gettysburg, Embossed, Pint 3.50
Milk, Gettysburg, Embossed, Quart 3.50
Milk, Greenleaf Dairy, Petersburg, Virginia, Maple Leaves, Green Pyro, Quart 8.00
Milk, Hatton Dairy, Lynneyville, Md., Tin Top, To Be Washed & Returned, Quart 25.00
Milk, Hilton Dairy, Madison, Maine, Pyro, Quart 3.50
Milk, Hygienic Dairy Co., Pyro, Red, 1/4 Pint 3.00
Milk, Hygienic Dairy, Watertown, N.Y., 1/4 Pint 3.00
Milk, J.J.Bowle's, Washington, D.C. 3.00

Milk, Sherer's Dairy, 1/2 Pint, 5 1/4 In.

Milk, Ohio Clover Leaf Dairy,
1/2 Pint, 5 1/4 In.
(See Page 146)

Milk, Brookfield, Double Baby Face, Quart

Milk, Jarosz Milk Co., Chicago, Ill., Embossed, Pint 2.00
Milk, John Gibas, Embossed, 1/3 Quart 2.50
Milk, John W.Boak & Son, Embossed, Quart 3.00
Milk, K.F.Yaeger, Eden, New York, Embossed Ken's Dairy, Pint 2.00
Milk, Kent Dairy, Red Pyro, 1 Ounce Creamer 3.00
Milk, Kenton Dunkirk Creamery Co., Embossed, 1/2 Pint 1.00
Milk, Kumysgen, Blue, Quart 450.00
Milk, Lady Pamela, Horseheads, N.Y., Pyro, Square, Amber, Quart 4.00
Milk, Land O'pines Dairy, Lufkin, Texas, Pyro, Square, Amber, Quart 4.00
Milk, Liberty Milk Co., Buffalo, Ribbed, Statue Of Liberty, Quart & Pint 15.00
Milk, Lincoln Highway Dairy, Delphos, Ohio, Orange Pyro 2.00
Milk, Mayer, Amber, Quart 50.00
Milk, Meadow Gold, Embossed, Square, Amber, Quart 9.00
Milk, Millner Dairy, Embossed Inside Star, Ribbed Neck, Pint 6.00
Milk, Mixon Diary, Hazelhurst, Ga., Embossed Cow's Head, Pint 10.00
Milk, Monterey Bay Milk Distributors Inc., Embossed, Round, 1/4 Pint 4.00
Milk, Muskalonge View Dairy, Fremont, Ohio, Brown Pyro, Pint 1.00

Milk, New Jersey Milk & Cream Co., Perth Amboy, N.J., Pint 3.00
Milk, Ohio Clover Leaf Dairy, 1/2 Pint, 5 1/4 In. .... *Illus* 3.00
Milk, Orchard Dairy, Dallas, Pennslyvania, Red Pyro 10.00
Milk, Painted, 7 1/2 In. .... *Color* 47.50
Milk, Palmerton Sanitary Dairy, Cream Top, Embossed, Quart 4.00
Milk, Parson's Jersey Dairy, Painted Square, 1/2 Pint .... .75
Milk, Parson's Jersey Dairy, Wellington, Ohio, Red Pyro, 1/2 Pint 1.00
Milk, Pettiet Dairy Inc., Cream Top, Painted Square 5.00
Milk, Pioneer Farms, Original Cap, Orange Pyro, Pint 5.00
Milk, Portage, Wisc., Amber, 1/2 Gallon 3.50
Milk, Quality Dairy, Best By Test, Red Pyro, 1 Ounce Creamer 3.00
Milk, Ravenswood Fresh Whole Milk, Pyro, Quart 5.00
Milk, Royal Creamery, Salinas, Monterey, Castroville, Embossed, 1/4 Pint 4.00
Milk, Sheffield & Arden Farms, Quart 4.50
Milk, Sherer's Dairy, 1/2 Pint, 5 1/4 In. .... *Illus* 1.00
Milk, Shoemake Guernsey Farms, Dayton, Ohio, Yellow-Brown Pyro, 1/2 Gallon 2.50
Milk, Single Baby Face, Pyro, Painted Square, Red, Quart 8.00
Milk, Smalley, Quart 30.00
Milk, Smalley, Tin Top, Quart 60.00
Milk, Stillicious, The Chocolate Dairy Drink, 1928, 7 Oz. 3.00

Millville Art Glass, Apollo, Soyus, Dark Amber, Front

Millville Art Glass, Lindbergh 50th Anniversary, Light Blue

Milk, Sulurlan Farm Dairy, Embossed Cow, Pint 10.00
Milk, Sunshine Dairy, Picture Of Sunrise, Baby Face, Square, Quart 11.00
Milk, Sunshine Farms, Pyro, Square, Amber, Quart 3.50
Milk, Sunshine Farms, Smiling Sun, White Pyro, Quart 4.00
Milk, Taylor Milk Co., Always A-Head, Cow's Head, Quart 6.50
Milk, Thatcher, No Glass Lid 185.00
Milk, Thatcher, With Top, Quart 275.00
Milk, Tin Top 12.00
Milk, Tonapah, Nevada, Embossed, 1/2 Pint 14.00
Milk, University Of California, Dairy Industry Division, Pyro, Quart 5.00
Milk, University Of Conn., Storrs, Conn., 1/2 Pint 2.50
Milk, University Of Delaware, Embossed, Clear, Pint 12.50
Milk, Vermont Dairy, Amber, Quart 3.50
Milk, Vonderhaar Bros., Cincinnati, Ohio, Pyro, Square, Amber, Quart 4.00
Milk, Vonderhaar Bros., Cincinnati, Ohio, White Pyro, Quart 5.00
Milk, Wakefield Dairy, Washington, D.C., Bust Of Washington, 1/2 Pint 4.00
Milk, Wauregan Dairy, Cream Top, Painted Round, Pint 4.00
Milk, Weckerl, Green, Quart 225.00
Milk, Weldonian Dairy, Jar, 12 Oz. 2.50
Milk, Winnisquam Farm, Amber, 1/2 Gallon 4.50

Milk, Witherdell's Dairy, Amber, Quart	4.50
Milk, Wm.Weckerle & Son, Inc. Dairies, Buffalo, N.Y., Amber, Quart	28.00
Millville Art Glass, Albert Eisenstein, Amethyst	10.00
Millville Art Glass, Amelia Earhart, Amber	10.00
Millville Art Glass, American Circus Bicentennial, Honey Amber	15.00
Millville Art Glass, American Freedom Train Bicentennial, Green	30.00
Millville Art Glass, American Freedom Train Bicentennial, Honey Amber	30.00
Millville Art Glass, Apollo, Soyus, Dark Amber, Front *Illus*	85.00
Millville Art Glass, Betsy Ross, Flag Day, Bicentennial, Amethyst	15.00
Millville Art Glass, Burgoyne, Saratoga Bicentennial, Amethyst 10.00 To	15.00
Millville Art Glass, Connecticut Bicentennial, Medium Blue	20.00
Millville Art Glass, Delaware Bicentennial, Light Amethyst	15.00
Millville Art Glass, Eleanor Roosevelt, Green	10.00
Millville Art Glass, Georgia Bicentennial, Yellowish Green	15.00
Millville Art Glass, Gerald R.Ford 38th President, Amethyst	40.00
Millville Art Glass, Good Buddy, Beaver Breaker, CBer, Amber	10.00
Millville Art Glass, Good Buddy, Beaver Breaker, CBer, Amethyst	10.00
Millville Art Glass, Good Buddy, Beaver Breaker, CBer, Blue *Color*	10.00
Millville Art Glass, Good Buddy, Beaver Breaker, CBer, Dark Green	10.00
Millville Art Glass, Good Buddy, Beaver Breaker, CBer, Light Green	30.00

Millville Art Glass, Viking I, Aqua
(See Page 148)

Millville Art Glass, 1978 St.Nick, Amethyst
(See Page 148)

Millville Art Glass, Susan B.Anthony, Medium Blue *(See Page 148)*

Millville Art Glass, Gra. Zeppelin 75th Anniversary, Amber 15.00 To	30.00
Millville Art Glass, Hawaii, Captain Cook Bicentennial, Amber *Color*	15.00
Millville Art Glass, Israel's 25th Anniversary, Honey Amber *Illus*	15.00
Millville Art Glass, Jersey Devil, Green *Illus*	10.00
Millville Art Glass, Jimmy Carter 39th President, Amber	10.00
Millville Art Glass, Jimmy Carter 39th President, Amethyst	10.00
Millville Art Glass, Jimmy Carter 39th President, Blue *Illus*	10.00
Millville Art Glass, Jimmy Carter 39th President, Green	10.00
Millville Art Glass, Jimmy Carter 39th President, Navy Blue	30.00
Millville Art Glass, Jimmy Carter 39th President, Sample, Blue	100.00
Millville Art Glass, John F.Kennedy 10 Year Memorial, Blue	50.00
Millville Art Glass, John F.Kennedy 10 Year Memorial, Cobalt Blue	40.00
Millville Art Glass, John F.Kennedy 15 Year Memorial, Light Green	25.00
Millville Art Glass, John F.Kennedy 15 Year Memorial, Light Yellow Brown	25.00
Millville Art Glass, July 4th Bicentennial, Honey Amber	35.00
Millville Art Glass, July 4th Bicentennial, Light Blue	45.00
Millville Art Glass, Lindbergh 50th Anniversary, Light Blue *Illus*	25.00
Millville Art Glass, Maryland Bicentennial, Amethyst	15.00
Millville Art Glass, Massachusetts Bicentennial, Green	20.00
Millville Art Glass, New Hampshire Bicentennial, Amber	15.00

Millville Art Glass, New Jersey Bicentennial, Medium Blue	20.00
Millville Art Glass, New York Bicentennial, Light Amber	15.00
Millville Art Glass, North Carolina Bicentennial, Green	15.00
Millville Art Glass, Panama Canal Treaty, Medium Amber	10.00
Millville Art Glass, Pennsylvania Bicentennial, Green	20.00
Millville Art Glass, Pope John Paul I Memorial, Medium Blue	10.00
Millville Art Glass, Pope John Paul II, Amethyst	10.00
Millville Art Glass, Pope John XXIII Memorial, Amber	10.00
Millville Art Glass, Pope Paul VI Memorial, Light Green	10.00
Millville Art Glass, Pope Paul VI Memorial, Light Yellow Brown	10.00
Millville Art Glass, Queen Elizabeth 25th Anniversary, Amethyst	100.00
Millville Art Glass, Rhode Island Bicentennial, Amethyst	15.00
Millville Art Glass, Richard M.Nixon 37th President, Amethyst	40.00
Millville Art Glass, Senator Hubert H.Humphrey Memorial	25.00 To 90.00
Millville Art Glass, Senator Sam Ervin, Senator Howard Baker, Topaz	15.00
Millville Art Glass, Skylab 3, Medium Cobalt Blue	10.00
Millville Art Glass, Skylab 3, Sample, Medium Cobalt Blue	175.00
Millville Art Glass, South Carolina Bicentennial, Medium Blue	15.00
Millville Art Glass, Special Apollo XI, Burnt Amber	45.00
Millville Art Glass, Special Apollo XI, Sample, Burnt Amber	215.00
Millville Art Glass, Spirit Of '76 Bicentennial, Honey Amber	35.00
Millville Art Glass, Spirit Of '76 Bicentennial, Light Blue	45.00
Millville Art Glass, St.John Neumann, Amethyst	30.00
Millville Art Glass, Susan B.Anthony, Medium Blue *Illus*	10.00
Millville Art Glass, Tall Ships & Wagon Train Bicentennial, Light Blue	15.00
Millville Art Glass, Tall Ships & Wagon Train Bicentennial, Olive Green	15.00
Millville Art Glass, U.S.Marine Corps Bicentennial, Dark Amber	15.00
Millville Art Glass, U.S.Navy Bicentennial, Blue	15.00
Millville Art Glass, U.S.Space Shuttle Enterprise, Light Amber	10.00
Millville Art Glass, Viking I, Aqua *Illus*	125.00
Millville Art Glass, Viking I, Light Green	15.00
Millville Art Glass, Virginia Bicentennial, Blue	15.00
Millville Art Glass, Watergate, Amethyst	175.00
Millville Art Glass, Watergate, Blue	50.00
Millville Art Glass, Watergate, Topaz	15.00
Millville Art Glass, Wright Brothers 75th Anniversary, Concorde SST, Blue	20.00
Millville Art Glass, 1794 Silver Dollar, Orange Amber	10.00
Millville Art Glass, 1840 Silver Dollar, Cobalt Blue	10.00
Millville Art Glass, 1878 Silver Dollar, Amber	10.00
Millville Art Glass, 1878 Silver Dollar, Amethyst *Color*	10.00
Millville Art Glass, 1878 Silver Dollar, Blue	10.00
Millville Art Glass, 1878 Silver Dollar, Green	30.00
Millville Art Glass, 1878 Silver Dollar, Light Green	10.00
Millville Art Glass, 1909 Model T Ford, Blue	10.00
Millville Art Glass, 1909 Model T Ford, Light Amber	30.00
Millville Art Glass, 1909 Model T Ford, Sample, Yellow Green	100.00
Millville Art Glass, 1921 Silver Dollar, Amethyst	30.00
Millville Art Glass, 1921 Silver Dollar, Blue	10.00
Millville Art Glass, 1932 Chevy, Cobalt Blue	30.00
Millville Art Glass, 1932 Chevy, Light Blue	10.00
Millville Art Glass, 1932 Chevy, Sample, Amber	100.00
Millville Art Glass, 1933 Duesenberg, Sample, Light Amber	100.00
Millville Art Glass, 1933 Duesenberg, Yellow Green	30.00
Millville Art Glass, 1971, Silver Dollar, Light Green	10.00
Millville Art Glass, 1973, St.Nick, Topaz	125.00
Millville Art Glass, 1974 St.Nick, Green	65.00
Millville Art Glass, 1975 St.Nick, Medium Blue	35.00
Millville Art Glass, 1976 Campaign Cabin, Carter & Ford, Emerald Green	85.00
Millville Art Glass, 1976 Democrat Campaign Cabin, Carter, Mondale, Aqua	80.00
Millville Art Glass, 1976 Democrat Campaign Cabin, Emerald Green	25.00
Millville Art Glass, 1976 Republican Campaign Cabin, Ford, Dole, Green	25.00
Millville Art Glass, 1976 St.Nick, Dark Amber	45.00
Millville Art Glass, 1976 St.Nick, Olive	90.00
Millville Art Glass, 1977 St.Nick, Honey Amber	25.00
Millville Art Glass, 1978 St.Nick, Amethyst *Illus*	75.00
Millville Art Glass, 1978 St.Nick, Medium Blue	15.00

Millville Art Glass, 1979 St.Nick 10.00

*Mineral water bottles held the fresh natural spring waters favored for
health and taste. Most of the bottles collected today date from the 1850-
1900 period. Many of thse bottles have blob tops.*

Mineral Water, A.W.Rapp, N.Y., Dyottville Glassworks, IP, Green	120.00
Mineral Water, Artesian Spring Co., Callston, N.Y., Olive Green	22.50
Mineral Water, Artesian, Louisville, Ky., Dark Amber, Pint	190.00
Mineral Water, B. & G., San Francisco, Superior, 10 Panel, IP, Cobalt	45.00
Mineral Water, Backus & Pratt, Binghampton, N.Y., Iron Pontil, Blue Green	45.00
Mineral Water, Beard's, Boston, Green, Quart	32.00
Mineral Water, Bitterquelle, Green, 9 1/4 In.	3.00
Mineral Water, Blount Spring's Natural Sulphur, Cobalt	29.50
Mineral Water, Buffalo Lithia Water, Lady With Pitcher	8.00
Mineral Water, C. & E.Hotchkiss & Son, Saratoga, Green	35.00
Mineral Water, Caledonia Spring, Wheelock, Honey Amber, Quart	190.00
Mineral Water, Capital Water Works, Cover, Del., Blue Aqua	45.00
Mineral Water, Careiner's & Co., Improved, Trade Mark, Moon & Stars	22.50
Mineral Water, Champion Sporting Spring Co., Aqua, Pint	30.00
Mineral Water, Chattolanee Co., Chattolanee, Md., ABM, Green, 1/2 Gallon	10.00
Mineral Water, Chemung, Embossed Indian, Porcelain Stopper, IBM, 1/2 Gal.	35.00
Mineral Water, Clarke & Co., Olive Green, Quart	30.00
Mineral Water, Clarke & Co., Saratoga, N.Y., Iron Pontil, Emerald Green, Pt.	120.00
Mineral Water, Clarke & White, Graphite Pontil, Olive Green	40.00
Mineral Water, Clarke & White, Green, Pint	30.00
Mineral Water, Clarke & White, N.Y., Bubbles, Olive Green, Pint	25.00
Mineral Water, Clarke & White, N.Y., Olive Green, Open Pontil, Quart	65.00
Mineral Water, Clarke & White, N.Y., Pontil, Pint	60.00
Mineral Water, Clarke & White, N.Y., Raised Dot, Bubbles, Citron Green, Qt.	45.00
Mineral Water, Clarke & White, N.Y., Seed Bubbles, Olive, Quart	45.00
Mineral Water, Clarke & White, New York, Olive Green	25.00
Mineral Water, Clarke & White, Quart	40.00
Mineral Water, Cold Indian Spring, Original Stopper	25.00
Mineral Water, Congress & Empire Spring Co., N.Y., Citron Green, Pint	35.00
Mineral Water, Congress & Empire Spring Co., N.Y., Citron, Qt. ...... 35.00 To 75.00	
Mineral Water, Congress & Empire Spring Co., N.Y., Green, Pint ...... 25.00 To 65.00	
Mineral Water, Congress & Empire Springs, Pottery, Green	12.00
Mineral Water, Cooper's Well, Miss., Amber, Pint	55.00
Mineral Water, Cure & Mineral Springs Co., S.Omaha, Neb., Aqua	20.00
Mineral Water, Cure & Mineral Springs, S.Omaha, Hutchinson	8.00
Mineral Water, D.H.Knowlton's, Saratoga, N.Y., Olive Green	35.00
Mineral Water, D.J.Whalen, Aqua, Quart	10.00
Mineral Water, Darien Mineral Springs, Tifft & Perry Darien, Green	155.00
Mineral Water, E.Bigelow & Co., Springfield, Iron Pontil, Green	135.00
Mineral Water, Ebberwein, 1882, Embossed Savh., Ga., Deep Cobalt	20.00
Mineral Water, Empire Spring, E, Saratoga, Green, Quart ...... 20.00 To 32.00	
Mineral Water, Empire Spring, Saratoga, N.Y., Dark Amber, Quart	45.00
Mineral Water, Eureka Spring, Saratoga, Torpedo	132.00
Mineral Water, Excelsior Spring, Saratoga, Green, Pint	28.50
Mineral Water, Excelsior Spring, Saratoga, N.Y., BIMAL, Green, 7 1/4 In.	12.50
Mineral Water, F. & B.Beard's, Boston, Green	24.00
Mineral Water, Fraser's Premium, Emerald Green, 1/2 Pint	130.00
Mineral Water, G.W.Weston & Co., Saratoga, N.Y., Dart Green	37.50
Mineral Water, G.W.Weston & Co., Saratoga, N.Y., Olive Green, Quart	45.00
Mineral Water, G.W.Weston, Embossed On Shoulder, Green, Quart	50.00
Mineral Water, G.W.Weston, Pontil, Olive Amber	30.00
Mineral Water, Geyser Spring, Saratoga Spouting Spring, Pint ...... 10.00 To 35.00	
Mineral Water, Gray's & Clark, Middletown, Green, Quart	85.00
Mineral Water, Great Bear Spring, Aqua Ice Blue, 11 1/2 In.	24.50
Mineral Water, Great Seal Spring, Chas.Decker & Bros., Aqua, 1/2 Gallon	15.00
Mineral Water, Guilford Mineral Spring Water, Guilford, Vt., Green	40.00
Mineral Water, Hathorn Spring, Saratoga, Black Amber, Pint	24.00
Mineral Water, Hathorn Spring, Saratoga, N.Y., Amber, Quart	15.00
Mineral Water, Hathorn Spring, Saratoga, N.Y., Black, Quart	30.00
Mineral Water, Hathorn Spring, Saratoga, N.Y., Green	14.50
Mineral Water, Hathorn Spring, Saratoga, N.Y., Olive Green, Pint	22.50

Mineral Water, Henderson's Bonanza, Mendocina, Cal. 28.00
Mineral Water, High Rock Congress Spring, Saratoga, N.Y., Green .... 59.00 To 75.00
Mineral Water, High Rock Congress Spring, Yellow Olive, Pint 50.00
Mineral Water, Hotchkiss, Congress & Empire Spring, N.Y., Light Yellow 150.00
Mineral Water, Hotchkiss, Congress & Empire Spring, N.Y., Olive Gold 77.00
Mineral Water, Humboldt Artesian, Eureka, Cal., Blob Top, Blue Aqua, 7 In. 8.75
Mineral Water, Hunyadi Janos, Label, Olive Green 10.00
Mineral Water, Ilnewone's, Embossed Eagle, Codd, Aqua 17.00
Mineral Water, Ingall's Bros., Portland, Me., Blob Top, 11 In. 8.00
Mineral Water, Isham's California Waters Of Life, 1/2 Gallon 12.00
Mineral Water, J. & A.Dearborn, D, N.Y., Iron Pontil, Cobalt Blue 90.00
Mineral Water, J. & A.Dearborn, New York, Union Glass Works, Cobalt 165.00
Mineral Water, J.C.Parker & Son, N.Y., Teal Blue 45.00
Mineral Water, J.G.Schoch, Philadelphia, S On Back, Iron Pontil, Green 35.00
Mineral Water, J.H.V.Premium Soda Or Mineral Water, Troy, Cobalt 75.00
Mineral Water, Jackson's Napa Soda, Aqua, 7 In. 10.00
Mineral Water, John Clarke, Embossed, 3 Piece Mold, Olive Green, Quart 40.00
Mineral Water, John H.Gardner & Son, Sharon Springs, Blue, Pt. .... 95.00 To 175.00
Mineral Water, John Ryan, Excelsior Mineral Water, Savannah, Ga., IP 42.00
Mineral Water, John Ryan, Excelsior Mineral Water, Union Glassworks, Cobalt 22.00
Mineral Water, John Ryan, Excelsior Union Glass Works, Cobalt 40.00
Mineral Water, John Ryan, Excelsior, Savannah, Ga., Union Glassworks, Cobalt 10.00
Mineral Water, John Ryan, 1852, Columbus, Ga., Deep Cobalt 50.00
Mineral Water, John Ryan, 1859, Cobalt 35.00
Mineral Water, John Ryan, 1866, Excelsior Sodaworks, Cobalt 28.00
Mineral Water, Keystone Water, E.Poland, Maine, Keystone Logo, Aqua, 1/2 Gal. 15.00
Mineral Water, L.E.Roussel, Phila., Iron Pontil, Dark Teal Green 60.00
Mineral Water, Lynch & Clarke, New York, Olive Green, Pint 80.00
Mineral Water, M.T.Crawford, Hartford, Union Glass Works, Mug Base, Cobalt 165.00
Mineral Water, Margillis Srontia, Baltimore, Embossed House, Aqua, 1/2 Gal. 17.00
Mineral Water, Mermont Springs, Nature's Remedy, Middletown, Green, Quart 135.00
Mineral Water, Middletown Healing Springs, Amber, Quart .... 36.00 To 50.00
Mineral Water, Middletown Mineral Springs, Middletown, Ut., Green, Quart 150.00
Mineral Water, Mineral Water Works, Dover, Del., Hutchinson 10.00
Mineral Water, Minnequa Water, Bradford Co., Honey Amber, Quart 65.00
Mineral Water, Missisquoi A Spring, Green, Quart 85.00
Mineral Water, Missisquoi, Seed Bubbles, Golden Amber, Quart 85.00
Mineral Water, New York, Monogrammed C, Dark Olive 22.50
Mineral Water, Panacea Spring Co., Littleton, N.C., Amber, 1/2 Gallon 64.50
Mineral Water, Pavilion & U.S.Spring, Emerald Green, Pint 35.00
Mineral Water, Pocahontas Spring Water, Ground Stopper, Embossed, 12 In. 17.00
Mineral Water, Poland Spring, Figural Moses, Aqua, Quart 70.00
Mineral Water, Poland Spring, Repro, Green, Honeymoon, Quart 25.00
Mineral Water, Portiv's Water Co., Montclair, N.J., Aqua, 1/2 Gallon 14.00
Mineral Water, R. & J.Adams, Druggist, St.Louis, Graphite Pontil, Aqua 75.00
Mineral Water, Red Spring, Emerald Green, Quart 32.00
Mineral Water, Red Wing Seltzer, Pump 10.00
Mineral Water, Sam.I.Nicholl, Leonard St., N.Y., Cobalt Blue 65.00
Mineral Water, Samuel Soda Springs, M In Triangle, Aqua, 6 1/2 In. 10.00
Mineral Water, Saratoga Carlsbad Water, Label, Amber, Quart 8.50
Mineral Water, Saratoga Star Spring, Amber, Quart 40.00
Mineral Water, Saratoga Star Spring, Dark Amber, Quart 45.00
Mineral Water, Saratoga Star Spring, Olive, Quart 45.00
Mineral Water, Schafer & Ebling, Hamilton, Ohio, Iron Pontil, Aqua 100.00
Mineral Water, Seitz & Bros., Easton, Pa, Premium, 8 Sided, IP, Cobalt 125.00
Mineral Water, Sheldon A.Spring, Sheldon, Vt., Blown, C.1870, Amber 150.00
Mineral Water, Solon Palmer, Florida Water, Aqua 5.00
Mineral Water, Southwick & Tupper, N.Y., 10 Panel, Iron Pontil, Clear Green 75.00
Mineral Water, St.Louis Superior, L.Block & Bros., Graphite Pontil, Green 95.00
Mineral Water, Star Spring Co., Saratoga, N.Y., Amber .... 35.00 To 42.50
Mineral Water, Star Spring Co., Saratoga, N.Y., Red Amber 15.00
Mineral Water, Sunset Springs Water, Catskill Mts., 1/2 Gallon 20.00
Mineral Water, Thomas Finegan, N.Y., Marble Stopper, Aqua 10.00
Mineral Water, Tryner & Hillier, N.Y., Iron Pontil, Clear Teal Green 40.00
Mineral Water, Turtle Hill Spring Water Co., Passaic, N.J., Aqua, 1/2 Gallon 17.00
Mineral Water, Tweddle's Celebrated Soda Or Mineral Waters, N.Y., Teal 55.00

Mineral Water, Tweddle's, Courtland Street, N.Y., Iron Pontil, Cobalt 165.00
Mineral Water, Twitchell, Band Lip, Large T, Green 25.00
Mineral Water, Twitchell, Phila., Light Green 30.00
Mineral Water, U.S.A. Hospital Dept., Olive, Quart 75.00
Mineral Water, Upper Blue Lick Water, Stanton & Pierce, Ky., Oval, Quart 300.00
Mineral Water, Vermont Spring, Saxe & Co., Sheldon, Green, Quart 40.00
Mineral Water, Vichy Springs Napa Co., Cal., Aqua, 6 1/2 In. 12.50
Mineral Water, W. & W., New Almaden Min L Water, Aqua 8.00
Mineral Water, W.Eagle Vestry, Union Glass Works, Iron Pontil, Teal Green 60.00
Mineral Water, Washington Lithia Well, Ballston Spa, N.Y., Aqua 18.50
Mineral Water, Washington, Saratoga, Green 60.00
Mineral Water, Weston String, Quart 40.00
Mineral Water, Witter Springs Water, Labels, BIMAL, Amber, 9 In. 15.00
Miniature, Alpa, Bugs Bunny 7.00
Miniature, Alpa, Daffy Duck 7.00
Miniature, Alpa, Elmer Fudd 7.00
Miniature, Alpa, Foghorn Leghorn 7.00
Miniature, Alpa, Grandma 7.00
Miniature, Alpa, Hippety Hopper 7.00
Miniature, Alpa, Honey Bunny 7.00
Miniature, Alpa, Little Big Horn, Set Of 5 .... 50.00
Miniature, Alpa, Petunia Pig 7.00
Miniature, Alpa, Porky Pig 7.00
Miniature, Alpa, Set No.1, Set Of 6 .... 24.95 To 32.50
Miniature, Alpa, Set No.2, Set Of 6 .... 32.50
Miniature, Alpa, Speedy Gonzales 7.00
Miniature, Alpa, Sylvester 7.00
Miniature, Alpa, Wile E.Coyote 7.00

Miniature, Beer, Conrad Seipp, Brg Co., 5 1/2 In.

Miniature, Beer, Conrad Seipp, Brg Co., 5 1/2 In. .... *Illus* 15.00
Miniature, Beneagles, Barrel 4.95
Miniature, Beneagles, Curling Stone 5.50
Miniature, Beneagles, Golden Eagle .... 3.95 To 5.95
Miniature, Beneagles, Haggis .... 3.95 To 5.95
Miniature, Beneagles, King Henry VIII, White 8.75
Miniature, Beneagles, King Robert The Bruce, Black 8.75
Miniature, Beneagles, Loch Ness Monster .... 3.95 To 5.95
Miniature, Beneagles, Mary, Queen Of Scots, Black 8.75
Miniature, Beneagles, Norman Tower, White 8.75
Miniature, Beneagles, Queen Elizabeth I, White 8.75
Miniature, Beneagles, Scottish Tower, Black 8.75
Miniature, Beneagles, Sir Francis Drake, White 8.75
Miniature, Billy's, Beer, ABM, Amber 4.00
Miniature, Black Bull, Angus 4.00
Miniature, Burnhama's Beef Wine Iron 7.00
Miniature, Case Gin, Clear, 5 In. 8.00

Miniature, Collectors Art, Afgan	10.95
Miniature, Collectors Art, Baltimore Oriole	15.95
Miniature, Collectors Art, Basset Hound	10.95
Miniature, Collectors Art, Black Angus Bull	10.95 To 13.00
Miniature, Collectors Art, Blue Jar	22.50 To 26.50
Miniature, Collectors Art, Blue Jay	20.00
Miniature, Collectors Art, Charolais Bull	10.95 To 12.95
Miniature, Collectors Art, Chipmunk	22.50
Miniature, Collectors Art, Dachshund	22.95
Miniature, Collectors Art, Dalmatian	10.95
Miniature, Collectors Art, Hummingbird	17.50
Miniature, Collectors Art, Meadowlark	29.50
Miniature, Collectors Art, Mexican Fighting Bull	36.50
Miniature, Collectors Art, New Polled Hereford	24.95
Miniature, Collectors Art, Old Polled Hereford	24.95
Miniature, Collectors Art, Original Cologne, Set Of 6	119.50
Miniature, Collectors Art, Painted Bunting	17.95
Miniature, Collectors Art, Parakeet	17.50
Miniature, Collectors Art, Pointer	24.95
Miniature, Collectors Art, Rabbit	35.00
Miniature, Collectors Art, Rabbits	29.95
Miniature, Collectors Art, Raccoons	25.50
Miniature, Collectors Art, Robin	16.50 To 19.00
Miniature, Collectors Art, Setter	25.50
Miniature, Collectors Art, Shepherd	24.95
Miniature, Collectors Art, Skunks	29.95
Miniature, Collectors Art, St.Bernard	22.95
Miniature, Collectors Art, Texas Longhorn	36.50
Miniature, Collectors Art, White Poodle	24.95
Miniature, Cream Pure Rye, Dallemand & Co.Rectangular, Amber, 2 3/4 In.	15.00
Miniature, Cream Pure Rye, Fluted Shoulders, Amber, 2 13/16 In.	5.00
Miniature, Crigler & Crigler Co., Distillers, Kentucky, Clear	6.00 To 13.00
Miniature, Crown Distilleries Co., Inside Thread, Amber	25.00 To 45.00
Miniature, Cyrus Noble, Assayer	14.50
Miniature, Cyrus Noble, Bartender	14.50
Miniature, Cyrus Noble, Blacksmith	14.50
Miniature, Cyrus Noble, Buffalo With Calf	15.50
Miniature, Cyrus Noble, Burro	14.50
Miniature, Cyrus Noble, Continental Navy, 1975	9.95 To 15.00
Miniature, Cyrus Noble, Faro Bank, 1975	12.00 To 15.00
Miniature, Cyrus Noble, Gambler	14.50
Miniature, Cyrus Noble, Gambler's Lady	14.50
Miniature, Cyrus Noble, Landlady	14.50
Miniature, Cyrus Noble, Miner	14.50
Miniature, Cyrus Noble, Miner's Daughter	14.50
Miniature, Cyrus Noble, Mountain Lion With Cubs	15.50
Miniature, Cyrus Noble, Music Man	14.50
Miniature, Cyrus Noble, Snow Shoe Thompson	14.50
Miniature, Cyrus Noble, Tonopah Saloon, 1975	13.00 To 15.00
Miniature, Cyrus Noble, Violinist	14.50
Miniature, Cyrus Noble, Whiskey Drummer	14.50
Miniature, Deep Spring, Tennessee Whisky, Amber	8.00
Miniature, Dr.Health Pain Expeller, Doctor In Formal Dress, German	75.00
Miniature, Dug's West Indies, Lucky Strike	17.95
Miniature, Dug's West Indies, Shamrock	20.95
Miniature, Fleming's Export Rye, Clear	20.00
Miniature, Foster Whiskey Figge, Doyle Milwaukee, Cylinder, Amber, 4 1/2 In.	10.00
Miniature, Fredericksburg Bottling Co., San Francisco, Amber, 5 1/2 In.	60.00
Miniature, Garnier, Butterfly	4.00
Miniature, Garrett & Co., Wine	17.00
Miniature, Garrett's American Wines, Clear	8.00
Miniature, Geo.Cohn, Louisville, Ky., Amber	12.50
Miniature, Geo.W.Torrey Co., Est. 1826, Amber, 5 In.	18.00
Miniature, Gold Camel	4.00
Miniature, Gold Horseshoe	4.00
Miniature, Gold Sphinx	4.00

Miniature, Good Old O.G.B., Winchell & Davis Co., Handled, Spout, 2 Tone	75.00
Miniature, Gortuna Whiskey, Paul Hollenlach & Co., Pottery Jug	29.00
Miniature, Grenadier, Fray Junipero Serra	13.95 To 18.00
Miniature, Grenadier, Shamrock	18.00 To 19.00
Miniature, Grenadier, Soldier, Dragoons	20.00
Miniature, Grenadier, Soldier, Grenadier Company, Tenth	20.00
Miniature, Grenadier, Soldier, Minute Man	20.00
Miniature, Grenadier, Soldier, Molly Pitcher	20.00
Miniature, Grenadier, Soldier, Moonlight Ranch	25.00
Miniature, Grenadier, Soldier, Mosby's Rangers	20.00 To 25.00
Miniature, Grenadier, Soldier, Nancy Holt	20.00
Miniature, Grenadier, Soldier, Pancho Villa & Rudolfo, 2 Horses	19.50
Miniature, Grenadier, Soldier, Pancho Villa On Horseback	12.00 To 15.50
Miniature, Grenadier, Soldier, Queen's Rangers, Tenth	20.00
Miniature, Grenadier, Soldier, Rhode Island Artillery, Tenth	20.00
Miniature, Grenadier, Soldier, Robert E.Lee	15.00
Miniature, Grenadier, Soldier, Stonewall Jackson	15.00
Miniature, Grenadier, Soldier, Teddy Roosevelt	15.00
Miniature, Grenadier, Soldier, Texas Ranger	15.00
Miniature, Grenadier, Soldier, U.S.Regulars, Tenth	20.00
Miniature, Grenadier, Soldier, Valley Forge, Tenth	20.00
Miniature, Grenadier, Soldier, Washington Blue Rifles	20.00 To 25.00
Miniature, Grenadier, Soldier, Washington's Guard, Tenth	20.00
Miniature, Grenadier, Soldier, Wisconsin Iron Brigade	17.00 To 20.00
Miniature, Grenadier, Soldier, 1st Regiment Virginia Volunteer	17.00 To 20.00
Miniature, Grenadier, Soldier, 4th Virginia Cavalry	17.00 To 20.00
Miniature, Grenadier, Soldier, 6th Alabama Raccoon Roughs	17.00 To 20.00
Miniature, Grenadier, Soldier, 1st Georgia Regiment, Tenth	20.00
Miniature, Grenadier, Soldier, 11th Indiana Zouaves	17.00 To 20.00
Miniature, Grenadier, Soldier, 14th Virginia Cavalry	17.00 To 20.00
Miniature, Grenadier, Soldier, 2nd Regiment U.S.Sharpshooters	17.00 To 20.00
Miniature, Grenadier, Soldier, 79th New York Highlanders	17.00 To 20.00
Miniature, Grenadier, Soldiers No.1, Set Of 3	35.00
Miniature, Grenadier, Soldiers No.2, Set Of 3	35.00
Miniature, Grenadier, Soldiers No.3, Set Of 3	45.00
Miniature, Hoffman, Bartender	11.00
Miniature, Hoffman, Beagle	16.00
Miniature, Hoffman, Bear & Cub	15.00
Miniature, Hoffman, Blacksmith	11.00
Miniature, Hoffman, Bobcat & Pheasant	15.00
Miniature, Hoffman, Boston Terrier	16.00
Miniature, Hoffman, Boxer	16.00
Miniature, Hoffman, Butcher	14.00
Miniature, Hoffman, Carpenter	14.00
Miniature, Hoffman, Charmer	11.00
Miniature, Hoffman, Cobbler	12.00
Miniature, Hoffman, Cocker Spaniel	16.00
Miniature, Hoffman, Dachshund	16.00
Miniature, Hoffman, Dancer	11.00
Miniature, Hoffman, Doctor	11.00
Miniature, Hoffman, Eagle	15.00
Miniature, Hoffman, Eagle & Fox	15.00
Miniature, Hoffman, Electrician	14.00
Miniature, Good Hoffman, Falcon & Rabbit	15.00
Miniature, Hoffman, Fiddler	11.00
Miniature, Hoffman, Fireman	12.00
Miniature, Hoffman, Generation Gap, Pair	23.00
Miniature, Hoffman, Green Winged Teal, Pair	18.00
Miniature, Hoffman, Guitarist	11.00
Miniature, Hoffman, Harpist	11.00
Miniature, Hoffman, Mailman	12.00
Miniature, Hoffman, Mallard, Pair	18.00
Miniature, Hoffman, Mechanic	14.00
Miniature, Hoffman, Mr.Lucky	12.00
Miniature, Hoffman, Mr.Lucky Series No.3, Set Of 6	79.00
Miniature, Hoffman, Mr.Lucky Series, No.4, Set Of 6	79.00

Miniature, Hoffman, Mrs.Lucky	11.00
Miniature, Hoffman, Owl & Chipmunk	15.00
Miniature, Hoffman, Pintail, Pair	18.00
Miniature, Hoffman, Pistol Series, Set Of 4	68.00
Miniature, Hoffman, Pistol, Civil War Colt	20.00
Miniature, Hoffman, Pistol, Dodge City Frontier	30.00
Miniature, Hoffman, Pistol, German Luger	20.00
Miniature, Hoffman, Pistol, 45 Automatic	20.00
Miniature, Hoffman, Plumber	14.00
Miniature, Hoffman, Policeman	11.00
Miniature, Hoffman, Red Head, Pair	18.00
Miniature, Hoffman, Sandman	11.00
Miniature, Hoffman, Saxophonist	11.00
Miniature, Hoffman, Schoolteacher	12.00
Miniature, Hoffman, Scotch Terrier	16.00
Miniature, Hoffman, Stockbroker	12.00
Miniature, Hoffman, Tailor	14.00
Miniature, Hoffman, Wildlife Series, Set Of 6	88.00
Miniature, Hoffman, Wolf & Raccoon	15.00
Miniature, Hoffman, Woman's Liberation, Pair	21.00
Miniature, Hoffman, Wood Duck, Pair	18.00
Miniature, International Pure Sour Mash, Jug	35.00
Miniature, Jesse Moore & Co., Cylinder, Amber, 6 1/8 In.	50.00
Miniature, Jon-Sol, Elvis, 1977	32.95
Miniature, Jug, Greybeard Scotch Whiskey, 2 Handled, 3 In.	20.00
Miniature, Just A Little Nip, Ceramic, 4 1/2 In. ...... Illus	32.00
Miniature, Kemp's Cough Balsam, Aqua	3.50
Miniature, Kontinental, Editor	15.00
Miniature, Kontinental, Gunsmith	15.00
Miniature, Kontinental, Pioneer Series No.1, Set Of 4	55.00
Miniature, Kontinental, Prospector With Burro	15.00
Miniature, Kontinental, Saddlemaker	15.00
Miniature, Liebeg Extract Co., N.Y., Jug	15.00
Miniature, Lionstone, Bird Series, Set Of 3	22.00
Miniature, Lionstone, Bird Series, Set Of 4	52.00
Miniature, Lionstone, Cardinal	10.00 To 12.50
Miniature, Lionstone, Circus Series, Set Of 9	90.00 To 125.00
Miniature, Lionstone, Dance Hall Girl	12.50
Miniature, Lionstone, Dog Series, No.1, Set Of 6	78.00
Miniature, Lionstone, Dog Series, No.2, Set Of 6	60.00 To 78.00
Miniature, Lionstone, Dog Series, No.3, Set Of 6	63.00 To 78.00
Miniature, Lionstone, Dove	10.00 To 12.50
Miniature, Lionstone, Firefighter Series, Fire Equipment, Set Of 6	39.95
Miniature, Lionstone, Koala Bear	11.00
Miniature, Lionstone, Mint Bar Scene	99.95
Miniature, Lionstone, Ring-Necked Pheasant	10.50
Miniature, Lionstone, Roadrunner	10.50
Miniature, Lionstone, Robin	10.00 To 12.50
Miniature, Lionstone, Safari Series, No.1, Set Of 7	66.00
Miniature, Lionstone, Safari Series, No.2, Set Of 6	63.00
Miniature, Lionstone, Shootout At OK Corral Series, Set Of 3	75.00
Miniature, Lionstone, Tropical Bird Series, Set Of 6	90.00
Miniature, Lionstone, Western Series, No.1, Set Of 6	60.00
Miniature, Lionstone, Western Series, No.2, Set Of 4	56.00
Miniature, Lionstone, Western Series, No.2, Set Of 6	72.00
Miniature, Lionstone, Woodpecker	10.00 To 12.50
Miniature, Luxardo, Gondola	4.00
Miniature, MBC, Banker	16.50
Miniature, MBC, Chinese Junk Plate	13.95
Miniature, MBC, Clipper Ship Plate	13.95
Miniature, MBC, Geishas, Set Of 6	34.95
Miniature, MBC, Gunfighter	6.95 To 9.95
Miniature, MBC, Japanese Lady, Set Of 3	29.95
Miniature, MBC, Mermaid	6.95 To 8.95
Miniature, MBC, Museum Vase, Pair	12.95
Miniature, MBC, Taj Mahal	6.95 To 8.95

Miniature, MBC, Wrangler	6.95 To 10.95
Miniature, McCormick, Bat Masterson	17.00
Miniature, McCormick, Benjamin Franklin	16.00
Miniature, McCormick, Betsy Ross	25.00 To 51.00
Miniature, McCormick, Billy The Kid	17.00
Miniature, McCormick, Black Bart	17.00
Miniature, McCormick, Calamity Jane	17.00
Miniature, McCormick, Charles Lindbergh	15.00
Miniature, McCormick, Confederates, Set Of 4	58.50 To 62.00
Miniature, McCormick, Doc Holliday	17.00
Miniature, McCormick, Elvis, No.1, In Concert	32.95
Miniature, McCormick, George Washington	25.00 To 37.95
Miniature, McCormick, Gunfighter Series, Set Of 8	110.00 To 114.95
Miniature, McCormick, Henry Ford	14.95 To 15.00
Miniature, McCormick, Jeb Stuart	14.00
Miniature, McCormick, Jefferson Davis	14.00
Miniature, McCormick, Jesse James	17.00
Miniature, McCormick, John Hancock	16.00
Miniature, McCormick, John Paul Jones	16.00
Miniature, McCormick, Mark Twain	14.95 To 15.00
Miniature, McCormick, Patrick Henry	16.00
Miniature, McCormick, Patriot Series, Set Of 8	230.50
Miniature, McCormick, Paul Revere	25.00 To 51.00
Miniature, McCormick, Robert E.Lee	14.00
Miniature, McCormick, Shriner Noble	14.95
Miniature, McCormick, Spirit Of '76	21.95 To 22.00
Miniature, McCormick, Stonewall Jackson	14.00
Miniature, McCormick, Thomas Jefferson	16.00 To 19.00
Miniature, McCormick, Wild Bill Hickok	17.00
Miniature, McCormick, Will Rogers	14.95 To 15.00
Miniature, McCormick, Wyatt Earp	17.00
Miniature, McCormick, 1776 Set	150.00
Miniature, McCormick, 1776 Set With Case	200.00
Miniature, Michter's, Death Mask Of King Tut, 1978, 1.6 Ounce	14.00 To 15.00
Miniature, Monkey	4.00
Miniature, Mt.Vernon Pure Rye	12.00
Miniature, Munyon's Paw Paw	7.00
Miniature, Muri & Co., Louisville, Whiskey, Amber	12.00
Miniature, Muri Whiskey, Louisville	13.00
Miniature, Nineteenth Hole, 4 In. ....Color	32.00
Miniature, Old Grand, 1913, Sealed, Medicinal	25.00
Miniature, Paul Jone's Pure Rye, Louisville, Amber, 4 5/8 In.	7.00
Miniature, Paul Jones, Louisville, Ky., Whiskey, Amber	4.00 To 8.00
Miniature, Penguin Borg	6.00
Miniature, Pennsylvania Dutch Foxes, Pair	12.00
Miniature, Potter's, Canada Goose	16.00
Miniature, Potter's, Dog Sled	30.00 To 39.95
Miniature, Potter's, Gold Panner	16.00
Miniature, Potter's, Polar Bear Cubs	30.00
Miniature, Potter's, Polar Bear With Cubs	30.00
Miniature, Quaker Whiskey, Pontil	4.50
Miniature, R. & G.A.Wright's, Phila., Open Pontil, Barrel, Aqua	325.00
Miniature, Rainier Beer, Seattle, U.S.A., Cylinder, Amber, 5 3/8 In.	40.00
Miniature, Raintree, Clown, No.1	14.00 To 17.50
Miniature, Raintree, Clown, No.2	14.00 To 17.50
Miniature, Raintree, Clown, No.3	14.00 To 17.50
Miniature, Raintree, Clown, No.4	15.95 To 17.50
Miniature, Raintree, Clown, No.5	15.00 To 17.50
Miniature, Raintree, Clown, No.6	15.00 To 17.50
Miniature, Red Top Whiskey, Round, Amber, 4 In.	18.00
Miniature, Rooster, White & Black	6.00
Miniature, Ski Country, Baltimore Oriole	14.75 To 21.50
Miniature, Ski Country, Barnum, P.T.	14.00 To 14.95
Miniature, Ski Country, Basset Hound	16.95 To 22.95
Miniature, Ski Country, Big-Horned Ram	18.00 To 23.50
Miniature, Ski Country, Birth Of Freedom	26.50

Miniature, Ski Country, Black Footed Ferret .... 14.95 To 15.00
Miniature, Ski Country, Black Lab With Pheasant 18.95
Miniature, Ski Country, Blackbird, Red Winged .... 15.50 To 17.00
Miniature, Ski Country, Blue Jay 22.95
Miniature, Ski Country, Blue Winged Teal Duck 19.95
Miniature, Ski Country, Bob Cratchit & Tiny Tim 17.00
Miniature, Ski Country, Bonnie 17.50
Miniature, Ski Country, Burro .... 12.95 To 19.95
Miniature, Ski Country, Caveman .... 11.00 To 11.95
Miniature, Ski Country, Chief On Horse, No.1 .... 18.95
Miniature, Ski Country, Chief On Horse, No.2 .... 18.95
Miniature, Ski Country, Cigar Store Indian .... 10.50 To 14.00
Miniature, Ski Country, Clown Bust 18.95
Miniature, Ski Country, Clyde 19.95
Miniature, Ski Country, Condor .... 17.00 To 20.00
Miniature, Ski Country, Coyote Family .... 13.75 To 17.95
Miniature, Ski Country, Duck, King Eider .... 17.00 To 22.95
Miniature, Ski Country, Duck, Mallard .... 21.00 To 26.50
Miniature, Ski Country, Duck, Mallard Family 20.95
Miniature, Ski Country, Duck, Pintail 19.95
Miniature, Ski Country, Duck, Red Head .... 17.00 To 36.50
Miniature, Ski Country, Ducks Unlimited 19.00
Miniature, Ski Country, Eagle On Drum 29.95
Miniature, Ski Country, Eagle, Harpy 45.00
Miniature, Ski Country, Eagle, Majestic 75.00
Miniature, Ski Country, Elephant On Drum .... 29.95 To 33.50
Miniature, Ski Country, End Of The Trail .... 19.95 To 26.50
Miniature, Ski Country, Falcon, White .... 18.00 To 22.50
Miniature, Ski Country, Hawk, Red Shouldered 31.50
Miniature, Ski Country, Hawk, Red Tailed .... 15.00 To 20.00
Miniature, Ski Country, Horse, Lipizzaner 24.95
Miniature, Ski Country, Horse, Palomino 23.50
Miniature, Ski Country, Indian Dancers Series, Set Of 6 .... 149.95
Miniature, Ski Country, Indian, North American, Set Of 6 .... 79.50 To 89.95
Miniature, Ski Country, Jenny Lind, Blue 22.95
Miniature, Ski Country, Jenny Lind, Yellow 36.50
Miniature, Ski Country, Kangaroo .... 13.00 To 26.50
Miniature, Ski Country, Ladies Of Leadville, Pair .... 22.00 To 32.95
Miniature, Ski Country, Lion On Drum .... 14.00 To 23.50
Miniature, Ski Country, Mountain Goat 19.95
Miniature, Ski Country, Mountain Lion .... 11.95 To 16.00
Miniature, Ski Country, Mrs.Bob Cratchit 27.95
Miniature, Ski Country, Mrs.Bob Cratchit 27.95
Miniature, Ski Country, Muskie .... 14.50 To 20.00
Miniature, Ski Country, Owl, Saw Whet .... 14.95 To 22.50
Miniature, Ski Country, Owl, Screech Family 29.95
Miniature, Ski Country, Owl, Snowy 50.00
Miniature, Ski Country, Owl, Snowy, Baby 26.50
Miniature, Ski Country, Owl, Spectacled 26.50
Miniature, Ski Country, Peace Dove .... 17.00 To 26.50
Miniature, Ski Country, Peacock 29.95
Miniature, Ski Country, Pelican .... 16.00 To 19.95
Miniature, Ski Country, Penguin Family .... 15.95 To 17.50
Miniature, Ski Country, Pheasant .... 17.95 To 43.95
Miniature, Ski Country, Political, Donkey 18.50
Miniature, Ski Country, Political, Elephant 18.50
Miniature, Ski Country, Prairie Chicken 21.50
Miniature, Ski Country, Raccoon .... 15.00 To 25.00
Miniature, Ski Country, Rainbow Trout .... 15.00 To 15.50
Miniature, Ski Country, Ringmaster .... 10.00 To 18.95
Miniature, Ski Country, Robin .... 19.00 To 29.95
Miniature, Ski Country, Sage Grouse 29.95
Miniature, Ski Country, Salmon, Landlocked .... 15.00 To 17.95
Miniature, Ski Country, Skier, Blue .... 16.00 To 20.00
Miniature, Ski Country, Skier, Red .... 9.00 To 16.00
Miniature, Ski Country, Skiers, Pair 29.95

Miniature, Ski Country, Skunk Family	19.50
Miniature, Ski Country, Spectacled Owl	26.50
Miniature, Ski Country, Submarine	15.00 To 19.95
Miniature, Ski Country, Swallow, Barn	15.50
Miniature, Ski Country, Swan, Black	15.00 To 15.95
Miniature, Ski Country, Tiger On Ball	15.00 To 24.95
Miniature, Ski Country, Tiny Tim	24.95
Miniature, Ski Country, Tom Thumb	10.00 To 18.95
Miniature, Ski Country, Wild Turkey	69.50

Miniature, Washington, Cherry Liqueur,
Cobalt, 4 1/2 In.

Miniature, Just A Little Nip, 4 1/2 In.
Miniature, Whiskey, Nineteenth Hole, Ceramic, 3 1/2 In.
(See Page 154)

Miniature, Ski Country, Woodpecker, Gila	16.50 To 18.00
Miniature, Ski Country, Woodpecker, Ivory Bill	19.95
Miniature, Smither's & Thurstone, Violet Glass, 2 1/2 In.	6.00
Miniature, Stein, Blue	8.00
Miniature, Stein, Brown	8.00
Miniature, Teddy's Pet Nurser	35.00
Miniature, Tu-Sano Cure	25.00
Miniature, Viking Ship, Bone China	14.00
Miniature, Viking Ship, Glass	6.00
Miniature, W.Hasekamp & Co., Case Gin, Full Label, Gin, 4 1/8 In.	100.00
Miniature, Washington, Cherry Liqueur, Cobalt, 4 1/2 In. ....*Illus*	15.00
Miniature, Wee Scotch, 5 In. ....*Color*	.
Miniature, Whiskey, Lady's Leg Neck, Olive Green, 4 3/4 In.	7.00
Miniature, Whiskey, Nineteenth Hole, Ceramic, 3 1/2 In. ....*Illus*	32.00
Miniature, Wisconsin Wildlife, Baby Robin	9.95 To 10.00
Miniature, Wisconsin Wildlife, Blue Jay	9.95 To 10.00
Miniature, Wisconsin Wildlife, Cardinal	10.95
Miniature, Wisconsin Wildlife, Hodags, Male & Female	27.90

Nursing, Rabbits, 7 In.

Miniature, Wisconsin Wildlife, Red Eyed Vireo	10.95
Miniature, Wisconsin Wildlife, Red Headed Woodpecker	9.95
Miniature, Wisconsin Wildlife, Red Winged Blackbird	10.95 To 11.00
Miniature, Wisconsin Wildlife, Totem Pole	3.50 To 6.50
Mitchter's, King Tut ....*Color*	51.50

Nursing bottles were first used in the second half of the 19th century. They are easily identified by the unique shape and the measuring units that are often marked on the sides.

Nursing, Baby Bunting, Rabbit, Round, ABM	15.00
Nursing, Boston Feeder, The, Embossed, Lies On Side, Marked Ounces, Clear	4.00
Nursing, Cat & Kittens, Round, ABM	6.50
Nursing, Cat, Round, ABM	6.00
Nursing, Good Luck, Clear	18.00
Nursing, Happy Baby, Round, ABM	6.50
Nursing, Hygienic Feeder, 2 Ends	25.00
Nursing, Kitten	8.00
Nursing, Marguerite Feeding Bottle, Inside Screw, Daisy On Top	35.00
Nursing, Mother's Comfort, Turtle Type, Clear	20.00
Nursing, O.K., 12 Ribs Vertically, Amethyst	29.50
Nursing, Oriental, The, Turtle Type, Clear	14.00
Nursing, Palace, Inside Screw Stopper, Nipple	40.00
Nursing, Papoose, Clear, 7 1/2 In.	3.50
Nursing, Peerless, Aqua	15.00
Nursing, Peerless, Turtle, Aqua	35.00
Nursing, Phoenix, Horizontal Ribs, Oval	12.00
Nursing, Phoenix, Round, ABM	5.00
Nursing, Rabbits, 7 In. ....*Illus*	3.00
Nursing, Rude Baby	6.00
Nursing, Sonny Boy, Embossed Baby	6.00
Nursing, Teddy's Pet, Peaceful Nights, Turtle, Clear, 4 Oz.	63.00
Nursing, The Favorite, Patented 1890, McKinnon & Co., N.Y.	150.00
Nursing, Turtle Shape, Embossed, Scotland, Aqua	25.00
Nursing, Turtle Shape, England, Aqua	25.00
Nursing, Turtle Shape, England, Pale Blue	40.00
Nursing, Turtle Shape, Scotland, Pale Blue	40.00
Nursing, Two Cats	6.00
OBR, Balloon, 1969	5.00 To 6.00
OBR, Caboose, 1973	15.00
OBR, Eastern Kentucky University, 1974	18.00
OBR, Fifth Avenue Bus, 1971	16.00
OBR, Football Player	10.00 To 20.00
OBR, Georgia Tech	15.00

OBR, Georgia University	15.00
OBR, Green Bay Packers	11.00
OBR, Hockey Player	9.00 To 14.00
OBR, Locomotive, General Sherman, 1974	17.00
OBR, Missouri University	20.00
OBR, NFL Football	15.00
OBR, Ohio State University	10.00
OBR, Pierce Arrow, 1969	20.00
OBR, Prairie Wagon, 1969	11.00
OBR, River Queen, Gold, 1969	20.00 To 22.00
OBR, River Queen, 1967	6.00 To 10.00
OBR, Santa Maria, 1971	14.00
OBR, Titanic, 1976	40.00
OBR, Trolley Car	32.00
OBR, W.C.Fields, No.1, Top Hat, 1976	12.00 To 19.00
OBR, W.C.Fields, No.2, Bank Dick, 1976	12.00 To 19.00
Oil, Bear's Oil, Open Pontil	30.00
Oil, Bear's, Content	20.00
Oil, Bear's, Open Pontil	25.00
Oil, Bear's, Picture Of Bear & Oil, Clear	12.00
Oil, British Troop, ABM, Clear	5.00
Oil, Gargling, Lockport, N.Y., Deep Green	10.00
Oil, Grover & Baker Extra Refined Machine, Clear	8.00
Oil, Hamilton's Old English Black	4.00
Oil, Healy & Bigelow Kickapoo Indian	9.00
Oil, Paskolay, Embossed Pineapple On Face, Amber	4.00
Oil, Rowland's Macassar, Crude Flared Lip	17.00
Oil, S.M.Kier, Petroleum, Pittsburgh, Blue Aqua, 6 3/4 In.	45.00
Oil, Shell Oil, Canadian, Embossed, ABM, Imperial Quart	13.00
Oil, Shell Penn Motor, Clear, 14 1/2 In.	8.00
Old Bardstown, Christmas Card, 1977	9.00 To 14.00
Old Bardstown, Foster Brooks, 1978	36.50 To 46.00
Old Bardstown, Ironworker	36.50 To 40.00

Old Fitzgerald, Cabin Still, Hillbilly, Pint, 1954
(See Page 160)

Old Fitzgerald, Cabin Still, Early American, 1970
(See Page 160)

Old Bardstown, Keg, With Stand, 1977	30.00
Old Bardstown, Kentucky Colonel, 1978	36.00 To 40.00
Old Bardstown, Kentucky Derby, 1977	9.00
Old Bardstown, Kentucky Wildcat, 1978	36.50 To 38.00
Old Bardstown, Surface Miner, 1978	36.00 To 63.00
Old Crow, Bugatti Royale, 1974	185.00 To 189.00
Old Crow, Chess Set, Rug	70.00
Old Crow, Chessman, Bishop	10.00
Old Crow, Chessman, King	10.00
Old Crow, Chessman, Knight	10.00
Old Crow, Chessman, Pawn	19.00 To 25.00
Old Crow, Chessman, Queen	10.00
Old Crow, Chessman, Rook	10.00
Old Crow, Crow, No Markings, 1974	14.00
Old Crow, Crow, Royal Doulton	47.00
Old Crow, Red Vest, 1974	13.00
Old Crow, Statue, We Pour It, Gold	200.00
Old Fitzgerald, America's Cup, 1970	21.00
Old Fitzgerald, American	4.00
Old Fitzgerald, American Sons Of St.Patrick, 1976	13.00 To 25.00
Old Fitzgerald, Birmingham, 1972	45.00
Old Fitzgerald, Birmingham, 2nd Edition	40.00
Old Fitzgerald, Blarney Bottle, 1970	12.00 To 25.00
Old Fitzgerald, Blarney Stone, 1970	11.00 To 25.00
Old Fitzgerald, Cabin Still, Anniversary, 1959	10.00
Old Fitzgerald, Cabin Still, Anniversary, 1960	9.00
Old Fitzgerald, Cabin Still, Bourbon, 1963	4.00
Old Fitzgerald, Cabin Still, Copper Still, 1957	5.00
Old Fitzgerald, Cabin Still, Deer Browsing, Double Image	14.00
Old Fitzgerald, Cabin Still, Deer Browsing, 1967	5.00
Old Fitzgerald, Cabin Still, Demijohn, With Rack, 1964	10.00
Old Fitzgerald, Cabin Still, Diamond, 1961	10.00
Old Fitzgerald, Cabin Still, Diamond, 1970	6.00
Old Fitzgerald, Cabin Still, Dog 1958, Right	8.00
Old Fitzgerald, Cabin Still, Dog, 1958, Left	12.00
Old Fitzgerald, Cabin Still, Ducks Unlimited, 1972	13.00
Old Fitzgerald, Cabin Still, Ducks Unlimited, 1973	11.00
Old Fitzgerald, Cabin Still, Early American, 1970	*Illus* 4.00
Old Fitzgerald, Cabin Still, Fish, Double Image, 1969	14.00
Old Fitzgerald, Cabin Still, Fish, 1969	4.00
Old Fitzgerald, Cabin Still, Gold Coaster, 1955	13.00
Old Fitzgerald, Cabin Still, Hillbilly, Fishing	79.00 To 100.00
Old Fitzgerald, Cabin Still, Hillbilly, Gallon	543.00
Old Fitzgerald, Cabin Still, Hillbilly, Pint	35.00 To 90.00
Old Fitzgerald, Cabin Still, Hillbilly, Pint, 1954	*Illus* 100.00
Old Fitzgerald, Cabin Still, Hillbilly, 5th, Dull Finish	9.00
Old Fitzgerald, Cabin Still, Hillbilly, 5th, Shiny Finish	15.00
Old Fitzgerald, Cabin Still, Hospitality, 1962	5.00
Old Fitzgerald, Cabin Still, Mallard, 1966	10.00
Old Fitzgerald, Cabin Still, Pheasant, 1956	5.00
Old Fitzgerald, Cabin Still, Pheasants Rising, 1964	11.00
Old Fitzgerald, Cabin Still, Quail, 1972	4.00
Old Fitzgerald, Candlelite, 1955	18.00
Old Fitzgerald, Candlelite, 1961	6.00 To 11.00
Old Fitzgerald, Cardinal	15.00
Old Fitzgerald, Classic, 1972	6.00
Old Fitzgerald, Colonial, 1969	5.00
Old Fitzgerald, Crown, 1957	9.00
Old Fitzgerald, Davidson, North Carolina, 1972	37.00
Old Fitzgerald, Diamond, 1959	10.00
Old Fitzgerald, Diamond, 1961	5.00
Old Fitzgerald, Double Candlelite, 1956	8.00
Old Fitzgerald, Eagle, 1973	4.00
Old Fitzgerald, Executive, 1960	7.00
Old Fitzgerald, Flagship, 1967	4.00 To 5.00
Old Fitzgerald, Fleur-De-Lis, 1962	10.00

Old Fitzgerald, Florentine, 1961	8.00 To 9.00
Old Fitzgerald, Four Seasons, 1964	4.00
Old Fitzgerald, Geese, 1970	4.00
Old Fitzgerald, Gold Coaster, 1954	13.00
Old Fitzgerald, Gold Coaster, 1955	15.00

Old Fitzgerald, South Carolina Tricentennial, 1970
(See Page 162)

Old Fitzgerald, Gold Web, 1953	16.00
Old Fitzgerald, Golden Bough, 1970	4.00 To 5.00
Old Fitzgerald, Hospitality, 1958	7.00
Old Fitzgerald, Hostess, 1977	5.00
Old Fitzgerald, Huntington, West Virginia, 1971	29.00
Old Fitzgerald, Illinois, 1972	17.00
Old Fitzgerald, Irish Counties, 1973	12.00 To 25.00
Old Fitzgerald, Irish Luck, 1972	15.00 To 25.00
Old Fitzgerald, Irish Patriots, 1971	13.00 To 25.00
Old Fitzgerald, Irish Wish, 1975	15.00 To 25.00
Old Fitzgerald, Jewel, 1951	8.00
Old Fitzgerald, Kentucky Sportsman	25.00
Old Fitzgerald, Kentucky University Wildcat	30.00
Old Fitzgerald, L.S.U., 1970	27.00
Old Fitzgerald, Lexington, 1968	6.00
Old Fitzgerald, Man-O'-War, 1969	6.00
Old Fitzgerald, Memphis, 1969	14.00
Old Fitzgerald, Monticello, Wrong Side	23.00
Old Fitzgerald, Monticello, 1968	5.00
Old Fitzgerald, Nebraska, 1971	32.00
Old Fitzgerald, Nebraska, 1972	22.00
Old Fitzgerald, Ohio State, 1970	17.00 To 18.00
Old Fitzgerald, Old Cabin Still, 1958	8.00
Old Fitzgerald, Old Cabin Still, 1972	8.00
Old Fitzgerald, Old Ironsides	5.00
Old Fitzgerald, Old Monterrey, 1970	12.00
Old Fitzgerald, Pheasant, 1972	4.00
Old Fitzgerald, Pilgrim Landing, 1970	15.00
Old Fitzgerald, Plase God, 1968	23.00 To 75.00
Old Fitzgerald, Prase Be, 1968	16.00 To 20.00
Old Fitzgerald, Ram, Bighorn, 1971	4.00

Old Fitzgerald, Richwood, West Virginia, 1971	35.00
Old Fitzgerald, Rip Van Winkle, Green Suit	25.00
Old Fitzgerald, Rip Van Winkle, 1971	34.00 To 50.00
Old Fitzgerald, Songs Of Ireland, 1974	9.00 To 25.00
Old Fitzgerald, Sons Of Erin, II, 1970	13.00 To 25.00
Old Fitzgerald, Sons Of Erin, 1969	12.00 To 25.00
Old Fitzgerald, South Carolina Tricentennial, 1970	*Illus* 11.00
Old Fitzgerald, Texas U, 1971	15.00 To 16.00
Old Fitzgerald, Tournament, 1963	8.00
Old Fitzgerald, Tree Of Life, 1964	5.00 To 6.00
Old Fitzgerald, Triangle Bond, 1977	4.00
Old Fitzgerald, Triangle Prime, 1976	4.00
Old Fitzgerald, Venetian, 1966	3.00
Old Fitzgerald, Vermont, 1970	17.00
Old Fitzgerald, Virginia, 1972	12.00 To 17.00
Old Fitzgerald, West Virginia Forest Festival, 1973	19.00
Old Grand Dad, see Whiskey, Old Grand Dad	
Old Mr.Boston, Amvet, Convention, Iowa	18.00
Old Mr.Boston, Amvet, Declaration Of Independence	17.00 To 20.00
Old Mr.Boston, Anthony Wayne	12.00
Old Mr.Boston, Assyrian Convention	22.00
Old Mr.Boston, Bart Starr, No.15	15.00
Old Mr.Boston, Berkeley, West Virginia	24.00
Old Mr.Boston, Bingo In Illinois	14.00
Old Mr.Boston, Bob White	13.00
Old Mr.Boston, Clown Head	20.00
Old Mr.Boston, Cog Railway	16.00
Old Mr.Boston, Concord Coach	18.00
Old Mr.Boston, Dan Patch, 1970	15.00
Old Mr.Boston, Dan Patch, 1973	16.00
Old Mr.Boston, Daniel Webster Cabin	18.00
Old Mr.Boston, Deadwood, South Dakota	14.00
Old Mr.Boston, Eagle Convention, Atlanta	13.00
Old Mr.Boston, Eagle Convention, Boston	13.00
Old Mr.Boston, Elkins, West Virginia Stump	19.00
Old Mr.Boston, Fire Engine	18.00
Old Mr.Boston, Green Bay, No.87	11.00
Old Mr.Boston, Greensboro Open, 1976, Golf Bag	40.00
Old Mr.Boston, Greensboro Open, 1978, Golf Shoe	40.00
Old Mr.Boston, Guitar, Music City	15.00
Old Mr.Boston, Hawk	18.00
Old Mr.Boston, Illinois State Capitol	12.00
Old Mr.Boston, Lamplighter	17.00
Old Mr.Boston, Lion, Sitting	16.00
Old Mr.Boston, Miss Madison Boat	16.00 To 17.00
Old Mr.Boston, Miss Nebraska	18.00
Old Mr.Boston, Mississippi Bicentennial	14.00
Old Mr.Boston, Molly Pitcher	14.00 To 16.00
Old Mr.Boston, Monticello	13.00
Old Mr.Boston, Mooseheart	10.00 To 13.00
Old Mr.Boston, Nathan Hale	17.00
Old Mr.Boston, National Guard	35.00
Old Mr.Boston, Nebraska Czechs	15.00
Old Mr.Boston, Nebraska, No.1, Gold	10.00
Old Mr.Boston, New Hampshire Frigate	13.00
Old Mr.Boston, New Hampshire Independence	15.00 To 19.00
Old Mr.Boston, New Hampshire Liquor Commission	15.00
Old Mr.Boston, Paul Bunyan	10.00 To 13.00
Old Mr.Boston, Paul Revere	18.00
Old Mr.Boston, Polish American Legion	18.00
Old Mr.Boston, President Inauguration, 1953	15.00
Old Mr.Boston, Prestige Bookend	8.00
Old Mr.Boston, Race Car, No.9	10.00 To 14.00
Old Mr.Boston, Red Dog Dan	17.00
Old Mr.Boston, Sherry Pitcher	4.00
Old Mr.Boston, Ship Lantern	18.00

Old Mr.Boston, Shriner AAONMS Camel	17.00
Old Mr.Boston, Shriner, Bektash Temple	18.00
Old Mr.Boston, Steelhead Trout	16.00
Old Mr.Boston, Tennessee Centennial	11.00
Old Mr.Boston, Town Crier	16.00
Old Mr.Boston, Venus	15.00
Old Mr.Boston, York, Nebraska	15.00
Pacesetter, Corvette, Dark Blue	24.00
Pacesetter, Corvette, Light Blue	24.00
Pacesetter, Corvette, Red	24.00

Perfume, Bears Oil, Merchant, Philadelphia, 5 In.
(See Page 166)

Perfume, Beck & Co., Cologne, 12 In.
(See Page 166)

Perfume, Bears Oil, Solon Palmer, Cincinnati, 4 In.
(See Page 166)

Pepper Sauce, Aqua, Open Pontil, 9 1/4 In.	32.50
Pepper Sauce, Cathedral, Amber, 9 In.	*Color* .
Pepper Sauce, Cathedral, Aqua	15.00
Pepper Sauce, Cathedral, Aqua, Hexagon, Open Pontil	33.50
Pepper Sauce, Cathedral, Aqua, Open Pontil	42.00 To 50.00
Pepper Sauce, Cathedral, Aqua, 8 In.	*Color* 20.00
Pepper Sauce, Cathedral, Aqua, 8 1/2 In.	*Color* 10.00
Pepper Sauce, Cathedral, Clear	16.00
Pepper Sauce, Cathedral, Hexagon, Aqua	14.50
Pepper Sauce, Cathedral, Hexagon, Iron Pontil	70.00
Pepper Sauce, Cathedral, Hexagon, Open Pontil	70.00

Pepper Sauce, Cathedral, Petal Shoulders, 3 Ring Neck, Open Pontil 14.50
Pepper Sauce, Cathedral, Spiral Ribs, Emerald Green, 8 In. 35.00
Pepper Sauce, Cathedral, St.Louis Spice Mills, Green, Embossed 200.00
Pepper Sauce, Cathedral, Western Spice Mills, Golden Amber 325.00
Pepper Sauce, Cathedral, 3 Rings Around Neck, Iron Pontil 35.00
Pepper Sauce, Cathedral, 4 Sided, Aqua, Open Pontil 60.00
Pepper Sauce, Cathedral, 4 Sided, Iron Pontil, Aqua 75.00
Pepper Sauce, Cathedral, 4 Sided, Smooth Base 28.50
Pepper Sauce, Cathedral, 6 Sided, Aqua 16.00
Pepper Sauce, Cathedral, 6 Sided, Iron Pontil 35.00
Pepper Sauce, Cathedral, 6 Sided, Open Pontil .... 39.00 To 42.00
Pepper Sauce, Cathedral, 8 Sided, Aqua, Open Pontil 20.00
Pepper Sauce, E.R.Durkee & Co., N.Y., Window For Label, Teal Green 40.00
Pepper Sauce, Fluted Vertically, Flare Lip, Open Pontil, Aqua 50.00
Pepper Sauce, Fluted, Open Pontil 19.00
Pepper Sauce, Gothic, Aqua, Paper Label, 8 1/2 In. ...._Color_ xxxx.xx

Perfume, Bell Shape, 3 In.
(See Page 166)

Perfume, Richard Hudnut, Deep Aquamarine, 5 In.
(See Page 167)

Perfume, Cut Glass, Elaborate Stopper, Clear, 7 In.
(See Page 166)

Pepper Sauce, Heathcote & Co., Pushed-Up Base, 10 Panels, Green 40.00
Pepper Sauce, Light Greenish Aqua, 9 3/8 In. 24.50
Pepper Sauce, Paneled, Pinched-In Lip, Aqua, 8 3/4 In. 10.00
Pepper Sauce, Petal Shoulders, Ribbed, 3 Ring Neck 7.50

Pepper Sauce, Pioneer, Embossed, Amber	45.00
Pepper Sauce, R.R.D. & Co., Patented Feb.'74, Embossed Base	16.00
Pepper Sauce, Ridgey, Embossed Base, Teal Green, 8 1/2 In.	17.00
Pepper Sauce, Ringed, Clear	7.00

Perfume, Milk Glass, Hand, 5 In.
(See Page 166)

Pepper Sauce, Roped Corners, 5 Stars On 3 Square Panels, Clear, 7 1/2 In.	15.00
Pepper Sauce, S. & P., Pat., Applied For, Tapered, 13 Spiral Ridges, Green	18.00
Pepper Sauce, S.& P., Patent, Teal Blue	18.00
Pepper Sauce, Spiral, Blue	65.00
Pepper Sauce, Spiral, Teal Green	35.00
Pepper Sauce, Swirled, 6 Sided, Aqua	14.00
Pepper Sauce, Well's, Miller, Embossed, Aqua	35.00
Pepper Sauce, 3 Panel Window Design, Open Pontil, Aqua, 6 1/8 In.	45.00
Pepper Sauce, 6 Sided, Aqua, Patented Feb.'74	14.00
Pepper Sauce, 8 Sided, Open Pontil, 3 Rings On Neck, Aqua	22.00
Pepper Sauce, 8 Vertical Ribs, 3 Ringed Neck, Double Ring Lip, IP, Aqua	24.50
Pepper Sauce, 20 Ring, Aqua, 8 1/4 In.	10.00
Pepsi Cola, Alabama Bicentennial, 1975	5.00
Pepsi Cola, Anderson Jr. College, 1976	3.00
Pepsi Cola, Arizona Sun Devils, 1973	4.00
Pepsi Cola, Cincinnati Reds, 1976	6.00
Pepsi Cola, Clemson Tigers, 1974	3.00
Pepsi Cola, Colorado Centennial-Bicentennial, 1975	5.00
Pepsi Cola, Dallas Cowboys, 1972	6.00
Pepsi Cola, Durham.N.C., Pinch Type, Aqua	8.00
Pepsi Cola, East Tennessee State, 1975	6.00
Pepsi Cola, Embossed Each Side In Script, Green, 12 Oz.	10.00
Pepsi Cola, Fiesta Bowl, 1972	9.00
Pepsi Cola, Florida Rowdies, 1976	8.00
Pepsi Cola, Furman University, 1975	3.00
Pepsi Cola, Iowa Vs Iowa State	3.00
Pepsi Cola, Jacksonville, Fla.	15.00
Pepsi Cola, Kentucky Celebration, 1975	3.00
Pepsi Cola, Macon, 1976	4.00
Pepsi Cola, Nebraska University, 1974	5.00
Pepsi Cola, New Bern, Birthplace	5.00
Pepsi Cola, New Bern, N.C., Clear 10 Oz.	5.00
Pepsi Cola, North Carolina, Tar Heel, 1975	7.00
Pepsi Cola, Ohio, Farming And Fort Bicentennial, 1976	4.50
Pepsi Cola, Ohio, Johnny Appleseed, 1976	5.00
Pepsi Cola, Ohio, Railroad And Canal Bicentennial, 1976	4.50
Pepsi Cola, Pensacola, Fla., Clear	225.00
Pepsi Cola, Richmond, Va., 8 Sided On 4 Panels, Aqua	30.00
Pepsi Cola, Savannah, Ga., Crown Top, BIMAL	6.25
Pepsi Cola, South Carolina, 1975	4.00
Pepsi Cola, St.Louis Blues, 1974	5.00
Pepsi Cola, Tar Heel, N.C., Bicentennial, Clear, 10 Oz.	5.00

Pepsi Cola, Virginia President, 1974	4.00
Pepsi Cola, W.Virginia, Famous Places, 1976	5.00
Pepsi Cola, W.Virginia, Mountain State, 1975	5.00
Pepsi Cola, Washington, D.C., Green, Embossed, 1976, 12 Ounce	10.00

Perfume, With Mirror, 4 In.

Pepsi Cola, Winter Bros., Buffalo, N.Y., Label, Amber	20.00
Pepsi Cola, 1905, New Born, BIMAL, Amber	28.00
Pepsi Cola, 1906, Goldsboro, N.C., BIMAL, Aqua	10.00
Pepsi Cola, 1906, Wilson, N.C., BIMAL, Amber	25.00
Pepsi Cola, 1906, 1906, Washington, N.C., BIMAL, Amber	35.00
Pepsi Cola, 1908, Fayetteville, N.C., Aqua Blue	10.00
Pepsi Cola, 1915, Rocky Mount, N.C., Aqua	8.00
Pepsi Cola, 75th Anniversary, Greenville, S.C., Clear, 12 Oz.	5.00
Pepsi Cola, 75th Anniversary, 1973	3.00
Perfume, see also Cologne, Scent	
Perfume, American Ideal Powder Sachet, Contents	30.00
Perfume, Bears Oil, Merchant, Philadelphia, 5 In. *Illus*	16.00
Perfume, Bears Oil, Solon Palmer, Cincinnati, 4 In. *Illus*	16.00
Perfume, Beck & Co., Cologne, 12 In. *Illus*	10.00
Perfume, Bell Shape, 3 In. *Illus*	4.00
Perfume, Betty Boop	10.00
Perfume, Bright Night, Felt Wrapper, Boxed, 1 Dram	13.00
Perfume, California Perfume Co., Fruit Flavors, Clear	16.00
Perfume, Cranberry Glass, Gold Decoration, 4 X 2 In.	100.00
Perfume, Crown Florida Water, Crown Perfumery Co., St.Louis, Amber	15.00
Perfume, Crown Perfumery Co., The, London, Emerald Green, 2 1/2 In.	6.00
Perfume, Cupid Bow, 1955, Boxed	50.00
Perfume, Cut Glass, Elaborate Stopper, Clear, 7 In. *Illus*	8.00
Perfume, Daphne Sachet, California, Full	68.00
Perfume, Elegante, Felt Wrapper, 1946, Boxed, 1 Dram	13.00
Perfume, Fair Lady, 1948, Boxed, Set	75.00
Perfume, G.W.Laird, Perfumer, New York, Milk Glass, Rectangular, 4 1/2 In.	8.50
Perfume, Lily Of The Valley Toilet Water, 1946, Boxed	35.00
Perfume, Lt.Piver, Paris & London, Wide Mouth, Pontil, Clear	15.00
Perfume, Lubin Parfumeur, Pairs, Pontil	5.00
Perfume, Luscious, Felt Wrapper, Boxed, 1 Dram	13.00
Perfume, Milk Glass, Hand, 5 In. *Illus*	65.00
Perfume, Nearness, Felt Wrapper, Boxed, 1 Dram	13.00
Perfume, Owl, Clear, 3 1/2 In.	9.00
Perfume, Palmer, Script, Emerald Green, 5 In.	6.50
Perfume, Pinaud, Paris, Londres, Bruxelles, Pontil, Clear, 3 1/2 In.	10.00

Perfume, Preston Of New Hampshire, Teal Green		8.00
Perfume, Red Roses, Paper Label, 4 1/2 In.	*Color*	4.00
Perfume, Richard Hudnut, Deep Aquamarine, 5 In.	*Illus*	22.00
Perfume, Rooster		8.50
Perfume, Rope Corners, Stars, Milk Glass, 9 1/8 In.		70.00
Perfume, Sunburst Scent, Cobalt, 2 3/4 In.		130.00
Perfume, Watkins' Rose, Box, 5 In.	*Color*	.
Perfume, With Mirror, 4 In.	*Illus*	8.00
Pickle, Aqua, Paper Label, 6 In.	*Color*	.
Pickle, Barrel, Dark Green		20.00
Pickle, Barrel, Green, 8 In.		25.00
Pickle, Barrel, Green, 9 1/2 In.		25.00
Pickle, Barrel, 6 Rings At Top & Bottom, Emerald Green, 10 In.		22.00
Pickle, Bunker Hill, Embossed Monument, Amber, Quart		15.00
Pickle, Bunker Hill, Embossed Monument, Citron, Pint		15.00
Pickle, Bunker Hill, Embossed Monument, Honey Amber, Pint		15.00
Pickle, Candy Bros., Mfg. Co., St.Louis, Glass Lid, Aqua Blue, 11 1/2 In.		22.50
Pickle, Cathedral Arches, Aqua, Pint, 7 1/2 In.		60.00
Pickle, Cathedral Arches, Aqua, 11 1/2 In.		15.00 To 45.00
Pickle, Cathedral Arches, Aqua, 6 1/2 In.		75.00
Pickle, Cathedral Arches, Blue Green, Quart		130.00
Pickle, Cathedral Arches, Bright Green, Hexagonal, 13 1/2 In.		120.00
Pickle, Cathedral Arches, Bulbous Ring, Floral Design, Square, 13 1/2 In.		75.00
Pickle, Cathedral Arches, Clear, 8 1/2 In.	*Illus*	22.50
Pickle, Cathedral Arches, Collared Mouth, Green, 8 1/4 In.	*Illus*	210.00
Pickle, Cathedral Arches, Deep Aqua		65.00
Pickle, Cathedral Arches, Design On 4 Panels, Blue Green, 1 1/2 Quart		130.00
Pickle, Cathedral Arches, Display, Deep Emerald		20.00
Pickle, Cathedral Arches, Dutch Porter, Embossed Wynand Fockink, Amsterdam		20.00

Pickle, Cathedral Arches, Collared Mouth, Green, 8 1/4 In.

Pickle, Cathedral Arches, Embossed S.J.G., Small	75.00
Pickle, Cathedral Arches, Emerald Green, Quart	110.00
Pickle, Cathedral Arches, Green, Gallon	150.00
Pickle, Cathedral Arches, Greenish Aqua, 1/2 Gallon	49.50
Pickle, Cathedral Arches, Ice Blue Aqua, 1/2 Gallon	97.50
Pickle, Cathedral Arches, Iron Pontil, Green, 9 1/2 In.	85.00
Pickle, Cathedral Arches, Light Green, 9 1/2 In.	115.00
Pickle, Cathedral Arches, Medium Green, 9 1/4 In.	175.00
Pickle, Cathedral Arches, Pale Yellow Green, 8 1/4 In.	210.00
Pickle, Cathedral Arches, Pontil, Dark Aqua, Pint	135.00
Pickle, Cathedral Arches, Pontil, Dark Aqua, 1/2 Gallon	185.00
Pickle, Cathedral Arches, Scalloped Design, Iron Pontil, Aqua, 1/2 Gallon	150.00
Pickle, Cathedral Arches, Teal Green, 8 3/4 In.	160.00
Pickle, Cathedral Arches, Unembossed, Square, Aqua, 7 1/2 In.	12.00

Pickle, Cathedral Arches, 3 Piece Mold, OP, Olive Green, Demijohn	25.00
Pickle, Cathedral Arches, 4 Different Sides, Iron Pontil, Aqua, 8 In.	125.00
Pickle, Cathedral Arches, 4 Sided, Aqua, Floral Design On Top, 8 3/4 In.	38.50
Pickle, Cathedral Arches, 4 Sided, Open Pontil, 1/2 Gallon	39.50
Pickle, Cathedral Arches, 5 In.Square Base, Light Green, 14 1/2 In.	575.00
Pickle, Cathedral Arches, 6 Sided, Aqua, 13 1/2 In.	48.50
Pickle, Cathedral Arches, 6 Sided, Clear, 13 1/2 In.	45.00
Pickle, Cathedral Arches, 6 Sided, Label, 13 1/2 In.	85.00
Pickle, Cathedral Arches, 6 Sided, Light Green, 13 In.	155.00
Pickle, Cathedral Arches, 6 Sided, Light Green, 13 1/2 In.	85.00

Pickle, Cathedral Arches,
Clear, 8 1/2 In.
(See Page 167)

Pickle, Cathedral Arches, 6 Sided, 1/2 Gallon	139.50
Pickle, Goofus Glass, Aqua, 13 In.	55.00
Pickle, Goofus Glass, Embossed Roses, Amethyst	9.00
Pickle, Goofus Glass, Statue Of Liberty	55.00
Pickle, H.J.Heinz, Gherkins, 8 In.	*Color*
Pickle, Hayward's Military	15.00
Pickle, Seville Packing Co., N.Y., Flower Vase Shape, Green, 8 3/4 In.	8.00
Pickle, Skilton Foote & Co., Bunker Hill, Honey Amber, 7 3/4 In.	28.00
Pickle, Skilton Foote & Co., Bunker Hill, Olive, Yellow, 8 In.	20.00
Pickle, Skilton Foote & Co., Bunker Hill, Yellow, Amber, 8 In.	20.00
Pickle, Stoddard Type, Golden Amber, 8 3/4 In.	140.00
Pickle, 16 Petals, 4 Recessed Panels, Quart, 8 7/8 In.	14.75

Poison bottles were usually made with raised designs so the user could feel the danger in the dark. The most interesting poison bottles were made from the 1870s to the 1930s.

Poison, Amber, 2 1/2 In.	2.00
Poison, Amber, 3 1/2 In.	2.00
Poison, Amber, 4 1/4 In.	2.00
Poison, Aqua, 3 In.	7.00
Poison, Cobalt, 3 1/2 In.	4.25 To 5.00
Poison, Cobalt, 4 In.	6.00
Poison, Cobalt, 4 1/2 In.	9.00
Poison, Cobalt, 5 1/2 In.	5.25 To 12.50
Poison, Cobalt, 6 Sided, 3 1/4 In.	3.00
Poison, Cobalt, 6 1/2 In.	5.00
Poison, Cobalt, 7 1/2 In.	22.50
Poison, Coffin, Amber, 3 1/2 In.	125.00
Poison, Coffin, Amber, 5 In.	175.00
Poison, Coffin, Cobalt, 7 1/2 In.	195.00
Poison, Demert, Embossed Skull & Crossbones, Cobalt, 10 1/2 In.	300.00
Poison, Diamond Shaped, Hobnails, Poison Embossed, Amber	10.00
Poison, Durflinger, ABM, Cobalt	8.00
Poison, Embalmer's Supply, Square	1.75
Poison, Embossed, Not To Be Taken, Emerald Green, , 8 1/2 In.	35.00

Poison, Emerald Green, 6 In.	14.50
Poison, Espy's Embalming Fluid, Springfield, Ohio, Clear, 1/2 Gallon	30.00
Poison, Flask, Hobnails, Open Pontil	29.00
Poison, Flask, Open Pontil, Light Green	75.00
Poison, H.K.Mulford Co., Chemists, Phila., Skull & Crossbones, Blue, 3 In.	55.00
Poison, H.K.Mulford, Hobnails, Embossed Skull & Crossbones, Cobalt Blue	10.00
Poison, Iodine, Cobalt, 3 In.	15.00
Poison, Jno Wyeth & Bros., Phila., Blue	35.00
Poison, Kilner Bros., Round Ribbed, Cobalt	50.00
Poison, Not To Be Taken, Hexagonal, Cobalt, 4 1/4 X 3 1/4 X 4 5/8 In.	8.00
Poison, Not To Be Taken, 6 Sided, Green, 7 In.	14.00
Poison, Olive Green, 8 1/2 In.	29.50
Poison, Owls, Triangular, Cobalt, 2 1/8 In.	8.00
Poison, Poisonous, Not To Be Taken, Oval, Aqua, 8 1/2 In.	30.00
Poison, Quilted Cobalt, No Stopper, 1/2 Gallon	100.00
Poison, Quilted, Cobalt, 7 In.	15.00
Poison, Quilted, Stopper, Cobalt, 4 1/2 In., Pair	42.00
Poison, Quilted, Stopper, Cobalt, 5 1/2 In.	9.00
Poison, Reese Chemical Co., Cleveland, Ohio, Cobalt Blue	10.00
Poison, Sellari, Skeleton	60.00
Poison, Sharp & Dohme, Honey Amber	85.00
Poison, Skull & Crossbones, ABM	3.00
Poison, Skull Shape, 4 In.	395.00
Poison, Strychnine Label, Triangle, ABM, Amber, 2 3/4 In.	12.00
Poison, Tincture Iodine, Skull & Crossbones, Amber	5.00
Poison, Triangle, Label, Contents, ABM, Blue	6.00
Poison, Triangle, Round Back, Amber	7.00
Poison, Triloids, Cobalt Blue, 3 1/2 In. *Illus*	2.00
Poison, Triloids, 3 Sided, ABM, Cobalt	8.00
Poison, Triloids, 3 Sided, Cobalt	3.50
Poison, Wyeth, Cylinder, Cobalt	6.00

Poison, Triloids, Cobalt Blue, 3 1/2 In.

Pottery, Ale, Australia, Brown & White, Embossed	7.50
Pottery, Book, Bennington Type, Multicolored Glaze, 5 1/2 X 4 1/8 X 2 In.	90.00
Pottery, C.& G.Chapin & Gore, Chicago.2 Handled Neck, Tan & Brown, 11 In.	45.00
Pottery, J.Eberly & Bro., Strasburg, Va., 1/2 Gallon	34.50
Pottery, Jar, Biscuit, Ivory, Gold Overlay, C.1875, New England	150.00
Pottery, Jug, Tacoma Crick Water, 5 1/2 In.	15.00
Pottery, Merril Pottery, Akron O., Ink, Pour Spout	9.50
Pottery, Moerlin's Old Jug Lager Beer, Cincinnati, O., Embossed Angels, Tan	26.00
Pottery, Peoria Crock, Quart	13.00
Pottery, Pig, Wtih Cork In End	39.00
Pottery, Pot, Clarke's Maraqulous Salve	18.00
Pottery, W.Smith, 8 Sided, Embossed Patent	10.00
Pottery, Weyman' Snuff	8.00
Purple Power, Football Player	11.00
Purple Power, Wildcat On Basketball	12.00

Purple Power, Wildcat On Football	12.00
Purple Power, Wildcat Walking	22.00
Raintree, Clown No.4	15.95
Raintree, Clown No.5	15.95
Raintree, Clown No.6	15.95
Raintree, Clown, No.1, With Pig *Illus*	19.00
Raintree, Clown, No.2, Tramp *Illus*	19.00
Raintree, Clown, No.3, With Car *Illus*	19.00
Rare Antique, Franklin	8.00
Rare Antique, Washington	10.00
Rebel Yell, Soldier On Horse	14.00
Sandwich Glass, see Cologne, Perfume, Scent	
Sarsaparilla, A.H.Bull's, Hartford, Aqua, Open Pontil	42.00 To 65.00
Sarsaparilla, A.M.Robinson, Jr., Bangor, Me., Aqua	22.50
Sarsaparilla, Allen Co., Woodfords, Maine, Rectangular, Aqua	18.00
Sarsaparilla, Atlas, For Tumors, Boils, Ringworms, Amber, 9 In.	15.00
Sarsaparilla, Ayer's Compound Extract, Rectangular, Aqua, 8 1/2 In.	4.25
Sarsaparilla, Bristol's Genuine, N.Y., Aqua, 10 1/4 In.	15.00
Sarsaparilla, Bristol's, 5 1/2 In.	50.00
Sarsaparilla, Brown's, For The Kidney, Liver & Blood, Embossed	18.00
Sarsaparilla, Bull's, Extract, Aqua, Open Pontil	20.00

Raintree, Clown, No.1, With Pig

Raintree, Clown, No.3, With Car

Raintree, Clown, No.2, Tramp

Sarsaparilla, Bull's, Pontil, Blue Green	50.00
Sarsaparilla, Charles Joly, Amber, 10 In.	25.00
Sarsaparilla, Dalton's Nerve Tonic, Label & Contents, Aqua	9.00 To 18.00
Sarsaparilla, Dana's, Belfast, Maine, Aqua, 8 1/2 In.	3.00 To 10.00

Sarsaparilla, DeWitts, Aqua	15.00
Sarsaparilla, Dr.Cronk's, 12 Sided, Stoneware, Quart	60.00 To 75.00
Sarsaparilla, Dr.Denison's, Oval, Open Colored Pontil, Base Crack, Green	120.00
Sarsaparilla, Dr.Green's, Aqua, 9 In.	14.00
Sarsaparilla, Dr.Guysott's Yellow Dock, Deep Aqua, 9 In.	150.00
Sarsaparilla, Dr.Guysott's Yellow Dock, Embossed	22.00 To 40.00
Sarsaparilla, Dr.Guysott's Yellow Dock, John Park, Cincinnati, IP, Aqua	125.00
Sarsaparilla, Dr.Hair's, Deep Aqua, Open Pontil	160.00

Sarsaparilla, Gooch, McCullough Drug Co., 9 1/2 In.

Sarsaparilla, Dr.Townsend's Improved Type, Pontil, Olive Green	72.00
Sarsaparilla, Dr.Townsend's, Albany, N.Y., Iron Pontil, Blue Green	145.00
Sarsaparilla, Dr.Townsend's, Albany, N.Y., Iron Pontil, Deep Green	80.00
Sarsaparilla, Dr.Townsend's, Albany, N.Y., Iron Pontil, Teal Green	135.00
Sarsaparilla, Dr.Townsend's, Albany, N.Y., Open Pontil, Blue Green	135.00
Sarsaparilla, Dr.Townsend's, Albany, N.Y., Open Pontil, Olive Amber	68.00
Sarsaparilla, Dr.Townsend's, Bright Green, 3/4 Quart	70.00
Sarsaparilla, Dr.Townsend's, Olive Amber, 3/4 Quart	55.00 To 90.00
Sarsaparilla, Dr.Wood's	7.00
Sarsaparilla, Emerson's, 3 Bottles Guaranteed To Cure	35.00
Sarsaparilla, F.Brown Sarsaparilla & Tomato Bitters, Open Pontil	95.00
Sarsaparilla, Gilbert's, Enosburg Falls, Vt., Honey Amber, 8 1/2 In.	325.00
Sarsaparilla, Gooch, McCullough Drug Co., 9 1/2 In. Illus	35.00
Sarsaparilla, Graefenberg Compound, N.Y., Open Pontil, Aqua, 7 In.	150.00
Sarsaparilla, H.H.Bull, Open Pontil	38.00
Sarsaparilla, Hartford, Connecticut, Aqua, Open Pontil	55.00
Sarsaparilla, Hood's, London, Sample	16.00
Sarsaparilla, Hood's, London, 5 1/2 In.	6.00
Sarsaparilla, Indian, A.F.Desautels, Honey Amber, 9 In.	70.00
Sarsaparilla, Iodine, Aqua, 9 In.	30.00
Sarsaparilla, John Bull Extract, Louisville, Ky., Lime Green	75.00
Sarsaparilla, John Bull, Extract, Louisville, Ky, Deep Aqua	95.00
Sarsaparilla, John Bull, Louisville, Ky., Beveled Corners, Aqua, Quart	55.00
Sarsaparilla, Joy's, E.W.Joy Co., Sunken Panels, Aqua, 8 1/2 In.	12.00
Sarsaparilla, King's Celery Compound, 4 Indented Panels, Amber, 10 In.	30.00
Sarsaparilla, Log Cabin	45.00 To 65.00
Sarsaparilla, Log Cabin, Amber	85.00
Sarsaparilla, Log Cabin, Dark Brown	75.00
Sarsaparilla, Log Cabin, Olive Amber	85.00
Sarsaparilla, Manner's Double Extract, Aqua, 8 In.	33.00

Sarsaparilla, Manner's, Binghamton, N.Y., Aqua 45.00
Sarsaparilla, McLean's, St.Louis, Mo., Aqua, 9 1/2 In. 30.00
Sarsaparilla, Old Doctor Townsend, Green 61.00
Sarsaparilla, Primley's, Aqua 10.00
Sarsaparilla, Recamir, Amber 55.00
Sarsaparilla, Rees Hughes', Redware, 10 In. 100.00
Sarsaparilla, Rush's 12.00
Sarsaparilla, Sand's, Open Pontil, Aqua .... 50.00 To 145.00
Sarsaparilla, Skoda's, Belfast, Maine, Amber .... 28.00 To 40.00
Sarsaparilla, Skoda's, Light Amber 28.00

Sarsaparilla, Yager's, Brown, 9 In.

Sarsaparilla, Wethersell's, Exeter, N.H., Aqua 55.00
Sarsaparilla, Yager's, Brown, 9 In. .... *Illus* 22.00
Sarsaparilla, Eyer's Compound Extract, Lowell, Mass., Aqua 3.00
     Scent, see also Cologne, Perfume
Scent, Moser, Gold Band, Flowers, Amethyst, 3 1/2 In. 90.00
Scent, Seahorse, Applied Rigaree, Sheared Mouth, Pontil, 3 In. 125.00
Scent, Violin, Screw Cap, Amethyst, 2 1/2 In. 30.00
Schlitz, Globe 15.00
Seal, A.Wertz Superior Rye Whiskey, Philadelphia, Amber 30.00
Seal, Ambrosial, B.M.& E.A.W.& Co., Open Pontil, Amber, 8 1/2 In. 125.00
Seal, Ambrosial, Handled Chestnut, Open Pontil 75.00
Seal, ASCR, Black, 11 In. 80.00
Seal, ASCR, Cylinder, Open Pontil, 10 3/4 In. 125.00
Seal, ASCR, Open Pontil, Black Glass, Olive, C.1795, 11 In. 75.00
Seal, B.B.Co. 135.00
Seal, Baker Bros., & Co., Baltimore, Md., Embossed On Bottom, Quart 22.00
Seal, Beni Wall, 1699, English, Olive Amber, Crack, 6 3/8 In. ...... *Illus* 850.00
Seal, Bob Taylor, Whiskey, Joseph Magnus On Back, Amber, Fifth 20.00
Seal, Constitution Class Of 1802, Trinity College 150.00
Seal, Daniel Visser, Gin, Case, Cobalt 18.00
Seal, Emanuel College, Cylinder, Iron Pontil, Black Glass, 11 1/2 In. 75.00
Seal, F.F. 1776, 11 X 6 In. 775.00
Seal, Montana Liquor Co., Butte, Olive Green 15.00
Seal, Nathan's Bros., 1863, Phil., Pa., Squat, Amber 45.00
Seal, Paul Jones Whiskey, Amber .... 8.00 To 12.00
Seal, Paul Jones Whiskey, Louisville, Red Amber 5.00
Seal, R.Greene, 1728, Olive Amber, Chips, 7 X 4 1/2 In. .... *Illus* 700.00
Seal, Sear's, Lime Green 135.00
Seal, Sm. & Co., N.Y., Handled, Open Pontil, Tapered, Amber 300.00
Seal, Sparkler, Handled, Open Pontil, Reddish Amber 165.00
Seal, Straight Sided, Case, 6 5/8 In. 300.00

Seal, T.M.1751, 9 3/8 X 4 3/4 In.	950.00
Seal, Van Dongurgh	45.00
Seal, Vieux Cognac, Laid On Ring, Green, 11 In.	30.00
Seal, W.Daubeny, 1776, 9 X 4 5/8 In.	950.00
Seal, W.M., 1733, Bulbous, Tooled Lip, Light Olive	800.00
Seal, W.Pooly, 1764, 9 X 4 3/4 In.	850.00
Seltzer, see also Mineral Water	
Seltzer, Coca-Cola Bottling Company, Pewter Top, Berlin, Pa., Clear	90.00
Seltzer, Joplin, Mo., Block Letter Coca-Cola	80.00
Seltzer, M.Silverstein, Brooklyn, N.Y., Etched Statue Of Liberty, Green	15.00
Seltzer, Meyer Bottling Co., San Francisco, No Siphon, Golden Amber	27.50
Seltzer, Puritan Beverage Co., Orange, N.J., Picture Of Pilgrim, Green	13.00
Seltzer, Royal Palm, Terre Haute, Ind., Clear, Green & Rust	90.00
Seltzer, Standard Bottling Co., Denver, Col., Rocky Mountain Beverage, Clear	15.00
Shoe Polish, Acme Blacking, Wolff & Randolph, Philadelphia	10.00
Shoe Polish, Eclipse French Satin Gloss, Olive Green, 4 1/2 In.	3.50
Shoe Polish, Jet Oil, Bixby's Friction Polish, 3 3/4 In.	*Illus* 2.50
Shoe Polish, Porter's, Free-Blown, C.1750	75.00
Shoe Polish, Race & Sheldon's Magic Waterproof, 8 Sided, Green	135.00 To 450.00
Shoe Polish, Shape Of Wagon Hub, Aqua	10.00
Sicilian Gold, David, Without Fig Leaf	25.00
Sicilian Gold, Moses	25.00
Sicilian Gold, Pieta	25.00
Ski Country, Basset Hound	35.00 To 39.95
Ski Country, Bear, Brown	18.50 To 27.00
Ski Country, Birth Of Freedom	45.00 To 65.00
Ski Country, Blackbird	36.75 To 43.95
Ski Country, Blue Jay	*Color* 46.00
Ski Country, Blue Winged Teal Duck	37.50 To 47.00
Ski Country, Bob Cratchit And Tiny Tim, 1977	*Illus* 45.00
Ski Country, Bonnie	35.00
Ski Country, Burro	35.00 To 47.00
Ski Country, Cardinal	47.50 To 49.00
Ski Country, Caveman	28.95 To 32.00
Ski Country, Charleston Centennial	55.00
Ski Country, Charolais Bull	20.00 To 35.00
Ski Country, Chukar Partridge	48.00

Seal, R.Greene, 1728, Olive Amber, Chips, 7 X 4 1/2 In.

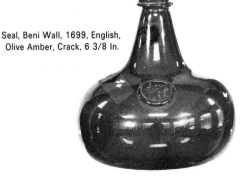

Seal, Beni Wall, 1699, English,
Olive Amber, Crack, 6 3/8 In.

Ski Country, Cigar Store Indian .... 21.00 To 27.00
Ski Country, Circus Tiger 20.00
Ski Country, Circus Wagon With Giraffe .... 25.00 To 33.95
Ski Country, Clown Bust .... 32.00 To 32.95
Ski Country, Clyde 32.00
Ski Country, Condor 36.50
Ski Country, Coyote Family 44.95
Ski Country, Dove .... 33.00 To 38.00
Ski Country, Duck, King Eider .... 36.00 To 45.00
Ski Country, Duck, Mallard .... 35.00 To 59.95
Ski Country, Duck, Mallard Family .... 29.95 To 58.00
Ski Country, Duck, Pintail 51.95
Ski Country, Duck, Red Head .... 45.00 To 49.00
Ski Country, Duck, Wood 115.50
Ski Country, Ducks Unlimited 52.00
Ski Country, Eagle-On-Drum 77.00
Ski Country, Eagle, Harpy .... 69.50 To 80.00
Ski Country, Eagle, Majestic .... 135.00 To 165.00
Ski Country, Eagle, Majestic, Gallon 400.00
Ski Country, Eagle, Mountain 60.00
Ski Country, Elephant-On-Drum 37.00

Shoe Polish, Jet Oil, Bixby's Friction Polish, 3 3/4 In.
(See Page 173)

Ski Country, Bob Cratchit And Tiny Tim, 1977
(See Page 173)

Ski Country, End Of The Trail .... 68.00 To 80.00
Ski Country, Falcon, White 54.00
Ski Country, Fox And Cubs .... *Illus* 70.00
Ski Country, Giraffe In Cage 33.00
Ski Country, Goose, Canada .... 37.00 To 55.00
Ski Country, Goose, Snow 150.00
Ski Country, Great Spirit .... 53.00 To 75.00
Ski Country, Hawk Eagle, Ornate .... 40.00 To 90.95
Ski Country, Hawk, Red Shouldered .... 45.00 To 60.00
Ski Country, Hawk, Red Tailed .... 45.00 To 49.95
Ski Country, Holstein Cow .... 14.00 To 37.00
Ski Country, Horse, Lipizzaner .... 35.00 To 38.00
Ski Country, Horse, Palomino .... 34.00 To 42.00
Ski Country, Indian Chief On Horse, No.1 .... 44.00 To 90.95
Ski Country, Indian Chief On Horse, No.2 .... 54.50
Ski Country, Indian Dancers, Set Of 6 .... 35.00

Ski Country, Fox And Cubs

Ski Country, Mountain Goat, 1975
(See Page 175)

Ski Country, Indian Eagle Dancer .... 42.50 To 58.50
Ski Country, Indian Lookout .... 17.00 To 55.00
Ski Country, Indian, North American, Set Of 6 .... 197.00 To 224.95
Ski Country, Jenny Lind, Blue .... 34.00 To 38.00
Ski Country, Jenny Lind, Yellow .... 39.95 To 55.00
Ski Country, Kangaroo 34.00
Ski Country, Koala .... 17.50 To 27.00
Ski Country, Labrador With Duck .... 43.00 To 98.95
Ski Country, Labrador With Pheasant .... 62.00 To 72.50
Ski Country, Ladies Of Leadville, Pair .... 45.00 To 45.50
Ski Country, Lady Of Leadville, Blue .... *Color* 20.00
Ski Country, Lady Of Leadville, Brown .... *Color* 20.00
Ski Country, Lion-On-Drum .... 24.95 To 30.00
Ski Country, Mill River Country Club .... 21.00 To 36.50

Ski Country, Mountain Goat, 1975 .... *Illus* 32.00
Ski Country, Mountain Lion .... 23.00 To 60.00
Ski Country, Mrs.Cratchit .... 43.00 To 60.95
Ski Country, Muskie .... 26.00 To 39.95
Ski Country, Oriole .... 14.95 To 43.95
Ski Country, Osprey Hawk .... *Color* 80.00
Ski Country, Owl, Horned .... 43.00 To 59.95
Ski Country, Owl, Saw Whet 43.95
Ski Country, Owl, Screech Family .... 36.30 To 44.00
Ski Country, Owl, Snow .... 65.00 To 107.50
Ski Country, Owl, Spectacled .... 39.95 To 45.00
Ski Country, P.T.Barnum .... 30.00 To 37.00
Ski Country, Peace Dove .... 35.00 To 42.00
Ski Country, Peacock .... 43.00 To 69.50
Ski Country, Pelican 39.50
Ski Country, Penguin Family .... 40.00 To 46.95
Ski Country, Pheasants Fighting .... 43.00 To 58.50
Ski Country, Political, Donkey .... 25.00 To 32.95
Ski Country, Political, Elephant .... 25.00 To 32.95
Ski Country, Prairie Chicken .... 29.00 To 32.00
Ski Country, Raccoon 47.00
Ski Country, Rainbow Trout .... 33.00 To 41.95
Ski Country, Ram, Bighorn .... 57.50 To 66.00
Ski Country, Ringmaster .... 24.95 To 26.00
Ski Country, Sage Grouse 45.00
Ski Country, Salmon, Landlocked .... 30.00 To 36.50
Ski Country, Skier, Blue 33.00
Ski Country, Skier, Gold .... 100.00 To 130.00
Ski Country, Skier, Red 25.00
Ski Country, Skunk Family 46.95
Ski Country, Snow Leopard 49.00
Ski Country, Swallow, Barn 43.95
Ski Country, Swan, Black .... 24.50 To 30.00
Ski Country, Tiger-On-Ball .... 31.00 To 43.00
Ski Country, Tiny Tim 57.95
Ski Country, Tom Thumb 27.00
Ski Country, Wild Turkey .... 95.00 To 135.00
Ski Country, Woodpecker, Gila .... 65.00 To 82.50
Ski Country, Woodpecker, Ivory Bill .... 34.00 To 41.50
Ski Country, Wyoming Bronco .... 59.50 To 66.00

Snuff bottles have been made since the eighteenth century. Glass, metal,
ceramic, ivory, and precious stones were all used to make plain or elaborate
snuff holders.

Snuff, American Snuff Co. Of N.Y., P.Lorillard Co.Jar, Amber, 6 1/2 In. 20.00
Snuff, Beveled Corners, Short Rolled Lip, Olive Green, 6 1/4 In. 115.00
Snuff, Chamfered Edges, Amber, Miniature 7.00
Snuff, Chinese, Hand-Painted 20.00
Snuff, Crude, Olive Green, 4 1/4 In. 20.00
Snuff, Dental Brand Scotch, Pat.1879, Lynchburg, Va., Tooth Picture, Small 25.00
Snuff, Doct Marshall's, Aqua, Open Pontil, 3 1/4 In. 15.00
Snuff, Doct Marshall's, Aqua, 3 In. 4.00
Snuff, Doct Marshall's, Label 3.00
Snuff, E.Roome, Green Amber 150.00
Snuff, E.Roome, Olive Green, Open Pontil 40.00
Snuff, E.Roome, Open Pontil 50.00
Snuff, E.Roome, Troy, N.Y., Olive Green, Open Pontil 75.00
Snuff, G.W.Gail & Ax, Baltimore, Soft Paste Ovoid Jar, Lid, Brown Lettering 300.00
Snuff, Honey Amber 20.00
Snuff, Lapis Lazuli, Carvings 375.00
Snuff, Levi Garrett & Sons, Label, Amber 8.00
Snuff, Lorillard, Fruit Jar Shape, Amber 15.00
Snuff, Lorillard's, Amber 25.00
Snuff, Maffaboy Snuff, Labels & Lid 12.00
Snuff, Octagon, Bubbles, Olive Amber, Small 28.00
Snuff, Open Pontil, Olive Green .... 20.00 To 25.00

Snuff, **Otto Landsbert & Co.**, Beroemde Celebrated Snuffer 20.00
Snuff, **Pontil,** Olive Green 50.00
Snuff, **Pontiled,** Light Olive Green 125.00
Snuff, **Rappee,** Miniature, Dense Amber, 2 1/2 In. 22.00
Snuff, **Rectangular,** Open Pontil, Olive Green .... 20.00 To 30.00
Snuff, **Stockholm,** Medium Amber, 5 In. 20.00
Snuff, **Stoddard,** Green, Open Pontil 25.00
Snuff, **True Cephalic,** Open Pontil 12.00
Snuff, **Tubular Pontil,** Amber, 4 1/4 In.Square 35.00

Soda bottles held soda pop or Coca-Cola or other carbonated drinks.
Many soda bottles had a characteristic blob top. Hutchinson stoppers and
coddball stoppers were also used.
    Soda, see also Mineral Water, Pottery
Soda, **A.D.Simmons,** Denver, Colo., Hutchinson, Embossed, Eagle .... 15.00 To 50.00
Soda, **A.F.Dietz Knowersville Albany Co.,** 1888, Hutchinson, Aqua 20.00
Soda, **A.F.Dietz,** 1888 Thief, Hutchinson 14.50
Soda, **A.J.Byrne,** New Britain, Conn., Hutchinson 6.00
Soda, **A.L.Hostman,** Plymouth, Wisc., Aqua 18.00
Soda, **A.P.Smith,** Charleston, Iron Pontil, Cobalt 30.00

Soda, Coca-Cola, Brown, 8 In.
(See Page 179)

Soda, **A.R.Cox,** Norristown, Iron Pontil, Squat, Green 110.00
Soda, **A.S.Miles,** Hutchinson, Aqua 9.00
Soda, **A.Van Hoboken & Co.,** Rotterdam, Blob Seal, Olive Green 28.00
Soda, **A.W.Meyer,** Savannah, Ga., Emerald Green 40.00
Soda, **Aba,** Fargo, N.D., Hutchinson, Aqua .... 20.00 To 38.00
Soda, **Adam Wieser,** Spokane, Hutchinson 14.00
Soda, **Aetna Bottling,** Concord, N.H., Hutchinson .... 8.00 To 10.00
Soda, **Ala-Cola,** Bessemer 25.00
Soda, **Alabama Bottling Co.,** Birmingham, Ala., Hutchinson, Embossed Eagle 15.00
Soda, **Albert Von Harten,** Savannah, Ga., Dark Teal 19.00
Soda, **Albert Von Harten,** Savannah, Ga., Green .... 7.00 To 20.00
Soda, **Albuquerque Bottling Works,** Hutchinson 200.00
Soda, **American Soda Fountain Co.,** Hutchinson, BIMAL 15.00
Soda, **Anchor Bottling Works,** Pittsburgh, Pa., Fluted Base 7.00
Soda, **Arctic Soda Works,** Honolulu 25.00
Soda, **Ardmore Bottling Works,** Ardmore, Okla., Hutchinson 90.00
Soda, **Arizona Bottling Works,** Phoenix, Arizona 200.00
Soda, **Ashland Bottling Works,** Hutchinson, Amber 17.75
Soda, **Aunt Ida,** Emerald Green, ABM 4.00
Soda, **Austin Bottling Works,** Austin, Tex., Hutchinson 15.00
Soda, **Austin,** Minn., Hutchinson 55.00
Soda, **B.B. & W.Bottling Works,** Hattiesburg, Miss., Hutchinson 30.00
Soda, **B.C.Brewing Co.,** Vancouver, B.C. 6.00

Soda, B.Ebberwein, Ginger Ale, Savannah, Ga., Yellow Amber 30.00
Soda, B.H.Woodbury & Co., Hutchinson, Aqua, 7 In. 15.00
Soda, B.R.Lippincott & Co., Stockton, IP, Cobalt 100.00
Soda, Baldwin's, Sole Agent, Arcadia, Cal., Clear 30.00
Soda, Ballanger, Tacoma, Hutchinson 11.00
Soda, Bayview Bottling Works, Seattle, Hutchinson 45.00
Soda, Beer's, Victoria Brewing Co., ABM, Amber, Quart 8.00
Soda, Beidenarn Candy Co., Vicksburg, BIMAL 50.00
Soda, Bennington Bottling Co., N.Bennington, Vt., Aqua .... 45.00 To 100.00
Soda, Birdsboro Bottling Works, Birdsboro, Pa., Amber, Pony 25.00
Soda, Boise, Idaho, Paneled Bottom, Hutchinson 99.00
Soda, Bolen & Byrne, Aerated Beverages, N.Y., Teal Green 12.00
Soda, Bolen & Byrne, N.Y., Aerated Beverages, Round Bottom, Aqua 8.00
Soda, Boley & Co., Union Glassworks, Iron Pontil, Cobalt 40.00
Soda, Boone Cola, Daniel Boone Shooting Gun, Embossed, Green 3.50
Soda, Boston Root Beer, Debossed 59.50
Soda, Boyland & Sturr Bottling Co., Blue Aqua, 6 3/4 In., Hutchinson 7.00
Soda, Bridgeton Glass Works, N.J.Green 24.00
Soda, Brock's Bottling Works, Comanche, Texas, Amethyst 50.00
Soda, Brown's Valley Bottling Co., Hutchinson, Aqua 6.00
Soda, Buffum & Co., Pittsburgh, Pontil, Aqua 17.50
Soda, C. & J.Dithmar Bottling Est., Pontil, Squat, Green 17.50
Soda, C. & K. Eagle Works, Sac City, Blob, Cobalt 45.00

Soda, Coca-Cola, Piqua,
Ohio, Aqua, 8 In.

Soda, C.B.Co., Concord, N.H., Hutchinson 21.00
Soda, C.C.& B., San Francisco, Calif., Iron Pontil, Cobalt 325.00
Soda, C.C.Knickerbocker, 10 Sided, Iron Pontil, Deep Cobalt 165.00
Soda, C.G.Habenight, Columbia, S.C., Aqua 25.00
Soda, C.H.Hutaff Bottler, Wilmington, N.C., Clear 20.00
Soda, C.J.Reasbeck, Martins Ferry, Ohio, Hutchinson 8.00
Soda, C.Schnerr & Co., Sacramento, Calif., Hutchinson .... 12.00 To 15.00
Soda, C.V.Naumann, Philada., Iron Pontil, Green 55.00
Soda, C.Valaer Bottling Works, Charlotte, N.C., Aqua, Hutchinson 35.00
Soda, C.W.Schlieper, St.Louis, Mo., Graphite Pontil 16.00
Soda, Cairns, Timmerman, Block & Co., St.Louis Soda Co., Squat, Green 22.50
Soda, California Soda Works, Embossed Eagle, Hutchinson, Aqua .... 20.00 To 30.00
Soda, Canada Dry, Carnival Glass 7.50
Soda, Capital City Bottling Works, Baton Rouge, La., Aqua .... 8.00 To 20.00
Soda, Catskill, N.Y., Embossed Rip Van Winkle, Clear 35.00
Soda, Cattle Post & Co., Portland, Oregon, Storage, Embossed Eagle, Green 60.00

Soda, Chadwick Rochdale, Ginger Beer, Dog Trade Mark, Honey Amber	10.00
Soda, Champion Bottling Works, Ironton, Ohio, Hutchinson, Aqua	7.00
Soda, Charles Clark, Charleston, S.C., Iron Pontil, Green	64.50
Soda, Charles E.Salfner, 210 E.4th St., Wilmington, Delaware, Aqua	20.00
Soda, Chas.Joly No.9, So.Seventh St., Phila., Green	18.00
Soda, Chase & Co., Green	65.00
Soda, Choctaw Bottling Works, Hutchinson, Aqua, 6 1/2 In.	6.00
Soda, Cincinnati Soda Water & Ginger Ale Co., Embosses Star	10.00
Soda, Claussen & Co., Pacific Sodaworks, Teal Green	25.00
Soda, Clinton Bottling Works, Augusta, Dark Amber	15.00
Soda, Coca-Cola, Brown, 8 In. .... *Illus*	20.00
Soda, Coca-Cola, Piqua, Ohio, Aqua, 8 In. .... *Illus*	12.50

Soda, D.Whiddelt, Tower Works,
Herne Bay, Codd, Green, 7 1/2 In.

Soda, Codd, Marble Inside, BIMAL, 1880-90, Aqua	24.00
Soda, Columbia Doa Works, San Francisco	50.00
Soda, Comstock Cove, C.C. & Co., Boston, Aqua	4.00
Soda, Concord Bottling Works, Concord, N.H., Hutchinson, Aqua	15.00
Soda, Concord Bottling, Hutchinson, Deep Aqua	13.00
Soda, Condarman, Philadelphia, Iron Pontil, Cloudy, Green	10.00
Soda, Constitutional Beverage, Scroll, Amber	165.00
Soda, Cordova Bottling Works, Cordova	25.00
Soda, Corry, Belfast, Round Bottom, Light Green	8.00
Soda, Cripple Creek Bottling, Cripple Creek, Colo., Aqua	12.50
Soda, Crystal Ice & Bottling Works, New Iberia, La., Aqua	12.00
Soda, Crystal Soda Water Co., Cobalt	130.00
Soda, Crystal Soda Water Co., Patented Nov.12, 1872	28.00
Soda, Cumaer & Barkman, Port Jervis, N.Y., Hutchinson	4.00
Soda, D.C.Fonda Boulder, Colo., Hutchinson	20.00
Soda, D.Denhalter & Son, Salt Lake City, Utah, Hutchinson	25.00
Soda, D.H.Baker, Davenport, Iowa	15.00
Soda, D.L.Clark & Co., Pitts., Pa., Blob Top, Stopper, Amber	50.00
Soda, D.T.Cox, Port Jervis, N.Y., Honesdale Glassworks, Pa., Green	95.00
Soda, D.Whiddelt, Tower Works, Herne Bay, Codd, Green, 7 1/2 In. .... *Illus*	6.00
Soda, Dan Gallagher, Texarkana, U.S.A.	25.00
Soda, Davis & Worchester, Birmingham	25.00
Soda, Delta Bottling Works, Yazoo City, Miss., Hutchinson	25.00
Soda, Delta Mfg. Co., Greenville, Miss., Hutchinson	35.00
Soda, Denhalter Bottling Co., Salt Lake, Utah, Sun Colored Amethyst	15.00
Soda, Diamond Bottling Co., West 15th St., N.Y., Aqua, 9 In.	6.00
Soda, Distilled Soda Water Co., Of Alaska	545.00
Soda, Distilled Soda Water Co., Valdez, Alaska, 10 Panel, Hutchinson, Aqua	50.00
Soda, Dyottville Glass Works, Ground Pontil, Green	30.00
Soda, Dyottville Glass Works, Iron Pontil, Blob Top, Deep Green	40.00

Soda, Dyottville Glass Works, Phila., Amber, Quart	10.00
Soda, Dyottville Glass Works, Phila., Aqua	15.00
Soda, Dyottville Glass Works, Yellow Amber	24.00
Soda, Dyottville Glass Works, 3 Mold, Honey Amber, Quart	10.00
Soda, E.J.Messall, Concordia, Hutchinson, Aqua	33.00
Soda, E.L.Billings, Sac City, Geyser Soda, Blue Green	27.50
Soda, E.L.Billings, Sacramento, Cal., Gravitating Stopper, Deep Aqua	15.00
Soda, E.Ottenville, Nashville, Tenn., Hutchinson, Blue	80.00
Soda, E.Schroder & Co., St.Louis, Aqua	10.00
Soda, E.Sheehan, Augusta, Ga., Amber	10.00
Soda, Eagle Bottling Works, Buffalo, N.Y., Embossed Spread Eagle, Clear	15.00
Soda, Eclipse Carbonating Co., St.Louis, Embossed Horseshoe, Amber	175.00
Soda, El Progresso De La Habana, Arsenal 12	50.00
Soda, Empire Soda Works, San Francisco, Blue	50.00
Soda, Engle Bottling Works, Lancaster, Mass., Lightning Stopper	4.00
Soda, Excelsior Soda Works, Los Angeles, Cal.	22.00
Soda, Extract, James Vernor, Detroit, Mich., Clear, 8 1/2 In.	5.00
Soda, F.A.Conant, Girod St., New Orleans, Iron Pontil, Green	35.00
Soda, F.Schmidt, Leadville, Colo., Aqua, Hutchinson	20.00
Soda, F.Schmidt, Leadville, Colo., Embossed, Aqua, Hutchinson	25.00
Soda, Fairbanks & Beard, Howard St., Boston, Embossed Star, Teal Green	30.00
Soda, Felix J.Quinn.Halifax, Nova Scotia, Soda Water Co.	35.00
Soda, Firth's Darlington, Ginger Beer, Locomotive Trade Mark	10.00
Soda, Florida Brewing Co., Tampa, Fla.	5.00
Soda, Fountain & Wells, Birmingham	25.00
Soda, Fred Schorr, Hutchinson	15.00
Soda, Fred W.Whitte, Brooklyn, Ginger Ale, Bail, Aqua	12.00
Soda, Frederik Meinke, Savannah, Ga., Ginger Ale, Amber	12.00
Soda, Friedrich Rau, Philada., Iron Pontil, Green	48.00
Soda, G.A.Cook & Bro., Phillipsburg, N.J., Iron Pontil, Green, Pony	180.00
Soda, G.A.Hohl Lamb's, N.Y., Iron Pontil, Emerald	45.00
Soda, G.Carl, LaCrosse, Wis., Aqua	17.50
Soda, G.Ebberwein, Savannah, Ga., Ginger Ale, Yellow Amber	30.00
Soda, G.Lomax, Chicago, Pontil, Light Blue	45.00
Soda, G.Norris & Co., City Bottling Works, Hutchinson, Blue	50.00
Soda, G.Thomas, Truckee, Cal.	100.00

Soda, Ginger Beer,
Smith & Clody, Pottery, 7 In.

Soda, G.W.Merchant's, Lockport, Green, 5 1/2 In.	40.00
Soda, Geo.Disbro & Co., Chicago, Hutchinson, Blue	80.00
Soda, Geo.Gemenden, Savannah, Ga., Eagle On Shield, IP, Emerald Green	100.00
Soda, Geo.Schmuck's Ginger Ale, Cleveland, Ohio, 12 Sided, Amber	90.00
Soda, Geo.Simons, Hartford, Ct., Green	165.00
Soda, Geo.T.Maginnis & Co., Seattle, Hutchinson	20.00

Soda, Gilbert Bottling Works, Gilbert, Minn., Greenish Aqua, 6 3/4 In.	7.50
Soda, Gimlich & White, Pittsfield, Mass., Aqua, Hutchinson	12.00
Soda, Ginger Ale, Buffalo Head On Bottle	3.25
Soda, Ginger Ale, J.A.Lomax, Aqua, Hutchinson	17.00
Soda, Ginger Ale, Olive Gold, 8 7/8 In.	15.00
Soda, Ginger Beer Co., Cleveland, Ohio, Pottery	6.00
Soda, Ginger Beer, Smith & Clody, Pottery, 7 In. *Illus*	3.00
Soda, Guaymas Bottling Works, Guaymas, Mexico	50.00
Soda, Guaymas Bottling Works, Guaymas, Mexico, Hutchinson	42.00
Soda, Guyette & Co., Detroit, Mich., Cobalt, Hutchinson	55.00
Soda, H.Burger, Frogtown, Ill., Aqua	30.00
Soda, H.Denhalter & Son, Salt Lake City, Utah, Aqua	60.00

Soda, Horn & Bros., Zanesville, Aqua, 7 1/2 In.
(See Page 182)

Soda, H.Grone & Co., St.Louis, Mo., Graphite Pontil	17.00
Soda, H.L. & J.W.Brown, Hartford, Ct., Dark Green	85.00
Soda, H.L. & J.W.Brown, Hartford, Ct., Olive Amber	65.00
Soda, H.Mau & Co., Eureka, Nevada, Blob Top, Aqua, 7 In.	38.00
Soda, H.Meis, Hazleton, Pa., Aqua	15.00
Soda, H.O.Krueger, Grand Forks, N.D., Hutchinson, Aqua	125.00
Soda, H.P.Beerer, Doylestown, Pa., Aqua	12.00
Soda, H.Salzler's, Springville, N.Y., Aqua	4.00
Soda, H.Sanders, Savannah, Ga., Amber	20.00
Soda, H.Weigel, York, Pa., Hutchinson, Green Aqua	15.00
Soda, Hadkins Bottling Co., Tottenville, N.Y., Clear, Hutchinson	8.00
Soda, Hamilton Glass Works, Metal Clip Top, Glass Ball, Round Bottom	30.00
Soda, Hamilton, Torpedo Shape, Embossed, 1880, Light Amber	250.00
Soda, Hamilton's Edward Patent, Metal Clip, Round Bottom	30.00
Soda, Hanigan Bros., Denver, Colo., Aqua	18.00
Soda, Hanigan Bros., Denver, Colo., Hutchinson, Embossed, Vertically	15.00
Soda, Harris Lithia Springs Co., Harris Springs, S.C., Crown Top, Amber	10.00
Soda, Harrisburg Bottling Works, Harrisburg, Pa., Honey Amber, Pony	45.00
Soda, Harvey & Bro., Hackettstown, N.J., Green, Squat	21.00
Soda, Harvey & Co., 204 Market St., Iron Pontil, Green	25.00
Soda, Hawaii Soda Works Co., Hutchinson, Aqua	25.00
Soda, Hayes Bros., Chicago, Ill., Paneled Base, Hutchinson, Blue, Quart	310.00
Soda, Hedlund & Co., Chicago, Ill., Graphite Pontil, Cobalt	85.00
Soda, Henry Kuck, Savannah, Ga., Green	17.50
Soda, Henry Lubs, 1885, Savannah, Ga., Green	17.00
Soda, Henry Winkle, Sac City, Reverse XX, Iron Pontil, Bubble, Aqua	65.00
Soda, Hew Hampton, Iowa, Hutchinson	55.00
Soda, Hickory Bottling Works, Hickory, N.C., Hutchinson, Aqua	22.00 To 35.00
Soda, Hico Soda Works, Aqua	28.00
Soda, Hires Root Beer, Aqua	6.00
Soda, Hires Root Beer, Hutchinson, Aqua	9.00

Soda, Hires, Raspberry Ade, Aqua, 9 1/2 In. ....*Color*

Soda, Hofman Bros., Cheyenne, Hutchinson 300.00

Soda, Hollamon Bros., Bottlers, Hope, Ark. 30.00

Soda, Hollister & Co., Honolulu, Aqua, Hutchinson 25.00

Soda, Horn & Bros., Zanesville, Aqua, 7 1/2 In. ....*Illus* 55.00

Soda, Horn & Bros., Zanesville, Graphite Pontil, Aqua 48.00

Soda, Houpert & Smuly, Birmingham, Ala., Hutchinson 10.00

Soda, Howell's Ginger Beer, Toronto 140.00

Soda, Hutchinson, Pine-Apple Nectar,
Curcia Bros., S.F., 7 In.

Soda, Hutche's, Standard, Fort Bragg 15.00

Soda, Hutchinson, Pine-Apple Nectar, Curcia Bros., S.F., 7 In. ....*Illus* 10.00

Soda, Imperial Bottling Works, Montgomery, Ala., Hutchinson 8.00

Soda, Independence Bottling Works, Independence, Mo., Aqua 7.00

Soda, Indian Root Beer Extract, Amber 5.00

Soda, Ingalls, Portland, Me., Squat, Green 23.00

Soda, J. & A.Dearborn, Albany Glass Works, N.Y., Cobalt Blue 89.00

Soda, J. & J.W.Harvey, Norwich, Conn., Green 145.00

Soda, J.A.Krusling & Huesmann, Cincinnati, Flag, Stopper, Hutchinson, Clear 6.00

Soda, J.C.Born Bottling Works, Canadian, Tex., Crown Top, Aqua 10.00

Soda, J.C.Parker & Son, Blue Green 23.50

Soda, J.F.Dalinger, Tacoma, Hutchinson 15.00

Soda, J.F.Herrmann & Sons, Washington, D.C., Hutchinson 25.00

Soda, J.G.Schooch, Phila., Iron Pontil, Blue, Pony 95.00

Soda, J.Grimshaw, Ltd., Burnley, Inside Screw Top, Olive 10.00

Soda, J.H.Boise, Idaho, Hutchinson, BIMAL, Aqua 120.00

Soda, J.J.Springer, Hollidaysburg, Pa., Graphite Pontil, Green 75.00

Soda, J.Kennedy, Pittsburgh, Iron Pontil, Light Green 95.00

Soda, J.Lake, Schenectady, N.Y., Bowling Pin Shape, Graphite Pontil, Blue 175.00

Soda, J.N., Boise, Idaho, Amethyst 125.00

Soda, J.N., Boise, Idaho, Apple Green 150.00

Soda, J.S.Francis, Avon Park, Fla., Coca-Cola Product, Green 12.00

Soda, J.W.Kidney, Defiance, Ohio, Whittled 20.00

Soda, J.Wahrenberger, New Haven, Conn., Aqua, Hutchinson 10.00

Soda, Jackson's Napa Soda Springs, Blob Top, Aqua 15.00

Soda, Jackson's Napa, Crown Top, Light Green 15.00

Soda, Jackson's Napa, San Francisco, Ring Top, BIMAL, Golden Amber, 12 In. 50.00

Soda, James A.Cramsey, E.Bethlehem, Pa. 5.00

Soda, James J.McGraw, Albany, Ny.Y. 10.00

Soda, James Pollack, Doylestown, Pa., Squat, Aqua 12.00

Soda, James Ray, Ginger Ale, Vertically Embossed, Cobalt Blue 30.00

Soda, James Ray, Savannah, Ga., Aqua, 7 In. 10.00

Soda, Jas.F.Taylor, New Bern, N.C., Hutchinson	30.00
Soda, Jean Hornig, Danbury, Conn., Hutchinson	8.00
Soda, John Forthoffer, Mt.Vernon, Ind.	18.00
Soda, John Graf, Milwaukee, Mug Base, Stopper, Amber	65.00
Soda, John Ryan, Savannah, Philadelphia Porter, Squat, Cobalt Blue	45.00
Soda, John Ryan, 1859, Excelsior, Savannah, Ga., Cobalt	20.00
Soda, John Ryan, 1866, Excelsior Soda Works, Savannah, Ga.	35.00
Soda, John Ryan, 1866, Savannah, Ga., Cobalt	25.00
Soda, John Ryan, 1899, Excelsior Soda Works, Savannah, Ga., Cobalt	22.00
Soda, Johnson & Corbett, Socarro, N.M., Dark Aqua	75.00
Soda, Jordan Water, Pan American Souvenir, 1901	15.00
Soda, Jos.James, Red Jacket, Mich.	6.00
Soda, Jos.Najemink, Chicago, Ill., Standing Lion	20.00
Soda, Jos.P.Bickar, Steubenville, Ohio	14.00
Soda, Jos.Scherrer, Moline, Ill.	6.00
Soda, Jos.X.Laube, Akron, O., Hutchinson, Blue	150.00
Soda, Jumbo Bottling Works, Cincinnati, Ohio, Hutchinson, 7 In. *Illus*	20.00
Soda, Jurgen's & Price Bottlers, Helena, Mont., Aqua	30.00
Soda, K.A.Lomax, Chicago, Cobalt, Hutchinson	25.00 To 45.00
Soda, K.A.Ruona & Co., Ishpeming, Mich., Clear	20.00
Soda, Kanter Bros. & Co., Hutchinson, Aqua	9.00
Soda, Kearney, Shamokin, Pa., Amber, Quart, Hutchinson	150.00
Soda, Keenan Mfg., Co., Butte, Mont., Crown Top	3.00
Soda, Kinkler & Co., LaSalle, Ill., Cobalt	160.00
Soda, Kleis & Ewing, Waterloo, Iowa, Aqua	17.50
Soda, Knicker Bocker, Iron Pontil	68.00
Soda, Korger Bros., Butte, Mont., Hutchinson	500.00
Soda, Kurtistown Soda Water Co., Aqua	50.00
Soda, L.Cohen & Son, Picture Of Beast, Pittsburg, Pa., Aqua	25.00
Soda, La Prueva Fabricade, Jerez Zab, Aqua Blue	15.00
Soda, Lahaina Ice Co., Lahaina, Maui, 4 Piece Molds, Aqua	28.00
Soda, Lancaster Glass Works, Light Violet Blue, 1/2 Pint	90.00
Soda, Lancaster Glassworks, N.Y., Iron Pontil, Sapphire Blue	30.00
Soda, Lougmout Bottling Works, Hutchinson	20.00

Soda, Jumbo Bottling Works, Cincinnati,
Ohio, Hutchinson, 7 In.

Soda, Luke Beard, Howard St., Boston, Iron Pontil, Emerald Green	40.00
Soda, Luke Beard, Pin Shape, Yellow Olive, 1/2 Pint	150.00
Soda, Lyman Astley, Cheyenne, Wyo., Hutchinson	100.00
Soda, M.Huls & Co., Hutchinson	11.50
Soda, M.J.Ryan, Mahanoy City, Pa., Amber, Pony	35.00
Soda, M.M.Battelle, Brooklyn, Green	42.50
Soda, M.Terzich, Sonora, Cal.	15.00
Soda, Mahaska Bottling Works, Hutchinson	10.00

Soda, Manke Co., Savannah, Green	40.00
Soda, Mansfield Bottling Works, Hutchinson, Light Aqua, 6 1/2 In.	25.00
Soda, Mansfield Bottling Works, Mansfield, Ark., Aqua, 6 1/2 In.	25.00
Soda, Mary Hayes, DuQuoin, Ill.	10.00
Soda, Maui Soda Works, Aqua	22.00
Soda, McKinney, Van Alstyne & Plano, Hutchinson, 6 1/2 In.	12.50
Soda, Meehan Bros., Hutchinson, Aqua Green, 6 1/2 In.	8.50
Soda, Memphis Bottling Works, R.M.Becker, Aqua	6.00
Soda, Merickle & Ebberwein, Savannah, Ga., Ginger Ale, Red Amber	30.00
Soda, Meridian Steam Bottling Co., Hutchinson, 6 1/2 In.	28.00
Soda, Merritt & Co., Helena, Montana, Graphite Pontil	30.00
Soda, Mission Dry, Carnival Glass	8.50
Soda, Missisquoi Springs, Green, Quart	32.00
Soda, Missoula Bottling Works, Hutchinson	5.00
Soda, Monroe's Distilled Soda Water, Eureka, Cal.	20.00
Soda, Morjarity & Carroll, Hutchinson, Aqua, 6 7/8 In.	10.00
Soda, Moxie, Glass Label, 12 1/2 In. ....Color	xxxx.xx
Soda, Moxie, Printed Label ....Color	xxxx.xx
Soda, Mrs.B.Zimmerman, New Brunswick, N.J.	56.00
Soda, Mt.Hood Water, Portland, Ore., Monogramed Bear Head, Hutchinson	25.00
Soda, N.Berns, Aviston, Ill.	8.00
Soda, N.Richardson, Trenton, N.J., Not To Be Sold, Iron Pontil	40.00
Soda, Napa Soda Phil., Cadoc, Cobalt	60.00
Soda, National Soda Works, Hutchinson	10.00
Soda, Negaunee Bottling Works, Negaunee, Mich., Aqua, Quart	25.00
Soda, New Century Soda Works, San Francisco, Cal., Bubble	26.00
Soda, New Iberia Ice & Bottling Co., Amethyst, Hutchinson	12.00
Soda, New Liberty Soda Co., Hutchinson	15.00
Soda, Neyhard & Jacoby, Bloomsburg, Pa., Teal Blue	35.00
Soda, Northrop & Sturgis Co., Portland, Oregon, Hutchinson, Blue Aqua, 6 In.	25.00
Soda, Northwestern Bottling Co., Hutchinson	20.00
Soda, O.S.Simonds, Granville, N.Y.	3.00
Soda, Ogden Bottling Works, Ogden, Utah, Hutchinson	25.00
Soda, Omaha Bottling Co., Hutchinson, Light Aqua, 6 1/2 In.	22.00 To 30.00
Soda, Orange Crush, Amber	3.00
Soda, Orange Crush, Brown	2.00
Soda, Osterberg & Wigert, Burlington, Iowa, Graphite Pontil	12.00
Soda, Otto Eberlin, Hermann, Mo.	12.00
Soda, Owen Casey Eagle Soda Works, Blue	25.00
Soda, P.D.F., Ferguson's Carbonated Water, Aqua, 7 In. ....Color	xxxx.xx
Soda, P.Ebner Bottler, Wilmington, Del., 10 Panel, Aqua	15.00
Soda, P.Hall, Phila., Iron Pontil, Aqua	35.00
Soda, P.J.Serwazi, Manayunk, Pa., Hutchinson, Olive Green	195.00
Soda, P.Schille, Columbus, Ohio	4.00
Soda, P.Schille, Columbus, Ohio, Bail, Sapphire Blue, Quart	150.00
Soda, Pablo Co., Blue Green	35.00
Soda, Pacific Soda Works, San Francisco	25.00
Soda, Peter Rumpf, Spokane Falls, Hutchinson	40.00
Soda, Philadelphia Porter XXX, Graphite Pontil, Green	55.00
Soda, Phoenix Bottling Works, Mobile, Ala., Aqua, Hutchinson	12.00
Soda, Pine-Apple Nectar, Curcia Bros., S.F., Hutchinson, 7 In. ....Illus	10.00
Soda, Pioneer Soda Works, Portland, Ore., Monogrammed Shield, Aqua	15.00
Soda, Pioneer Soda Works, San Francisco	15.00
Soda, Poplar Bluff, Mo.	15.00
Soda, Popular Soda Water Co., Hutchinson	8.00
Soda, Port Townsend Soda Works, Hutchinson, Aqua	145.00 To 190.00
Soda, Porter XXX, Graphite Pontil, Green	55.00
Soda, Pride Bottling Co., Hutchinson, Aqua	16.00
Soda, Priest Natural Soda, Embossed Priest's Head, Aqua	15.00
Soda, Purdy Bottle Co., Hutchinson, Aqua	14.50
Soda, R.K.Duffield, Philada., Iron Pontil, Green, Squat	35.00
Soda, R.M.Becker, Memphis Bottling Works, Aqua	6.00
Soda, R.M.Jones, Portmadoc, Codd, Marble, Aqua	15.00
Soda, R.Riddle, Philadelphia, Teal Blue	7.00
Soda, R.Weller, Saratoga, N.Y., Aqua, 6 1/2 In., Hutchinson	7.00
Soda, Rader Bros., Kent, Washington	20.00

Soda, Rainier Soda & Bottling Works, Seattle, Hutchinson 20.00
Soda, Razorback Ginger Ale, Emerald Green 10.00
Soda, Rocky Mountain Bottling Co., Butte, Mont., Star On Bottom, Aqua 15.00
Soda, Rolfe Bottling Works, Rolfe, Iowa, Hutchinson 9.00
Soda, Royal Crown, Copyright 1936 .... 2.00
Soda, Ryan Bottling Works, Chicago, Hutchinson 6.00
Soda, S. & B.Co., Natchez, Miss. 20.00
Soda, S.C.Palmer, Washington, D.C., Hutchinson, Embossed, Amber 125.00
Soda, S.Doschfranci, One Inch Letters, Cobalt 30.00
Soda, S.W.Co., Oakland, California, Open Pontil 35.00
Soda, Salina Bottling Co., Hutchinson, Aqua 30.00
Soda, San Francisco Soda Works, Hutchinson .... 9.00 To 10.00
Soda, Sandberg Bros., Hutchinson 8.00
Soda, Saratoga Bottling Works, Blue Paneled Base, Hutchinson 39.00
Soda, Scammon Bottling Works, Scammon, Kansas, Hutchinson .... 27.00 To 40.00
Soda, Schweppe's, Hutchinson, Emerald Green, 5 In. 37.50
Soda, Seattle Soda Works, Hutchinson .... 12.00 To 15.00
Soda, Seitz & Bro., Easton, Pa., 8 Sided, Iron Pontil, Blue .... 75.00 To 95.00
Soda, Silver Springs Brewing Co., Victoria, B.C. 8.00
Soda, Sisseton Bottling Works, Hutchinson, Aqua 20.00
Soda, Sloup-Sherry Bottling Co., Omaha, Neb., Hutchinson 15.00
Soda, Smith & Clody, Ginger Beer, Pottery, 7 In. ....*Illus* 3.00
Soda, Smithe & Co., Premium Sodawater, Charleston, S.C., 8 Sided, Green 90.00
Soda, Sorsoran Bros., Pittston, Pa., Blue Aqua 10.00
Soda, Southern Bottle Company, Atlanta, Ga., Hutchinson 8.00
Soda, Speidel Bros., Hutchinson, Aqua 25.00
Soda, Spencer & Butler, Des Moines, Iowa, State Capitol, Hutchinson 75.00
Soda, Spring Garden Glass Works, Anchor, Cabin, Tree, Aqua, Pint 500.00
Soda, Standard Bottling Co., Denver, Colo., Aqua, Hutchinson 15.00
Soda, Standard Bottling Co., Denver, Colo., Hutchinson, Clear .... 10.00 To 15.00
Soda, Standard Bottling Works, Minneapolis, Minn., Hutchinson, Amber 95.00
Soda, Star Bottling Works, New Haven, Conn. 20.00
Soda, Star Bottling Works, St.Paul, Minn. 7.50
Soda, Star Bottling Works, Star, N.C., Hutchinson .... 30.00 To 40.00
Soda, Stoddard, 3 Piece Mold, Light Olive Amber 20.00
Soda, Success Bottling Works, Hutchinson 12.00
Soda, Sweeny & Cherry, 33 Norfold St., New York, Cobalt 16.00
Soda, T.J.Tanner, Port Townsend, Washington, Hutchinson .... 195.00 To 230.00
Soda, T.Shotbolt, Lemonade, Victoria, B.C., Bubbly, Aqua 100.00
Soda, T.W.Gillett, New Haven, 8 Sided, Iron Pontil, Dark Teal 58.00
Soda, Taylor & Co., Sodawater, San Francisco, Eureka, Iron Pontil, Cobalt 50.00
Soda, The Haas Co., Chicago, Hutchinson, Aqua 6.00
Soda, Thomas Leonard Sonora Soda Works, Sonora, Cal. 45.00
Soda, Thos.Bragell, West Gardner, Mass, Clear 8.00
Soda, Thos.Brandon, Topeka, Hutchinson, Clear 38.00
Soda, Thos.Maher, Dyottville Glass Works, Phila, Green, Squat 18.00
Soda, Thos.Maher, Dyottville Glass Works, Squat, Emerald Green 40.00
Soda, Thos.Maher, Savannah, Embossed Rising Sun, Green 40.00
Soda, Thos.Maher, Slug Plate, Emerald Green, Iron Pontil 25.00
Soda, Turner Brothers, Buffalo, N.Y., & San Francisco, Cal., Green, Square 100.00
Soda, Twin City Bottling Works, Grand Forks, N.D., Clear 33.00
Soda, Twin City Bottling Works, Texarkana, Ark., Green 18.00
Soda, Tyler Union Bottling Works, Amethyst, Hutchinson 26.00
Soda, Tyler Union Bottling Works, Tyler, Texas, Amethyst 26.00
Soda, Uncle Jo, Amber, ABM 4.00
Soda, Union Bottling Co., Seattle, Hutchinson 25.00
Soda, Union Bottling Co., Wilmington, Del. 25.00
Soda, Union Bottling Works, Aqua, Hutchinson 55.00
Soda, Union Brewing Co., Nanaimo, B.C. 9.00
Soda, Union Glass Works, Iron Pontil, Green 29.00
Soda, Usona Bottling Works, Ft.Smith, Ark., Aqua 45.00
Soda, Usona Bottling Works, Ft.Smith, Ark., Clear 30.00
Soda, Valley Falls Bottling Works, Valley Falls, Kas. 20.00
Soda, Van Harten & Grogen, Ginger Ale, Blob, Teal 95.00
Soda, Vieregg, Grand Island, Neb., Hutchinson 30.00
Soda, Vincent Hathaway & Co., Boston, Ginger Ale, Round Bottom, Aqua 8.00

Soda, Virginia Spring Water Co., Davis & Douglas, Rumford Falls, Me. 3.00
Soda, W.B.Mew & Langton Co., Hutchinson, Emerald Green, 6 In. 19.50
Soda, W.E.Brockway, N.Y., Iron Pontil, Green 23.00
Soda, W.E.Rumming, Nanaimo, B.C., Inside Screw Top, Aqua 12.00
Soda, W.H.Cawley & Co., Dover, N.J., Aqua, Hutchinson 8.00
Soda, W.H.Darling & Sons, Newport, Vt., Contents, Hutchinson .... 50.00 To 85.00
Soda, W.H.H., Chicago, Ill., Cornflower Blue 80.00
Soda, W.H.Hutchinson & Son, Chicago, BIMAL, Aqua, 13 1/2 In. 32.00
Soda, W.Olmstead & Co., N.Y. Constitution Beverage, Yellow 185.00
Soda, W.P.Knickerbocker Sodawater, N.Y., 1848, 10 Panels, Iron Pontil, Cobalt 80.00
Soda, W.S.Wright, Blob, Dark Aqua 50.00
Soda, W.W.Lake, Jackson Bottling Works, Aqua, Hutchinson 25.00
Soda, Wagner, Sidney, Ohio, Amber, Pint 4.00
Soda, Walalua Soda Works, Aqua 28.00
Soda, Waldron Bottling Works, Hutchinson, 6 1/2 In. 25.00
Soda, Waldron Bottling Works, Waldron, Ark., Sun Colored Amethyst 14.00
Soda, Washington Springs, Green, Pint 35.00
Soda, Waxahachie, Texas, Hutchinson 25.00

Tonic, Standard, Aqua, 11 In.

Soda, Weisbach Bros., Alton, Ill. 6.00
Soda, Wesley Cunningham, Hutchinson, 7 1/2 In. 25.00
Soda, Western Soda Works, With Elk 22.00
Soda, Whittaker's Altham, Inside Screw Top, Aqua 7.00
Soda, William & Severance, Iron Pontil, Squat, Cobalt 60.00
Soda, William's Town, N.J., Iron Pontil, Teal 65.00
Soda, Wilmington, N.C., Hutchinson, Purple Tint 30.00
Soda, Winchester Bottling Works, Winchester, Md. 25.00
Soda, Witmer & Helt, Lykens, Pa., Teal Blue 35.00
Soda, Wm.A.Kearney, Shamokin, Pa., Hutchinson, Red Amber, Quart 125.00
Soda, Wm.Aylmer, Fargo, Hutchinson, Blue 300.00
Soda, Wm.Eagle, Premium Soda Waters, 8 Sided, Iron Pontil, Cobalt 175.00
Soda, Wm.J.Lager, Aviston, Ill. 8.00
Soda, Wm.S.Kinch, Paterson, N.J. 5.00
Soda, Yuncker Bottling Co., Tacoma, Wash., Hutchinson 8.00
Soda, Zeis & Sons, Redding, Cal. 25.00
Soda, Ziegers Soda Works, Tucson, Ariz., Hutchinson 185.00
Stiegel Type, Rectangular, Flint, German Half Post, Engraved Bullrushes 28.00
Stoneware, A.A.Chickering, Paneled, Stamped 16.50
Stoneware, Bottle, L.House, Incised, Blue Writing 30.00
Stoneware, Dr.Jug's Medicine For Lungs, Liver & Blood, 6 1/4 X 3 1/2 In. 160.00
Stoneware, E.Ferris, Blue Slip, Quart 36.00
Stoneware, Fred Stengel, Ludlow St., N.Y., This Bottle Not To Be Sold 20.00
Stoneware, G.S.Twitchell, Beer 13.00

Stoneware, Galloway's Everlasting Jar, Pat.1870, Clamp	38.00
Stoneware, Ginger Beer, Buffalo, N.Y.	7.00
Stoneware, IXL, Paneled, Stamped	18.50
Stoneware, Jug, Handled, Eagle On Staff With Banner, 2 Gallon	110.00
Stoneware, L.House, Incised, Blue Writing, Small	30.00
Stoneware, Meyer's, Paneled, Stamped	19.50
Stoneware, Schroder Renzs	18.00
Stoneware, Wagner Ginger Beer, Youngstown, Ohio	16.00
Stoneware, Walker & Co., Boston, Mass., Molded Handles, Blue Leaf Paint	50.00
Stoneware, Weyman & Bro., Pittsburgh, Gray & Blue	69.00
Toilet Water, see Cologne, Perfume, Scent	
Tonic, Atwoods Quinine	29.00
Tonic, Bownlow & Raymond, Federal, Cobalt Blue	225.00
Tonic, Columbo Peptic	18.00
Tonic, Dr.Bock's Restorative Paducah, Haze	20.00
Tonic, Dr.Harrison's Chalybeate, Blue Green, Label	90.00
Tonic, Dr.Kurnitzkis Aromatic Wire Grass	40.00
Tonic, Mull's Grape, Amber	12.00

Wheaton Commemorative, Andrew Jackson
(See Page 188)

Tonic, Rehrer's Expectoral Wild Cherry	135.00
Tonic, Schenk's Seaweed	15.00
Tonic, South American Nervine, Haze	50.00
Tonic, Standard, Aqua, 11 In. *Illus*	55.00
Tonic, Todd's, ABM, Stain	20.00
Tonic, Veno's Seaweed, Rectangular, Blue Aqua, 5 1/8 In.	6.50
Tonic, Wait's Wild Cherry, The Great, Square, Amber, 8 1/2 In.	28.00
Trenton Spirits Limited, George Washington	10.00
Trenton Spirits Limited, James Madison	10.00
Trenton Spirits Limited, James Monroe	10.00
Trenton Spirits Limited, Thomas Jefferson	10.00
Vinegar, Champion	12.00
Vinegar, Mayfield Co., Mayfield, Ky., Fine Family & Pickling	35.00
Vinegar, Monroe Cider & Vinegar Co., Eureka, Cal.	22.00
Vinegar, Southern Fruit Product Co., Rogers, Ark., Get The Best, 4 1/2 In.	35.00
Vinegar, White House, Apple Shape, Handled, Clear, 1/2 Gallon	10.00
Vinegar, White House, Embossed On Side, ABM, Clear, 8 1/2 In.	6.00
Vinegar, White House, Lighhouse	30.00
Vinegar, White House, Pitcher, Embossed On Base, Ribbed, Clear	8.00
Vinegar, White House, Spout, Pint	5.00 To 8.00
Vinegar, White House, Spout, Quart	5.00
Vinegar, White House, World's Fair	35.00
Vinegar, White House, 2 Embossed Buffalo Heads	3.00
Vinegar, World's Fair, 1939, Label, Milk Glass	10.00

Warner Brothers, see Alpa
Water, Mineral, see Mineral Water
Water, Moses, see Mineral Water, Moses

Wheaton Commemorative bottles have been made by hand since 1977 at Wheaton Village, Millville, New Jersey. Earlier commemorative bottles were machine made and sold under the name Wheaton Nuline.

Wheaton Commemorative, Abraham Lincoln	9.00
Wheaton Commemorative, Alexander Graham Bell	6.00
Wheaton Commemorative, Andrew Jackson ....*Illus*	6.00
Wheaton Commemorative, Andrew Johnson	7.00

Wheaton Commemorative, Ben Franklin

Wheaton Commemorative, George Washington

Wheaton Commemorative, Apollo 11	20.00
Wheaton Commemorative, Apollo 12	44.00
Wheaton Commemorative, Apollo 13	8.00
Wheaton Commemorative, Apollo 14	5.00
Wheaton Commemorative, Apollo 15	5.00
Wheaton Commemorative, Apollo 16	5.00
Wheaton Commemorative, Apollo 17	10.00
Wheaton Commemorative, Ben Franklin ....*Illus*	5.00
Wheaton Commemorative, Betsy Ross	6.00 To 15.00
Wheaton Commemorative, Billy Graham	5.00
Wheaton Commemorative, Charles Evans Hughes	5.00
Wheaton Commemorative, Charles Lindbergh	5.00
Wheaton Commemorative, Christmas, 1971	11.00
Wheaton Commemorative, Christmas, 1971, Not Frosted	12.00
Wheaton Commemorative, Christmas, 1972	5.00
Wheaton Commemorative, Christmas, 1973	6.00
Wheaton Commemorative, Christmas, 1974	7.00
Wheaton Commemorative, Christmas, 1975	10.00
Wheaton Commemorative, Christmas, 1976	10.00
Wheaton Commemorative, Christmas, 1977	10.00

Wheaton Commemorative, Christmas, 1978	10.00
Wheaton Commemorative, Clark Gable	6.00
Wheaton Commemorative, Democrat, 1972, Eagleton, McGovern	10.00
Wheaton Commemorative, Douglas MacArthur	4.00
Wheaton Commemorative, Franklin D.Roosevelt	9.00
Wheaton Commemorative, General Eisenhower	6.00
Wheaton Commemorative, General Patton	5.00
Wheaton Commemorative, George Washington *Illus*	20.00
Wheaton Commemorative, Gerald Ford	7.00
Wheaton Commemorative, Harry Truman	6.00
Wheaton Commemorative, Helen Keller	5.00
Wheaton Commemorative, Herbert Hoover	5.00

Wheaton Commemorative, Richard Nixon

Wheaton Commemorative, Humphrey Bogart	5.00
Wheaton Commemorative, Humphrey, Muskie, 1968 Democrat	11.00
Wheaton Commemorative, James Madison	10.00
Wheaton Commemorative, Jean Harlow	5.00
Wheaton Commemorative, James Carter	10.00
Wheaton Commemorative, John Adams	7.00
Wheaton Commemorative, John Kennedy	29.00
Wheaton Commemorative, John Paul Jones *Illus*	5.00
Wheaton Commemorative, John Quincy Adams	10.00
Wheaton Commemorative, John Tyler	10.00
Wheaton Commemorative, Lee Minton	10.00
Wheaton Commemorative, Lyndon Johnson	5.00
Wheaton Commemorative, Mark Twain	5.00
Wheaton Commemorative, Martin Luther King	6.00
Wheaton Commemorative, Martin Van Buren	10.00
Wheaton Commemorative, McGovern, Schriver, 1972 Democrat	7.00
Wheaton Commemorative, Nixon, Agnew, 1968 Republican	11.00
Wheaton Commemorative, Nixon, Agnew, 1972 Republican	6.00
Wheaton Commemorative, Paul Revere	6.00
Wheaton Commemorative, Pope Paul VI	10.00
Wheaton Commemorative, President Eisenhower	8.00
Wheaton Commemorative, Richard Nixon *Illus*	7.00
Wheaton Commemorative, Robert E.Lee	4.00
Wheaton Commemorative, Robert Kennedy	5.00
Wheaton Commemorative, Sheriff's Association	14.00
Wheaton Commemorative, Skylab 1	6.00
Wheaton Commemorative, Skylab 2	7.00
Wheaton Commemorative, St.John	13.00
Wheaton Commemorative, St.Luke	13.00
Wheaton Commemorative, St.Mark	13.00

Wheaton Commemorative, St.Matthew	13.00
Wheaton Commemorative, Theodore Roosevelt	5.00
Wheaton Commemorative, Thomas Edison	5.00
Wheaton Commemorative, Thomas Jefferson	7.00
Wheaton Commemorative, Ulysses S.Grant	5.00
Wheaton Commemorative, Vietnam	10.00
Wheaton Commemorative, W.C.Fields	6.00
Wheaton Commemorative, Will Rogers	4.00
Wheaton Commemorative, William McKinley	8.00
Wheaton Commemorative, Wm.H.Harrison	10.00
Wheaton Commemorative, Woodrow Wilson	9.00
Wheaton Commemorative, 1976 Mother's Day	10.00
Whiseky, Udolpho Wolfe's, Schiedam, Aromatic Schnapps, Bubbles, Dark Olive	15.00

Whiskey bottles came in assorted sizes and shapes through the years. Any container for whiskey is included in this category.

Whiskey, see also modern manufacturers by brand name

Whiskey, A.McGinn's Co., Baltimore, Maryland, Clear, Sample	8.00
Whiskey, Adolph Harris Co., Inside Screw Threads, Stopper, Amber, Quart	25.00
Whiskey, Ag.Marchuetz, N.Y., Label, Embossed	10.00
Whiskey, Anderson, Ohio, 1880, Pure Bourbon	*Color*
Whiskey, Applied Handle, Tubular Pontil, Dark Amber, Quart	60.00
Whiskey, Atlas Bourbon, Hohn's & Kaltenbach, San Francisco	45.00
Whiskey, B.M. & E.A.Whitlock & Co., Club Shaped, Aqua	65.00
Whiskey, Barnet & Lumley, Mist Of The Morning, Barrel, Amber	235.00
Whiskey, Bear Grass, Braunschwieger & Co., San Francisco	45.00
Whiskey, Belle Of Anderson, Sour Mash, Milk Glass, 7 In. *Illus*	85.00
Whiskey, Bennett & Carrol, Pittsburgh, Barrel, Olive Yellow, 3/4 Quart	200.00
Whiskey, Berry's Diamond Wedding	10.00
Whiskey, Bertin & Lepori, San Francisco, Amber, Quart	30.00
Whiskey, Bininger, see Bininger	
Whiskey, Black & White, Olive Green, Quart	6.00
Whiskey, Black Glass, C.1830, Open Pontil	20.00
Whiskey, Black Glass, C.1840, Blue, Pontil, Quart	12.00
Whiskey, Blakes, Reynold's, Olive Amber	350.00
Whiskey, Boldner's Aromatic Schnapps	45.00
Whiskey, Bourbon, Raspberry Puce	165.00
Whiskey, Buchanan's Black & White, Applied Top, Green	10.00
Whiskey, C.C.G., Rochester, N.Y., Aqua, Pint	30.00
Whiskey, C.O.Blake's Rye & Bourbon, Adams Taylor & Co., 13 In. *Illus*	4.00

Wheaton Commemorative, John Paul Jones
(See Page 189)

Whiskey, Campus Gossler Bros., The, Handled Cylinder	110.00
Whiskey, Carroll & Carroll, Pepper Distillery, Sole Agents, 4 Piece Mold	65.00
Whiskey, Carroll Rye, Rectangular, 1/2 Pint	5.00
Whiskey, Cartan McCarthy & Co., San Francisco	95.00

Whiskey, Carter's Spanish Mixture, Iron Pontil, Olive 75.00
Whiskey, Casper's, Cobalt, Quart .... 175.00 To 220.00
Whiskey, Cedarhurst, Flask Type, Label, Amber 10.00
Whiskey, Chapin & Gore Sour Mash, 1867, Barrel, Amber 60.00
Whiskey, Chas.S.Grove Co., Liquor Merchants, Boston, Mass., Jug, Sample 25.00
Whiskey, Chase & Duncan, Barrel 55.00
Whiskey, Chestnut Grove, Applied Handle, Bubbly, Funnel Pontil 137.50
Whiskey, Chestnut Grove, C.W. On Seal, Handled Jug, Open Pontil, Amber 125.00
Whiskey, Columbian, Cordial, Quart ....*Color* 25.00
Whiskey, Conrad Stottin Grunhof, Kummel, Amber, 9 1/2 In. 10.00
Whiskey, Cottage Brand, Cabin, Mint Green 165.00
Whiskey, Covington Kentucky, Aqua, Gallon 32.50
Whiskey, Crown Distilleries Co., Light Orange Amber 12.00
Whiskey, Crown Distilleries, Blob Top, Red Amber 75.00

Whiskey, Belle Of Anderson, Sour Mash, Milk Glass, 7 In.

Whiskey, Crown Distilleries, Inside Thread, Stopper, Amber, Fifth 11.00
Whiskey, Crown Distilleries Co., BIM, Inside Screw, Fifth 23.00
Whiskey, Cutter Old Bourbon, Amber, Fifth 15.00
Whiskey, Cutter Old Bourbon, Sole Agents 45.00
Whiskey, Cutter, Crown Shoulder, Swirls, Amber 390.00
Whiskey, Dallemand & Co., Chicago, Fluted Shoulder, Amber 15.25
Whiskey, Dave D.Gibbon's & Co., San Francisco, Tool Top, Fifth 25.00
Whiskey, Davy Crockett, Hey Grauerholtz & Co., Sole Agent, Amber 30.00
Whiskey, Detrick Distilling Co., Pottery, 5 In. ....*Illus* 22.00
Whiskey, Dewar's Scotch, 5 Reservoir, Gold Lettering, Pontil, Clear 30.00
Whiskey, Driving Club Rye, Amber, 12 In. ....*Color*
Whiskey, Duffy Malt, Amber, Quart, 10 In. 5.00
Whiskey, Duffy Malt, Amber, 8 1/4 In. 7.00
Whiskey, Duffy Malt, Label, Pint .... 9.00 To 20.00
Whiskey, Duffy Malt, Rochester, Olive Amber 30.00
Whiskey, Duffy Malt, 6 In. .... 25.00 To 28.00
Whiskey, Dyottville Glassworks, Cylinder, Iron Pontil, Citron 30.00
Whiskey, Dyottville Glassworks, Phila., Honey Amber 22.00
Whiskey, Dyottville Glassworks, Phila., Yellow 27.00
Whiskey, E.P.Middleton Wheat Whiskey, 1825, Blob Seal, Amber, Quart 24.50
Whiskey, E.R.Betteron, Chattanooga, Tennessee, Embossed, Amber, Pint 4.50
Whiskey, E.R.Betteron, Chattanooga, Tennessee, Embossed, Amber, 1/2 Pint 3.50
Whiskey, Edolpho Wolfe's Schiedam Aromatic Schnapps, Amber, 9 1/2 In. 18.00
Whiskey, Elvis Presley No.1, Musical Decanter 95.00
Whiskey, F.Brown's Ess., Of Jamaica Ginger, Phil., Aqua, Open Pontil 8.50
Whiskey, Fible & Crabb's Handmade Sour Mash, 1876, 15 Swirl, Clear, 11 In. 65.00
Whiskey, Figg, Doyle, Milwaukee, Cylinder, Clear, Quart 6.00
Whiskey, Finsbury Distillery Co., Embossed Dragons, Coat Of Arms, Aqua 8.00

Whiskey, Forest Lawn, J.V.H., Squat, Pontil, Green 175.00
Whiskey, Frank Abadie, Eureka, Nev., Pumpkinseed, 1/2 Pint 85.00
Whiskey, Fulton, Aqua, Gallon 25.00
Whiskey, G.A.Shift, Saloon, Pottery, 7 1/2 In. .... *Illus* 125.00
Whiskey, Gold Dust, Hohn, Glob Top, Honey Amber 100.00
Whiskey, Golden Wedding, Carnival Glass, Fifth 10.00
Whiskey, Golden Wedding, Carnival Glass, Pint 10.00
Whiskey, Goldsberg, Bowen & Co., San Francisco, Oakland, Purple, Quart 18.00
Whiskey, Goldwater Schnapps, Applied Lip, 8 3/4 In. 45.00
Whiskey, Greeley's Bourbon, Barrel 140.00
Whiskey, Griffith Hyatt & Co., Open Pontil, Handle, Red Amber 425.00
Whiskey, Griffith Hyatt, Handled Jug, Open Pontil, Deep Red Amber 550.00
Whiskey, H.Munzer & Co., Paterson, N.J., Quart 20.00
Whiskey, Hall-Luhrs Co., Sacramento, Inside Screw Threads, Amber, Fifth 17.50
Whiskey, Hall's, Barrel, Burst Bubble, Yellow Amber 99.00
Whiskey, Harper, Embossed 4.50
Whiskey, Hawkin's Rye, Green, Quart 10.00
Whiskey, Hayner, Bar, Combination Lock Stopper 25.00
Whiskey, Hayner, Dayton, Ohio, Embossed 11.00
Whiskey, Hayner, Four City, Embossed, BIMAL .... 9.00 To 11.00
Whiskey, Hayner, 1897, Clear 2.75

Whiskey, C.O.Blake's Rye & Bourbon, Adams Taylor & Co., 13 In.
(See Page 190)

Whiskey, Detrick Distilling Co., Pottery, 5 In.
(See Page 191)

Whiskey, Heather Blossom Malt, Square, Amber, 1/2 Pint 8.50
Whiskey, Hollywood, Amber, 11 3/4 In. 18.00
Whiskey, Holtz & Freystedt, N.Y., Amber 35.00
Whiskey, Horse, Gentry, Slote & Co., New York, Deep Olive Amber, Pint 460.00
Whiskey, House Of Lords, Aqua, Quart 15.00
Whiskey, House Of Lords, William Whitley, Leith, Scotland 8.00
Whiskey, I.W.Harper, Amber, Paper Label, 6 1/2 In. .... *Illus* 2.00
Whiskey, I.W.Harper, Deep Red Amber, 9 1/2 In., Quart 7.50
Whiskey, J.F.T. & Co., Handled, Amber 310.00
Whiskey, J.H.Cutter, Amber, Vertical, 11 1/2 In. 4.75
Whiskey, J.H.Cutter, E.Martin & Co., Midcrown, Amber 150.00
Whiskey, J.H.Cutter, Extra Old Bourbon, Glob Top, BIMAL, Star On Bottom 50.00
Whiskey, J.H.Cutter, Extra Old Bourbon, Star & Shield, Amber, Fifth 50.00
Whiskey, J.H.Cutter, Light Amber, Tooled Top 55.00
Whiskey, J.H.Cutter, Old Bourbon, A No.2 In Circle, Amber, Fifth 15.00
Whiskey, J.H.Cutter, Old Bourbon, Clear Tooled Top, Barrel 75.00
Whiskey, J.H.Cutter, Old Bourbon, Light Amber, Crude 80.00
Whiskey, J.H.Cutter, San Francisco, Cal., Amber, Fifth 20.00

Whiskey, G.A.Shift, Saloon, Pottery, 7 1/2 In.

Whiskey, J.H.Cutter, Yellow Amber, Th-46, 4 Piece Mold 65.00
Whiskey, J.J.Stump & Co., Cumberland, Maryland, Jug, 1/2 Pint 28.00
Whiskey, J.J.W.Peter's, Hanburg, Embossed Dog, Amber, Quart 32.00
Whiskey, J.Moore, Chielovich, Amber 600.00
Whiskey, J.Oppenheimer & Co., San Antonio, Texas, Amber, Quart 150.00
Whiskey, J.Rieger's & Co., Distributors, Kansas City, Miss., Purple, Sample 8.00
Whiskey, J.Walker's V.B., Aqua, 7 1/4 In. 10.50
Whiskey, Jesse Moore, Hunt Co., San Francisco, Calif., Amber, Quart 15.00
Whiskey, Jesse Moore, Moore Hunt & Co., Honey Amber 15.00
Whiskey, John Scoufe, San Francisco, Cal., Strapside, Thread, Amber, Quart 10.00
Whiskey, Jones Garrim & Co., Amber, 8 1/2 In. 75.00
Whiskey, Jug, The Golden Hill, Toledo, Ohio, 4 1/2 In. .... *Illus* 40.00
Whiskey, Jug, Umpire Club Bourbon, Etched On Clear, Applied Handle 22.00
Whiskey, Julius Kessler & Co., G.R.Sharpe, 6 In. .... *Illus* 7.50
Whiskey, Julius May, Brunswick, Ga., 1880-90, Aqua, 7 3/4 In. 50.00
Whiskey, Kahn Liquor & Grocery Co., Shreveport, La., Cylinder 25.00
Whiskey, Kellog's Nelson County, Kentucky Bourbon, Golden Amber, Fifth 50.00
Whiskey, Kellog's Nelson County, Kentucky Bourbon, W.L.Co., Sole Agent 20.00
Whiskey, Kellogg's Wilmerding-Loew Co., San Francisco, Tool Top, Fifth 15.00
Whiskey, Kreielsheimer Bros., Seattle, Wash., Tool Top, Dark Amber 35.00

Whiskey, Lady's Leg, Olive Amber, Quart 35.00
Whiskey, Lancaster Glass Works, Amber, 3/4 Quart 120.00
Whiskey, Lancaster Glass Works, Barrel With Staves, Amber 150.00
Whiskey, Lillienthal & Co., Distillers, Amber, Fifth 60.00
Whiskey, Lillienthal & Co., S.F., Golden Amber 90.00
Whiskey, Lone Creek Distillery Co., Newport, Ky., Amber, Quart 10.50
Whiskey, Louis Lassig, San Francisco, Inside Thread, Stopper, Clear 8.00
Whiskey, Macy & Jenkins, N.Y., Handled, Embossed Base, Amber 22.50
Whiskey, McCully & Co., Dark Olive 15.00
Whiskey, McDonald & Cohn, Inside Screw Threads, Golden Amber, Fifth 20.00
Whiskey, Melcher's Aromatic Schiedam Schnapps, Label, Square, Green, Quart 50.00
Whiskey, Melcher's Old Crown, Toledo, O., Acid Etched Barrel & 2 Crows 175.00
Whiskey, Meredith's Diamond Club, 8 In. ....*Color* 75.00
Whiskey, Merry Christmas & A Happy New Year, 8 In. ....*Illus* 15.00
Whiskey, Miller Game Cock, Boston, Pale Aqua, Pint 7.00
Whiskey, Millionaire's Club, Olive Green 9.00
Whiskey, Mist Of The Morning, Barnett & Lumley, Barrel, Amber 235.00
Whiskey, Mist Of The Morning, Barnett, Barrel, Light Amber 300.00
Whiskey, Mist Of The Morning, Barrel, Golden Amber, 3/4 Quart 150.00
Whiskey, Mist Of The Morning, Barrel, Light Yellow Olive 400.00

Whiskey, I.W.Harper, Amber, Paper Label, 6 1/2 In.
(See Page 193)

Whiskey, Monk's Lion, Embossed Figures, Amber .... 50.00 To 85.00
Whiskey, Monticello Rye, Jug, Pottery, 8 1/2 In. ....*Illus* 20.00
Whiskey, Mount Vernon Pure Rye, Lady's Leg, Amber, Quart 8.00
Whiskey, Mount Vernon Pure Rye, Square, Amber, Quart .... 10.00 To 14.00
Whiskey, Mount Vernon, Labels 5.50
Whiskey, Mountain Anthrust Distillery, Kansas City, Miss., Lady's Leg, Quart 14.00
Whiskey, Nelson's Old Bourbon, Maysville, Ky., Barrel, Amber, 7 1/8 In. 485.00
Whiskey, Old Bourbon For Medicinal Purposes, Pint 6.00
Whiskey, Old Cabinet Kentucky Bourbon, San Francisco, Cylinder, Amber 265.00
Whiskey, Old Castle, Amber 20.00
Whiskey, Old Crow Rye, H.B.Kirk & Co., Label, Amber 12.00
Whiskey, Old Father Time Manhattan, Amber, Quart 15.00
Whiskey, Old Grand Dad, Glass Stopper, Medium Purple 5.00
Whiskey, Old Judge, Kentucky Whiskey, San Francisco, Cal. 35.00
Whiskey, Old Kentucky Valley, Amber, Paper Label, 11 1/2 In. ....*Color* xxxx.xx
Whiskey, Old Kentucky, Taylor Blend, Embosses, Amber, Quart 12.00
Whiskey, Old McBrayer, J.H.McBrayer Distilling Co., Clear, Quart 8.00
Whiskey, Old Pioneer, Spears & Co., Braunschweiger & Co., Sole Agents 115.00
Whiskey, Old Times Whisky, 1893 World's Fair, Clear, Quart 10.00
Whiskey, P.Hoppe's Schiedam Schnapps, Deep Green, Quart 20.00
Whiskey, P.Schille, Columbus, Ohio, Blue, 10 In. ....*Color* xxxx.xx
Whiskey, Paul Jones Pure Rye, Red Amber 12.00
Whiskey, Paul Jones, Amber, Label, Cork Stopper 20.00
Whiskey, Paul Jones, Aqua, Rectangular, 1/2 Pint 5.00

Whiskey, **Paul Jones,** Embossed Glass, Label 10.00
Whiskey, **Pett's Bald Eagle,** Clear, 6 In. 3.00
Whiskey, **Pink Striations Through Glass,** Pinkish Puce, Fifth 65.00
Whiskey, **Porcelain,** 6 In. .... *Illus* 35.00
Whiskey, **Premier Blend,** Grand Old Highland, Square, Aqua, Fifth 17.00
Whiskey, **Pure Old North Carolina Corn,** Roanoke, Va., 3 Piece Mold, Quart 10.00
Whiskey, **Qui Rye,** Dr.Koch, Berlin, Picture Of Dog Head 72.00
Whiskey, **Quinine,** Lady's Leg, Amber, Quart 5.00
Whiskey, **R.D.Westheimer & Sons,** Red Top, 6 1/2 In. 5.00
Whiskey, **Rheinstrom Bros.,** Emerald Green, Flake, Pint 25.00
Whiskey, **Rheinstrom Bros.,** Olive Green, Quart 20.00
Whiskey, **Rittenhouse,** Straight Rye, Amber, 10 In. .... *Illus* 1.00
Whiskey, **Rosenberg & Jackson,** N.Y., Amber, Quart 10.00
Whiskey, **Roth & Co.,** Amber 12.00
Whiskey, **Roth & Co.,** Chocolate 95.00
Whiskey, **Roth & Co.,** San Francisco 100.00
Whiskey, **Rum,** Free-Blown, C.1790, Fired Pontil, Olive Green, 7 1/2 In. 12.00
Whiskey, **S & M Wheat,** Honey Amber, 1/2 Gallon 659.00

Whiskey, Jug, The Golden Hill, Toledo, Ohio, 4 1/2 In.
(See Page 193)

Whiskey, Julius Kessler & Co., G.R.Sharpe, 6 In.
(See Page 193)

Whiskey, Merry Christmas & A Happy New Year, 8 In.

Whiskey, S.A.S.Devine, Roxbury, 6 In. .... *Illus*   35.00
Whiskey, S.F.Petts & Co., Purity Guaranteed, Boston, Mass., Slug Plate, Quart 12.00
Whiskey, S.Grabfelder & Co., Louisville, Ky. 3.50
Whiskey, S.McKee & Co., Cylinder, Embossed, Amber 5.00
Whiskey, Saltzman & Siegelman, Stenciled, Rye Whiskey, Jug, 7 In. 30.00
Whiskey, Samuel Bros., Louisville, San Francisco, Square, Quart, BIMAL 15.00
Whiskey, Schlesinger & Bender Inc., Pure California Wine & Brandies, Quart 18.00
Whiskey, Scranton Distributing Co., Colonial Figure Under Glaze, Gallon 29.50
Whiskey, Sheehan Malt, Clear 6.00
Whiskey, Sherry, Brassy & Co., Amber, Fifth 35.00
Whiskey, Smokine, Cabin, Embossed, Amber, Quart .... 150.00 To 175.00
Whiskey, Smokine, Cabin, Winnipeg & Minneapolis, Amber, Quart 200.00
Whiskey, Spider & Fly, Embossed, Amber, Quart 17.50

Whiskey, Monticello Rye, Jug, Pottery, 8 1/2 In.
(See Page 194)

Whiskey, Porcelain, 6 In.
(See Page 195)

Whiskey, S.A.S.Devine, Roxbury, 6 In.

Whiskey, Rittenhouse,
Straight Rye, Amber, 10 In.
(See Page 195)

Whiskey, **Spruance Stanley & Co.**, Horseshoe, Amber .... 28.00 To 45.00
Whiskey, **Star,** Handle, Amber 335.00
Whiskey, **Stout Dyer & Wicks,** N.Y., Calabash, Aqua, 8 1/2 In. .... 25.00 To 45.00
Whiskey, **Taylor & Williams,** Embossed, Miniature 5.00
Whiskey, **That's The Stuff,** Barrel, Amber, Chips, 3/4 Quart .... *Illus* 240.00
Whiskey, **The Cinter Company,** ABM 3.00
Whiskey, **The F.Chevulier Co.,** Old Castle Whiskey, San Francisco 25.00
Whiskey, **Theo.Gier Co.,** Oakland, Calif., Loop Top, Fifth 15.00
Whiskey, **Theodore Netter,** Barrel, 8 Oz. 25.00
Whiskey, **Thos.Taylor,** Virginia, Amber 190.00
Whiskey, **Treadwell,** San Francisco, Amber, Quart 35.00

Whiskey, That's The Stuff, Barrel, Amber, Chips, 3/4 Quart

Whiskey, Van R-X-7, Bininger's
Knickerbocker, Amber, Pint

Whiskey, Van R-X-5, A.M.Bininger & Co.,
Green, Chip, 3/4 Quart

Whiskey, **Turner Brothers,** Barrel, Yellow Green, 3/4 Quart 500.00
Whiskey, **Turner Brothers,** N.Y., Barrel, Amber, 3/4 Quart 110.00
Whiskey, **U.S.Mailbox Rye,** Clear, Quart 65.00
Whiskey, **Udolpho Wolfe's,** Aromatic Schnapps, Honey Amber 12.00
Whiskey, **Udolpho Wolfe's,** Aromatic Schnapps, Iron Pontil 30.00
Whiskey, **Udolpho Wolfe's,** Aromatic Schnapps, Olive Green, Open Pontil, Pint 35.00
Whiskey, **Udolpho Wolfe's,** Golden Yellow, Pint 20.00
Whiskey, **Udolpho Wolfe's,** Schiedam, Aromatic Schnapps, Olive, Tapered Lip 72.50
Whiskey, **Udolpho Wolfe's,** Schnapps, Olive Green, Iron Pontil 23.50
Whiskey, **Uri,** Louisville 13.00
Whiskey, **Utah Liquor Co.,** Salt Lake City, Utah, Full, 1/2 Gallon 65.00
Whiskey, **Van R-X-5,** A.M.Bininger & Co., Green, Chip, 3/4 Quart .... *Illus* 550.00
Whiskey, **Van R-X-7,** Bininger's Knickerbocker, Amber, Pint .... *Illus* 550.00
Whiskey, **Voldner's Aromatic Schnapps,** Olive Green, Quart 30.00
Whiskey, **W.B.Sanxay,** Grocer, Newburg, Cylinder, Amber, Fifth 12.00
Whiskey, **W.C.Peacock & Co.,** Honolulu, Wine & Liquor Merchants, Amber, 11 In. 75.00
Whiskey, **Week's Glassworks,** Cylinder, Red Amber 75.00
Whiskey, **Wharton's Chestnut Grove,** 1850, Cobalt Blue, 1/4 Pint 245.00

Whiskey, Wheat, Amber, Quart, 16 1/2 In. ....*Color*   135.00
Whiskey, Whitney's Glass Works, 2 Piece Mold, Applied Top, Olive Green 15.00
Whiskey, Wichman, Lutgen Co., San Francisco, Inside Threads, Stopper, Quart 7.00
Whiskey, Wilmerdin-Lowe Co., Inside Screw Threads, Aqua, Fifth 25.00
Whiskey, Wilson Fairbanks, Old Bourbon, For Medicinal Purposes 35.00
Whiskey, Wm. Cully & Co.Patent On Shoulder, Citron, Fifth 22.00
Whiskey, Wm.Edward's Pure Rye, Inside Screw, Stopper, Stoneware, Quart 100.00
Whiskey, Wolf Wreden Co., Golden Amber 125.00
Whiskey, Wright & Taylor Distillers, Louisville, Ky., Amber, 6 In. 18.00
Whiskey, Wright & Taylor, Amber .... 4.00 To 5.00
Whiskey, Zimmerman Mail Order House, Portland, Ore., Clear, Quart 15.00
Whyte & MacKays, Bagpipe Player 8.00
Whyte & MacKays, Duffer Cheater 10.00
Whyte & MacKays, Duffer Driver 10.00
Whyte & MacKays, Duffer Putter 10.00
Whyte & MacKays, Duffer Slicer 10.00
Wild Turkey, Backbar, Gold 200.00
Wild Turkey, Charleston Centennial .... 45.00 To 61.00
Wild Turkey, Crystal Anniversary-55 .... 1880.00

Wild Turkey, No.4, 1974, With Poult

Wild Turkey, No.5, With Flags

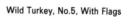

Wild Turkey, Liggett & Meyers	350.00
Wild Turkey, Mack Truck	9.50 To 17.00
Wild Turkey, No.1, Male	125.00 To 360.00
Wild Turkey, No.2, Female	150.00 To 270.00
Wild Turkey, No.3, On The Wing	65.00 To 150.00
Wild Turkey, No.4, With Poult	55.00
Wild Turkey, No.4, 1974, With Poult	*Illus* 55.00
Wild Turkey, No.5, With Flags	*Illus* 35.00

Wild Turkey, No.6, Striding

Wild Turkey, No.6, Striding	*Illus* 30.00
Wild Turkey, No.7	22.00 To 35.00
Wild Turkey, No.8	*Color* 60.00
Wildcatter, Oil Well	6.00
Willett, see Old Bardstown	
Windsor, Guardsman	14.75
Wine, Clarke's Sherry, Rectangular, Aqua	40.00
Wine, Cylinder, Black Glass, C.1770	25.00
Wine, Dutch Onion, Black Glass	65.00
Wine, Dutch Onion, String Neck, Open Pontil	55.00
Wine, E.Pernod Couvet, Pontiled Seal	14.00
Wine, F.Cazanove, Bordeaux, Embossed, Seal	9.00
Wine, F.Dolin & Cle Chambery, Back Bar, Acid Etched	9.00
Wine, Face Under Glass, 14 In.	*Color* xxxx.xx
Wine, Free-Blown, C.1800, Quart	30.00
Wine, Free-Blown, Open Pontil, Italian Green	10.00
Wine, Garrett's, Embossed Eagle, Sample	8.00
Wine, Goldberg, Bowen Co., Wine Merchants, Dark Purple, Pint	50.00
Wine, Hock, Amber	1.75
Wine, Hock, Green, 11 In.	2.50
Wine, Hock, Green, 13 In.	2.50
Wine, Hock, Red Amber, 11 In.	4.00
Wine, Hock, Red Amber, 13 In.	4.00
Wine, Hock, Spin Mold, Midnight Blue, 14 In.	8.00
Wine, Hock, Teal, 11 In.	5.00
Wine, Hock, Teal, 13 In.	5.00

Wine, Hogarth, Squat, English 225.00
Wine, L.Rose, Sample, Aqua, 6 1/2 In. 8.00
Wine, Leon Greenbert & Co., 1/2 Pint 23.00
Wine, Milano Vermouth, Green, Seal, 13 1/2 In. 5.00
Wine, Tester, Free-Blown, Blue Green 5.00
Wine, W.H.Jones & Co., Imported Wines, Spirit & Cordials, Green, Quart 12.00
Wine, Wilson's Invalid's Port Wine, Cylinder, Olive 20.00
Wisconsin Wildlife, Baby Robin, Bisque Finish, 4 1/4 In. .... 9.95 To 11.00
Wisconsin Wildlife, Blue Jay, Bisque Finish, 5 In. .... 9.95 To 11.00
Wisconsin Wildlife, Cardinal .... 10.95 To 11.00
Wisconsin Wildlife, Hodag, Female, 1976 .... 15.00
Wisconsin Wildlife, Hodag, Male, 1976 .... 15.00
Wisconsin Wildlife, Red Eyed Viro 11.00
Wisconsin Wildlife, Red Winged Blackbird 11.00
Wisconsin Wildlife, Redheaded Woodpecker, Bisque, 5 In. .... 9.95 To 11.00
Zanesville, Swirls, Open Pontil, Light Blue, Quart 115.00
Zanesville, 10 Diamond, Chestnut, C.1815 ....*Color* xxxx.xx
Zanesville, 24 Swirled Ribs, Globular, Amber, 8 In. ....*Illus* 325.00
Zanesville, 24 Swirled Ribs, Globular, C.1815 ....*Color* xxxx.xx
Zanesville, 24 Swirled Ribs, Globular, Chestnut, C.1815 ....*Color* xxxx.xx